DATE DUE			
JAN 9 MAY 2 2			

POWER and POLITICS

in LABOR LEGISLATION

POWER and POLITICS
in LABOR LEGISLATION

by Alan K. McAdams

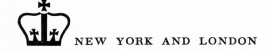 NEW YORK AND LONDON

COLUMBIA UNIVERSITY PRESS 1964

Alan K. McAdams is Assistant Professor at the
Graduate School of Business and Public Administration
of Cornell University.

64714

TO ANN AND THE BOYS

PREFACE

THIS study is directed to the general public, or more accurately to that anonymous but hopefully large group of readers, the "intelligent laymen." It has been written to inform the reader about the processes of his government and, in turn, the impact of the government on certain aspects of the economy, using as a vehicle a law which aroused passions on all sides, the Landrum-Griffin Act. The major thesis of the study is that the public, in ways which were sometimes direct and sometimes indirect, decided the outcome of the battle over labor reform legislation in 1959. It is hoped that a more complete understanding of the processes of our government and of the many and varied interactions which are involved therein will make more rational the participation of the public in future major issues on which its influence could be decisive.

Men charged with responsibility by various groups which hope to influence the actions of their legislators are among the many who might read this study with profit. The lessons to be learned are transferable to other questions of major import, but they may also be applicable to more mundane questions as well. These lessons are of direct relevance to laymen such as the leaders of the labor unions of this country and their counterparts in management. The merits of issues, at least as perceived by the public, did have great influence with legislators in the major confrontation which resulted in the Landrum-Griffin Act. It is clear that great ingenuity is required to transmit accurately to the public the essence of complex issues so that the public influence can be brought to bear in a reasoned and intelligent manner. It is also clear that the professional politician has an important influence on the effectiveness of the efforts of any interest group.

The study was carried out mainly through interviews with the major participants and their staffs. It would not have been possible had it not been for the great reservoir of good will toward scholars which exists among people in all segments of the American society. With few exceptions men of responsibility in public and private organizations were generous with their time and trust. The individuals are too numerous to name, and the conditions which made it possible for them to provide frank answers to blunt questions preclude their being named.

The interviews were carried out from an interview list prepared after an extended study of the background of the legislation. One major personality, who had participated closely in the development of Landrum-Griffin, criticized and added to the author's interview list of important participants on all sides of the question. The list as revised proved to be an excellent guide. It was augmented at various stages by suggestions made by successive interviewees. Each topic in the study was followed individually with several participants until the facts were substantiated and the ambiguities resolved. Data from written and published records was simultaneously analyzed and used to check the time relationships and accuracy of the perceptions of interviewees. Staff persons often were more knowledgeable and informative than their principals.

Interviewees were assured that they would not be identified as the source of the information which they provided. This presented them with a dual opportunity: they could inform or mislead in anonymity. There were many who accepted one of these opportunities and many who accepted both. In most instances there was sufficient data available through cross-checking to make it possible to judge which presentation fitted which category. Where this was not true, qualification has been presented in the body of the study.

Six individuals and organizations offered to open their files to my inspection; five of these offers were accepted. The minutes and other records of the executive sessions of certain committees were made available to me for perusal and note-taking, for which I am grateful. Two organizations, including one union, offered to provide me with office facilities during the extended period of interviewing in Washington, D.C., but these were respectfully declined.

Certain information was provided on the basis that it not be published before a given date. This stipulation has been met.

The bulk of the published material on the development in Congress of the Labor-Management Reporting and Disclosure Act of 1959 appeared in the general news or periodical literature of the period. This published data was used for three purposes: to serve as the basis for leads to be followed up in interviews, to state certain matters which can be more gracefully said by quotation from existing published sources than boldly stated without attribution, and to substantiate data gathered through interviews. Where specific references have not been given, the source of more general substantiating material has often been indicated.

It should be noted that government publications are available from the Superintendent of Documents, Government Printing Office, Washington, 25, D.C. From the same source all the major bills, reports, and hearings, as well as the pertinent sections of the *Congressional Record,* are available in bound form in the NLRB publication *Legislative History of the Labor-Management Reporting and Disclosure Act of 1959,* Volumes I and II. The excerpts from the *Congressional Record* in that publication are from the *Daily Congressional Record* for the period, the paging of which is different from that of the bound Record which appeared subsequently. All references in the present study for the year 1959 are to this *Daily Congressional Record.*

For the reader whose recollection of the specific legislative procedures of the federal government are dim, an excellent guide for review is available through the Superintendent of Documents in the pamphlet by Charles J. Zinn, *How Our Laws are Made* (86th Cong., 1st Sess., 1959, House Doc. 156; Washington, U.S. Government Printing Office, 1959). A second source available at most libraries is the *Congressional Quarterly Almanac* for any given year (Washington, Congressional Quarterly, Inc.), two sections of which are directly relevant, "How a Bill Is Passed" and "Glossary of Congressional Terms."

Certain of the major conclusions expressed in the body of the study rely for their support on the qualitative perceptions of individual participants or on circumstantial evidence. For complete verification of these conclusions controlled conditions would have been required, before and after the fact or techniques employed, which were beyond the time and monetary resources available to me. The conclusions are therefore more accurately classed as hypotheses for which some supporting evidence exists. The study presented here is an interpretation of the event in light of all the data that I was able to marshal. In the presentation a shorthand classification of the various parties as "liberal" and "conservative" is used more for convenience and conformance with common usage than as a true characterization of political philosophies (which is not intended).

I would like to express my appreciation to Professors Theodore Kreps, John Troxell, and John Bunzel, all of Stanford University, who provided guidance, direction, and encouragement in the earlier stages of this study. I would also like to express appreciation to Dr. Cornelius Cotter, formerly of Stanford University and formerly with the Republican National Committee, who provided invaluable assistance in arranging certain important interviews. My appreciation also goes to the Social Science Research Center of Cornell University (supported by an unrestricted grant from the Ford Foundation), its Director, Professor Wayne Thompson, and to the Graduate School of Business and Public Administration for their support in the later stages of this study and the preparation of the manuscript. A number of colleagues at Cornell and labor leaders who have participated in programs there have provided criticism, encouragement, and support. Many members of Columbia University Press have worked patiently and have wrought myriad improvements to this manuscript. For their assistance I am grateful.

The preface would not be complete without acknowledgment of the assistance and understanding of my wife, Ann, who has acted as a sounding board for ideas and presentation, typed earlier drafts, and proofread this one. As is true in many other cases, the costs of this effort have been at least as high for her and for our three young sons as they have been for me.

Responsibility for any errors and omissions remaining in this study is mine.

ALAN K. MC ADAMS

CONTENTS

TABLES

POWER and POLITICS
in LABOR LEGISLATION

I. INTRODUCTION

THE Labor-Management Reporting and Disclosure Act of 1959, the final version of what had been the Landrum-Griffin bill of the House of Representatives, was signed into law by President Dwight D. Eisenhower on September 14, 1959. This was the first legislation to deal directly with the relationships between management and labor since the passage of the Taft-Hartley Act twelve years before.

Taft-Hartley had represented a swing of the pendulum away from full support by the federal government for the aims and desires of the labor movement, an earlier trend which had culminated in the passage of the Wagner Act another twelve years previously, in 1935. Landrum-Griffin represented a further swing of the pendulum toward government regulation of unions.

Among the major stipulations of the law as passed by the Congress were provisions specifying certain rights of members of labor organizations, requiring reports to the Secretary of Labor by labor organizations and employers, regulating the establishment and functioning of trusteeships over local unions by international unions, prescribing certain procedures and regulations for union elections, defining fiduciary responsibilities for officers of labor organizations including a requirement for bonding of particular officers and employees, dealing with such miscellaneous subjects as a ban on extortionate picketing, and, most important of all, providing a number of amendments to the Taft-Hartley Act of 1947.

The law was regarded by most union leaders as an antilabor act. Passage of legislation of this tenor was almost totally unexpected, even by well-informed observers, as little as three months before Landrum-Griffin became the law of the land. In fact, the prevailing climate of opinion would have indicated that any legislation to emerge from the Eighty-sixth Congress would have been at the bidding of the union leaders themselves. This feeling grew out of an analysis of the election of 1958.

Elections of 1958

The fall of 1958 was an interesting period in the history of this country. National pride had already taken a heavy setback the year before when the Russians orbited the world's first artificial earth satellite. Then the economy began to slump after the 1955–56 boom. The newspapers were filled with reports of corruption in various sectors of the society: the television quiz scandals, "payola" in popular music ratings, alleged racketeering in labor-management affairs. It was an unsettled time to have a national election, but by law the election would take place on November 4, 1958.

To members of the Republican Party and to conservative strategists in general it appeared to be a propitious time to place the question of the so-called "right-to-work" laws before the voters in a number of states.[1] Senate hearings had produced evidence of corruption in some unions, had generated a good deal of mail on the subject, much of it reported to have been from union members and their families, and had been partially responsible for the passage of legislation in the summer of 1958 to regulate the handling of employee welfare and pension funds.

Senator William F. Knowland, Republican of California and Senate Minority Leader, judged the time to be ripe to make an issue of the internal reform of unions and the passage of right-to-work laws. Knowland staked his political future on his support of the right-to-work referendum in California in his bid for the governorship of that state.

In the waning months of summer 1958 and into the fall of that

[1] The right-to-work laws proposed in a number of states differed in the specifics of their provisions but had the common objective of outlawing agreements between unions and employers requiring, as a condition of continued employment, that employees join the union in question. The terms of such agreements usually provide that newly hired nonunion employees be given a specified period after employment in which to join the union. After the expiration of the grace period, they, like all other employees, must be members of the union in order to retain their jobs. Such arrangements are known as union shop agreements.

year the economy continued a downward trend. Unemployment totals reached 4.5 million persons, or 5.8 percent of the civilian work force. The Federal Reserve Board index of industrial production dropped to 133, a decrease of 9 percent from its peak in 1957. This was the second recession during the Eisenhower Republican Administration and the third of the postwar era. This was the second recession under the Administration of the party of Hoover.

The reaction of unions to the increasing level of unemployment, to the possibility of deepening recession, and to the threat of legislation outlawing union shop agreements was vigorous. They threw their man power and resources into the election campaign to defeat the proposed right-to-work laws and to carry out their stated policy of electing their "friends" and defeating their "enemies."

When, on November 5, the election results were tabulated, a startling fact became apparent. There had been a landslide for the Democratic Party in both the Congress and the state capitals. The proposed right-to-work laws were defeated by the voters in all but one state. Senator Knowland was soundly trounced by Democrat Edmund G. (Pat) Brown for the governorship of California. Seventy percent of the candidates backed by the AFL-CIO in congressional contests were elected. The Senate, which in 1958 had been fairly evenly split with 50 Democrats to 46 Republicans, was transformed into a lopsided body with 64 Democrats and 34 Republicans. The House of Representatives, which at the close of the Eighty-fifth Congress had had 231 Democratic members to 200 Republicans, now had 283 Democratic congressmen-elect to 153 Republicans.

The election was a heavy blow for the Republican Party and especially for the Eisenhower Administration. The result led a number of highly placed and apparently well-informed officials to issue public statements bordering on despair. Perhaps the most eloquent of these was made by Postmaster General Arthur Summerfield before the National Association of Manufacturers on December 5, 1958. The event was reported by the New York *Times* and is quoted in part as follows:

It was "union bosses" who assured the Democratic sweep in the November elections, Mr. Summerfield said. As a result, he added, "America teeters on the precipice of a labor-bossed Congress. . . ."

"Americans will watch with fascinated interest these next two years as the minions of this rampaging political combine move to reward their masters."

"I know of no time in our nation's history when the forces of intelligent Conservatism have been in greater danger of obliteration." [2]

The reaction was shared by the labor leaders themselves, but with elation rather than despair.

Election Impact on Congressional Committees

The election results had a direct impact on the committees which controlled the development of labor legislation in both the House and the Senate. In 1958 the Committee on Labor and Public Welfare of the Senate was made up of 13 members, with 7 Democrats opposing 6 Republicans. In 1959 the advantage for the Democrats in an enlarged committee shifted to 9 to 6. The Subcommittee on Labor of the Committee on Labor and Public Welfare, chaired by Senator John Kennedy, remained strongly in the control of liberals, although conservative Republican Senators Barry Goldwater and Everett Dirksen were members of this subcommittee. In the House of Representatives the shift was more dramatic and apparently more significant. Speaker Sam Rayburn had long been struggling to provide liberal representation on the Committee on Education and Labor, a committee which in 1958 had a membership of 17 Democrats and 13 Republicans. In each past year the Republican members of the committee had tended to vote as a bloc, but the Democrats had been split according to the usual sectional division of the Party, the two Southern Democrats, Chairman Graham Barden and Representative Philip Landrum, voting generally with the Republican bloc. As a result, in the Eighty-fifth Congress there had been a 15 to 15 deadlock on most major issues. The 1959 representation was to be 20 Democrats and 10 Republicans. Thus, even if the Southern Democrats voted with a solid bloc of Republicans, the result would be 18 Democratic votes, all of them of apparently liberal leanings, versus 12 conservative votes—with some labor representation among the Republicans.

To the leaders of organized labor these changes appeared to be significant and, perhaps, crucial. The influence of the McClellan

[2] New York *Times*, Dec. 6, 1958, p. 1.

Committee (to investigate improper activities in the labor-management field) on the election in 1958 had apparently not been strong. The Congress of 1959 looked to the representatives of labor like just the one for which they had been hoping. Their enthusiasm was shared in other quarters. Among the Democratic congressional leadership there was buoyant talk of "congressional initiative," the proposed direction of the policies of the nation by the Congress. The Senate Majority Leader was to go so far as to prepare his own "State of the Union Message."

The Central Question

In this study the anatomy of the 1959 statute and of the forces which brought it about are analyzed. The question is this: How could a law so out of character with what was expected have emerged from the Eighty-sixth Congress?

Stages in the Development of the Law

There were three main stages in the development of the law. The first covered the period of expected dominance by labor up through the surprise passage in the Senate of a group of provisions opposed by labor. In effect, the outcome of the final struggle over reform legislation was previewed in the Senate on the evening of April 22, 1959, when, following an emotional oration by a senator of the old Southern school, John L. McClellan, the liberal Senate passed by a single vote the so-called McClellan "bill of rights" for the laboring man. There were many unusual facets of this particular vote, but the most unusual of all was its final tally. Virtually no one would have predicted this outcome. It demonstrated the potential for conservative victory on an issue the labor movement felt it controlled completely. The shock effect of this vote was not long sustained after the new bill of rights was substantially amended. The vote was treated as a temporary aberration, but it was in fact a signal—a straw in a breeze which would grow to be a hurricane. It was a signal which the labor movement failed to anticipate, dismissed from its judgment the moment the substance of the bill of rights had been modified, and continued to ignore as the legislative battle shifted to the House of Representatives.

Stage two represented the climax to the struggle, a climax which took place on August 13, 1959, on the floor of the House of Representatives. The House floor was the apex of the massive forces which were brought to bear by the all-out effort of liberals and conservatives alike to influence the outcome of the struggle. On that day in August a decision was made between the conservative-sponsored Landrum-Griffin version of labor reform and the Elliott bill, which had emerged from the House Committee on Education and Labor with the blessing of Speaker Rayburn.

Stage three was, in effect, a postlude representing a partial balancing of the scale of power. It took place in the conference between the House and Senate to resolve their differing versions of the reform bill. Here the "worst" of Landrum-Griffin was removed, concessions were made to particular unions which were sufficiently powerful in their own right to stall and perhaps halt the final passage of any reform legislation, and the labor movement recognized both its own weakness and its own strength. We shall review the sequence of these events in their proper context. But first we must touch upon the major factors which determined the content of the bill as well as the outcome of the struggle over its passage.

Major Determinants of the Outcome

As we shall see, this issue was not decided directly by pressure groups. The legislation does not represent the ratification by Congress of a balance of power achieved among a temporary coalition of forces among the pressure groups (or even interest groups) in the nation's capital.[3] It does not represent a political double cross of the

[3] Latham describes the American political process in the following terms: The principal social values of modern life are realized through group action. Groups organize for security and advantage, to control the environment in which they exist, in order to make it predictable and safe. Organization begets counter-organization. Coalitions, constellations, and combinations of groups struggle with each other for security and the advantage of their members. The struggle takes place in the official as well as the private fields of controversy. The distinction between "official" and "private" is the social understanding that the first have the right to give known and knowable orders to the second. In the struggle for security and advantage, private groups enlist the support of official groups in their behalf when the added leverage of official power is required. A principal function of legislators is to referee the group struggle, to ratify the victories of successful coalitions, and to record the terms that define the compromises, surrenders and victories in the form of statutes. Legislative

labor movement by the Democratic congressional leadership, an interpretation often heard in interviews with Washington representatives of some unions. It does represent the result of an all-out power struggle among various groups in our society; it does reflect the underlying conservative bias of our national legislature; it does reflect certain misconceptions of power relationships, actual and potential, by the leaders of the labor movement; [4] but, most of all, it represents an issue which was decided by the American public itself. This is the major conclusion to be drawn from the analysis of the Labor-Management Reporting and Disclosure Act of 1959. The role of the American public was crucial to the final outcome.[5]

votes tend to represent the composition of strength, i.e., the balance of power, among the contending coalitions at the moment of voting. What may be called "public policy" is the equilibrium reached at any moment in the struggle of contending coalitions, an equilibrium which factions of groups constantly strive to weight in their favor.

The above is summarized from Earl Latham, *The Group Basis of Politics, A Study in Basing Point Legislation* (Ithaca, N.Y., Cornell University Press, 1952), Chapter I.

Latham's abstraction from the reality of American politics is rich in insight, but it fails to take into account two dimensions of the body politic: the first is what David Truman calls the "rules of the game," the generally accepted values and mores which cannot be violated without high cost to the violator; the second is the role of the general public in a politico-economic power struggle. As will be stated, it is my thesis that the latter forces were in fact the dominant forces. The border line between the power of interest groups and the power of the general public is indeed fuzzy, especially in light of the interaction of the two groups, but the distinction can be drawn and must be drawn in order to understand the passage of this law.

David Truman's interpretation of groups in politics is broader than that of Latham, but it, too, falls short as a theory for the interpretation of the passage of this law.

For a more comprehensive elaboration of his theory see David Truman, *The Governmental Process: Political Interests and Public Opinion* (New York, Knopf, 1951).

[4] The motivations of various segments of the labor movement were extremely complex, but a goal shared by most was the attainment of a new respectability for labor unions. This aspect of their motivation lies outside the usual theories of the political process. It will be explored as a substudy in this analysis.

[5] The title of E. E. Schattsneider's book, *The Semisovereign People: A Realist's View of Democracy in America* (New York, Holt, Rinehart, and Winston, 1960), suggests also that only on certain issues does the public become involved in deciding the outcome. Schattsneider suggests that the dynamics of the situation proceed from the stage when the weaker side in a private struggle seeks the aid of governmental groups to strengthen its position. Then the weaker of the combined private and governmental groups seeks further "socialization" (as contrasted to "privatization") of the issue by enlisting the general public in the dispute. Only on major conflicts does the general public

Such a conclusion would appear to be an optimistic one for a democratic society. Yet, this is not necessarily the case. To state that the general public was instrumental in determining the final direction of the decision on this issue is not to state that the decision was made optimally, nor even that the decision was made in the right direction under the existing circumstances. As the analysis proceeds, the reader will see the basis on which the attitude of the public was formed, the means by which it was made known to the Congress, and the degree of understanding the public displayed. Many qualifications about the process must be expressed before one can determine his own attitude toward the event.

Nevertheless, the conclusion is an important one, both in terms of the support which it lends to particular theories of political decision making and in terms of the weight it lends to the refutation of other such theories. It is highly significant even if limited to its negative aspects. These judgments will be spelled out as the study unfolds.

The election of 1958 gave organized labor, through congressmen of liberal leaning, unprecedented representation on the labor committees of both houses of Congress. The Senate was most clearly under control of the liberal group. The Subcommittee on Labor was chaired by Senator John F. Kennedy, who, with the aid of Senators Wayne Morse, Pat McNamara, and Jennings Randolph, had automatic voting control over the actions and recommendations of the subcommittee. Liberal representation on the full committee was strong even on the Republican side of the group. Yet, this committee recommended to the Senate legislation which would regulate the internal affairs of labor unions. For the first time a clear majority of the House Committee on Education and Labor was favorably disposed to the position of the labor movement. That committee also reported such a bill. These actions would not have been taken had they not been a "political necessity."

At this point let us pause a moment. The political necessity that

in fact take part. Robert A. Dahl, political scientist from Yale University, suggests a supporting theory of the involvement of the public which will be referred to later. To Schattsneider the awareness of conflict brings about the interest of the public.

there be a labor reform bill presented to and acted on by both the House and the Senate existed at two levels. First, it was essential to the Democratic Party, which had overwhelming numerical control over the Congress, that it demonstrate its "responsibility" by passing labor reform legislation. (This, in effect, is one of the "rules of the game" conditioning the behavior of major participants.) The Presidency in the election of 1960 loomed as the goal for at least four individual Democrats: Majority Leader Lyndon Johnson, Senator John Kennedy, Senator Hubert Humphrey, and Senator Stuart Symington. The partisanship of House Speaker Rayburn for the Johnson presidential cause was a further strong stimulus for the lower house to follow the path of responsible government.

The second major political necessity was that faced by the AFL-CIO itself. The labor movement in the United States has experienced a long, uphill struggle for legitimacy and prestige. Its zenith was reached, perhaps, during the final years of the Roosevelt Administration—at least in terms of prestige relative to that of the businessman, who was suffering at that time a temporary eclipse as a result of general reaction to the Great Depression of the thirties. In 1959, as a result, first, of the hearings of Senator McClellan's Senate Select Committee on Improper Activities in Labor-Management Affairs and, second, of the ineffectiveness of the weapons available to the labor movement for purging itself of an aura of guilt or, indeed, to correct the conditions which brought the need for formal action by the AFL-CIO, some further convincing steps were necessary to rebuild the waning prestige of labor as a law-abiding group worthy of public respect.[6] Since the problem was not amenable to correc-

[6] Sociologists and social psychologists would interpret this as the search by the labor movement for a new "identity." A more commonly used term for a closely related concept would be a new "public image." No matter what the phrase, the dynamics of the situation are the same. Ward Goodenough of the University of Pennsylvania sets forth six steps necessary for change in identity to take place. First, there must be a desire on the part of the group for change; second, there must be a commitment to change; third, there must be understanding on the part of the members of the group of the changed role; fourth, there must be the ability on the part of the group to perform the changed role; fifth, there must be recognition and acceptance by others that the change has taken place; and sixth, there must be a conception by the members of the group that they indeed have achieved a new condition. See Ward H. Good-

tion from within the labor movement itself, the necessity for action by the federal government was clearly indicated.

In saying this we are saying that the power of the public and its collective opinion is great. Political necessity derives from the need to adjust to or modify the opinion of the public (no matter how it has been gauged).

It became a fact of the environment in 1959 that labor reform legislation had to be passed in the Eighty-sixth Congress. The greatest genius attributed to Lyndon Johnson was his reputed ability to gauge the temper of the country and of the Senate in order to select the proper moment to bring legislation to the floor for formal decision. The first session of the Eighty-sixth Congress was the time selected by him for labor reform. (In 1958 the attempt at passage of legislation had been sufficient; in 1959 actual passage was necessary.)

A member of the leadership of the House also stated candidly that an attempt (halfhearted) was "good enough" for the closing moments in the House of Representatives in 1958 but "would not do" for 1959. Speaker Rayburn was quoted by several congressmen in interviews with the author as stating repeatedly "there's got to be a bill." This was a reflection, through the perception of congressional leaders, of the mood of the public.

On most issues before the Congress, however, the public remains apathetic, thus exerting little if any influence. We must then account for the degree of participation by the public in the legislative struggle over Landrum-Griffin. There are two major factors which brought about the participation of the public: the activities of the McClellan Committee and the intervention of the President of the United States. The influence of each of these was different in timing and function; the influence of both was essential to the particular embodiment of the outcome.

---

enough, "Education and Identity," in Frederick C. Gruber, ed., *Anthropology and Education* (Philadelphia, University of Pennsylvania Press, 1961), pp. 84–102.

The desire on the part of labor for respectability represented its commitment to achieve social change, the change in its identity. Federal legislation appeared to be the only feasible method of bringing about the change. This helps explain the actions of labor and its stake in legislation.

The Influence of the McClellan Committee

Eminent political scientists have documented the usual political apathy of the general public.[7] A factor contributing to this usual role of the public is ignorance: first, ignorance of the existence of the issue itself; second, ignorance of the proper direction of action to resolve an issue once known. Ordinarily, the private citizen tends to leave the resolution of complex technical issues to his elected representatives, hoping that the elected official will invest sufficient time and effort to acquaint himself with the substance of issues and the proper direction for their resolution.

In brief outline we can point to the role of the McClellan Committee on Improper Activities in Labor-Management Affairs—commonly called the Labor Rackets Committee—as the underlying cause of public awareness that there was some wrongdoing in the internal operation of unions which had to be righted. The influence of President Eisenhower was required to translate awareness into action.

For two and one-half years the McClellan Committee trumpeted report after report of alleged corruption and the misuse of funds in labor-management affairs. The committee's discoveries and pronouncements were amplified and transmitted in the mass media of communication until the Teamsters Union, its one-time President (and present inhabitant of a federal prison) Dave Beck, and President-elect Jimmie Hoffa became household names. Here were disclosures of questionable activities which did not merely flash into headlines and then disappear from public awareness. Here were disclosures, which occurred with increasing regularity, of alleged wrongdoing which was continuing. This was not all. Specific actions —the indictment of Dave Beck, the expulsion of the Teamsters and certain other unions from the AFL-CIO—provided confirmation that there was substance to the claims of corruption and wrongdoing.

From its beginning the McClellan Committee had taken elaborate pains to maintain impartiality between labor and management contexts for seeking out wrongdoing in labor-management affairs. Then, gradually and subtlely, the committee's activities changed in char-

[7] See, for example, Robert A. Dahl, *Who Governs?: Democracy and Power in an American City* (New Haven, Yale University Press, 1961).

acter. A single, most able protagonist emerged. The activities of the committee came to be aimed more and more at alleged corruption in a single union, the Teamster's Union, and at a single man, Teamster's president, James Hoffa.

The drama took on new interest for the public and the press as Hoffa proved to be at once able, articulate, and arrogant. Frequent and violent encounters between Senator McClellan or his chief committee investigator, Robert Kennedy, and Hoffa always made colorful reading and received generous coverage in the news. The droning in the mass media of the message of the McClellan Committee approached in intensity the repetitive message of cigarette advertisers —only the singing jingles were missing. The average citizen was made thoroughly aware that there was an issue, that the issue was before the Congress, and that it should be resolved in 1959.

But, again, there is ample evidence that awareness of a problem is not in itself sufficient for the resolution of the problem. A prominent antecedent to the hearings of the McClellan Committee, the investigations of the Kefauver Crime Committee, had produced equally sensational coverage in the mass media. In fact, the hearings of that committee were the first to receive the coverage of television and thus directly reach the homes of millions of Americans. Yet, in that case no legislation effectively combating the organized network of crime in this country was passed by the Congress. The average citizen is perhaps not aware of this. His apparent tendency has been to equate public exposure of an issue with resolution of the issue. There continues to be ample, though piecemeal, evidence that the evils exposed by Senator Estes Kefauver have not been overcome.

The McClellan Committee accomplished two things for the private citizen. It provided him with information—the condensed and sensationalized information of the mass media, but information nonetheless—on the existence and nature of a problem in labor-management relations. It also provided him, throughout the extended investigations over almost three years, with evidence that the problem presented had not been resolved. In fact, the McClellan Committee issued statements during the spring and summer of 1959 urging the passage of particular legislation which was "required" to resolve the problem.

The importance attributed here to the McClellan Committee is apparently at variance with the election results of 1958, especially on the union shop issue. The apparent contradiction can easily be resolved because it did not exist. Congressional and state election contests did not constitute an appropriate scale by which to measure the impact of the Rackets Committee activities. These contests appear to have been decided on the basis of local personalities and issues and on the usual voter reaction to the state of the economy.

The defeat of the right-to-work laws, however, is somewhat more difficult to explain. A combination of several factors seems to have been important. First, labor unions appear to be quite effective in directly influencing voting. Their greatest strength is in the numbers of their members, their local organization, and their ability to use their man power in election campaigns. Second, the unions directed their efforts toward the general public in condemning the proposed right-to-work laws as representing no more than an attempt to destroy labor unions. Third, the right of the working man to organize in unions and to pursue his goals through collective bargaining is now an accepted tenet of our economic system. It is an accepted "rule of the game." Thus, an open, almost blatant attempt to shift radically the balance of power between labor and management would not be (and was not) received with favor. The recession and the high level of unemployment were no doubt also of considerable importance in reinforcing these factors.

It will be seen that the misinterpretation of the election results was a major error on the part of the leaders of labor. It resulted in a false evaluation of their power and, thus, in a number of strategic and tactical mistakes.

The Role of the President

At a crucial moment, just before the various proposals for legislation were presented to the House of Representatives for a vote, Dwight David Eisenhower, the President of the United States, addressed the nation by radio and television.

In August of 1959 President Eisenhower was in his last two years of office. By constitutional amendment he could not succeed himself. He was a "lame duck." Factors of similar import to the careers of

many men before him had led them to lethargy and inaction; to
Eisenhower these factors proved to be a spur. The change in the
President in his last two years was dramatic. The press began gradually to speak of the "new Eisenhower," the man of energy, power,
and action.

The man was not entirely "new," however. The President was still
the father image to millions of Americans, still the nonpartisan arbiter of disputes over the public interest, still the man of character,
honor, and duty. The fact that he could not be re-elected enhanced
rather than detracted from these facets of the Eisenhower image.
Here was a man who could have no political motivation because he
could not run again for political office. Eisenhower was seen, and
saw himself, as the man elected by all the people, seeking only the
good of the nation.[8]

In this context his plea to the public in a rare radio and television
appeal—the only time he was to mention a piece of proposed
legislation by name—was a very powerful stimulus indeed for the
Landrum-Griffin bill in the House of Representatives. Eisenhower's
endorsement of the conservative-sponsored legislation brought about
a great response on the part of the general public. Eisenhower's request for support of "strong" labor legislation gave legitimacy to the
Landrum-Griffin bill and to those who supported it.

This was directly important within the Congress as well as to the
public at large. Landrum-Griffin had been introduced as a substitute
for a bill duly passed through the process of House committee action.
Now the substitute had a public, presidential blessing.

While the hearings of the McClellan Committee had cultivated
the environment for labor reform legislation, informing the public
that "something should be done," the Eisenhower speech brought the
commitment of the "little man" to flower. It provided him with the
second ingredient he needed to bring his political influence to bear
on the issue—a clear direction for the resolution of the problem.
When the President, who had stood throughout his term in office
above the battle of partisan politics, took an explicit stand on the

[8] See Richard Neustadt, *Presidential Power: The Politics of Leadership*
(New York, Wiley, 1960), for an excellent sketch of Eisenhower's self-image.

issue of labor reform legislation, he informed the public that the resolution of the problems of labor corruption lay in the passage of "strong" legislation and that such legislation took the form of the Landrum-Griffin bill.

The change in character of the mail which reached congressional offices following the Eisenhower speech was important to a number of congressmen. Earlier mail, while heavy, had clearly been sent in response to organized campaigns. This mail had indicated the strength of feeling of various organizations on the issue, but the mail which came after the speech was clearly from the average citizen who felt strongly enough as an individual to write to his congressman.[9] A further factor supporting the conclusion that the mail was not from organized sources was the fact that both houses of Congress were engulfed in the avalanche of messages from the electorate. The Senate had already acted on its version of labor reform. Only the House of Representatives could act or not act on the Landrum-Griffin bill. Yet, both senators and representatives were contacted and given the opinions of the writers. The mail sent to senators was not totally wasted, as we shall see; it was important in the final phases of the legislative struggle.

Public Influence on the Congress

When it became clear that the general electorate was aware of the issue of labor reform and was sufficiently informed to take a stand for or against a particular piece of legislation, the congressmen were on the spot. They could not afford to ignore the issue, nor could they afford to weigh lightly a vote not in agreement with the expressed wishes of their constituents.

The power of the public pressure for labor reform was clearly demonstrated in the House of Representatives. Of the 434 congressmen eligible to vote on the issue, 430 cast their votes. With but one exception this was the largest percentage of those eligible who voted

[9] These comments necessarily represent qualitative judgments. They are based on evidence reported to the author during interviews with congressmen and also with congressional staff members whose job it was to gauge the reactions of the public. Estimates of mail volume on particular dates were also given by Capitol postal authorities.

on any question in this century. Further quantitative measures of the influence of the public became available at certain stages of the voting on the law. These will be highlighted in turn.

Much of the discussion in the chapters which follow details maneuvers of the two major protagonists in the range of tactics—with much that can be seen and learned at this level. But the tactics of the groups and their impact were limited by the factors alluded to thus far. There would be labor reform legislation in 1959; this had been determined. The legislation would embody regulation of the internal affairs of unions. The question of whether there would be changes to the Taft-Harley Act was open and at certain stages could have been resolved in the negative, but the thrust of events forced the issue to be resolved in the positive. The particular type of Taft-Hartley changes and the degree of severity in the reforms of internal union affairs were the questions which had to be resolved in the interaction of the two major protagonists. But the degree to which the protagonists could influence the outcome was severely limited; this will be documented as the study unfolds.

It is now necessary to step back and recognize the preceding comments for what they are: an interpretation of the events which took place in 1959. They necessarily represent abstraction from the extended, rich interactions which took place at the time the act was being considered. It must also be recognized that the role of the interest groups was highly significant, especially in certain specifics. Both management and labor recognized the 1959 session of the Eighty-sixth Congress as a crucial one for legislation affecting their interests. Each committed its major resources to the battle, and each had a significant effect on the final outcome. This was to be expected and to be desired. The parties at interest in a dispute over major legislation should make their views known to the Congress, and only these two groups had the ability to predict the impact that certain legislative provisions would have in practice. But the interest groups did not decide the issue. They were unable even to control the basic strategy (the content of the legislation) employed once the process was under way. The effective impact of these groups was really achieved through the electorate. The people decided the issue.

Further Questions

There are a number of subissues on which much light can be shed in the course of this study. One of them has been suggested already: the complex motivation of the labor movement in supporting a law which would regulate its internal affairs. The difficulties for the AFL-CIO which arose over the legislation resulted from their inability to understand and control the dynamics of the changes which they were seeking. A second subissue was the impact of the organization of the interest groups on their effectiveness in achieving their goals. Clearly, the organization of the AFL-CIO was an important factor which influenced its ability to deal with the dynamics of change, while unusual management coordination was achieved on the other side of the issue. The workings of the legislative process is the third subissue which can be studied at close range in the pages to follow. There are hazy border lines among these subissues, but for most purposes distinctions can be made.

One startling fact which emerges from this study is that real controversy did not develop over the question of labor reform per se once it had been settled that there would be changes to the Taft-Hartley Act appended to the reform sections of the legislation. Rather, the major differences and the sources of controversy were found in issues outside the areas of reform, outside the areas of comment and recommendation of the McClellan Committee. Controversy centered on those questions related directly to the balance of power between labor and management, the direction and degree of changes to the Taft-Hartley Act. Yet, the battle was joined and fought by both sides in the name of labor reform.

This illustrates a fact of life in our democratic society which many authors have recognized. We in the United States do not make changes involving major power groups (or other important changes for that matter) except under conditions of crisis or alleged crisis. It took the Great Depression before the federal government regulated known abuses in the securities markets. It took the mass unemployment of the thirties to bring the federal government to give full sanction to union organizations. It took the challenge of the

Russian sputniks before we acted on the whole question of our educational process, and so forth. In a period of crisis, when the public is aroused to the point of demanding that "something must be done," it is also true that the action which is taken often bears little relation to the questions nominally at issue.[10]

There is no doubt that this was the case in 1959. Both sides recognized that the time to make all desired changes in labor-management legislation was the time when the Congress had such questions —any facet of such questions—before it. The justification for the inclusion of any particular change was unnecessary.

In the chapters to follow the development of the Labor-Management Reporting and Disclosure Act in the Eighty-sixth Congress is analyzed. In Chapter II the background of the labor movement in this country is sketched, a brief history of attempts to change the law of labor-management affairs from the time of the Wagner Act through 1959 is presented, and the origin and initial impact of the McClellan Committee is given. In this context the law of 1959 can be seen as the continued development of a familiar pattern, even in the continuity of personalities involved in the process. (But the leaders of labor did not perceive it to be so.) In Chapters III through IX the development of the 1959 statute is analyzed in chronological sequence, with occasional digressions to provide significant perspective. In Chapter X the conclusions to be drawn from this analysis— many of them previewed in the preceeding pages—are discussed.

---

[10] To Schattsneider this is "substitution of issues," the process of cloaking a desired (and perhaps unpalatable) objective in the more acceptable garb of the solution to some pressing issue which is before the public. A variation on the procedure is the presentation of the desired objective as a representation of an acceptable homily. See Schattsneider, *The Semisovereign People*. Similar observations are made by Dahl and J. K. Galbraith in other contexts.

II. THE MILIEU

LEGISLATION grows from a substantive environment; it grows from an economic, social, and political fabric. It grows as an addition to and modification of history. Therefore we must trace a number of diverse factors if the particular legislation which is the subject of this study is to be understood fully. Even with the considerable passage of years the reader will note the continuity of behavior patterns and perhaps one cause thereof, the many repeat performers among the major actors in the continuing labor-management struggle in the political arena.

The American Labor Movement: An Historical Sketch

The general philosophy of the American labor movement has been to seek improvement in the lot of the working man within the system of private property and private capital.[1] It has avoided a purely class identification, partly because the prevailing attitude among the workers was that everyone had the opportunity someday to become a capitalist. Thus, the working groups viewed their position in the hierarchy of employment to be temporary. Unions were viewed mainly as a means of achieving improvement in the temporary economic condition of the worker. The result was what became known

[1] This section is intended only as a sketch to provide background for the material which follows. A complete history of the labor movement and the complex of tenets which underly its philosophy are beyond the scope of this work. The readers interested in delving further should see Philip Taft, *The A.F. of L. in the Time of Gompers* (New York, Harper, 1957), Harry A. Millis and Royal E. Montgomery, *Organized Labor* (New York, McGraw-Hill, 1945), especially Chapters 1–5, and similar works. For an interesting compilation of documents see also Neil W. Chamberlain, *Sourcebook on Labor* (New York, McGraw-Hill, 1958).

as "business unionism": the concentration on wages, hours, and conditions of work. There was no attempt on the part of the labor movement to organize a political party or to make itself felt on broad social issues through political means. However, especially as a result of the actions of the courts, the labor movement gradually recognized the necessity to bring pressure in the political arena in order to achieve the ends of business unionism. Even then, the leaders of labor were content to work through the existing parties in seeking their goals.

A number of attempts at the formation of national unions had met with failure. It was not until the concentration on organizing along craft lines, which allowed the union to capitalize on the common bonds of similar skills, that a national union became truly effective. The craft union, or trade union, became the predominant means of organization until new pressures grew with the growth of industrialization in the country.

Certain basic features have characterized the American labor movement for over a century. The first is jurisdictional disputes as a source of friction. The rivalry among various unions for the allegiance of particular workers has led to internal strife from the labor movement's early days. The vehemence with which the rivalry has been pursued stems from the economic significance of jurisdiction over certain types of employment. Without the ability to control the supply of workers available to a business the union is essentially powerless. Overlapping jurisdiction means at least alternative sources of supply for the businessman and can mean that a rival union would displace one's own as sole bargaining agent.

The second feature of the American labor movement is the rivalry of the craft union versus the industrial union and its attendant animosity, again stemming from the economics of jurisdictional questions. With the widespread organization of whole industries by a single union, which occurred in the 1930s, jurisdictional warfare became greatly accentuated.

Industrial unions sought to represent all the workers in a given industry no matter what their level of skill or trade. A major stumbling block to such efforts was that many of the highly skilled tradesmen in these industries were already represented by a trade union.

Yet, experience had shown the futility of bargaining by many independent unions in a loose federation of crafts (leaving a large segment of the unskilled workers in the industry not represented at all) with a single unified management. Industrial unions appeared to be the only feasible alternative. Acceptance of the alternative brought with it the violent reaction of the craft unions whose ranks were raided with the emergence of each new industrial union.

The third major feature has been the functioning of the international unions as centers of influence and power. The parent federation (AFL, CIO, or AFL-CIO) has often been looked upon as monolithic, power-wielding "labor," but the word has cloaked a many-headed group of mutually competitive, independent leaders preoccupied with their own internal political problems—the leaders of the international unions.

The first national federation of unions in the United States which was to demonstrate an ability to survive, the AFL, was organized by Samuel Gompers in December, 1886. The constitution of the American Federation of Labor incorporated many of the features which characterize unions to this day. International unions were the main structural units; state and local bodies were subordinate to the Executive Council, which had only one full-time salaried member, the president. The parent federation had three main functions: the protection of the jurisdiction of its affiliates, the encouragement of legislation favorable to wage earners, and assistance to the constituent groups in organizing new unions.

When it became clear that direct political action would be necessary to achieve the goals of the AFL, Gompers developed the approach through the Democratic and Republican parties of "rewarding his friends and punishing his enemies."

Gompers himself was not a sophisticated student of the federal government. On various occasions he would accept form for substance in negotiations with the Congress. The fortunes of labor ebbed and waned with changes in the political and economic climate of the times. The decisions of the conservative courts of the 1920s caused the labor movement to look more and more toward the Congress as the means to improve its lot in the society.

The industrial growth of the United States posed a number of fur-

ther problems for the trade union movement. It tended to accentuate
the jurisdictional problems faced by the AFL. Gompers developed
certain techniques for attempting to deal with these disputes. The
Building Trades Department set up by him in 1901 was designed to
help solve disputes between the trade unions. Now an especially
important sociological problem, the question of organizing the unskilled and the foreign-born, was added to the earlier questions. The
prevailing attitude among skilled craftsmen in the AFL, based both
on prejudice and experience, was that the unskilled could not be
organized and perhaps should not be organized in the same unions
with the skilled Anglo-Saxon and Scandinavian tradesmen. In any
case, the mechanics of attempting to organize an entire industry presented great problems of coordination to the AFL. Such a wide range
of trades and activities were encompassed that it was necessary to
gain the cooperation of fourteen to twenty-four international unions
in the effort to organize a single industry. These cumbersome arrangements were completely ineffective in the sometimes open-
warfare of the organizing drive. The failure of the AFL to organize
whole industries generated great internal pressure, a pressure for
changes in the approach to organization.

While the record of the trade union movement in achieving improvement for child and female laborers, in hours and working conditions, and for certain social legislation was good, its achievement
of legislation directly favorable to unions as such had been minimal
through the 1920s. The Railway Labor Act of 1926 was the first major
law of benefit to a trade union as an institution. It represented the
first time that the federal government had gone on record in encour-
aging union growth. Though it applied to a particular, relatively
small group of workers, it was a forerunner of legislation to come.
Employers were compelled by law to negotiate exclusively with
representatives of employees who had been chosen freely and without limitation. They were required to negotiate on matters of rates
of pay, rules, and working conditions.

The Emergence of the CIO

The economic, political, and social upheaval of the depression
period brought great changes both in the legislation relating to labor

and in the labor movement itself.[2] It is interesting to note that, at
the time when the federal government was nurturing the comparatively powerless labor movement, the internal warfare of the movement had reached its greatest height. In 1934 the split in the labor
movement became quite clear, although it was compromised in the
convention of that year. By 1935 compromise was no longer possible,
and John L. Lewis, resigning his vice-presidency of the AFL, formed
an independent group to bring about the new approach to organization of industrial unions, the Committee for Industrial Organization.

The Norris-LaGuardia Anti-Injunction Act had been followed in
the early 1930s by the National Industrial Recovery Act (NIRA),
Section 7 of which specifically called upon employers in all industries engaged in interstate commerce to recognize the right of their
employees to bargain collectively. Though NIRA was found unconstitutional by the conservative Supreme Court in 1935, the federal
government reacted almost immediately with the passage of the
Wagner Act in that same year. This truly established a new era for
the American labor movement. With the confirmation in 1937 that
the Wagner Act was constitutional, organization by unions became
most effective. Armed with the provisions of the Wagner Act, which
provided firm guarantees of the rights of employees to join into
unions, to bargain collectively, and to strike without fear of reprisal
from employers, and prohibited employer interference with union
activities, nonrecognition of unions, or refusal to bargain, the Committee for Industrial Organization brought about the organization of
literally millions of previously nonunion people. The spectacular
success of the organization of industrial unions exceeded even the
dreams of the leaders. Evidence indicated, however, that it was not
merely the method of organization or the personalities of the leaders
of the Committee which led to its success, for the AFL itself grew at
a very rapid pace during the 1930s.

From the beginning, John L. Lewis and his fellow leaders of the
Committee had not intended to split the labor movement asunder.
Their objective was a reorganization within the parent group. This
had been frustrated from the start, and animosity had grown in

[2] These sections dealing with the conditions leading up to and including the
merger of the AFL and the CIO rely heavily on Arthur J. Goldberg, *AFL-CIO,
Labor United* (New York, McGraw-Hill, 1956).

intensity, especially as the Committee proved its ability to succeed. In 1938 the split, with its resultant jurisdictional warfare, was insitutionalized when the Committee for Industrial Organization became the Congress of Industrial Organizations.

The first president of the CIO was John L. Lewis himself. He served in this capacity until 1940, when, after a series of policy disputes, he resigned the presidency, to be succeeded by Philip Murray. In 1942 Lewis took his United Mine Workers out of the CIO entirely.

Impact of World War II

A new factor, a major source of understanding and cooperation, came into being with the onset of World War II. At that time the leaders of organized labor were afforded unprecedented recognition by the federal government. They were made members of boards and panels; they worked together in many capacities and agencies; they associated intimately and grew in mutual confidence. Personal animosities began to fade with the passage of time and the recognition of the mutuality of interests between the two groups. Now, with the new atmosphere, Philip Murray, the second president of the CIO, made a series of efforts and overtures to achieve unity in the labor movement. These were partly in response to efforts by President Franklin Roosevelt to bring about such unity during the war period.

By 1938 and 1939 pressure for the amendment of the Wagner Act had begun to build. The pressure came from an interesting source, the AFL itself.[3] The AFL had become increasingly unhappy with the actions of the National Labor Relations Board (NLRB) because of its alleged favoritism toward the CIO in union-representation decisions. The AFL directed its efforts toward modification of the statute as a means of achieving treatment it felt would be more favorable to its interest.

Three types of bills were introduced in the Congress as proposed modifications of the Wagner Act. The first group would have redefined agricultural labor in order to exclude from coverage certain workers otherwise covered. The second group would have left the

[3] See Harry A. Millis and Emily Clark Brown, *From the Wagner Act to Taft-Hartley: A Study of National Labor Policy and Labor Relations* (Chicago, University of Chicago Press, 1950), especially Chapters 8 and 9, for a complete summary of this legislation. The discussion here is based on this book.

spirit of the Wagner Act intact while modifying the letter sufficiently to improve the position of the AFL in representation elections. Bills resulting from the AFL pressure mentioned above fell into this category. The third category, supported by business and industrial groups, would have greatly changed the character of the Wagner Act and the NLRB. It included provisions which would have restricted and regulated the activities of labor unions. Certain provisions were designed to provide "balance" by specifying unfair labor practices for unions, allowing management to "counsel and advise" employees on organization questions, and so forth.

Extensive hearings were undertaken in the Congress on these questions. While hearings were being held, a bit of familiar legislative strategy was undertaken. Representative Howard Smith, a conservative Southerner who was to have great influence in labor legislation throughout his lifetime—especially in the development of the Landrum-Griffin Act in 1959—introduced a resolution in the House to authorize an investigation of the NLRB. Smith was not a member of the House Committee on Education and Labor, but of the Rules Committee of the House. He was a known opponent of labor and the Wagner Act, against which he had voted because he "felt it was unconstitutional." The formation of the committee to carry out the investigation was supported by the AFL! The resolution was approved by the House and a select committee formed.

The members appointed to the committee were Smith (D, Va.), chairman; Arthur Healey (D, Mass.); Abe Murdock (D, Utah); Charles Halleck (R, Ind.); and Harry Routzohn (R, Ohio). Representative Halleck was to have an important role in later labor legislation, as were members of the House Labor Committee itself: Graham Barden, Clare Hoffman, Fred Hartley, and others.

The select committee conducted extended hearings over the period of a year, the record of which was published in over thirty volumes. The committee issued an interim report calling for legislation, legislation which Chairman Smith himself introduced in the House (H.R.8813) in March of 1940. The committee utilized isolated cases from the files of the NLRB to level general condemnation at the board. (A more extensive, unbiased study conducted by the Columbia University Law School strongly supported the board and its actions.) The AFL backed the committee in its charges of favoritism in the administration of the law and supported many of the provisions of the Smith bill. The CIO violently opposed both. The Committee on Education and Labor, being charged by the House with the organizational responsibility of expertise in labor affairs, meantime proposed legislation on its own, the Norton bill, which business groups, supporters of the Smith bill, labeled a "red herring." The Rules Committee provided a rule allowing the substitution of the Smith bill for the Norton bill when it was considered on the floor. And the House sidetracked the latter while passing the former. The tactic would become familiar to observers of the Congress. It was repeated several times, including one instance in August, 1959. The Senate took no action on the subject.

The Smith-Connally Act of 1943 was the first legislation successful in modifying the Wagner Act. Representative Smith, bathed in prestige from his committee investigation, had become an authority on labor matters in the House. Though at no time a member of the Committee on Education and Labor, Smith was able to use his authority in labor matters to push legislation through the House. He was instrumental in the passage by the lower chamber of the War Labor Disputes (Smith-Connally) Act over the veto of President Roosevelt. Senator Tom Connally shepherded the bill through the Senate. Feeling against work stoppages in the bituminous coal industry during wartime had generated public support for restrictive labor legislation.

An interesting sidelight on the passage of Smith-Connally was the number of important amendments proposed but not passed during debate over the act. These proposals were direct harbingers of provisions that were to become law in the Taft-Hartley Act. At this stage they were evidence of growing sentiment which favored changes in the Wagner Act. The most important were the proposals for the use of injunctions by the Attorney General in national emergency disputes, the use of "cooling-off" periods prior to major strikes, and the prohibition of major strikes.

Smith-Connally, as passed, had four major provisions: (1) the requirement for twenty-day notice prior to strikes in private plants, (2) the provision of statutory authority for the War Labor Board,

(3) the prohibition of strikes in government-held plants and mines, and (4) prohibition of political contributions by unions in federal elections.

Further bills were proposed in the Congress prior to the advent of Taft-Hartley. Millis and Brown summarize:

Several observations can be made: first, there were few major provisions in Taft-Hartley which did not find counterparts in legislation previously introduced; second, a relatively small number of points in the NLRA and its administration were severely and consistently criticized by a minority of representatives and senators during the ten-year period; third, important members of this minority were the same members who consistently proposed restrictive amendments that would have changed the basic law of labor; fourth, it was the views of this minority, substantially unchanged, which became the predominantly accepted view of the Congress as a new Republican majority joined hands with die-hard southern Democrats; and, lastly, despite the lengthy hearings of the Senate and House labor committees at two widely separated times, and the investigation by the highly controversial Smith Committee in 1939–40, there was never any systematic, nonpolitical study or investigation authorized or undertaken by Congress before it acted on many complex and technical matters about which it had relatively little accurate information.[4]

The example of the passage of the Smith Bill in the House had chastened the leaders of the AFL. As the war progressed the leaders of various labor groups were gradually to know and understand each other better, and the basis for a new relationship among union people gradually became established.

Taft-Hartley and a New Climate

While the internal problems of the labor movement appeared to be abating, its relationships to the society as a whole were deteriorating. The activities of the United Mine Workers and the publicity attendant to their wartime strikes were interpreted by the public as union arrogance and an expression of the tremendous economic power of a single union leader. The jurisdictional disputes leading to industrial strife, the round of postwar strikes in basic industries, all of these contributed to a changing atmosphere and a changing perception of the union movement in this country. The press and the

[4] Millis and Brown, *From the Wagner Act to Taft-Hartley*, p. 362.

political spokesmen identified the union movement with John L. Lewis, the personification of labor arrogance and power.

When, in this atmosphere, the Taft-Hartley Act was being considered by the Congress during 1947, there were a number of overtures between the labor groups toward joint action in opposition to what they considered to be antiunion legislation. However, the tactics of the labor movement were not successful; coordinated effort was not achieved. Each union supported proposals in its own narrow self-interest.

It can be argued that, given the mood of the public and the Republican control of the Congress, the actions of labor would have been ineffective. In any case, the passage of the law in 1947 over the veto of the Democratic President, Harry Truman, indicated the ineffectiveness of those actions that were taken.

The Taft-Hartley Act was a very complex piece of legislation with a number of major provisions. The three main titles dealt with: (1) amendments to the National Labor Relations Act, contained in eighteen of the law's twenty-eight pages and covering a number of sections, including those modifying the functioning of the NLRB, redefining unfair labor practices to include a number of union activities, prescribing procedures for selection of union representatives and their election, and prescribing procedures for prevention of unfair labor practices (including the use of injunctions); (2) provision of a conciliation service independent of the Department of Labor and a procedure for dealing with national emergency strikes through the now-familiar eighty-day injunction; (3) suits by and against labor organizations, restrictions on payments to employee representatives, on boycotts, and other unlawful combinations, restrictions on political contributions, and the prohibition of strikes by government employees.

Millis and Brown have classified the Act into four major categories, based on the impact and apparent intent of the various provisions.[5] The first group includes those provisions which achieved a real and necessary equalization of the effects of the Wagner Act. Among provisions of this type were the prohibition of coercion of employers and/or employees by unions or union leaders, of extortion and feath-

[5] Millis and Brown, *From the Wagner Act to Taft-Hartley*, Chapter 17.

erbedding, or refusal to bargain, and of strikes or boycotts in furtherance of jurisdictional disputes. The second group they call "that long
list of provisions" made in the name of fairness which had desirable
psychological effect if not substantive impact. In this category were
included provisions making clear the responsibility of unions for
their conduct, reassurances for employers in a free speech amendment (though it went too far), provisions strengthening democratic
tendencies and the acceptance of decisions through various election
procedures, and a number of administrative changes made in furtherance of impartiality. The third group of changes tended to promote
conflict and litigation which were inclined to weaken the collective
bargaining process and in fact upset established practices previously
worked out by labor and management. Some of these major changes
included were the outlawing of the union shop—and, apparently,
the hiring hall as well—restrictions on payments to unions and on
the administration of joint welfare funds, the sixty-day notice clause
for strikes, the encouragement of damage suits, and the proscription
of bargaining units for certain classes of workers (especially super-
visors). The fourth classification includes a longer list of unfair and
discriminatory provisions which reflected bias against unions and
collective bargaining in general. This group provided weapons to an
employer who wished to fight a union and included the free speech
amendment, which could be extended almost to coercion, the ban on
boycotts and sympathy strikes, the use of injunctions (some of which
were mandatory, requiring priority treatment by the NLRB), the
one-sided pressure on unions in "national emergency" strikes, and
the ban on union expenditures of dues in national elections. The
major effect of such provisions fell on weak unions which faced
powerful employers.

The public had reacted to the presumed power of labor unions
with support of Taft-Hartley legislation. Yet, even in this time of
crisis, the two major union groups could not bury their differences
sufficiently to act in a common cause. Immediately from its passage,
the Taft-Hartley Act was labeled as a "slave labor law," and its repeal
became the stated objective of every union leader. Suggestions to
compromise some of those sections of the law which had been
drafted in hasty fashion were not supported by the union groups.

Senator Robert A. Taft's efforts to bring about a compromise package of changes favorable to both labor and management were rebuffed.

Attempts at Revision and Repeal

In light of the apparent paradox alluded to in Chapter I, a brief glance at the history of attempts to modify Taft-Hartley in the years immediately following its passage will be instructive. An excellent summary and appraisal of these events was made at the symposium on the Taft-Hartley Act conducted in 1958 at Cornell University. The substance of the analysis was published in the *Industrial and Labor Relations Review*.[6]

Benjamin Aaron, of the University of California, one of the major participants in the symposium, analyzed at length the history of such attempts at revision. The first of the proposed modifications came in 1949, shortly after the upset election which returned President Truman to office. Though it may be premature so to state, the similarity between the events of 1959 and those of 1949 is remarkable.

Aaron presents labor's interpretation of the election of Truman as a popular mandate for the repeal of the Taft-Hartley Act. The legislative events which in fact took place in 1949 are summarized in the following quotation:

> The "popular mandate" for repeal went unrecognized in both Houses of Congress, where a coalition of Republicans and Southern Democrats put the quietus on organized labor's illusion of a return to the good old days of the Wagner Act. The process was a painful one for the union leaders, who greatly overestimated their congressional support from the outset, and who seemed reluctant—one might say, unable—to descend from the cloudland which they had inhabited since Truman's reelection.
>
> Leading from what they erroneously thought to be a position of strength, both the AFL and the CIO publicly urged Congress to follow a "two-package approach: an immediate repeal of the Taft-Hartley Act and restoration of the status quo under the Wagner Act; then consideration of the amendments favored by the Administration."

Congress ignored the "two-package" approach and in the House proceeded to pass a bill making slight concessions to labor but substantially re-enacting the main Taft-Hartley provisions which had

[6] Benjamin Aaron, "Amending the Taft-Hartley Act: A Decade of Frustration," *Industrial and Labor Relations Review*, Vol. XI, No. 3 (April, 1958), 327–38. The quotations in this section are from the Aaron article.

been specifically opposed by the Truman Administration and the labor movement. By a very slim majority this bill re-enacting Taft-Hartley was returned to the committee—a tactical victory which signaled the loss of the war to repeal the "slave labor act."

The Administration bill in the Senate never reached a vote; a substitute bill sponsored by conservative senators led by Senator Taft was passed in its place. Aaron states:

Thus, a congressional session which organized labor had looked forward to with such roseate hopes ended in complete disaster. Faced with the equally unappetizing alternatives of keeping Taft-Hartley on the books or replacing it with the Senate-approved measure, which probably could have cleared the House, the Administration elected the former. AFL and CIO leaders, embittered by the great "betrayal," licked their wounds and vowed to make the defeat of Senator Taft in the 1950 elections their prime objective.

Clearly, Truman's election had not been the "popular mandate" which the labor movement had viewed it to be. The election did little to change the conservative make-up of the Congress even in Truman's own party. The Southern Democrats were beyond the political reach of unions, were needed by the Administration for the passage of the rest of its program, and thus were free to follow their own path on the labor issue. An important factor contributing to the total defeat of the labor program was the union strategy itself. In the words of Aaron:

Their "all or nothing" demands seemed arrogant and unreasonable, especially when contrasted with the deceptively conciliatory proposals of Taft to discuss and, if need be amend or eliminate any provisions of the existing law that were demonstrably unworkable or prejudicial to labor's legitimate interests. Whatever slight hope there might have been for popular support of substantial revision of Taft-Hartley was shattered by the unions' intransigent position.

By following this strategy labor lost a good deal. The conservative side had made a number of suggested concessions designed to gain the support of a broad spectrum of legislators in the revisions of the law. These included proposed provisions:

limiting liability of unions for the acts of their agents, restricting the authority of the General Counsel of the National Labor Relations Board to seek injunctions against unfair labor practices, increasing the protection of job rights of economic strikers, and expressly validating secondary strikes and boycotts initiated pursuant to "hot cargo" provisions in collective agreements.

In retrospect, these would have been highly beneficial to certain unions, while the provisions which were unpalatable to labor and thus the real barriers to agreement did not in practice prove to be as bothersome as anticipated.

The realities of congressional sentiment and power brought adjustments in the type of proposals for changes in labor legislation. Specific adjustments were advocated in place of outright repeal of Taft-Hartley: certain management groups joined and threw their weight behind some of the proposals made by particular unions, and individual unions began independently to press for changes most vital to their own interests. The result of these new trends was legislative stalemate, generally ensured by opposition within the labor movement by one union to proposals made by a rival union.

For example, the opposition of the Sailors' Union of the Pacific to legislation strongly advocated by the International Longshoremen's and Warehousemen's Union (and the Pacific Maritime Association) was instrumental in preventing action on the proposal involving hiring-hall procedures. Also, the Building and Construction Trades Department of the AFL saw its attempts to adjust the Taft-Hartley provisions relating to union-representation elections to fit the peculiarities of the construction industry frustrated by opposition from within the labor movement: the CIO objected to the fact that the proposed legislation would do nothing for the maritime unions, and the International Association of Machinists felt that the proposal would eliminate its members from all job opportunities in the construction industry. The United Mine Workers, whose District 50 was active in the organization of construction workers, was also opposed.

General stalemate prevailed until the time of President Eisenhower's Administration. Even then, early hopes of revision in the basic structure of labor legislation were soon to fade with the death of Senator Taft and the resignation of Labor Secretary Martin P. Durkin.

By 1954 labor was definitely on the defensive, devoting itself to defeating proposals for amendments strengthening to Taft-Hartley.

Proposals for legislation from 1954 to 1958 were not major:

The Administration has officially focused its attention on two points, the right of economic strikers to vote in representation elections and the requirement that employers, as well as union officers, sign non-Communist affidavits.

Aaron concludes his article with a section entitled "1958 and Beyond: No Major Changes." He attributes to Labor Secretary James Mitchell a statement that the Administration would actively oppose a national right-to-work law, legislation to put unions under antitrust laws, and any legislation designed to bust unions. On the positive side the Administration supported the following:

Repeal of the non-Communist affidavit requirement and the provision disenfranchising permanently replaced economic strikers in representation elections, and the addition of provisions permitting the NLRB, under appropriate circumstances, to certify building and construction trades unions as bargaining representatives, thus validating some prehiring agreements. Other proposals outlined by the Secretary relate chiefly to new and expanded reporting and disclosure requirements for unions.

More familiar are recommendations to tighten up on certain types of boycotts; and a new departure is the proposal to outlaw a type of organizational picketing which the Secretary earlier characterized as "blackmail" picketing, that is, "the use of a picket line to force an employer or his employees to have a union against their will.

As quoted below, the final two sentences of the article help to add perspective. The statements were made by one student of the field without qualification and apparently without objection from his many colleagues assembled for learned discussion of labor law.

Major changes must await a massive shift in alignments, accompanied, perhaps, by a series of significant related events, such as occurred in 1946–47. Whether 1960 will prove to be the crucial year is a question that invites speculation; but at least until then it is apparent to the most inexperienced entrail-reader that the likelihood of any major changes being made in the law is slight.

With the advantage of hindsight this statement is ironic.

Toward a Merger

Overtures to achieve unity in the labor movement continued during the postwar period. In 1949 the CIO took a very important step when it expelled from its ranks its Communist-dominated affiliates. This removed a major point of controversy between the rival federations. Also in 1949 the two United States labor organizations joined and worked together in the newly formed International Confederation of Free Trade Unions.

It was two otherwise unhappy events, however, which hastened the achievement of unity: in November, 1952, CIO President Philip Murray died of a heart attack; less than a month later William Green, President of the AFL, also passed away. With the death of these two pioneers, an era in United States labor history came to a close.

George Meany was selected by the Executive Council of the AFL to be its new president. He lost no time in indicating that his major aim would be to achieve peace in the labor movement, peace with honor.

The CIO faced greater difficulty in its succession: Walter Reuther was elected only after an open fight on the floor of the convention in which he defeated Allan S. Haywood, for a number of years the executive vice-president of the CIO.

Both Meany and Reuther demonstrated that there was more than words in their calls for unity. Reuther expressed support for Meany's suggestion of unity, but set forth four basic requirements for any solution to the issue: (1) the basic industrial structure of the CIO would have to remain intact; (2) agreement would be necessary on the machinery for resolving jurisdictional conflicts; (3) membership in all unions in a united labor movement would have to be open to all workers without regard to race, color, or creed; (4) racketeering influences would have to be eliminated.

Progress was made slowly on specific issues, but the momentum toward unity began to build. The first step agreed on by the two leaders was a no-raiding pact. Statistics had shown that, though 366,500 workers had been involved in raiding and 62,000 workers had changed affiliations, the net change was 2,800 members. A committee of six men—Meany, William Snitzler, and Mathew Woll for the AFL and Reuther, James Carey, and David McDonald for the CIO—agreed on a formula for arbitration enforceable in the courts. The agreement was unanimously approved by the conventions of the two federations, but not by all the international unions. Several of the major unions of the AFL, especially the Teamsters and the Carpenters, were opposed to such an agreement.

Attempts to implement this agreement are instructive in their message about the power and organization relationships of the labor "bosses": Meany and Reuther. The agreement was approved by a sufficient number of CIO unions to make its terms binding within that federation. When the AFL failed to get sufficient support among its international unions, however, the CIO Executive Council in March, 1954, voted to "deep freeze" the agreement. It was not until June of 1954 that the agreement became sufficiently thawed by the ratification by 65 of the 110 unions of the AFL and 29 of the 32 unions of the CIO to be put into effect. Even at this point, two of the largest internationals of the AFL, the Teamsters and the Carpenters, and an important CIO union, the Steelworkers, had not agreed to abide by the terms of the agreement. Though the committee had negotiated in good faith, it was necessary to convince the international unions that they should comply with the provisions of the pact before the agreement could become meaningful.

Once the agreement was implemented, the remaining steps toward unification proceeded more rapidly. By October 15, 1954, the joint committee met and announced by resolution a decision for unity through merger. The presidents of the two federations were authorized to appoint a joint subcommittee to draft details of the arrangement. The group did not attempt to settle all outstanding issues in advance. Instead its members decided that the merger would be by the "short method," through the admission and guarantee of integrity to all unions of the united federation. Problems and future mergers of individual unions would be worked out by voluntary means. The four criteria set forth earlier by Walter Reuther were accepted as the basis for the detailed arrangement.

The merger agreement was negotiated in early February of 1955 at Miami Beach, Florida. The conflicts and duplications entailed in automatic admission of unions affiliated with both federations could be eliminated only by agreement of the unions involved. The question of craft and industrial unions was settled by the recognition that both were "appropriate, equal, and necessary as methods of trade organization." Internal machinery was called for to assure that there would be no discrimination in affiliated unions and that racketeering and subversion would be kept out of the new federation. An industrial union department was provided on an equal footing with the other departments of the old AFL. The craft unions made significant sacrifices in the agreement. They gave up certain aspects of their autonomy, and they actually abandoned their basic doctrine of exclusive jurisdiction over certain occupations. The independence of the international unions was assured throughout the document on the special insistence of the AFL.

Thus, formal unity was achieved by swallowing the basic problems of jurisdiction and hoping to digest them gradually. In the words of Arthur Goldberg:

After lunch the two full committees reassembled in a palm-decorated terrace room just off the lobby of the Roney-Plaza Hotel. The merger agreement recommended by the joint subcommittee was formally submitted and read to the full committee, and was approved and ratified by it in less than an hour. While aides scurried to reproduce the agreement on the nearest mimeograph machine—a half mile away—the two committees participated in the most cordial social meeting that the two branches of organized labor had seen in eighteen years. George Meany moved to an elegant grand piano in a corner of the room to demonstrate his musical prowess. But the eagerness to announce the agreement to the assembled press corps was too great to wait for the mimeographed copies. The press was called in, and in the form of two somewhat bedraggled carbon copies, the historic merger agreement was made public. The speed with which agreement had been reached surprised not only the press but, it seemed, the negotiators themselves.[7]

At the state and local level the merger was in fact to take much longer than the merger in form at the federation level.

The McClellan Committee

By the time the two major labor organizations joined hands in merger, congressional investigations already in progress had demonstrated that there had been improper use of the pension and welfare funds of some labor unions. In the Senate the Government Operations Committee and the Committee on Labor and Public Welfare had each touched on the question of the handling of pension and welfare funds, and each had discovered some evidence of misman-

[7] Goldberg, *AFL-CIO*, p. 89.

agement. Various senators appraised these indications of wrongdoing with a wary political eye. The potential for a well-publicized, full-fledged investigation was not overlooked. The decision about which committee would have jurisdiction over any investigation and who would do the investigating was extremely important, since investigations have long served as means for bringing about publicity, pressure, and even legislation itself.

There was little doubt that, in terms of the substance of the question, an investigation would more appropriately have fallen within the jurisdiction of the Committee on Labor and Public Welfare. Since they were familiar with the workings of such investigations, however, the representatives of management groups felt that leaving the question to this committee and its liberal membership would lead to a "whitewash." Union groups, aware of the investigations conducted by the rival Government Operations Committee, the staff of which was little changed from its days under Senator Joseph McCarthy, were even more adamant that any investigation not be conducted by that body. The solution to the impasse between the standing committees represented an adept bit of political strategy, a compromise arrangement calling for the appointment of a select committee to carry out the investigation.

An analysis of the make-up of the appropriate subcommittees of the committees in question, as of 1957, brings certain facts to light.[8]

Labor Subcommittee of the Committee on Labor and Public Welfare

Kennedy (Mass.), chairman

Neeley (W.Va.)	Ives (N.Y.)
McNamara (Mich.)	Goldwater (Ariz.)
Morse (Ore.)	Purtell (Conn.)

Permanent Subcommittee on Investigations of the Committee on Government Operations

McClellan (Ark.), chairman

Jackson (Wash.)	McCarthy (Wis.)
Symington (Mo.)	Mundt (S.D.)
Ervin (N.C.)	Revercomb (W.Va.)

[8] U.S. Congress, *Congressional Directory*, 85th Cong., 1st Sess., 1957.

The Labor Subcommittee had four members "friendly to labor" on the Democratic side, plus the liberal Republican and former dean of the Cornell University School of Industrial and Labor Relations, Irving Ives of New York. Only two members of the subcommittee would have been classed as "unfriendly to labor." The Permanent Subcommittee on Investigations presented a situation which was almost the reverse of this.

The Select Committee on Improper Activities in Labor-Management Affairs appointed as a compromise had eight members, equally divided as to party and including an equal number from each subcommittee. The men from the Subcommittee on Investigations were: John L. McClellan, Sam J. Ervin, Jr., Joseph R. McCarthy, and Karl E. Mundt. Those from the Labor Subcommittee were: John F. Kennedy, Pat McNamara, Irving Ives, and Barry Goldwater. One understanding reached in discussions prior to the organization of the committee was that Robert Kennedy, younger brother of Senator Kennedy, would be made its chief counsel.

Labor still had some "friends," but the combined impact of equal party representation, ostensibly to provide a "nonpartisan committee," and the inclusion of the two Southern Democrats gave majority representation to a coalition of conservative senators. If this coalition was not "unfriendly" to labor, it was known to be "friendly" to management. The selection of Senator McClellan as the chairman, with the powers which accrue to the chairman, made this virtually certain. The resulting select committee was little changed in representation from the Permanent Subcommittee on Investigations.

In discussing the appointment of this committee, a man who was active in management circles at the time said:

You have to look at the subtleties in these things. The appointment of four Republicans and four Democrats was very important in the balance of power. Management groups knew that the conduct of these investigations would make all the difference in the kind of legislation that we would get. Labor thought that with Kennedy and McNamara on there, and with Kennedy's brother, young Bob, as chief counsel, they would be all right. You should have heard them yell when they saw what we had done to them. There is no question about it, the labor boys were out-maneuvered on that one.

When shown this comment, a labor representative took issue with the interpretation it presents. His view was that any knowledgeable person would recognize the implications of the committee make-up, but at the time it was the best that labor could get.

The role of the McClellan Committee in the history of labor-management-government relations in this country was extremely complex and would itself be a suitable topic for extended research. Its importance to the legislation passed in 1959 has already been stated. It was clearly the motivating force in bringing about the passage of legislation in that year.

The findings of the committee and certain legislative recommendations were included in its first interim report. The recommendations called for: (1) legislation to regulate and control pension, health, and welfare funds; (2) legislation to regulate and control union funds; (3) legislation to insure union democracy; (4) legislation to curb the activities of middlemen in labor-management disputes; and (5) legislation to clarify the "no man's land" in labor-management relations (the disputes which were not included in the jurisdictional standards adopted by the NLRB, but which were pre-empted by federal jurisdiction from being handled by state courts).[9]

Though ostensibly set up to deal with both labor and management misconduct, the activities of this committee, at least as perceived by the public, were decidedly more one-sided. Initially, this was not a result of the activities of the committee itself. It resulted more from the reporting bias of the mass media than from the actual hearings themselves.

On days when the activities of Nathan Shefferman and other labor-management consultants were being heard by McClellan's committee, the news media had a more colorful and interesting personality to report—James Hoffa.

To many Americans "labor" came to mean Teamsters, Teamsters to mean Hoffa, and Hoffa to mean arrogance and bossism. In the

[9] U.S. Senate, Select Committee on Improper Activities in the Labor or Management Field, *Interim Report*, 85th Cong., 2d Sess., 1958, Report No. 1417, p. 450. The reader will note that the name of the select committee is presented with minor variations from time to time. These differences appear in the basic source documents themselves.

simplification and generalization process which becomes a part of any complex society the hearings of the committee had "proved" that "labor was corrupt" and had demonstrated that "something ought to be done." In the words of Senator Williams of Delaware, in reference to one of Hoffa's many statements: "This statement by Mr. Hoffa demonstrates the great need for Congress to pass adequate legislation curbing the power of such arrogant and irresponsible individuals." [10]

AFL-CIO Attempts at Purification

The AFL-CIO itself had been stirred to action. It laid down additional codes of ethical practices. It expelled the Teamsters Union, the Bakery and Confectionery Workers' Union, the Textile Workers' Union, and the Laundry Workers' International Union for corrupt practices. Later it restored the United Textile Workers' Union to membership, in view of the steps that union took to eliminate internal corruption. The AFL-CIO referred the case of the International Union of Operating Engineers to its Ethical Practices Committee for formal investigation.[11] These steps were noted by the media of mass communication, often in a manner unflattering to the labor movement.

Thus, it was recognized on all sides that there was some fire beneath the smoke of publicity surrounding the McClellan Committee investigations. Disagreement centered on the degree to which the discovered abuses were present in the labor movement as a whole. At this point the Congress itself began to move toward action.

Labor-Management Legislation in the Eighty-fifth Congress

The bulk of investigating in the field of labor-management affairs had been done by the Senate.[12] In addition to the McClellan Committee, the Senate Subcommittee on Labor had carried out three years of investigations into the handling of employee welfare and pension funds. It was to be expected, then, that the upper house would be the scene of labor reform legislation.

[10] U.S. Congress, *Daily Congressional Record*, 86th Cong., 1st Sess., May 21, 1959, p. 7,922.
[11] U.S. Senate, Select Committee, *Interim Report*, 1958, pp. 456, 457.
[12] This discussion is based on the *Congressional Record*, 85th Cong., 2d Sess., 1958, Part 6.

Two major pieces of legislation, S.2888, a bill "to provide for registration, reporting and disclosure of employee welfare and pension benefit plans," [13] and S.3974, a bill "to provide for the reporting and disclosure of certain financial transactions and administrative practices of labor organizations and employers, to prevent abuses in the administration of trusteeships by labor organizations, to provide standards with respect to the election of officers of labor organizations, and for other purposes," [14] were favorably acted on by the Senate. The two bills are closely related to each other and together form the direct antecedents to the 1959 labor-management statute.

The first, S.2888 (known as the Kennedy-Douglas-Ives bill), was introduced by Senator Paul Douglas in August of 1957 in the first session of the Eighty-fifth Congress. It was favorably reported on April 21, 1958, by the Labor Subcommittee, then under the chairmanship of Senator Kennedy. It was given minor amendments and passed by the Senate, 88 to 0, on April 28, an apparently uneventful passage. A closer look at the *Congressional Record* reveals quite another picture, however.

Republican members of the Senate repeatedly attempted to include in the bill all of the five areas covered in the recommendations of the McClellan Committee. Senators Mundt, Goldwater, and Knowland, among others, had introduced their own bills of that tenor. The stated purpose of the proposed amendments to S.2888 was to carry out the recommendations of the Select Committee on Improper Activities in Labor-Management Affairs. By referring to the authority of the select committee's recommendations the Republican senators hoped to open the whole field of labor-management relations to further scrutiny. Senator Knowland personally proposed a series of amendments which he called a bill of rights for the laboring man. All of these proposals were defeated, but the prodding led Senator Lyndon Johnson to remark in the *Congressional Record* that, if the bill on pension and welfare fund reporting were passed, he hoped,

[13] U.S. Senate, *To Provide for Registration, Reporting and Disclosure of Employee Welfare and Pension Benefit Plans*, 85th Cong., 2d Sess., 1958, S.2888.

[14] U.S. Senate, *To Provide for the Reporting and Disclosure of Certain Financial Transactions and Administrative Practices of Labor Organizations and Employers, etc.*, 85th Cong., 2d Sess., 1958, S.3974.

since the Senator [Kennedy] is chairman of the Subcommittee on Labor of the Committee on Labor and Public Welfare, that the Senator will continue the hearings into the general subject of labor legislation, with the thought that perhaps we shall have other labor legislation before this body before we adjourn.[15]

Those amendments which did pass the Senate had the prior approval of Senators Kennedy, Douglas, and Ives.

The fact that 1958 was an election year provides a clue to the significance of this jockeying. The Senate membership included a number of presidential aspirants. Public awareness of corruption in some labor-management relationships could be very important to their aspirations, but some of them were faced with a dilemma. While they did not wish to offend politically powerful groups in the labor movement, they could not allow themselves to be identified publicly as responsible for blocking "labor reform" legislation. The question was important to at least one senator, Senator Knowland, from a different point of view. As already mentioned, his whole political strategy in a bid for the governorship of California was based on his assessment of the appeal of "right-to-work" and related labor-management issues.

S.2888 had been passed without a dissenting vote and had been referred to the House Committee on Education and Labor, chaired by Representative Graham Barden. It was turned over on July 22 to a subcommittee under the chairmanship of Representative Ludwig Teller of New York, with instructions to take a "fresh look" at the questions involved. Within six days the subcommittee reported its own bill, H.R.13507, a bill "to provide for the reporting and disclosure of employee welfare and pension benefit plans."[16] In the floor discussion of the Committee of the Whole, Barden and Teller criticized the Senate bill for attempting to do "too much," delegating too much authority to the Secretary of Labor, and dealing with problems on which too little was known. Their own bill was considerably watered down from the Senate version. The majority of the welfare

---

[15] *Congressional Record*, 85th Cong., 2d Sess., 1958, Part 6, p. 7,055.
[16] U.S. House of Representatives, *To Provide for the Reporting and Disclosure of Employee Welfare and Pension Benefit Plans*, 85th Cong., 2d Sess., 1958, H.R.13507.

plans covered by S.2888 were administered by employers. A management spokesman stated that the bill as passed by the Senate would have been excessively burdensome for management-run pension funds. The revised bill was not.

H.R.13507 was passed by the House of Representatives on July 28, 1958. A joint conference committee met and recommended a compromise which was essentially the House version.[17] Graham Barden told the Senate, in effect, that it could take the House version or leave it. Both houses passed the compromise version and the bill became Public Law 836, to become effective January 1, 1959.[18]

Something of the temper of the two houses can be seen from the brief discussion of this legislation. More light is shed by following S.3974, the Kennedy-Ives bill.

Several Republicans, including the Minority Leader, had called for broad labor reform legislation. The Democratic leadership answered this call with S.3974 and the statement that it had been its intention all along to consider the bill. On June 2, S.3974 was introduced in the Senate under the most auspicious of circumstances.

A nonpartisan blue ribbon committee of experts in the field of labor relations, under the chairmanship of Professor Archibald Cox of the Harvard Law School, had met and made recommendations which were included in the bill. This committee, and the one which was set up in 1959 to study changes to the Taft-Hartley Act, provided the Congress (technically the Senate) with the systematic, non-political study of the "many complex and technical matters" of labor practices and law that had usually been lacking in earlier congressional dealings with labor issues. This, by the way, met one of the major criticisms of Taft-Hartley that had been leveled by Millis and Brown (see p. 27).

The bill had both a Democratic sponsor, Senator Kennedy of Massachusetts, and a Republican sponsor, Senator Ives of New York. Its terms were so written that they received the formal ap-

[17] U.S. House of Representatives, *Conference Report, Welfare and Pension Plans Disclosure Act*, 85th Cong., 2d Sess., 1958, Report No. 2656.

[18] U.S. Congress, *Welfare and Pension Plans Disclosure Act*, 85th Cong., 2d Sess., 1958, Public Law 836. This law has often been criticized as ineffective. In 1962 it was amended to correct its deficiencies.

proval of the AFL-CIO, and, by the time the bill was reported out of committee, it also had the strong endorsement of a key Southern Democrat, Senator McClellan.

The bill had six titles, the content of which were as follows: [19]

Title I: Reporting and Disclosure. Definition of the organizations and officers thereof who were required to report, what was to be reported, when, and penalties for noncompliance with the provisions.

Title II: Trusteeships: Prescription of the conditions under which a national or international union could place a local under trusteeship, the legal time limit to such trusteeships, and standards and limitations for their operation.

Title III: Elections. Prescription of conditions and standards for the election of officers by various union jurisdictions.

Title IV: Codes of Ethical Practices. Essentially, a statement of the codes of ethical practices which the AFL-CIO had previously adopted to govern its affairs.

Title V: Definitions and Miscellaneous. The subject matter of this title is obvious and led to little controversy.

Title VI: Amendments to the Labor-Management Relations Act of 1947, as amended. This was the most controversial title. It included: a definition of the word "supervisor"; a provision to correct the so-called no man's land [20] of cases over which the NLRB refused jurisdiction and state courts were unable to assume jurisdic-

---

[19] Throughout this study, discussion of the substance of legislation is designed to provide the reader with the general content of a bill without burdening him with excessive detail. It is hoped that the discussion is sufficiently precise so that the technician or specialist can gain the full significance of the development of the Act.

[20] The NLRB had set arbitrary standards for the size of case it would consider (based on dollar amount of interstate commerce). Up through 1957 state courts dealt with some cases which the NLRB had refused to consider. The Supreme Court, in the case *Guss v. Utah Labor Relations Board*, 353 U.S. 1 (1957), held that federal law pre-empted the field and thus state courts were denied jurisdiction. This led to what has been called the no man's land. Management groups desired to have the problem solved by allowing the more conservative state courts to have jurisdiction, while labor would have preferred to have federal law applied throughout. The first solution would put what is technically interstate commerce under state jurisdiction, while the second runs into difficulties of administration.

tion because of federal pre-emption; a provision to make picketing to achieve personal profit illegal; provisions that an agreement made by an employer engaged primarily in the building and construction industry with a union before that union's majority status had been decided in an NLRB election not be considered an unfair labor practice, that such an agreement require, as a condition of employment, membership in the union within seven days, that the union have the right to refer applicants for employment, that minimum apprenticeship times be set, and that priority in employment be allowed to those with seniority with the employer, in the industry, or in the geographical area. The title also required, under certain conditions, non-Communist affidavits of employers, made illegal certain payments from employers or their agents to representatives of unions, made demanding or accepting such payments illegal for the union representatives, and made it legal for an employer engaged primarily in the building or construction industry to make payments to a trust fund for pooled vacation benefits or apprenticeship training programs of employees.

The first five titles dealt with areas which were directly related to abuses shown in the inquiry of the McClellan Committee. The sixth included "sweeteners," changes to the Taft-Hartley Act desired by particular unions as the price for their cooperation in the consideration of the bill. The major beneficiaries of the sweeteners were the building and construction trade unions and, for the new definition of "supervisor," the Communications Workers of America.

The bill provided for reporting and disclosure of information in the same manner as earlier legislation, such as the Securities and Exchange Act of 1933 had done. The proposed law would make it possible for union members to police their own organizations by giving them (and the public) the information necessary for the task. This type of reform has often been called the "goldfish-bowl" approach to regulation. A major portion of the actual drafting of Kennedy-Ives was done by two members of the blue ribbon committee: Chairman Archibald Cox and AFL-CIO Special Counsel Arthur Goldberg.

It was not long before a political storm blew up around the proposed legislation; attempts were made to make it a partisan issue. The Secretary of Labor, James Mitchell, raised a number of questions about the provisions of the bill.

Senator Ives, who planned to retire at the close of the Eighty-fifth Congress, said in a news conference:

It looks to me as if somebody is trying to make a Republican thing out of this when we were trying to make it bi-partisan. I never believed labor relations should be partisan. I'm not going to close my legislative career with that kind of monkey business.[21]

Senator Kennedy later pointed out that the provisions to which the Secretary appeared to object most strongly were identical to those in a rival bill offered by Senator Goldwater of Arizona on behalf of the Administration itself! The bill was passed in early June, 1958, by the Senate by the vote of 88 to 1, Senator Goldwater dissenting.

The issues with which Kennedy-Ives dealt were controversial and probed deeply into old wounds. The economy had reached its low point in April and was showing signs of rebounding, but the high level of unemployment persisted and added its own supply of sparks for the potentially explosive issue. In this context it is surprising that the Senate had been able to muster such an overwhelming vote for the bill. This is especially so if the public stand of each of several important groups is examined.

On the side of labor, the AFL-CIO had expressed its backing of the Kennedy-Ives bill, but only after President George Meany made the often-quoted statement, "God save us from our friends."

Behind the image of solidarity conveyed by the word "labor" there were, of course, many differing views. The Railroad Brotherhoods opposed the bill, and the powerful Steelworkers Union was cool toward it. The independent unions such as the Teamsters and the Mine Workers expressed themselves as completely opposed to all forms of government regulation. The effectiveness of such "labor backing" can be easily inferred.

Secretary of Labor Mitchell's position vacillated considerably, but at no time was he strongly in favor of the passage of the bill, which he considered "reasonably satisfactory" at best. The Presi-

[21] New York *Times*, June 10–20, 1958, is the source for the quotations in this section.

dent took note of flaws of omission, especially in relation to secondary boycotts and what he called "blackmail picketing." The Republicans' position appears to have been that reform was necessary, but no reform would probably be better than not enough reform. And there was an additional deterrent in a bill which would bear the name of a potential Democratic presidential candidate. The National Association of Manufacturers (NAM) and the Chamber of Commerce took positions similar to that of the Administration but stressed the need to "bring the unions' monopoly power under the Antitrust laws." Senator McClellan was on record as favoring the bill, but earlier he, too, had expressed a desire for stronger legislation. The only legislators who took a firm stand for the Kennedy-Ives bill were Senators Kennedy and Ives.

The treatment given S.3974 in a campaign year is not surprising. In the House of Representatives it was not referred to committee until after it had been on Speaker Sam Rayburn's desk for well over a month.

Rayburn tried to bring the bill to the floor in the closing days of the session under a special suspension-of-rules procedure requiring a two-thirds majority to institute. The provisions of the procedure would forbid amendment of the Kennedy-Ives bill if it were considered at all. The vote on the proposal was 190 to 198, less than a majority.

The House leadership and other supporters could say they tried; those who voted against the procedure could say they favored the principle of the reform bill but not the conditions under which they had to consider it; each could look to the coming elections to give his side more leverage for the next time around. The situation allowed all parties to blame the others, and they did. Liberals blamed an "unholy alliance" between the NAM and the Teamsters; Kennedy blamed the Administration. The NAM and Chamber of Commerce said labor didn't want any reform. The Administration blamed the Democratic congressional leadership. And almost everyone was happy.

At his news conference President Eisenhower issued a prepared statement which listed his objections to the Kennedy-Ives bill and called for further attempts at reform. He stated that the shortcom-

ings of the bill were the following: (1) its failure to provide adequate machinery to enforce the standards necessary for proper
handling of labor union funds; (2) its failure to deal with boy-
cotting and blackmail picketing; (3) its weakening of certain aspects of the Taft-Hartley Act; (4) its failure to move at all toward
recognizing appropriate state responsibilities in labor matters; and
(5) its presentation to the House on a take-it-or-leave-it, no amendment basis. He then called on Congress to make another effort. No
further action was taken.[22]

In this context the results of the elections of 1958 would appear
to have given vindication to labor's supporters. Those favoring
strong reform, such as Knowland, were soundly beaten. Right-to-
work proposals were defeated in all but one state. Seventy percent
of labor-backed candidates were successful. The reaction of conservative spokesmen reflected their concern, a sample of which we
have seen along with an analysis of the inaccuracy of the reasoning
it represented.

Perhaps the apparently contradictory expressions of the public in
voting as in 1958 and acting as in 1959 can be further explained by
the public attitude toward labor unions, which has been one of
ambivalence. The ambivalence appears to result from a dual image
of labor.[23] On the one hand, unions have been seen as the instru-
ment through which the worker achieves some measure of independence and dignity in industry; they represent the workers'
"alternative to serfdom" and thus were defended by the public in
1958. On the other hand, they have been seen as the instruments
of labor "bosses," who wield great economic power and live in
plush comfort off the dues which their followers are forced to pay.
In the latter view unions are organizations over which the members
have little control and thus required federal regulation in 1959.
The success of a particular public appeal may well be determined
by the degree to which it evokes one or the other of these images.

[22] New York *Times*, Aug. 28, 1958, p. 10.
[23] See "The Public Image of Unions" in Chamberlain, *Sourcebook on Labor*,
p. 225.

III. THE SENATE COMMITTEE

THE development of the Labor-Management Reporting and Disclosure Act of 1959 was an extremely complex process. To report
such a process in a clear fashion entails abstraction from the events,
yet care must be exercised to ensure against oversimplification. To
be understood the Act and its development must be shown in context. Much of the material of Chapter II was intended to make this
possible, and this is the objective of including in the chapters to
follow certain passages which provide significance and perspective
to seemingly simple or straightforward events. In one sense these
passages are digressions—digressions from the chronology of the
main presentation—but in another sense they are essential to an
understanding of the development of the law.

The Legislative Strategy

We have seen that the Kennedy-Ives bill passed the Senate by
an overwhelming vote. And we have also seen the reaction to the
bill in the House of Representatives. Management groups were in
violent opposition to the sweeteners included in the legislation at
that stage. In light of this experience of the year before, Democratic
congressional leaders wished to propose in 1959 what was called a
"straight reform" measure, leaving out sweeteners. They proposed
to begin consideration of the bill in the House rather than the
Senate and then, after the reform bill was passed, to consider a
second "package" dealing with a series of amendments to the
Taft-Hartley Act desired by both labor and management. A blue
ribbon committee of experts in the field of labor-management affairs
would be set up, as had been done in 1958, this time to recommend
terms for the amendment of the Taft-Hartley Act.

Such a strategy would isolate the issue of labor reform—over which much heat had been generated—from the question of changes to the Taft-Hartley Act, which directly affected the vital interests of both labor and management. It would be reasonable to assume that, with a reform law to assuage the clamor of the public that "something be done" about labor-management problems and to prove the responsibility of the Democratic Party, the major interested groups could sit down around a committee table and attempt to resolve their differences over the Taft-Hartley Act in a calm and rational atmosphere. There was no question that both sides wished changes in the law, and it appeared to be quite possible that some mutually acceptable formula could be reached.

Since the management people had demonstrated and continued to make clear that they would hotly oppose any changes to Taft-Hartley which did not include the changes they sought, an approach of this type would be necessary if a heated battle over the bill embodying labor reform measures were to be avoided and the issue expeditiously resolved.

The Substance of the Taft-Hartley Proposals

Of particular interest to the building and construction trades were changes stipulating that it would no longer be an unfair labor practice for a contractor to negotiate the terms of a contract with a construction union before the union's status as representative of a majority of workers on the job was established by NLRB election or even before workers had been hired for the job (known as pre-hire agreements). The Taft-Hartley Act provision requiring NLRB certification was not workable in an industry of transient and rapidly changing employment and job opportunities. The unions also wanted specifically stated the right for the union to refer employees to the employer on request (the union hiring hall procedure) and to require reasonable qualifications in terms of training and/or experience for certain jobs. In addition, they hoped to have the thirty-day grace period, allowed an employee hired under a union shop agreement (including a prehire union shop agreement) before he would be required to join the union, reduced to seven days for their industry (the seven-day union shop).

A major issue between unions and management was the question of the applicability of federal law to labor disputes in interstate commerce. The National Labor Relations Board was given jurisdiction over all such cases, but, because of the limitations of its staff and resources, the board had, from time to time, voluntarily relinquished its jurisdiction over disputes which it considered to be too small or unimportant to deal with. A number of courts, however, had ruled (and were upheld on their decision by the Supreme Court) [1] that, since Congress had passed legislation on the question, Federal law pre-empted the field, and state law would no longer apply. This left an area, the no man's land, in which neither state nor federal law was applicable. Unions wanted federal law to apply to these questions, since, on the whole, state laws on labor-management affairs are more conservative than are federal. Management groups, especially those in the South, preferred to have the state laws applied.

All unions wanted to change the application of the Labor Management Relations Act (LMRA), Section 9(c)(3), which prohibited strikers not eligible for reinstatement from voting in a representation election. The unions wanted such employees on strike (economic strikers) to be able to vote in these elections.

The Wagner Act had specified a number of unfair labor practices by employers in their dealings with their employees and unions. Among its major provisions the Taft-Hartley Act specified a number of unfair labor practices by labor unions. One major action designated as an unfair labor practice was the secondary boycott (see Section 8(b)(14) of the Labor Management Relations Act, 1947).

A strike is a primary boycott. The employees refuse to supply their services to the employer. The strikers may also refuse to purchase the goods of the employer. If the strikers bring pressure on a second employer or group of individuals to prevent them from purchasing the goods of the first employer, this is a secondary boycott and would be an unfair labor practice subject to injunction under the Taft-Hartley Act. As the section is written and as it has

[1] As discussed in footnote 20, Chapter II, the Supreme Court, in the case *Guss v. Utah Labor Relations Board*, 353 U.S. 1 (1957), held that federal law pre-empted the field of labor-management disputes (included in Taft-Hartley); thus, state law could not apply, and state courts were denied jurisdiction.

been interpreted by the courts, however, there are a number of secondary boycotts which are not covered by the Act. The courts had interpreted that the words "induce or encourage employees" (not to purchase the goods of an employer) specified employees and not employers and thus did not apply to pressure brought by unions directly on other employers. The term "concerted refusal" (to deal with an employer or in the goods of an employer) is a term of art at law and, in order to be judged an unfair labor practice, specifically would require the refusal by employees as a group to perform a prohibited act, and not such refusal by a single key employee. The term "in the course of employment" was held by the courts specifically not to apply to the practice of convincing workers not to accept or undertake employment as long as they had not begun work on the job.

In addition to the above loopholes stemming from court interpretations, several other exceptions to the provisions of this section existed. Agricultural workers and firms subject to the Railway Labor Act were specifically excluded from coverage of the provisions of the Taft-Hartley Act. The acceptance by the NLRB of the practice of "roving picketing" under the Act (whereby pickets follow the products of the company from place of manufacture to place of sale) made this type of pressure on the seller of the goods of the primary employer possible. Hot cargo contracts, by which an employer agrees in advance not to handle goods declared by the union to be "unfair," are another exception. Thus, many secondary boycotts had been beyond the reach of Taft-Hartley prohibitions. Management groups hoped to close these loopholes to make all secondary boycotts unfair labor practices.

The management groups also hoped for restrictions on certain union picketing activities. For example, if, as a part of its effort to organize the workers in a given business, a union uses a picket line to bring pressure on the employer to induce him to recognize the union, the practice is known as organizational picketing. The effectiveness of such organizational picketing often depends on the actions of other unions in refusing to cross such lines. If other unions refuse to cross the picket lines, the business may be cut off from needed services or the pickup and delivery of materials. If the picketing can also be extended to secondary sites—the customers of the primary employer—the economic impact of the union's effort can be magnified. It has just been stated that one means of such extension is the hot cargo or unfair goods provisions of some collective bargaining agreements. These tactics are thus interrelated and have all been opposed by employers.

As already stated, secondary boycotts have proven to be powerful economic weapons in the hands of unions. Unquestionably, they have been subject to abuse, as have many other tactics in labor-management relations. In some areas of the country where there is staunch opposition to unions of any type, often the boycott has been the only effective tool available to the union in its attempt to exercise its right to organize workers. Because of both their effectiveness and their misuse, boycotts have been staunchly opposed by management groups, which have long worked to have them all declared unfair labor practices.

It should also be recognized that technicalities may often transform what are essentially primary picketing and primary boycotts into secondary boycotts at law. This is true especially in process industries, such as the clothing and apparel, and the construction industries.

Organizational picketing has also been misused. One example of misuse has been extortion picketing, the use by a union leader of a picket line to exact personal consideration from an employer or to force the recognition of his union against the wishes of both employee and employer.

It is obvious that the legal proscription of weapons such as these would greatly alter the balance of power between management and labor, a balance which has gradually been turning against the unions under existing legislation.

A further comment is necessary. The effectiveness of any of these devices often depended on the cooperation of the Teamsters Union. For example, a white-collar union may find that it can exert little economic pressure on an employer even though it is able to enlist the entire clerical staff to its ranks. If, however, it can gain the cooperation of the Teamsters Union, it can, by picketing the firm, cut off pickup of finished goods and delivery of raw materials and supplies. With the power derived from cooperation with their huge brother, even a union small in numbers can be extremely effective in bargaining.

In summary: management people hoped to make all secondary boycotts and all hot cargo agreements unfair labor practices. They hoped also to eliminate organizational picketing as a union weapon.

The Stakes

While strong management opposition to the sweeteners as the only changes to Taft-Hartley [2] did not appear to involve much of a threat to passage of legislation in the Senate, there was always the problem of getting a Senate-passed bill through the House of Representatives, where the coalition of Republicans and Southern Democrats was still very powerful. The Democratic leadership knew well that issues on which there is a good deal of public involvement could become difficult to handle, especially if they were not resolved until the closing days of the congressional session. The leadership hoped to avoid such a situation if it was at all possible.

There is evidence which shows, and one member of Congress flatly stated, that the leaders of the AFL-CIO had agreed to the so-called "two package" approach of first passing a reform law and then considering a separate bill embodying changes to the Taft-Hartley Act. The agreement was allegedly reached at a meeting of the leaders of the AFL-CIO with Democratic congressional leaders in the first week in January, 1959.

It soon became evident, however, that some union leaders strongly opposed any reform measure which was not made more palatable by the inclusion of the sweeteners. Their reasoning was simple. After an overwhelmingly successful election and after the proposal by the Eisenhower Administration of such desired features as the reversal of the Denver building trades doctrine [3] by the Eisenhower

[2] As shown above, sweeteners in Title VI of Kennedy-Ives included the application of federal law to cases in the no man's land, the legalization of prehire union shop agreements and associated provisions desired by the building and construction unions, the provision of a vote to economic strikers, and the revision of the definition of the word "supervisor" as desired by the Communication Workers of America.

[3] This reference is to *NLRB v. Denver Building and Construction Trades Council*, 341 U.S. 675 (1951), which held what is known as "common situs

Administration (along with several Taft-Hartley changes desired by management), why should the unions accept less than they had been offered a year earlier? To do so would expose them to possible regulation of their internal affairs without any *quid pro quo*, or, in the event that both "packages" were to pass the Congress, regulation plus changes to Taft-Hartley that they would prefer not to see enacted in exchange for those Taft-Hartley changes which they sought, the sweeteners. Either possibility would represent a failure to exploit the position of strength which these labor leaders perceived themselves to have achieved in the elections of 1958.

No doubt there was also some residual feeling lingering from the earlier squelching by rival unions of attempts by the building and construction and other unions to go-it-alone with their pet legislative proposals. One argument which had been used against independent action was that the labor movement should present a united front, that individual unions or groups of unions should coordinate their legislative programs. The prospect of reform legislation meant that the momentum to pass a major labor-management bill would be developed. Clearly, this was the opportune moment to press for the provisions they desired. The historical record shows that these union men did stand firm and demanded the sweeteners as their price for cooperation on a labor reform measure.

As the fortunes of one side or the other ebbed or waned in the struggle over this legislation, however, that group's position on the question of including Taft-Hartley Act changes along with basic reform provisions in the proposed law shifted in opposite measure. Before the legislative session was out, both sides were to have come full circle on the question. By the time the content of the Act of 1959 was finally decided, many labor people wished that some of their colleagues had been less certain of their strength at the outset.

The differences among the various union leaders were not finally resolved until the Executive Council meeting of the AFL-CIO in February. In the meantime the Democratic leadership felt compelled to act.

---

picketing" to be illegal. That is, it was held illegal to picket and thus prevent work by all employees on a single site. Thus, it would be illegal for carpenters striking on a given site to interfere with the work of plumbers on the site. The impact of such a ruling on the construction trades is obvious.

The First Moves

After various discussions, the decision was made that legislation should begin in the Senate as before and progress as rapidly as possible. Buoyed by the election and the mood of optimism it generated, Senator Kennedy, who was chairman of the Subcommittee on Labor and thus charged with the responsibility for preparing the legislation, publicly expressed hope that a bill could be passed by the Congress within a few weeks. Over-all strategy would be to include the labor-backed sweeteners on the basis that they were "noncontroversial" (that is, some had the backing of President Eisenhower, and all had been recommended by the late Senator Taft and had been passed by an overwhelming majority of the Senate in the Kennedy-Ives bill the year before). The second blue ribbon committee was appointed to study further changes to Taft-Hartley in the interim. (See Appendix A for the biographical sketches of the members of this committee.) The total content of the legislation as proposed would closely parallel the Kennedy-Ives bill.

Since one of the major changes to Taft-Hartley which management people hoped to bring about was the prohibition of secondary boycotts, any provisions which might open such questions to amendment from the floor of the Congress were specifically excluded from the proposed legislation. It was on this basis that the reversal of the Denver building trades doctrine was excluded in favor of the provision for prehire arrangements mentioned earlier.

On January 20, 1957, the Kennedy-Ervin Bill, S.505, again drafted in major part by Cox and Goldberg and again containing the sweeteners in Title VI, was introduced in the Senate. A few days later the usual machinery for considering legislation was set in motion. All major groups (with the exception of the Teamsters Union) were invited to appear before the Subcommittee on Labor for hearings, but it was anticipated that this would be little more than a formality. The ground had been thoroughly covered the year before.

The introduction of the Kennedy-Ervin bill was followed by the introduction of a large number of other bills in the Senate, several of which are briefly summarized in Table 1. The make-up of the

Table 1. Major Senate Bills on Labor-Management Reform
(Eighty-sixth Congress, First Session)

Bill	Major Sponsors	Some Identifying Features
S.505	Senators Kennedy and Ervin	Six-title bill which, when introduced, had the support of the AFL-CIO. Similar to Kennedy-Ives bill of 1958.
S.748	Senator Goldwater	The Administration's bill, drafted by the Labor Department on the general model of the Kennedy-Ives bill. Contained revisions to Taft-Hartley desired by both labor and management. Would make NLRB services contingent on compliance with reporting requirements. An omnibus bill.
S.1137	Senator McClellan	A bill including provisions for equal rights within a union; often called a union licensing bill. Contained no amendments to Taft-Hartley Act. Such amendments were proposed as separate bills: S.1384, S.1386, S.1387. Another separate bill, S.1385, would have prohibited hot cargo agreements.
S.1555 (as reported)	Senators Kennedy, Ervin, Javits, Cooper	Six-title bill representing extent to which AFL-CIO was willing to compromise. A version of S.505 modified to gain Republican support and to anticipate potential opposition on the Senate floor. Became commonly known as the "Kennedy bill."
S.76	Senator Curtis	A bill dealing with the problems of boycotts. Similar to Senator McClellan's S.1387.
S.1555 (as passed by) the Senate)	Senator Kennedy	A seven-title bill now known as the "Kennedy bill," with bill of rights as new Title I. Included a prohibition against some hot cargo contract provisions.

Senate Committee on Labor and Public Welfare and of the Subcommittee on Labor were such that the AFL-CIO could expect close attention to its wishes. (See the line-up of the committee membership presented in Table 2 on p. 58.)

The AFL-CIO Committee on Political Education (COPE) evaluated the voting records of the congressmen for the edification of union members. The scores given by COPE to the members of the Senate Subcommittee on Labor are indicated below. The number given first indicates the number of votes considered "right" by AFL-CIO standards on issues of importance to labor in the Senate in 1958; the number given second indicates "wrong" votes.[4]

[4] The COPE evaluations can be found in the AFL-CIO Committee on Political Education publication, *How Your Senators and Representatives Voted, 1957–58* (Washington, AFL-CIO, 1958).

Kennedy 15 - 0

McNamara 16 - 0	Goldwater 0 - 13
Morse 15 - 1	Dirksen 5 - 11
Randolph *	Prouty *

* Not members of the Senate in 1958.

The Hearings and Their Significance

The AFL-CIO, the major management groups, and the Secretary of Labor appeared at the hearings before the Subcommittee on Labor. Little of special note transpired. The hostile reception given by the majority to several representatives of management associations, the rambling discussions certain senators carried on with some witnesses, the short notice given some groups expected to be unsympathetic to the Kennedy-Ervin bill—these things were routine.

The labor side had participated closely in the preparation of the Kennedy-Ervin bill. At the hearings Senator Kennedy continued to solicit openly the suggestions of the AFL-CIO for changes and revisions to the language of the bill. This provided legitimacy and prestige to the representatives of the group in their overt participation. The only comment of note was the statement at the hearings

Table 2. Senate Committee on Labor and Public Welfare
(Eighty-sixth Congress, First Session)

Lister Hill, Alabama, *Chairman*

James E. Murray, Montana	Barry Goldwater, Arizona
John F. Kennedy, Massachusetts	John Sherman Cooper, Kentucky
Pat McNamara, Michigan	Everett McKinley Dirksen, Illinois
Wayne Morse, Oregon	Clifford P. Case, New Jersey
Ralph W. Yarborough, Texas	Jacob K. Javits, New York
Joseph S. Clark, Pennsylvania	Winston L. Prouty, Vermont
Jennings Randolph, West Virginia	
Harrison A. Williams, Jr., New Jersey	

Stewart E. McClure, *Chief Clerk*

SUBCOMMITTEE ON LABOR

John F. Kennedy, Massachusetts, *Chairman*

Pat McNamara, Michigan	Barry Goldwater, Arizona
Wayne Morse, Oregon	Everett McKinley Dirksen, Illinois
Jennings Randolph, West Virginia	Winston L. Prouty, Vermont

John S. Forsythe, *General Counsel of Committee*
Ralph Dungan, *Professional Staff Member*
Samuel Merrick, *Special Counsel*
Michael J. Bernstein, *Minority Counsel*

SOURCE: U.S. Congress, *Congressional Directory*, 86th Cong., 1st Sess., 1959.

by the official labor spokesman, Andrew Biemiller, that the labor movement would oppose "at this time" any reform legislation which did not include the desired Taft-Hartley changes (sweeteners).

Because of their earlier stand on internal regulation, management groups could not gracefully take an active part in the portion of the proposed legislation dealing with union reform. Their stake was not great in the reform titles in any case, but the possible passage of changes in Taft-Hartley desired by labor would remove the incentive for compromise in further consideration of labor-management questions and thus would make it difficult to bring about those changes desired by management. This was the reason for the staunch opposition of management and farm groups to the inclusion of the sweeteners. The management groups and their allies stressed their willingness to work with a five-title bill, with an omnibus bill including all Taft-Hartley revisions, or with a two-package bill, but not a bill like the Kennedy-Ervin bill.

The general views of the management side were put forth at the hearings by Charles H. Tower of the National Association of Broadcasters, the first management witness to appear. In speaking to Senator Randolph, who was presiding, he stated, in part: [5]

Senator, I might say at the outset that we were called on Wednesday afternoon and asked if we would be willing to fill a spot on Friday morning. We agreed to this if we would not be burdened with the problem of preparing a written statement for this morning's appearance. . . .

As to our position on S.505, the Kennedy-Ervin bill, first the association is for corrective legislation in the area of union internal corruption; there is no question about that.

Secondly, we are against the inclusion of nonrelevant Taft-Hartley amendments in a bill like S.505, which is primarily a corruption bill, unless all needed Taft-Hartley amendments are included at this time.[6]

Later management witnesses made essentially the same points but included statements that trade unions should be placed under the antitrust laws, should not be allowed to participate in politics, and so forth. The question of including curbs on secondary boycotts

[5] Note that Senator Randolph was the only member of the majority to be present at this session of the hearings and that he was the junior Democrat on the committee.

[6] U.S. Senate, Subcommittee on Labor, *Hearings*, 86th Cong., 1st Sess., pp. 145, 146.

and organizational picketing if any changes to the Taft-Hartley Act were contemplated was perhaps the strongest recurring theme.

Secretary of Labor James Mitchell was given unusually severe treatment on the day of his testimony. One person from the Labor Department commented: "We sure had a rough time that day." And this was no exaggeration.

Senator Kennedy, who had become a student of labor law, and Senator Morse, former dean of the University of Oregon Law School, were armed with a series of hypothetical situations by which to test the scope of application of the Administration bill, S.748. These hypothetical cases were prepared in part by staff lawyers of the AFL-CIO, a bit of support typical of that supplied by interest groups. Apparently Mitchell and his general solicitor, Stuart Rothman (later general counsel for the NLRB), were not prepared for the onslaught. As a result, the Secretary was placed in the position of either not knowing or having to admit the applicability of the Administration bill to unfavorable and embarrassing circumstances.[7] He later gave prepared answers for the hypothetical questions by memorandum.

Finally, a Teamsters representative, Sidney Zagri, had requested through Senator Morse that he be allowed to testify during the Senate hearings. There was a possibility that this would be done, but at the last minute the Teamsters withdrew their request.[8]

Perhaps the most surprising thing about the hearings was that they lasted as long as they did. Senator McClellan introduced a bill of his own after the formal closing of the hearings on proposed legislation on February 16. McClellan's prestige in the field of labor relations, deriving from his chairmanship of the Senate select committee, made it necessary that his views be heard before the full Committee on Labor and Public Welfare could report a bill to the Senate. This led Senator Kennedy to prolong the hearings of his subcommittee. Once the hearings were in effect reopened, Senators Mundt and Curtis also requested to be heard. This could not be arranged before March 9, 1959.[9] The time consumed in the hearings was much greater than expected.

[7] *Ibid.*, pp. 255–317.
[8] U.S. Congress, *Daily Congressional Record*, 86th Cong., 1st Sess., April 24, 1959, p. 5,895.
[9] U.S. Senate, Subcommittee on Labor, *Hearings*, pp. 675, 729.

In the Subcommittee on Labor there had been little question that liberals were in control. Kennedy and his able staff, which included Professor Archibald Cox of Harvard Law School, who sat in as "arbiter" in the executive sessions of the subcommittee, had determined the content of the bill in close consultation with the AFL-CIO. It was, however, desirable to have bipartisan support for the bill in the hope that strictly party issues would not interfere with its passage. Among the Republicans on the subcommittee neither Senator Goldwater nor Senator Dirksen could be expected to serve as cosponsors, and Senator Winston Prouty was a freshman.

By February 18 the subcommittee had carried S.505 about as far as it was politically profitable in light of the sharp division between its Republican and Democratic members. The only significant change that was made from proposed language was the deletion of the exemption of small unions from reporting requirements. Motions to substitute the Administration's bill had been defeated. At this point, on a motion from Senator Morse, the bill was referred to the full committee for consideration of the most controversial questions (although the subcommittee was to continue its hearings under its extended schedule).

The Committee Amends the Kennedy-Ervin Bill

The first executive session of the full Committee on Labor and Public Welfare was a little more than routine. Senator Dirksen introduced a surprise motion for delay in the Senate until the House had acted on the bill, a tactic which was to be used with success in the passage of the Civil Rights Act of 1960.[10] This was defeated. Senator Goldwater next introduced a motion to substitute the Administration bill for S.505, Kennedy-Ervin; this was defeated. Then Senator Morse moved that the committee report S.505 directly to the floor of the Senate. This, too, was defeated, and the committee settled in for a lengthy debate which represented a tactical defeat for Senator Kennedy.

After Senator Goldwater's motion to substitute the Administration bill had failed, he presented its provisions as individual amendments numbering approximately a hundred. For each amendment

[10] See Daniel M. Berman, *A Bill Becomes a Law: The Civil Rights Act of 1960* (New York, Macmillan, 1962).

a statement of justification and legal argument had to be prepared. Lengthy discussions were often engendered on these points. Senator Goldwater, no lawyer himself, relied heavily for his presentations on Michael Bernstein, minority counsel for the Labor subcommittee. Bernstein was allowed more freedom than other regular staff members on either side. On not infrequent occasions Senator Goldwater would turn the entire discussion over to Bernstein, who would make the presentation and then answer questions. For these and other reasons his fellow staff members began jokingly to call him "Senator Bernstein."

Senator Kennedy preferred to conduct discussions himself after being briefed by his staff. There were exceptions to this general rule. When Professor Archibald Cox was present, he participated directly in committee discussions. Many times he was called on to interpret the meaning and impact of proposed language. His academic prestige made him the final arbiter on questions of law during this stage of the legislation. Other Democratic senators were generally content to let Senator Kennedy carry the ball and acted as a group to support him on most questions.

Senator Prouty and his assistants were gradually making their presence known. As a freshman senator and a newcomer to the committee, Prouty's initial impact was limited. Yet, he developed a series of "common-sense" compromises to some of the problems which were raised and presented them to the committee. His knowledge grew as the session wore on, and, by the time the legislation reached the conference committee, he was to play a very important role.

To gain the backing of liberal Republican senators from the full committee, concessions were made in substance and language; for example, in the fiduciary sections of Title V. With the inclusion of relatively minor amendments Senators Jacob Javits and John Sherman Cooper were willing to join as cosponsors of the bill. Some other changes were made in anticipation of stronger amendments expected from the floor. These concessions were felt by labor representatives to be the maximum concessions they could reasonably be asked to make.

Early estimates had indicated that the Senate would have a "labor reform" bill to the floor by the end of February. The actual process of laborious discussion and amendment took a good deal longer. On March 25 the committee voted, 13 to 2, to report S.505 as amended to the Senate, Senators Dirksen and Goldwater dissenting. A total of fifty-six amendments had been made but the over-all substance and impact was not greatly changed.

Kennedy then introduced a "clean" bill embodying the amended version of his earlier bill.[11] The new bill, numbered S.1555,[12] was referred to the committee and technical perfecting amendments added. S.1555 was reported favorably to the Senate with amendments on April 14.

Though the preceding discussion has appeared rather perfunctory, the report of the committee illustrates the effects of the enormous pressures brought to bear on the committee. As a part of the report submitted by Senator Kennedy there were minority, supplemental, and individual views.

The minority views submitted by Senators Goldwater and Dirksen opposed passage of S.1555 in its existing form. The view included legal analyses developed by Washington management representatives and also a very obvious courting of Senator McClellan. Administration proposals and McClellan's proposals came in for approximately equal play and praise as necessary modifications to make S.1555, the Kennedy bill, effective. It is significant that this dissenting opinion recommends four revisions to Taft-Hartley:

First, elimination of the loopholes in the [Taft-Hartley] ban against secondary boycotts;

Second, some limitations on the right of minority unions to engage in organizational and recognition picketing;

Third, elimination of the "no man's land" in labor disputes and the solution of the problems which the existence of the "no man's land" have given rise to; and

Last, the revision of section 302 of the Taft-Hartley Act to prevent certain abuses involving so-called middlemen and possible subversion

[11] It is common practice for a committee or subcommittee chairman to introduce, in his own name, a so-called "clean" bill in place of the amended version of a bill which had been considered by his committee. Such a bill is treated technically as a new bill.

[12] U.S. Senate, *To Provide for the Reporting and Disclosure of Certain Financial Transactions and Administrative Practices of Labor Organizations and Employers, etc.*, 86th Cong., 1st Sess., 1959, S.1555.

along the lines unsuccessfully proposed in committee by the minority.

We cannot think of any other provision of the Taft-Hartley Act or any relevant or legitimate amendment thereto which has or could have even the slightest significance for, or be in the slightest degree necessary to, the achievement of an effective labor reform program. *For that reason we believe that all other proposed amendments to the Taft-Hartley Act such as are contained in both the committee and administration bills are entirely irrelevant to the professed objective of labor-reform legislation.* [Italics added] [13]

This section is interesting for several reasons. Despite statements to the contrary, it contradicted the earlier position that "controversial" Taft-Hartley amendments should not be included in a reform bill. It also specifically repudiated Administration recommendations. In effect, it would have substituted management sweeteners for the labor sweeteners, used reasoning parallel to Kennedy's to justify this, and then claimed its own position was entirely consistent. It should be noted that the strongest reaction in this minority-of-the-minority view was to Taft-Hartley changes proposed by the AFL-CIO. Since Taft-Hartley changes had been proposed, however, the conservative senators argued strongly for those which were felt to be of benefit to management.

Two other sets of minority comments were included. Senators Javits and Cooper submitted their own views. While they agreed that S.1555 was not perfect, they pointed out that no legislation is. Their statement in effect disavows the Goldwater-Dirksen view in particular.[14] Senator Prouty took an independent path. He voted to report S.1555 as the only vehicle by which to get the question of reform before the Senate.[15] He thus fell about midway between the opposing views of his Republican colleagues.

When the bill was reported to the floor, it again had bipartisan sponsorship. But it had no truly active supporter of the stature in labor-management affairs of Senator Ives to aid Senator Kennedy. Senator McClellan's role was also considerably changed from the year earlier. In the Senate, with its great shift in party alignment,

[13] U.S. Senate, Committee on Labor and Public Welfare, *Labor-Management Reporting and Disclosure Act of 1959*, 86th Cong., 1st Sess., 1959, Senate Report No. 187 to accompany S.1555, p. 84.
[14] *Ibid.*, p. 117.   [15] *Ibid.*, pp. 118, 119.

it seemed doubtful that these differences from the year before would
have significance.

Digressions

On the floor of the Senate the legislative battle would be fought
by three main groups, led by three prominent and interesting political personalities: Senators Kennedy, Goldwater, and McClellan. The
three represented the main power blocks in the Congress, the so-
called liberal Democrats, the (conservative) Republicans, and the
Southern Democrats.

In a precedent-shattering speech in 1963 Senator Joseph Clark
of Pennsylvania overtly expressed on the floor of the Senate a conviction which has long been shared by observers of the Senate and
a fact illustrated by the development of this particular piece of legislation four years earlier: that the Senate is controlled by its "Establishment," which "is almost the antithesis of democracy." It is
"a self-perpetuating oligarchy" made up mainly of Southern Democrats and conservative Republicans, who jointly decide (partly
through control of key committee assignments) the fate of major
legislation. Few if any liberal spokesmen achieve membership in
the Senate "Establishment." [16]

At the time of the consideration of labor legislation in 1959 Majority Leader Lyndon Johnson, Minority Leader Everett Dirksen,
most probably Senator McClellan, but most probably not Senator
Kennedy, were members of the "Establishment." The significance
of this will become clear as the drama unfolds.

The objectives, personnel, and functioning of the three senate
power groups will be examined, but first it is appropriate to look at
two primary groups of interest, the labor movement and the management groups, as they were organized in 1959.

Labor: Internal Vignette

At the time the Kennedy-Ervin bill was about to be brought
before the Senate, the labor movement was locked in one of its

[16] *Daily Congressional Record*, Feb. 19, 1963, p. 2,413. Clark's account of
Republican participation is given on p. 2,529.

continuing internal struggles. It is an interesting phenomenon that internal conflict comes most readily to the surface in groups which feel powerful in relation to their environment. The current disarray of the alliances in the world's major power blocks attests to this fact at a time of military stalemate, and this was apparently true of the labor movement in February, 1959.

The sketch in Chapter II of the history of the merged labor movement suggests the lines of schism which had developed and remained just beneath the surface even on the most harmonious of occasions. The corruption issue, the jurisdictional disputes, the old craft-versus-industrial-union problems, and the weakness of the federation vis-à-vis the international union were in the forefront of the disputes which upset the unity of the united labor movement as the Executive Council of the AFL-CIO met in San Juan, Puerto Rico, in mid-February.

Among the other pressures bearing in upon the leaders of labor at their winter meeting was the continuing widespread unemployment despite the budding recovery from the recession of 1957–58. By February, 1959, industrial production had increased from its recession low by 76 percent, but employment had increased only by 26 percent. The McClellan Committee continued its investigation of improper activities in labor-management affairs. The case of the president of an old-line trade union who had been indicted in a road construction scandal was coming before the Executive Council for decision. A jurisdictional dispute between James Carey's International Union of Electrical Workers (IUE) and the Sheet Metal Workers' International Association was at the boiling point. There were clear signs that a major test of strength would develop in the negotiations of the steel companies with the United Steelworkers Union. The question of labor policy toward reform legislation also had to be resolved. The interrelationships of these factors made their resolution difficult. Another complicating factor was George Meany's illness, which kept him from attending the first day of the meetings in San Juan.

Despite the absence of Meany, Walter Reuther, chairman of the federation's Economic Policy Committee, called a meeting of his group to discuss the question of the unemployed. Reuther wanted to dramatize their plight by a mass march on Washington under the sponsorship of the AFL-CIO. The decision to do so was taken by the committee, at least temporarily.

When Meany arrived, news of the meeting's decision made him extremely angry, especially since it was known that he opposed the idea of a march on Washington. He exchanged sharp words with Reuther. Meany wanted the committee to reverse itself. The reaction of Reuther was that Meany was too "dictatorial." He threatened to resign as chairman of the Economic Policy Committee, an act which could have led to dissolution of the AFL-CIO.

James Carey also clashed with Meany. He apparently felt that the AFL-CIO President would side with the sheet metal workers in the jurisdictional dispute, which had come to a boil. Carey threatened to disaffiliate the IUE from the federation if his dispute were lost.

In an interview with the New York *Times* Meany is quoted as conceding that there had been "a little heated discussion," [17] but he was later able to smooth over the differences with Reuther and Carey.

One major job faced by Meany during this session of the council was to deal with the question of the union president charged with involvement in the highway scandal without blowing the issue wide open. Though the man had stated that no union funds were at issue in the case, many members of the Executive Council were opposed to keeping him in his post as AFL-CIO vice-president. They were prepared to react strongly at any indication of temporizing on Meany's part.

In fact, the council took no action on the accused president, pending the outcome of the court proceedings. It adopted a compromise action—a conference on the unemployed, to dramatize the unemployment situation; it investigated the merits of the major jurisdictional dispute; it demanded in the strongest terms it had yet used that Title VI remain in the labor reform legislation since it was "impossible to make an effective assault on labor management corruption without some changes in the Taft-Hartley Act" (a true statement perhaps, but one unrelated to the provisions in Title VI);

[17] New York *Times,* Feb. 19, 1959, p. 22.

it voted support for the 600,000 steelworkers; and it strongly advocated the $1.25-an-hour minimum wage. Thus it can be seen that the minds of the leaders of the AFL-CIO were occupied with many vital issues, including the survival of the federation itself. Though important, the issue of labor reform legislation was not seen as the overriding priority question for decision.

The Management Groups

Much attention has been given to the labor movement and its organization and conflicts. No strictly parallel development is possible for management groups, since they have not formally attempted to unite and could not legally or practically do so. Yet, on matters such as the legislation under study, the management representatives achieved a greater degree of coordination and unity than did labor at any stage, and they appeared to pursue successfully long-range goals over extended periods of time. An important example of the long-range effort was the committee formed to seek legislative relief from secondary boycotts.

Early in 1951 a small group of management representatives set up an informal organization to work for a change in the law of secondary boycotts. The effort was independently financed, although it did receive some of its support from the United States Chamber of Commerce. One member was established as administrative head, and the group became known as the Secondary Boycott Committee.

At the end of the first year the committee was formally absorbed into the National Chamber of Commerce itself. Permanent staff support was provided and an executive secretary, Harry Lambeth, was appointed. The scope of its interests were broadened to include the field of organizational picketing as well as secondary boycotts. Membership of the committee gradually increased, until it reached a total of thirty-eight in 1959.

The long-range goal was to bring about relief from boycotts through legislation. The committee decided to concentrate on a series of intermediate but essential steps. The first was a major program of education aimed at the business community, the natural leaders of opinion (magazine and newspaper editors, prominent citizens, and educators), and the Congress.

The committee functioned as a clearinghouse for information and materials. Local chambers of commerce sponsored "Secondary Boycott Meetings" based on educational materials supplied through the committee. Two subcommittees were formed to give special attention to areas of greatest importance: the Subcommittee on Legislation, to concentrate efforts on the Congress, and the Subcommittee on Public Relations, to direct activities aimed at the general public. The members of the full committee augmented these activities through their personal efforts.

Each year the Subcommittee on Legislation drafted bills, arranged for their introduction, and informed various members of Congress about their provisions and the problems they were designed to cure. Eventually, Senator Carl Curtis of Nebraska cooperated in introducing in the Senate the drafts of the Secondary Boycott Committee's bills. Representative Graham Barden did so in the House.

The chairman of the full committee from 1955 to 1958 was Hoyt S. Steele, at that time president of the Benjamin Electric Company and prominent member of the National Electrical Manufacturer's Association. One of his colleagues termed him "the man most responsible for 'effective labor legislation.'" In 1959 he was vice-president for government relations of the General Electric Company.[18]

A program which commenced during Steele's first year in office was the collection of "atrocity cases," accounts of secondary boycott or organizational picketing situations which had great emotional appeal. These cases were the basis for much of the literature and publicity emanating from the committee. Some of the individuals involved in these cases became witnesses in congressional hearings on labor questions.

The degree of success that the Secondary Boycott Committee attributed to its efforts can be measured by the comment one member made:

We generated a change in the Administration program. The first four years the Administration made no mention of secondary boycotts; then

[18] Steele later headed the team for attempting settlement of the damage suits brought against General Electric for antitrust violation.

during these last two years the President's message began saying that boycott protection was necessary. I was a little surprised by Secretary Mitchell's going along with this. . . .

Editorial comment changed radically over the last few years, too. The Washington *Post* changed its position, as did the St. Louis *Post-Dispatch*. This just shows what you can do if you are essentially right, present your case well and often with drive and imagination.

In another frank comment, however, a spokesman stated that, without the McClellan Committee hearings, all efforts of this group would have meant little. But, when combined with the publicity generated by the McClellan investigations, the boycott program was able to direct public reaction into desirable channels. "The McClellan hearings," he said, "gave us the train to ride on; they were the bulldozer clearing the path." In slightly less colorful terms he summed up his feelings: "The disclosures of the McClellan Committee made it politically acceptable to move toward the conservative position in relation to labor unions." The membership of the committee and its subcommittees in 1959 are shown in Appendix B.

There was general concurrence among management groups in opposition to boycotts and organizational picketing. This made coordination of the program comparatively simple. On many other questions of policy, however, it was very difficult for the management side to get together in a coherent program. While the AFL-CIO appears to be organized for internal conflict (that is, it often faces the necessity, and impossibility, of presenting a common front on a number of issues on which its major power centers, the international unions, are almost hopelessly divided), the management groups have lacked any formal coordinating machinery. Issues have been handled by ad hoc committees, coordination "achieved" through luncheon sessions, and so forth. But follow-up and execution of decisions have been difficult.

Each staff of a major management interest group faces the problem of justifying its existence to its own clientele. This has sometimes led to rivalry and jealousy rather than concerted effort, even on questions of common interest. On many issues the legitimate interests of different management groups have clashed, further complicating a coherent "management viewpoint." Yet, a number of observers have noted the tendency, already exemplified in the particular case of an attitude toward boycotts—the tendency for management groups to close ranks on questions involving labor relations.[19] Nonetheless, even here, when the will to coordinate was present, the actual mechanics for effective coordination were lacking. This void was filled by the Eisenhower Administration through two of its administrative arms, the legislative liaison branch of the White House staff and the Cabinet secretariat (the secretariat more because it was there and could take on the additional load than for any other reason).

Management's Ally: The Administration

Prior to the first session of the Eighty-sixth Congress in 1959 a number of shifts had taken place in the administrative staff of the President. The former governor of New Hampshire, Sherman Adams, had resigned as assistant to the President just before the elections in 1958, following discussion in the press of his relationship with Bernard Goldfine, New England industrialist, who was later convicted on charges of income tax evasion. His place was taken by General Wilton B. ("Jerry") Persons, and a number of other changes were made. The formal organization of the presidential staff as of 1959 is indicated below.

Wilton B. Persons
Assistant to the President

Gerald D. Morgan
Deputy Assistant to the President

Bryce N. Harlow
Deputy Assistant to the President for Congressional Affairs

Jack Z. Andersen *Administrative Assistant* *to the President*	Edward A. McCabe *Administrative Assistant* *to the President*	Clyde A. Wheller, Jr. *Staff Assistant to* *the President*

The changes in personnel also brought changes in procedure. An article in *Time* magazine described "Jerry" Persons and the workings of the administrative office of the President under him. "The difference between Sherman Adams and 'Jerry' Persons is more of

[19] See David Truman, *The Governmental Process: Political Interests and Public Opinion* (New York, Knopf, 1951).

manner than of mettle. . . . Adams was the stern, testy New Eng-
lander, all business and no chit chat." Persons was very nearly the
opposite. "Staff Chief Persons works on the theory that the way to
lead Congress is to exploit the natural desire to work and plan for
common ends." [20]

Deputy Assistant to the President Gerald Morgan also played an
important role in White House liaison with the Congress. David
Truman pointed to one reason for this in the following comment
about White House legislative meetings:

Informants report a more formalized arrangement during most of the
Eisenhower Administration, with attendance at the meetings by the
Assistant to the President and the Deputy Assistant to the President,
and apparently with minutes taken at least concerning the agreements
reached.[21]

Morgan's long association with the Congress as assistant legislative
counsel to the House of Representatives intimately acquainted him
with the Congress and its leaders. His unusual role in the preparation of the Taft-Hartley Act (discussed below) is of interest in
view of his position during the consideration of the Labor Management Reporting and Disclosure Act of 1959.

It was brought out in debate on the floor of the House of Representatives in the first session of the Eighty-first Congress that Morgan had been the chief draftsman of the Taft-Hartley Act. At the
time he was not employed in any official capacity but did receive
compensation for his efforts under somewhat unusual circumstances.
After some passage of time, he was paid $7,500 by the Republican
National Committee for his part in drafting Taft-Hartley. The details of this were confirmed by Representative Charles Halleck, who
had been Majority Leader in the House in the Eightieth Congress.[22]

The record of each of these two top administrative aids to the
President showed them to be Democrats, conservatives, and oriented
toward the Congress. Their influence became especially important
for the labor law fight. Labor legislation became a vital political
issue in the Eighty-sixth Congress. Therefore, control of congres-

[20] *Time*, Vol. LXXIII, No. 14 (April 6, 1959), 18, 19.
[21] David Truman, *Congressional Party: A Case Study* (New York, Wiley,
1959), p. 296.
[22] *Congressional Record*, 81st Cong., 1st Sess., 1949, Part 4, pp. 5,872, 5,873.

sional liaison was shifted from the particular department, especially the Departments of Labor and Commerce, to the White House presidential staff. This is not to say that the departments were not consulted on the strategy and impact of the legislation; rather, it is that consultation with these departments was mainly on technical matters and on interpretations expected in their particular spheres of competence. In any case, the increased involvement of the White House staff was of major importance in determining the impact of the Administration on proposed legislation.

When asked his opinion on why the Eisenhower Administration in its actions in support of a labor reform bill appeared to go against a number of policy pronouncements made by the Secretary of Labor, a management spokesman rejected the hypothesis that the advice of the Secretary of Commerce, the natural rival of the Secretary of Labor, had been taken over the advice of the Secretary of Labor. He said: "This was not a question of Secretary Mitchell's being outmaneuvered by the Secretary of Commerce. This was a question of the Secretary of Labor being outmaneuvered by the White House staff." The suggestion appears to be plausible in light of the events of 1959.

Edward McCabe, one of three legislative assistants under Bryce Harlow, was normally responsible for White House liaison with the Senate. However, his earlier background as counsel to the House Committee on Education and Labor and as friend of its chairman, Graham Barden, led to a shift in his responsibilities to allow his close participation in the development of labor legislation in both houses.

The Eisenhower Administration had two major legislative objectives in 1959. The first of these was the achievement of a balanced budget, an objective which became almost an obsession with Eisenhower. The second was the passage of labor reform legislation.

One Administration spokesman stated that, to capitalize on existing attitudes among interest groups, "we enlisted the support of those groups which felt as we did in attaining our legislative goals. This was done partly by bringing about liaison between the White House and the people concerned. This required the time and efforts of staff personnel."

The man who apparently had the time to devote to liaison with interest groups was Robert Gray, secretary to the Cabinet. The Cabinet secretariat had been established by Max Raab earlier in the Eisenhower Administration. Under Gray it had been assigned tasks seemingly unrelated to its title, including District of Columbia affairs as well as interest group liaison. The objective of the Cabinet secretary's efforts in relation to the economy-in-government questions and the labor reform issue was to generate public support for the Administration's objectives.

For the economy-in-government program 142 organizations were selected as being roughly representative of the 4,000 with offices in Washington, D.C., and were contacted for support, generally in the form of letters to and from the groups on the questions.

The organizations which supported the Administration program for labor reform legislation were the groups which would ordinarily have been working to this end in any case. Their number was a good deal smaller than for the other program, and their activities were more narrowly focused. The function of the Cabinet secretary was to provide that coordinating link which was so often missing in management approaches to issues. As one participant stated: "It took someone bigger than all of us to get us to work together." That someone was the President of the United States.

The White House served as the coordinator of effort and clearinghouse of ideas and planning in the attempts to generate public support for labor reform legislation. More will be said about this organization and its activities in later chapters.

In commenting on the twin program of the Cabinet secretary, an Administration source said:

We received good support on the labor question by such groups as the Chamber of Commerce. However, in spite of their formal support for the economy in government program, we couldn't get them to keep their people off Capitol Hill testifying *in favor* of airport construction or anything else for their local areas.

Uniform cooperation for all phases of both programs could not be enforced.

The management groups were also active on another level in the Congress. In response to the assistance in analysis and provision of questions which the labor lawyers were able to provide in support of the majority staff of the Senate Labor Subcommittee, several management representatives set up on their own a loosely-knit group which gained the somewhat inaccurate title of the "task group." The group was made up of "technicians" (a word which has a certain mystique in Washington, meaning those who really know the substance of issues as contrasted with those interested only in "politics"). Their objective was to supply more comprehensive technical assistance to the minority side. The minority counsel, Michael Bernstein, with the other minority staff members, was working far into the night to provide technical support and information for his side. The management people parceled out sections of various bills for analysis and comment.[23] They supplied their analyses to the minority members. In addition, several lawyers were contacted for research on specific subjects during the Senate committee consideration of the bill. Two prominent Washington attorneys supplied memoranda on the fiduciary question, the question of government intervention in the internal affairs of the organizations, and the role of state courts in labor-management affairs. One of them also did considerable research for the secondary boycott portion of the minority report of the committee. The assistance provided by management people was somewhat less open than that supplied by the labor representatives.

John Fitzgerald Kennedy, Junior Senator from Massachusetts

The hopes of the labor movement rode on the shoulders of the young and vigorous junior Senator from Massachusetts, John F. Kennedy. As chairman of the Subcommittee on Labor of the Senate Committee on Labor and Public Welfare, he would be the floor leader charged with shepherding the Kennedy-Ervin bill through the senior house.

This young man, the first Catholic in over a decade seriously considered for the nomination of his party for the Presidency, had

[23] This effort was undertaken quite informally. It so happened that the Internal Revenue Service was investigating one association in question to determine the extent of its lobbying activity (which is not a tax-deductible expense). It was stated that the representative of this group participated without the knowledge of his superiors.

in his own mind committed himself to seek the nation's highest office following the defeat of Adlai Stevenson by President Dwight D. Eisenhower in the election of 1956. At the time labor legislation was to reach the floor of the Congress his campaign for the nomination of his party was already under way.

The participants in the earliest stages of the Kennedy campaign for the Presidency had been Theodore Sorensen, who was Kennedy's administrative assistant, and the potential candidate himself. However, following the senatorial campaign in Massachusetts in 1958, a campaign which ended in a victory presenting Kennedy with approximately 74 percent of the popular vote—an incredible total of 1,362,928 to his opponent's 488,318—the effort and the staff were expanded. In January of 1959 Stephen Smith, brother-in-law to Kennedy, had quietly opened the first of the presidential campaign headquarters in Washington, D.C.

On April 1, 1959, just two weeks before the opening of the Senate debate, a meeting to survey the requirements for achieving the Democratic nomination took place at the home of Joseph P. Kennedy, father of the Senator, in Palm Beach, Florida. Already the decision had been made to open headquarters space for clerical help in the Esso Building, a short distance from Capitol Hill. Plans were under way to expand the staff to include Robert F. Kennedy, brother to the potential candidate, as campaign manager, Pierre Salinger for press relations, and Lewis Harris, public opinion analyst, to head up the research staff.

Certain facts were well understood by the group at the meeting in Palm Beach. Although firm decisions had not yet been made, the inevitable result of the noted facts would lead in but one direction. In the words of Ted Sorensen:

> Now the basic difficulties always boiled down to the facts that the country had never elected a Catholic, that the country had never elected a forty-three-year-old, that the country had only selected one Senator to be President in this century.
> This being true you had to examine the nominating process, which is not a free open popular vote, but a process which is dominated and influenced by all the groups in the Democratic coalition—the farmers, labor, the South, the big-city people, et cetera. These groups are more influential in a convention than they are in the country as a whole.

Therefore he [Kennedy] had to prove to them that he could win. And to prove that to them, he'd have to fight hard to make them give it to him, he couldn't negotiate it. If the Convention ever went into the back rooms, he'd never emerge from those back rooms. So it evolved from the top down that you had to go into the primaries.[24]

Kennedy had assumed responsibility for the content of legislation in one of the most complex and potentially explosive areas of American political life, labor-management relations, as part of his bid to prove that he was worthy of the Presidency. A law successfully passed would represent major legislation bearing his name, the goal of every legislator.

For this congressional fight, as for each of the others that he would wage, Kennedy had assembled the best group of minds available to him. Professor Archibald Cox, whose earlier participation has already been indicated, was at his side throughout the Senate floor consideration of the bill. Ralph Dungan, young attorney and strategist, would continue his efforts as chief staff assistant for legislation and liaison with the labor groups vitally interested in the outcome of the Senate action. As one participant put it: "It was Dungan's job to hold labor's hand throughout this whole ordeal. He had to calm them down and quietly explain to them the reasons various decisions were made. He did quite a job." The same could be said for a number of others.

As the debate opened, labor was confident that the Senate would produce no real surprises and that the "votes were there." This would be a logical interpretation of their dealings with Senator McClellan, which are discussed below. This conclusion is further supported by direct evidence from interviews. However, other groups were making feverish preparations for the debate. Senators Goldwater and Dirksen and their staffs were assembling for the new fight the ammunition which had been used earlier. Senator McClellan and his assistants were splitting his major bill, S.1137, into a series of individual amendments. Senators Kennedy and Johnson were each preparing independently to meet the expected heavy barrage of proposed amendments.

[24] Theodore H. White, *The Making of the President, 1960* (New York, Atheneum, 1961), p. 65.

The Goldwater Camp

Barry M. Goldwater, like John Kennedy, was elected to the Senate in 1958 by an overwhelming majority; like Kennedy he had served on the Senate Committee on Labor and Public Welfare from his first year in the Senate (Senator Taft personally sought him as a conservative representative on the committee) and had been a member of the Select Committee on Improper Activities in Labor-Management Affairs, the McClellan Committee, from the beginning. The two men are sons of wealthy families. Both are third-generation Americans: Goldwater's grandfather was an immigrant from Poland, Kennedy's an immigrant from Ireland. The two men are energetic and forceful. Kennedy was already a presidential candidate. Goldwater's name had been prominently mentioned on the Republican side.

But here the likeness ends. Barry Goldwater has earned for himself the title of "Mr. Conservative," formerly the mantle of Senator Robert A. Taft. Kennedy is a liberal. Goldwater's rhetorical archfoe is Walter Reuther, President of the United Auto Workers' Union. Kennedy and Reuther are personal as well as political friends. Goldwater completed one year of college at the University of Arizona. Kennedy is a *cum laude* graduate of Harvard and a Pulitzer Prize winning author. The one man is a handsome, rough-and-ready Westerner, the other a handsome and urbane Easterner.

Barry Goldwater's first taste of political activity came in his home town of Phoenix, Arizona, where, as president of Goldwater's Department Store, he energetically campaigned in his state in favor of the right-to-work law which was passed in the late 1940s. From there he went on three years later to become a member of the Phoenix "reform" City Council. Then, after managing the 1950 campaign of the first successful Republican candidate for governor of Arizona, Howard Pyle, Goldwater himself ran for a major political office—against Senate Majority Leader Ernest W. McFarland. It was the Eisenhower landslide which carried Goldwater to the Senate in 1952, but it was the Goldwater personality and convictions which brought him national prominence and re-election in 1958.

Goldwater is quick to pin the label of "socialist" on those who seek the more active role of government in our society. It was this label which he cast against McFarland in his election campaign. It is the label he has used to classify Walter Reuther, but also men of much milder liberal leanings.

The intensity of the personal vendetta against Walter Reuther and later against labor leaders in general, plus the history of support for right-to-work legislation, for Senator McCarthy (whose views he shared, though whose tactics he sometimes deplored), and for the investigations of the McClellan Committee have won Goldwater the animosity of the labor movement.

Goldwater had little if any personal knowledge or experience with unions or their leaders. This fact was stated in one of his biographies:

Aware that he had only convictions—and precious few facts—about organized labor's activities, Goldwater had sat back and listened in his early meetings with his fellow Labor Committee members. He read avidly in the literature of labor relations, and he questioned labor experts at every opportunity.

The man who did most to give him facts, figures, and a developing philosophy of labor was Mike Bernstein. A brilliant young attorney and a recognized authority on labor relations, Bernstein was Republican counsel on the committee. He and Goldwater became close friends, and, with Bernstein's help, Goldwater began to gain a better understanding of labor and its power.[25]

Some of the views later firmly espoused by Goldwater are expressed by him in the following quotation, also from his biography:

Congress has still to come to grips with the real evil in the labor field. . . . Graft and corruption are symptoms of the illness that besets the labor movement, not the cause of it. The cause is the enormous economic and political power now concentrated in the hands of union leaders.[26]

Goldwater is a striking man with graying hair and a winning smile. He is a natural salesman and politician. It has been said of him that even "those who hate him, like him." Few people have been able to retain a personal grudge against this man, who has

[25] Rob Wood and Dean Smith, *The Biography of a Conservative, Barry Goldwater* (New York, Avon Book Division, The Hearst Corporation, 1961), p. 96.
[26] *Ibid.*, p. 101.

demonstrated his straightforward reaction to personal and political questions. He often fights hard and fights to win, but he has done so without deceit or guile. This is the man who led the Administration fight for reform in the Senate, but he did not fight alone.

For staff support Goldwater and the Republicans had relied on Mike Bernstein and the others of the minority staff of the Senate Subcommittee on Labor. Management groups also supplied technical support on certain questions, as mentioned above. On most questions of language, interpretation, or impact before the committee or on the floor of the Senate, it was Archibald Cox for the liberals against Michael Bernstein for the conservatives.

Senator Goldwater was the lead man for the Eisenhower Administration on the labor issue. Goldwater was in close contact with his colleague Everett Dirksen, but the latter was engrossed in his duties as Minority Leader. The Administration faced an uphill battle, especially in the Senate. Let us view the odds as seen from their vantage point.

Early 1959 was a sober period from the viewpoint of the Republicans, outnumbered as they were in both houses of Congress. In this situation the President and his Administration decided to direct a major effort to the people of the nation. As a matter of fact, their only other choice would have been to abandon their program. The major weapons of the Administration were the power of veto and the popularity of the President. Whatever part of the Administration program would be salvaged in this session would result from aroused public opinion, providing leverage to a close-knit nucleus of Republican (and Southern Democratic) votes.

One key to the chances for passing the type of labor legislation the Administration desired was the position of Senator McClellan. A conscious attempt was made to cultivate his lead in the fight for a "strong" bill, and it was not a coincidence that he was the only Senator singled out by name in the President's State of the Union Message. It would be preferable by far to have McClellan lead the battle against a Kennedy bill than to have Barry Goldwater, labor's archfoe leading the forces of opposition.

In explaining Senator McClellan's support for the Kennedy-Ives bill of 1958, an Administration source stated:

McClellan had given his word to Kennedy that he would support the bill; he was a good Democrat, and at the time lacked a deep understanding of the questions of boycotts and organizational picketing. After more education on these questions he came to the view that such a bill would be inadequate.[27]

McClellan's voting record shows that it would not be inconsistent for him to assume a leading role in such a fight. David Truman, speaking about voting behavior in the Eighty-first Congress, states:

McClellan . . . stood apart from the consolidation of the minority bloc [of Democratic Members] with the center of the party and continued to vote, individually but fairly regularly, with a Republican faction. On the second-session set McClellan, Robertson, McCarran, Byrd, and Frear continued voting patterns which placed them individually and in varying degrees closer to a Republican grouping than one of the Democratic blocs.[28]

Throughout the period of consideration of the bill in the Senate the Republican minority sought to cast itself in the role of the group interested in strengthening the Kennedy-Ervin bill to meet the abuses shown by the McClellan Committee. It would fight every inch of the way, requesting record votes and delaying the action of the committee to underscore its position in the public eye.[29]

Senator John L. McClellan of Arkansas

Two years of investigation and hearings by the Select Committee on Improper Activities in Labor-Management Affairs had established the chairman of the committee, John McClellan, as an expert on the internal affairs of the labor movement. He thus became a crucial center of power in the Senate. He was not a member of the standing Committee on Labor and Public Welfare, but in some ways this could enhance rather than detract from his prestige.

Investigator McClellan had represented the state of Arkansas in the Senate for sixteen years. Prior to his service in the Senate his career had been marked by his admission to the bar (despite his

[27] In November of 1958 the McClellan Committee began an investigation of secondary boycotts in labor-management affairs.

[28] Truman, *Congressional Party*, pp. 66, 67.

[29] This strategy lends support to E. E. Schattsneider's view that it is those who perceive themselves to be weak who seek to enlist the support of outsiders, in this case the public, to aid them in a conflict and thus achieve what he terms the socialization of the conflict.

tenth-grade education) at the age of seventeen—making him the youngest lawyer in the country—his service in World War I with the Army Air Corps, and, after extended experience in the practice of law, his two terms as a congressman.

McClellan firmly believed in the reforms he would champion for labor unions. He has often been quoted as stating that he would, if a workingman, unhesitatingly join the ranks of the union movement. Though his voting record had on many occasions been closer to Republican groups than to his Democratic senatorial colleagues, he was generally a supporter of his party as an institution.

McClellan is a soft-spoken Southern gentleman with an air of the patrician about him. People who worked with him found him to be warm and friendly. They found him to be the type of man who could inspire intense loyalty and devoted service. They found him sincere in his motivations and conscientious in his efforts. He is a man who is known to have strong loyalties to others. He has often been known to join the members of his staff at lunch in the Senate dining room—a practice not shared by many of his colleagues.

In his personal life McClellan has experienced a number of tragedies. His first marriage ended in divorce. Then, after his former wife had died, he married for a second time in 1922. His second wife died of spinal meningitis in 1935. For two years after this he totally immersed himself in his work. Then, in 1937, he remarried and embarked on a grueling election campaign for the Senate. He was beaten by 10,000 votes and within a week following the election collapsed from pernicious anemia, an illness which had affected him throughout the campaign. He recovered and in 1942 was elected to the Senate.

McClellan's oldest son, Max, died of spinal meningitis while on active duty with the Army in North Africa in 1943. In March of 1949, on the evening before he and his wife were to rebury Max, whose body had been brought back from overseas, they received word that their second son, John, had been in an automobile accident. He died in the hospital one-half hour before his parents arrived. In 1958 McClellan's only remaining son, Jimmy, was killed in an airplane accident.

The Senator has overcome all his personal tragedies and has used his work as a purifying and redeeming process. The loss of his sons, two of them young and successful lawyers, left a void in personal attachments that was filled to a great extent by the chief counsel for his committee, Robert Kennedy. McClellan was a frequent visitor to the home of young Kennedy, where Kennedy's family and numerous children provided a friendly haven for him.

From the beginning of the session of the Eighty-sixth Congress Senator McClellan was preparing for a major role in the fight over the Kennedy-Ervin bill. He retained a recent graduate of Harvard Law School, Professor Monroe Freedman of George Washington University Law School,[30] as his legal advisor. McClellan set plans in motion to work out common ground with Representative Barden, chairman of the House Committee on Education and Labor, and with the former counsel for Barden's committee, Edward McCabe, then serving as administrative assistant to the President.

Meetings with Barden proved fruitless, due in large part to the intransigence of Charles Ryan, counsel for Barden's committee and draftsman of H.R.4473 [31] and H.R.4474,[32] the so-called Barden bills. One participant stated that Ryan's pride of authorship was too great to allow even minor revisions or deletions of language, let alone of substance. The meetings arranged with McCabe were not held (and the appointments were specifically denied by an Administration spokesman). The introduction of the Administration's bill, S.748,[33] prepared by the staff of the Department of Labor, came sooner than expected and foreclosed the value of discussion. McClellan nevertheless went ahead with the preparation of his own bill, S.1137.[34]

The personality of Professor Monroe Freedman is important to

[30] Professor Freedman is not to be confused with Monroe Mark Friedman, a man thirty-four years his senior.
[31] U.S. House of Representatives, *To Provide a Constitutional Bill of Rights to Guarantee and Protect the Inherent Natural Rights . . . of Members of Labor Organizations Within Their Labor Organizations, etc.,* 86th Cong., 1st Sess., 1959, H.R.4473.
[32] U.S. House of Representatives, *To Amend the Labor-Management Relations Act of 1947 as Amended and for Other Purposes,* 86th Cong., 1st Sess., 1959, H.R.4474.
[33] U.S. Senate, *Providing Further Safeguards against Improper Practices in Labor Organizations and in Labor-Management Relations, etc.,* 86th Cong., 1st Sess., 1959, S.748.
[34] U.S. Senate, *To Provide Minimum Standards Guaranteeing Basic Rights of Labor Union Members and Insuring Ethical Practices in the Conduct of Union Affairs, etc.,* 86th Cong., 1st Sess., 1959, S.1137.

an understanding of McClellan's bill. Freedman was a dedicated adherent of the philosophy of the American Civil Liberties Union (ACLU). His wife was a staff economist for a trade union.[35] He has been described as "a radical of the left." It was Professor Freedman who initially suggested the necessity for including a statement of the basic rights for the workingman as a member of a trade union in any reform legislation. The pamphlet of the ACLU prepared by Clyde Summers of Yale University attacking the Kennedy-Ives bill as inadequate to the task of ensuring union democracy contained the model from which was developed what came to be known as the McClellan bill of rights, although the latter differed considerably from Summers's proposals.

We have seen that the Eisenhower Administration had looked upon the Senator from Arkansas as the key to its hopes for legislation in the Senate. The AFL-CIO also recognized Senator McClellan as a potential power center outside the standing committee. Thus, in late February George Meany, accompanied by Andy Biemiller and other aides, called on the Senator. The purpose of the visit was to seek common ground on the provisions of a reform bill. Meany felt that McClellan would play an important role in the consideration of the Kennedy-Ervin bill on the floor of the Senate. McClellan indicated that he was willing to reach agreement on issues which apparently divided them. There was some discussion of the salient features of McClellan's proposed legislation. Meany is reported to have indicated that he didn't see anything so terrible about the statement of basic rights or other features of the bill. He suggested that a later meeting be scheduled by members of his staff with McClellan's to work out the terms of a satisfactory arrangement.

This meeting took place a few days later. Professor Freedman visited the headquarters of the AFL-CIO and met with Tom Harris, associate general counsel of the AFL-CIO, and other members of the federation's legal staff. For two hours they discussed McClellan's views on the various features of his bill. At the end of this discussion Professor Freedman commented to the effect that he saw no

[35] When apprised of this fact, McClellan is reported to have stated words to the effect: "I'm hiring Freedman, not his wife."

reason that they could not reach a mutually acceptable agreement. Tom Harris replied that, on the contrary, he saw no common ground at all. Further, he added that he would be strongly opposed if McClellan persisted with his proposed section on the basic rights of workers as members of unions.

This unexpected turn of events closed further discussion with the AFL-CIO. It also led McClellan to modify the language of Section 101 (1), the equal rights provision, of his bill.

The short title of S.1137 indicated some of the major ways in which the bill differed from Kennedy's bill. It was called the Labor-Management Basic Rights, Ethical Standards, and Disclosure Act of 1959.

In mid-April, at the office of Senator McClellan, the Senator, Professor Freedman, and Ed Dupree, McClellan's administrative assistant, were gathered with other staff members to prepare their part for the coming floor battle in the Senate. Mike Bernstein, from the minority staff, stopped by to convey a message from Senator Goldwater—a message that he would defer to amendments to the Kennedy bill proposed by McClellan if McClellan so desired. This visit lasted for seven hours, during which Bernstein observed the preparations, answered questions, and occasionally offered advice from his indisputedly vast knowledge of the field of labor law. From all accounts of this session the basic rights section of McClellan's bill did not come up for discussion. It was not until later that the title of the amendment was changed from "Basic Rights" to the emotionally appealing "Bill of Rights," a change reflecting political insight which may well have meant the margin between victory and defeat when the proposed amendment was voted on in the Senate.

The Republicans still hoped to avoid the possible embarrassment of having Senator Barry Goldwater lead the opposition to Kennedy's bill. McClellan, the chairman of the anti-corruption crusade, who was both a Democrat and a close personal friend of Senator Kennedy, would be much more likely to attract the votes of the uncommitted.

But McClellan had supported the bill proposed in the Senate the year before and early in this session had told Kennedy that he would support the legislation proposed by the Committee on Labor and Public Welfare when it came to the Senate for consideration. Nonetheless, the actual situation which developed turned out more auspiciously than the Administration strategists could have hoped.

The COPE evaluation of the voting records of several other senators who would be important during consideration of the bill will be of help to the reader. This evaluation is as follows: [36]

McClellan	7 - 7
Johnson	13 - 3
Humphrey	14 - 0
Douglas	16 - 0

[36] For explanation of the scores see p. 57.

IV. THE SENATE PASSES
THE KENNEDY BILL

ON April 14 the Committee on Labor and Public Welfare issued Senate Report No. 187 [1] to accompany the Kennedy-Ervin bill (now S.1555) to the floor of the Senate. Some difficult issues, including the question of the no man's land, had not been solved but merely tossed in the lap of the blue ribbon committee in hopes that that group could reach a solution before the issue was voted on the floor. [2]

On April 15, 1959, the Senate opened debate on S.1555, the proposed Labor-Management Reporting and Disclosure Act of 1959.

Behind the scenes McClellan and Senator Sam Ervin proposed to Kennedy that the two-package approach to legislation be used in the Senate. They offered to give strong support to the reform titles, Titles I–V, of S.1555 if labor's sweeteners were dropped from the bill—if Title VI was not included. If Senator Kennedy would agree to this, then McClellan would stick to his earlier promise to support Kennedy's reform bill, Ervin would rejoin as active cosponsor of the bill, and both would use all their influence to prevent any amendments opposed by labor from being added to the reform measure. If Kennedy would not agree, then McClellan would feel

---

[1] U.S. Senate, Committee on Labor and Public Welfare, *Labor-Management Reporting and Disclosure Act of 1959*, 86th Cong., 1st Sess., 1959, Senate Report No. 187 to accompany S.1555, p. 84.

[2] One member of the blue ribbon committee stated that the group was on the verge of resolving this issue when the situation suddenly changed and negotiations became impossible. The report of the committee finally filed in 1960 was perfunctory.

relieved of his pledge, and Ervin would withdraw his sponsorship. If he would not agree, they would attempt to get the Senate to adopt their approach to legislation.

The leaders of labor again refused to accept a two-package approach to reform; Senator Kennedy did not agree to the terms suggested by his colleagues.

Early Debate

The early debate centered on a few technical matters. Then the following parliamentary situation developed: the first amendment to be considered would be that of the nominal cosponsor of S.1555, Senator Ervin, to delete Title VI, the Taft-Hartley sweeteners. The vote on this amendment would be taken Tuesday, April 21; a total of six hours of debate would be allowed. (These stipulations were adopted by unanimous consent, the usual procedural device of the Senate.)

The next days were filled with much speechmaking. A vast number of amendments were submitted. They were dated by the legislative day of receipt and given a letter to indicate the order of receipt. Before debate was over, Senator Goldwater alone had introduced more than seventy amendments, and McClellan at least half that number. The desks of all senators were piled high with well over a hundred of them. The speechmaking continued for the record; quorum calls were suggested and rescinded, while conferences were conducted or speakers lined up. An air of expectancy began to build.

The Ervin amendment came to a vote at the appointed time on April 21. McClellan joined Ervin in a plea for the removal of Title VI. Both proposed to be bound by a gentleman's agreement: not themselves to propose, and actively to oppose, any amendment to the Taft-Hartley Act suggested by others if Title VI was dropped. The decision, however, had been made two months before by the AFL-CIO in San Juan. Labor's threat to withdraw support for all reform if Title VI, the Taft-Hartley sweeteners, was struck had made this clear. Kennedy argued for defeat of his cosponsor's amendment. It was defeated, 27 to 67.

Senator Dirksen then proposed an amendment to substitute Title

V of the Administration bill (containing Taft-Hartley revisions desired by both labor and management) for Title VI of what was now definitely called the Kennedy bill. The amendment was defeated, 24 to 67. So the expected pattern emerged. Senator Ervin, even with the backing and prestige of Senator McClellan, had been defeated. The Republican-sponsored effort had also been voted down. Kennedy had prevailed.

The Second Day

April 22 was to be an important day in the consideration of the Kennedy bill. A significant factor in the development of legislation is the confidence of the members of Congress in the ability of a bill's floor manager to get his program through. The bulk of lawmaking follows the recommendations of the committee which had jurisdiction and of its chairman, but the floor manager must guard against the first breach in his armor, since it can be the prelude to a host of changes.

The greatest concern of union people was the possibility that undesirable amendments to Taft-Hartley, which were sure to be offered, might be passed. At noontime on April 22, however, AFL-CIO legislative representatives were talking about the eight to thirteen Republican votes which could be counted on in any showdown. They were confident that as many as seventy votes would be available to defeat such amendments, although they were aware of the absence of two staunch supporters. Senator Douglas had left for Canada to keep a long-standing appointment with the Prime Minister to discuss the water level of Lake Michigan, a question of great concern to both; Senator Humphrey was on the West Coast making a campaign speech.[3]

[3] There remains some controversy over the absence of these men on this date. Various informants stated that both had the approval of the AFL-CIO for their absence. There seems to be agreement that both had the "go-ahead" from the Majority Leader, Lyndon Johnson. My judgment is that the AFL-CIO was at least aware of their leaving and gave at least tacit approval. A participant who was present quoted Humphrey as claiming to have "paired" on the issue with a senator of conservative persuasion. Whatever the facts of the matter the senator named did vote for passage of the bill of rights.

The Bill of Rights

The early part of the session on April 22 was devoted to providing S.1555 with a definition of the word "officer," which Senator Goldwater called essential. Then, in the early afternoon, Senator McClellan was recognized.

McClellan apparently felt that he had fulfilled the obligations of a gentleman to his friend by offering to support Kennedy's bill as modified by removal of the sweeteners. With the rejection of this overture he was free to introduce his own amendments.

The Senate floor was only sparsely populated. McClellan and his legal aide, Professor Freedman, hadn't decided on a firm order for calling up proposed amendments. Freedman rummaged in his brief case to select one from the group of amendments that had been drafted, as McClellan commenced an emotional two-hour discourse on the necessity for labor reform.

McClellan's approach to specific amendments is shown in the following quotation:

> Whether the retention of title VI and the Taft-Hartley revisions it contains, and such amendments in that area as may now be added to the bill, will jeopardize the final passage of the bill, I do not know. But those who favor amendments or revision of the Taft-Hartley Act have no alternative but to seek to have adopted amendments which they think important when the occasion is offered for revision of the Taft-Hartley law.
> It will not be the first amendment I shall offer to the bill, but the second or certainly the third amendment will be to revise certain sections or provisions of the Taft-Hartley law.[4]

Senator Ervin joined with McClellan in the discussion, supplying leading questions in a colloquy. It was only at the end of this two-hour period that a specific amendment was presented. Before its number could be read by McClellan, several senators—Frank Lausche, Barry Goldwater, Styles Bridges, Carl Curtis, and Gordon Allott—rose to pay tribute to McClellan and the accomplishments of his committee. This bipartisan group generally voted with the most conservative members of each party.

It was only then that the Senate knew for sure what amendment

[4] U.S. Congress, *Daily Congressional Record*, 86th Cong., 1st Sess., April 22, 1959, p. 5,804.

McClellan would call for: his amendment numbered 4-20-59-M. One modification was requested by its author: "On page 5, between lines 6 and 7, insert Title I: *Bill of Rights* of Members of Labor Organizations [italics added]." [5]

At about 4 p.m. Senator Johnson proposed a unanimous-consent agreement that debate be limited to two hours, with one hour under the control of McClellan, who favored the amendment, and one hour under the control of the Majority Leader, who opposed it. This was not agreed to. Some other arrangement would be necessary.

In the meantime Senator Kennedy spoke in opposition to Mc-Clellan on the grounds that the amendment was unnecessary and indeed would pre-empt the field for federal jurisdiction, thus denying more extensive rights now available to union members under state law. Senator Thomas Kuchel asked if McClellan would accept a perfecting amendment to close this possibility. As originally drafted, McClellan's bill of rights contained such a clause. It had been purposely left out to simplify the debate. McClellan made reference to this, then, after some discussion, proposed the revision to the amendment himself.

During later debate Senator John Carroll of Colorado brought out a feature of McClellan's amendment which was similar to a proposal made in the fight over civil rights legislation in an earlier session of Congress:

Then if we now agree to this amendment we are conferring a power on the Secretary of Labor and the Attorney General of the United States to institute suits in behalf of private plaintiffs—"for such relief as may be appropriate, including, but without limitation, injunctions to restrain any such violations". . . .

And so forth. I thought we crossed that bridge two years ago. I remember the great debate on the floor of the Senate about instituting the supposedly new device of injunction proceedings without a jury trial. Here I find a provision in the McClellan amendment offered to a bill not dealing with constitutional democracy, not dealing with political democracy, but dealing with economic democracy. I wonder why proponents of this amendment were unwilling to accept a parallel remedy to enforce the most basic constitutional rights of citizens.[6]

[5] *Ibid.*, April 22, 1959, p. 5,810. By presenting his amendment as a bill of rights McClellan made it difficult for colleagues to vote against him.
[6] *Ibid.*, April 22, 1959, p. 5,819.

Kennedy amplified this in his own remarks a few minutes later. These statements, with their implied references to civil rights applications of such procedures, apparently fell on deaf Southern ears. Perhaps this was because, during these early discussions, there were few senators on the floor.

McClellan then stated his willingness to agree to a specific time for a vote on his amendment. In rephrasing his unanimous-consent request, Johnson suggested 6 p.m. as the time for the vote, with the intervening period to be equally divided between McClellan and Kennedy.[7]

Outside the chambers the AFL-CIO was telling its representatives that they could leave. "You fellows can go home; there is no need for you here, and there are too many of you around. . . . We have the votes. You can leave now."

On an elevator a union lobbyist was telling a correspondent from a great newspaper: "This is one of over a hundred amendments. They can't have read it, much less vote for it." The amendment itself was considered so unimportant that no analysis or statement of implications had been made by anyone for distribution to the senators. Administration aides felt that their vote would be higher than the labor people had estimated but conceded that there was little chance for victory.

Back on the floor senators rising in opposition to McClellan's amendment were in a difficult position. They were opposing a bill of rights—something that is difficult for any senator to oppose— and the leading senatorial authority on labor corruption at the same time. All sought to disassociate themselves from such an impression of opposing recognized authority by stating their own admiration for the Senator from Arkansas and his work. They, like Kennedy, sought legal loopholes and technicalities on which to base their opposition.

Senator Javits was one of the opponents. He based his opposition on his "conscience as a lawyer." He stated that the wording made law, rather than being declaratory of law, and that it was vague:

[7] Minor shifts, such as this one in the person to control the opposition time, are sometimes significant. Here the shift placed the junior Senator from Massachusetts in opposition to McClellan, where before the Senate Majority Leader was nominally in charge of the opposition.

I point out also that on page 4, line 22, provision is made for a written transcript of the hearing, by an impartial person or persons. Who? Appointed by whom? Passed on by what? Is a union officer to be at the risk of going before a jury because a jury is finally to decide that a person was or was not impartial? In addition to criminal penalties there is included the provision for injunction suits for 16 million people who would be subject to the law.[8]

A quorum call had brought a large number of senators to the floor. To close the debate Kennedy summarized his position before the Senate in five points. The most important of these was the last:

> Last of all, I point out that the pending amendment would give the Secretary of Labor power, through the Attorney General, to obtain injunctions against any personage in the Nation, on behalf of any of the 15 million union members who might feel that their rights had been abused.
> I think any Member of the Senate who voted for the protection of jury-trial rights and for the protection of the other civil rights of Americans would find it difficult to vote for section 103 of the amendment, in its present form. . . .
> Therefore, on every count—despite the fact that I know the Senator from Arkansas wishes to do the right thing and wishes to provide proper protection for union members, I believe that his amendment is badly drawn; and if his amendment were to be adopted, union members would have fewer rights, rather than more rights.[9]

McClellan had four minutes left for his own summary. It was very close to 6 p.m. The galleries and the Senate floor were filled. McClellan blasted forth with his devastating rejoinder:

> Mr. President, some of the arguments I have listened to this afternoon have been backed up by or have been based on less than the basis or backing up of any of the other many arguments I have heard during my 16 or 17 years of service in this Chamber.
> We propose that the Secretary of Labor be allowed to obtain injunctions in order to prevent the doing of injustice to the dues-paying members of unions; but some Senators say that will be awful and will be making the Secretary an agent of the Congress. However, the same senators include similar provisions in two sections of their own bill. We have copied word for word, down to the point of the injunction provision.
> Why is it wrong to obtain an injunction to protect the rights of such

[8] *Daily Congressional Record*, 86th Cong., 1st Sess., April 22, 1959, p. 5,825.
[9] *Ibid.*, April 22, 1959, p. 5,827.

workers? Why is it wrong to give the Secretary the right to bring a suit to secure an injunction to enforce the rules he makes? Is it better legislation and sounder legislation to state what the rights of such persons are, and then not give the Secretary the right to enforce them?

But if we do provide for enforcing them, and if this provision applies to union members, but does not give some benefit to a union boss, then some Senators condemn us.

As McClellan's oratory gained force, certain Republican senators had just entered the chamber. One whispered to another. "Say, this might be our chance to vote against Kennedy." "Don't you think I know that?" replied the other.

McClellan continued, his voice at one moment filling the chamber, at another reduced to hardly more than a whisper:

I say that the union members have rights; and tonight we shall either protect them by legislative means, or Senators will vote against every dues-paying union member in the country who tonight is being exploited and abused. Senators must take their choice; no other issue is now before us.

Senators can argue about technicalities, including some I heard mentioned a moment ago; but let me say that never before have I heard so ridiculous an argument by one who has so much intelligence.

The distinguished Senator from New York said he could not vote for the amendment because his conscience would not let him do so. What is bothering his conscience, Mr. President? When we propose that if union members are being dealt with for some misconduct, and if some disciplinary action is being taken, they be given a right to have their case heard by an impartial person or persons, the Senator from New York says his conscience will not let him vote for such a provision because it is indefinite.

Listen to the next part of the amendment, Mr. President: "(i) agreed to by such organization and the accused, or (ii) designated by an independent arbitration or mediation association or board."

Mr. President, how can we arrive at a better way to be fair and to obtain honest adjudications than by having two men agree to let a third man settle their differences.

If such a provision is wrong, if it is an imposition, if it is unjust to union members, let Senators vote against it. But in dealing with such matters, I should like to find a more honest and a fairer way than to give the union and the accused the right to select the jury. That is what we do all the time.[10]

[10] *Ibid.*, April 22, 1959, pp. 5,826, 5,827.

Spectators could actually feel the Senate respond to the speech delivered in the grand manner reminiscent of the oratory of the century before. It was clear that senators had been moved.

The time for a vote had come. A few stragglers hurried into the chamber, inquiring as they went of the issue that had transfixed their colleagues. They were briefed summarily as the process continued.

Just prior to the vote it was announced that two senators, J. Allen Frear and Theodore Green, were absent because of illness, and three others, Douglas, Humphrey, and A. Willis Robertson were absent on "official business."

The roll call commenced. When the clerk called their names the first time, several of the more liberal Republicans passed, hoping to see how the vote was going before committing themselves.

The tabulation indicated a startling fact: the McClellan bill of rights had passed the Senate, 47 to 46! The first breakdown is shown in Table 3.

The presence of Douglas and Humphrey could have made the difference! But there were other, more intriguing questions about this vote. Republicans had closed ranks to a greater degree than on any other controversial questions. Only two Republicans, Jacob Javits and William Langer, had voted against the bill of rights. Among the yeas on the Democratic side were men known to the press as "Johnson men." Many Southerners had voted for extension of federal jurisdiction and use of injunctions, by the Attorney General on request of the Secretary of Labor, for the rights of the individual.

There was immediate uproar in the galleries. Legislative representatives of many unions poured into the lobbies to voice their protests to each other and to the Senate. Earlier, a realization of the potential of the situation had stirred Kennedy. Hurriedly he consulted with Andy Biemiller to see if the apparent tide could be stemmed, but it was too late. Now Cy Anderson, who was the legislative representative of the Railroad Brotherhoods and a key man in representing the labor movement to the Congress, got on the phone and contacted Senator Douglas, informed him of the situation, and requested his return. Douglas's administrative assistant

Table 3. Vote on McClellan Bill of Rights

Yeas—47

Aiken	Dirksen	Morton
Allott	Dodd	Mundt
Beal	Dworshak	Prouty
Bennett	Eastland	Russell
Bridges	Ervin	Saltonstall
Bush	Fulbright	Schoeppel
Butler	Goldwater	Scott
Byrd, Va.	Hickenlooper	Smathers
Capehart	Holland	Smith
Carlson	Hruska	Stennis
Case, N.J.	Jordan	Talmadge
Case, S.D.	Keating	Thurmond
Chavez	Kuchel	Wiley
Cooper	Lausche	Williams, Del.
Cotton	McClellan	Young, N.D.
Curtis	Martin	

Nays—46

Anderson	Hill	Morse
Bartlett	Jackson	Moss
Bible	Javits	Murray
Byrd, W.Va.	Johnson	Muskie
Cannon	Johnston	Neuberger
Carroll	Kefauver	O'Mahoney
Church	Kennedy	Pastore
Clark	Kerr	Proxmire
Ellender	Langer	Randolph
Engle	Long	Sparkman
Gore	McCarthy	Symington
Gruening	McGee	Williams, N.J.
Hart	McNamara	Yarborough
Hartke	Magnuson	Young, Ohio
Hayden	Mansfield	
Hennings	Monroney	

Not Voting—5

Douglas	Green	Robertson
Frear	Humphrey	

SOURCE: U.S. Congress, *Daily Congressional Record,* 86th Cong., 1st Sess., April 22, 1959, pp. 5,826, 5,827.

chartered a plane and sent it to pick up the Senator. There was a six-hour delay in reaching Senator Humphrey on the West Coast, but he, too, returned to the Capitol.

On the floor the drama was continuing to unfold. The Senate was going through the parliamentary maneuver to make its action final. The vote on the amendment had taken place at approximately 6:05. Senator Goldwater's motion to table a motion to reconsider the vote was voted on about twenty to twenty-five minutes later. At this time there were three more senators absent. Senator James Murray had returned to his home. As could be expected for a man of his advanced years, he was simply tired. The two other absentees were Senators James Eastland and B. Everett Jordan. Murray had voted against the bill of rights. His absence would merely increase the margin of loss. The other two supported the bill of rights. Their absence, combined with that of Murray, led to a tie vote on the motion to table, making it necessary for another presidential hopeful, Vice-President Richard Nixon, to commit himself on the issue. Nixon broke the tie and the motion to table was carried. The Senate adjourned at 6:40 p.m. The final forty minutes had had an impact which led to a series of violent repercussions.[11]

Newsweek carried the following analysis:

It was when baffled Democrats began analyzing the votes that they made an interesting discovery. Two of the Democrats who had joined with McClellan were freshman Thomas Dodd of Connecticut and veteran Dennis Chavez of New Mexico. Both are known as "Johnson Men," the kind the Majority Leader calls on when he badly needs votes.

Did this mean that Johnson, who nurses presidential hopes of his own, deliberately rigged the vote to embarrass his rivals?

To many in the Senate it certainly seemed so.

Johnson branded the speculation, "lies," then he proceeded to do an about face. Overnight a memorandum circulated among Southern Democrats warning that McClellan's bill of rights, by banning racial discrimination, could lead to integration of white and negro members of Southern Unions. The document bore the name of Olin Johnston of South Carolina, but actually it was prepared by the office of Lyndon Johnson.[12]

[11] Many people in Washington credit Lyndon Johnson with forcing the Vice-President to commit himself on this by requesting the two Southerners to remain in the cloakroom. I was unable to confirm or deny this, but it is unlikely that these seasoned legislators were unaware of the impact of their absence.

[12] *Newsweek*, Vol. LI, No. 18 (May 4, 1959), 26. In reality, the document was

The Substance of the Bill of Rights

We have noted that the major principle on which legislation had been drafted was regulation through disclosure, a common principle in this country. A second important principle had been followed in the drafting of the Kennedy-Ervin bill, and that was one of minimum interference in the internal affairs of unions. The bill had only two titles which impinged on such affairs—Title II (Title III after the inclusion of a new bill of rights as Title I), dealing with the conduct of local unions placed under trusteeship by their internationals, and Title III (now Title IV), dealing with the conduct of union elections. Both of these areas had been subject to abuse, as shown in the McClellan Committee hearings.

Now a third sweeping area had been added, in which detailed prescription of the conduct of internal affairs would be provided by statute. The catalogue of subtitles does indeed read like a bill of rights, but a bill of rights stated in absolute language, much of it arbitrary and some of it capricious. The headings were as follows: Title I: Bill of Rights of Members of Labor Organizations; Section 101 (a) (1) Equal Rights; (2) Freedom of Speech; (3) Freedom of Assembly; (4) Freedom from Arbitrary Financial Exactions; (5) Protection of the Right to Sue; (6) Safeguards against Improper Disciplinary Action; (7) Inspection of Membership Lists. Section 102 provided that, if officers interfered or attempted to interfere with the enumerated rights, they would be subject to $10,000 fine or two years in prison, or both; Section 103 provided that the Secretary of Labor could bring action in federal court to enforce the provisions of the Title; Section 104 provided the effective date of the provisions of the Title.

Then, in addition, the amendment would define the word "member":

"Member" or "Member in good standing" when used in reference to a labor organization, includes any person who has fulfilled or tendered the lawful requirements for membership in such organization, and who neither has voluntarily withdrawn from membership nor has been expelled or suspended from membership after appropriate proceedings

unsigned. Further, there was some evidence of a personal dispute between Chavez and George Meany which may account for the vote cast by Chavez.

consistent with lawful provisions of the constitution, bylaws, or other governing charter of such organization.[13]

As interpreted by lawyers for various unions, the wording of Title I would place unions in technical strait jackets, would make more difficult the elimination of corrupt elements, would make possible membership in unions by Communists and other undesirables, and would subject any union officer attempting to conduct a meeting to the constant threat of fine or imprisonment because of a faulty ruling or procedure.

For example, as interpreted, the "Freedom of Speech" and other provisions would prohibit any restraint, limitation, or modification whatsoever of the expressed right—in contrast with the court-established modifications and limitations to the Bill of Rights in the U.S. Constitution. Some of the language, such as "Freedom from Arbitrary Financial Exactions," was offensive to honest union men, especially since, as worded, a referendum of the entire union membership would be required before dues could be lowered as well as raised.[14]

The Significance of the Voting

As the initial confusion began to settle, several things stood out. First, and perhaps foremost, the bill of rights in its present form made the Kennedy bill unacceptable to the AFL-CIO. Senator Kennedy himself could not support the bill. Thus, his ambition to sponsor major legislation, with the increased stature this would bring, was all but dead. For the Democratic Party the possibility that its second attempt at labor reform legislation might fail despite its overwhelming majority in the Congress was not a welcome one. The situation would also reflect directly on Lyndon Johnson and his image as the "master congressional strategist." On the other hand, the strongly partisan vote of the Republicans could prove embarrassing to them if the voters could be made to feel that Republican action, in effect, killed labor legislation in 1959.

From another point of view, the minority's battle had been some-

[13] *Daily Congressional Record*, 86th Cong., 1st Sess., April 22, 1959, p. 5,810.
[14] For an analysis of the bill of rights as it developed in the Senate and House and was included in the final act see Edward Joseph Hickey, Jr., "The Bill of Rights of Union Members," *The Georgetown Law Journal*, Vol. XLVIII, No. 2, 226–56.

thing of a sham, with little hope of success until the vote on the bill of rights. On this their forces coalesced, and there was now some indication of a real chance that they could succeed. This impression was buoyed by the way the votes were breaking on other subsequent amendments, each of which was a moral victory in a Senate so much more liberal than the year before. Evidence accumulated that the bill of rights vote was the turning point.

Stated in terms of the sociology of the Senate, the standing committee had lost control of its bill. McClellan, a nonmember of the Committee on Labor and Public Welfare, was leading the floor fight against the bill, and successfully so at this point. The conservative coalition which had been successful in earlier sessions of Congress was again in control.

The loss of control by the committee does not seem like such a great change from the pattern of legislative action if a few facts are kept in mind. Speaking in general terms, a congressman finds it much easier to defend a vote in favor of something than a vote against something. This was a natural strength of the bill of rights for workingmen. Then, too, influence of committee members stems in large part from their expertise on the question before the full house. They have lived with the legislation from its inception and are in a position to understand all its ramifications. McClellan's experience, though he was not a member of the Labor Subcommittee, certainly provided the expertise from which influence derives. In addition, he had no identifiable ambitions beyond the legislation itself. These factors strengthened his position. Thus, the establishment of a select committee to conduct the investigation of improper activities in the labor-management field also produced an alternate legitimate authority on labor legislation in the Senate, as had been done by the Smith Committee in the House several years earlier.

Another factor to recognize is that the substance of the bill of rights was true reform, legislative recognition of rights of individuals as members of unions. Unless one was to accept the interpretations advanced by some union people that the amendment as drafted was designed to cripple unions with procedural snares, it was free of perceptible benefits to management. To this day the draftsman of the language of the bill of rights, Monroe Freedman, strongly denies that, even with biased interpretation, could it have had adverse effects on unions as institutions. He contends that there were implied limitations in his (as in all such) language. His letter to the New York *Times* made this clear.[15] It seems certain that harassment was not his intent, nor was it the intent of McClellan.

The Repercussions

When the Senate adjourned, a large number of people descended on Lyndon Johnson's office. The labor representatives wanted McClellan's amendment stricken from the bill. Discussion centered on whether this should be done, and, if so, how?

Individual labor representatives made their feelings known to as many senators as they could. The potential effects of the absolute language used in the statement of individual rights were stressed. Andy Biemiller asked the assistance of several of the lawyers and representatives of various AFL-CIO unions in making their objections specific. Dave Fellor, Ken Meikeljohn, Lou Sherman, and Bob Connerton were among them. They began to pinpoint their objections.

Without explicit qualifications, many courts, at least on the district level, would probably interpret the statement of rights literally. The labor lawyers felt that limitations on constitutional guarantees developed over years of litigation would not be applicable in, or at least not applied by, such courts.

The definition of the word "member" stated that "any person who has fulfilled *or tendered* the lawful requirements of membership" (italics added) would be considered a member. This could lead to the legally enforced membership of Communists, criminals, or management stooges in unions merely by their having offered to join.

The authorization of criminal penalties for interference with the member's exercise of the rights to which he would be entitled marked the first time that other than civil penalties would have been included in law for such violations in any field. Generally, labor's lawyers felt that the bill of rights was poorly drafted.

[15] New York *Times*, May 8, 1959, p. 26.

Senator Olin Johnston prepared a talk later in the evening for transmission to his home state of South Carolina. In this talk he cited his reasons for voting against the bill of rights. He explicitly referred to the powers granted to the Secretary of Labor, and thus in reality to the Attorney General, as being a dangerous precedent. Other Southern senators were taking a hard look at what had been passed. They held a caucus on the floor of the Senate, during which some sharp questions were asked of Senator McClellan. By this time the Democratic Policy Committee, a creature of the Majority Leader, had prepared its legal analysis of the bill of rights and began to circulate it. Its more "folksy" memorandum was not ready until the next morning.

The Majority Leader came to the conclusion that from a parliamentary point of view it was possible to strip out the bill of rights as long as contiguous matter was stricken as well. This possibility was discussed with labor representatives. Another approach was possible, however. In the Kennedy camp Professor Cox stayed up a good part of the night preparing a revised draft of the bill of rights, removing what he considered obvious weaknesses or undesirable features.[16]

Thursday, April 23

At about 9 a.m. Senator Johnson distributed the "folksy" version of the memorandum prepared for him.[17] This unsigned document was circulated among Southern senators, ostensibly through the office of Senator Johnston of South Carolina. In emotional and exaggerated terms it brought the civil rights implications of the bill of rights to the attention of Southerners who may have missed them up to that point. Had it been prepared eighteen hours earlier, it would probably have brought the defeat of the bill of rights amendment itself.

After an evening's consideration a decision was reached by Ken-

[16] A very few years earlier Professor Freedman, the draftsman of the McClellan bill of rights, had been one of Professor Cox's students.

[17] The memorandum was typed on a manual typewriter and had many strikeovers and even misspelled words; it was reproduced by a photographic process for distribution.

nedy and Johnson that it would not be desirable to yank the bill of rights out of S.1555. Although there were enough votes and the requisite parliamentary rules to do so, that course was felt to be too blatant and likely to leave too great a scar. The preferable course would be to make the amendment "livable" by a series of modifications. To this end Professor Cox asked the views of the AFL-CIO lawyers on minimum changes required to make it palatable to them.

By this point the tide had definitely changed. When accusations were made that the bill of rights might work to the advantage of Communists, or might upset the social balance in the South, or could work unreasonable hardship on the honest unions, or would lead to the all-out opposition of the AFL-CIO to S.1555 itself, then a good number of senators took notice. Many senators regarded as "fair-minded" in labor matters had misgivings about their earlier vote.

In view of these criticisms of the amendment, it is only fair to trace further McClellan's role. We have seen that McClellan was fully aware of the civil rights precedents and implications in his amendment. As a matter of fact, his bill, S.1137, as originally drafted, would have gone much further. Criminal penalties for denial of individual rights were felt to be desirable by both McClellan and Freedman. At no point did McClellan dogmatically demand his own language or provisions if they appeared to threaten the chances of passage of the legislation. This attitude will be further illustrated in the pages to follow.

It must also be remembered that a union, as a private organization, is entitled to select its members on a discriminatory basis.[18] Thus, without the requirement of McClellan's bill that "every person who meets the reasonable qualifications for membership uniformly imposed shall be eligible for, and admitted to membership in a labor organization," there was little substance to accusations against the section.[19] As presented to the Senate in the bill of rights, the definition of "member" was "anyone who has fulfilled or

[18] See *Pacific Maritime Association,* 10 NLRB 1647 (1954), for example.
[19] See S.1137, p. 9, lines 7–10, and *Daily Congressional Record,* 86th Cong., 1st Sess., April 22, 1959, p. 5,810.

tendered the *lawful* [as opposed to 'reasonable'] requirements for membership in such organization [italics added]." It would be "lawful" for a private association to discriminate, but it would not be "reasonable."

Further Senate Action

On the floor of the Senate a series of amendments were introduced and over thirty accepted during this eventful week. Some order was introduced into the procedure by the floor leaders of the two parties. A unanimous-consent agreement was reached limiting debate on any amendment to one hour, duplicating amendments were combined or withdrawn, and the order of call-up was specified. This last point was accomplished after a plea from Senator Kennedy:

Mr. President, it would be extremely helpful to the members of the committee and the committee staff if we could have some idea of the order in which, for example, the next three or four amendments will be called up. This will prevent our slowing up the work of the Senate. The amendments are extremely complicated. An amendment offered by the Senator from Arizona [Mr. Goldwater] was rewritten and a substitute offered. It was finally accepted after a period of 45 minutes. Since numerous amendments are at the desk, it would help us if we could have advance knowledge of the order in which they will be called up.[20]

Senator Javits assumed the role of "honest broker" during a good portion of this debate. He proposed compromise language to make provisions acceptable to Kennedy or to the proponent of the amendment. This procedure inhibited Senator Goldwater and his staff from attacking Kennedy on a partisan basis. Javits's label of Republicanism served as a shield in the debate.

The bill of rights vote had opened the gates to several changes which were not expected to carry, but it also put Kennedy and Johnson on notice that no issue could be overlooked. Support efforts were stepped up considerably, and all issues considered significant enough to warrant a record vote were decided in accordance with the wishes of the Democratic leadership, consistent with the necessity to pass a law on labor reform.

Some of the major proposed amendments not previously discussed here were:

[20] *Daily Congressional Record*, 86th Cong., 1st Sess., April 23, 1959, p. 5,849.

Amendment	Yea	Nay	Outcome
Case (S.D.) provision that economic strikers could vote in representation elections under NLRB rules (agreed without vote)			Agreed
McClellan-Curtis-Allot no man's land amendment	39	52	Rejected
Gore amendment making common (motor) carrier union hot cargo contract an unfair labor practice (agreed without vote)			Agreed
Prouty's amendment to Cooper's no man's land amendment	40	53	Rejected
Cooper-Javits-Morse no man's land amendment allowing state agencies to apply federal law	78	15	Passed
Ervin's amendment to McClellan's picketing amendment to legalize peaceful picketing	25	67	Rejected
McClellan's amendment to bar organizational picketing unless 50 percent show interest. Included criminal penalties for "shakedown" picketing and all other union unfair labor practices	30	59	Rejected
McClellan amendment providing detailed procedures for conduct of union elections (agreed without vote)			Agreed
McClellan's amendment to bar secondary boycotts	41	50	Rejected
Prouty's amendment to allow organizational picketing unless: (1) another union recognized; (2) the union lost an NLRB election during previous nine months. Included provision that an employer unfair labor practice would be defense against charge of illegal picketing	86	4	Passed
Dodd's amendment to allow trusteeships for one year only, and only if need proven	41	51	Rejected
Eastland's amendment to require secret-ballot strike votes	28	60	Rejected
McCarthy's amendment to allow union to pay defense costs in trials of leaders	7	85	Rejected
Mundt's amendment providing further detailed procedures for conduct of union elections (agreed without vote)			Agreed
Holland's amendment to prevent strikes in public utilities	27	64	Rejected

In addition, Senator Morse raised a series of amendments of a generally minor nature, which he stated grew out of a discussion the evening earlier, a discussion he held with "a Teamsters lawyer." To some of these Senator Kennedy agreed, on others he took issue. The former were passed and the latter rejected.

The size of the opposition vote was in many cases a victory for opponents of the Kennedy bill. The changes wrought by the 1958 elections have been discussed. Yet, the more liberal 1959 Senate was not able to muster anywhere near the majorities that had prevailed in 1958. The vote comparison before and after the bill of rights is also interesting. The Ervin-McClellan group could only muster 27 votes to remove Title VI sweeteners. But now the votes were running as high as 41 against a five-member majority (i.e., 50 to 41, with a shift of 5 votes capable of changing the decision).

These votes were quite significant. It was clear that the mood of the Senate—which reflected the temper of the country as a whole—had been misjudged. The labor people had made their "maximum" concessions in the Senate Labor Committee to gain the support necessary for rapid passage of the bill. Yet, this had proved not to be enough. Specific limits on organizational picketing had been passed by the Senate. Hot cargo clauses for common (motor) carriers had been included as unfair labor practices in the bill, along with further regulations of election procedures and bonding requirements for certain union offices and employees. A shift of five votes would have meant passage of Senator McClellan's proposals on secondary boycotts as well. All of this was in addition to the major stunning factor, the McClellan bill of rights.

One important factor in the developments on the reform law was the role of Senator McClellan. His prestige with the public was very high. It was also high with his colleagues. In addition, he continued to present his amendments with a judicious aura of fairness. It is doubtful if Senator Goldwater (who nonetheless had had a number of proposed amendments approved) could have been as successful on the major issues.

But another factor was also important. Many senators now felt politically free to vote for more sweeping prescriptions and proscriptions for union activities. The political atmosphere had changed from the year earlier; their respective electorates were now prepared to accept more in the way of "reform."

The Senate "Off the Record"

During this period of proposal and consideration of amendments on the floor of the Senate, a great deal of activity was taking place behind the scenes. One draft of revisions in the McClellan bill of rights has been referred to. Before the revision reached the floor of the Senate, several versions were prepared. One was prepared by lawyers representing the AFL-CIO. Senator Kennedy, through Professor Cox, had requested their views on desirable changes. On

Thursday afternoon, April 23, four or five labor representatives got together to hammer out their proposal. During the evening Professor Cox joined them with his draft of revisions. This group worked through much of the night. All reports indicate that this was an evening of hard discussion ("quite a tussle"). Some agreement was reached on certain areas of the amendment. Friday morning Senators Frank Church and Joseph Clark contacted Professor Cox and discussed with him their draft of compromise language.[21] At his suggestion they went to talk it over with the union lawyers.

At about this point a mimeographed version of proposed language was distributed among interested parties. This did not represent agreement among all the parties, but was considered a reasonable document from which to work. Several copies were taken to the Senate chamber, where further negotiations were carried on. At the rear of the chamber near Senator Kennedy's desk a group of senators and staff people gathered. The group included Senators Kennedy, McClellan, and Johnson and advisers Cox, Dungan, and Freedman. The situation and the group were not static. As action on the floor demanded, individuals came and went. From time to time one of those present in the chamber suggested the absence of a quorum and, with the drone of the clerk's voice calling the roll in the background, the negotiations continued.

The discussion centered around McClellan's willingness to go along with proposed revisions. Certain areas were agreed to; others were discussed at length. The mimeographed sheets were cut and various sections combined in a new draft. Freedman had gone over the provisions and indicated his feelings to McClellan. The type of things McClellan resisted were changes in the effective date of the amendment, a change in the section negating federal pre-emption of jurisdiction over the questions included in the amendment, and further changes in the definition of "member." He readily accepted explicit limitations on the statement of rights and new language which would discourage dual unionism.

On the Republican side there had been many second thoughts

[21] For those interested in colorful anecdotes, a story went around Washington that these two, after several cocktails at dinnertime, decided, "We can do better than that," (meaning they could draft a better title than had McClellan), and set to work to prove it, coming up with the version herein referred to.

on the bill of rights. Several of the more liberal senators had discussed possible ways to change the features they considered undesirable. On Friday morning Senator Kuchel, the minority whip, joined the group at the back of the senate floor. The consensus of those present was discussed, and Kuchel left with a copy of the draft as it stood at that stage.

Friday afternoon a bipartisan group, including Senators Kuchel, George Aiken, Javits, Church, Clark, and Clifford Case (N.J.), met in the office of the Minority Leader (Senator Dirksen was not present). The group made changes in the language of the draft; Senators Kuchel and Javits were active in the actual rewriting of the provisions. The measure came out of this session in the form of the so-called "Kuchel compromise." The Los Angeles *Times* carried an article which discussed the role of Senator Kuchel in these proceedings. It quotes Kuchel as stating that Kennedy had asked him to reconsider his vote on the McClellan bill of rights and that he had conferred with Andrew Biemiller, described as "former Democratic Representative (Wisc.), now top congressional lobbyist for the AFL-CIO," and two "officials" of the AFL-CIO Building and Construction Trades Department. It further quotes Kuchel as saying that "he found some of their objections 'sound', but denied that they had drafted his substitute." The article then continues:

Kuchel denied that Kennedy personally urged him to introduce the "Kuchel Compromise" which saved the day for Democrats, but other capital sources insist that the decision to present it as a bipartisan solution was Kennedy's. Kuchel said Aiken was the unofficial chairman at the Friday afternoon huddle. . . . "Of course I saw Andy Biemiller [Kuchel said], but the language was the work of Republican Senators and Clark and Church. This was drafted by Case, Javits, Aiken and Kuchel. We did take some of the language Clark and Church had been improvising." [22]

It was not until late on this Friday evening, April 24, that Senator Kuchel came forward with his compromise on behalf of the bipartisan group. When he did so, the introduction of the Kuchel compromise on the floor apparently came as a surprise to some of those present, and there was an immediate reaction. So strong were the feelings on this issue, and the debate thereon so hard upon

[22] Robert Hartman, Los Angeles *Times*, April 28, 1959, pp. 1, 10.

the cocktail hour, that the halls of the self-styled "most dignified deliberative body in the world" resounded with the booing of one honorable senator by another. This was not the only manifestation of reaction. Later in the Republican cloakroom this same (booing) senator took a roundhouse swing at Kuchel (but missed). This raises the question of the type of reception the Senate might have given the stark removal of the bill of rights!

The reaction is understandable if a few earlier comments among some senators are noted. During the period following the passage of the initial McClellan bill of rights they had said, in their private conversations: "Well, you can't call it the Kennedy bill now," and "No, and he doesn't want it called that either."

With the inclusion of the bill of rights a presidential candidate had been dealt a heavy blow. Now the introduction of a compromise brought the possibility of his resurgence. This was bad enough, but to have the minority whip carry the floor battle and lend his name to the compromise was quite a shock to anyone who had not followed the elaborate preparations for the change and had not perceived the enormous pressure building behind the change. The Los Angeles *Times* article continued:

(Kuchel's actions were described as) "bailing the Democrats out of a disastrous dilemma" as one administration official put it privately. . . . Kuchel said it didn't occur to him to consult Senator Styles Bridges (R–N.H.) the senior Republican Senator and head of the powerful G.O.P. Senate Policy Committee and that he saw no need to "clear" his proposal with Senator Goldwater (R–Ariz.) ranking minority member of the Labor Committee and lone holdout on the 90-1 final passage of the modified Kennedy-Erwin labor reform bill.

But Kuchel added: "This was cleared with (Minority Leader) Everett Dirksen (Ill.) and John McClellan and then we sat down with Barry Goldwater and went over it point by point." [23]

A bill of rights revision was necessary and would in any case have been passed by the Senate, or the labor people would have used all their energy to prevent the passage of any bill in the Senate. Kuchel's action merely assured that the final version of the bill of rights would have close Republican scrutiny. The attack on Kuchel by this newspaper was based more on emotion than understanding.

[23] *Ibid.*, p. 10.

The Kuchel Compromise in the Senate

To make the Kuchel compromise feasible parliamentarily, contiguous material would also have to be changed in substantive fashion. This would circumvent the prohibition against consideration of the "same" material, which had been locked into the bill by tabling the motion to reconsider.

The introduction of the Kuchel compromise had thrown the Friday evening session of the Senate into disorder. Four times the presiding officer had to gavel for order in the chamber. Senator Johnson made reference to "the latest demonstration" in his statements. Of the four points of order raised in quick succession, the one raised by Senator Styles Bridges of New Hampshire, chairman of the Republican Policy Committee, was the most significant. It challenged the validity of the Kuchel compromise on grounds that the matter had already been voted on. The presiding officer ruled that the compromise was in order in that it dealt with contiguous matter and was substantially different from the original bill of rights. Senator Bridges appealed from the ruling of the chair.[24] In this situation it was up to the Senate to decide the question by majority vote. But there were no copies of the compromise available for distribution to the senators. They would thus be voting blindly on the point of order, as well as on the amendment itself. After a good deal of acrimonious debate the Senate adjourned until the next day, Saturday, April 25, at noon. The hope that the bill could be passed sometime Friday evening was not realized. The delay made it possible to print, distribute, and discuss the compromise, and also to determine the merits or demerits of the point of order.

At noon, with the Vice-President in the chair, the Senate reconvened. Vice-President Nixon, the presiding officer, made a statement citing precedents supporting the proposition that the amendment was in order. Senator Bridges was not present, but Minority Leader Dirksen, speaking for him, asked that his point of order and appeal from the ruling of the chair be withdrawn. There was no objection to this request. It was clear that the Republicans, at

[24] *Daily Congressional Record*, 86th Cong., 1st Sess., April 24, 1959, p. 6,001.

least the Administration supporters, were not willing to use parliamentary tactics against the compromise.

With this out of the way the Senate was free to discuss the compromise on its merits. At this point in the debate Senator Kuchel made a rare admission of a well-known phenomenon:

On the basis of the debate, I concluded—as did many other Senators —to support the bill of rights amendment offered by the Senator from Arkansas. It was a long amendment; and we had been debating long and hard, for many, many hours, in trying to arrive at a labor reform bill which would have bipartisan support, which would represent progress by the Congress in the field of labor reform, and which would become the law of the land.

The next day, I, like many of my colleagues, *read the text of the amendment* offered by the Senator from Arkansas for which I had voted [italics added]. It was several pages long. Certainly, with more than 100 printed amendments on our desks, it was physically impossible for any of us to read, let alone to study, the amendments, as, one by one, they were offered with rapidity and we were required to vote each one either up or down.

Others of my colleagues on both sides of the aisle did what I did —read and studied the amendments. It became apparent that there were some obvious questions as to parts of the language used. I concluded that in this proposed legislation there were provisions which were imperfectly drawn, which should be improved, and changed.

Thus, with some of my colleagues on this side of the aisle and with some of my colleagues on the other side of the aisle, I began to explore the possibility of keeping that which the Senator from Arkansas advocated, namely a bill of rights for labor, but of writing those rights in clear, unmistakable, reasonable, and just terms. That is what we tried to do.[25]

The close participation in the preparation of this amendment by some of labor's best legal minds, and the strong feelings of the labor people against the McClellan Title I which would be replaced, were important factors in bringing the AFL-CIO to back the Kuchel compromise. As has been pointed out, the Southern senators backed it; the Democratic leadership and Senator McClellan did likewise.

After discussion the amendment passed, 77 to 14. The principal changes from the original McClellan language were:

[25] *Ibid.,* April 25, 1959, p. 6,020.

(1) Qualifying language in the equal rights subsection making a member's participation privileges in all union nominating, election, referenda, and union membership meetings "subject to reasonable rules and regulations";

(2) The inclusion within the subsection on freedom of speech and assembly of similar qualifying language, with direct application to union meetings;

(3) An important provision to all the rights granted by the above subsection that they be subject to the union's right to "adopt and enforce reasonable rules as to the responsibility of every member toward the organization as an institution and to his refraining from conduct that would interfere with its performance of its legal or contractual obligations." [26]

A few other amendments were dealt with in perfunctory fashion, but the compromise essentially closed debate on the bill. There were the usual complimentary references for the performance of the major participants and their staffs, and then the amended S.1555 was passed by the Senate, 90 to 1 (Senator Goldwater dissenting). The AFL-CIO expressed its approval of the vote for the bill through its legislative representatives.

This marked the close of the first phase of the consideration of labor reform legislation. The content of the bill at this point was quite different from what had been anticipated. But the major breach opened by the bill of rights passages had been closed, at least with a makeshift structure, the Kuchel compromise. The union threats to withdraw support had had the anticipated result.

Yet, the careful analyst would have recognized from the start that the Senate was much more liberal-minded than the House of Representatives, and that the labor side had greater access to power in the Senate. He would also have noted that the greatest response on the part of the Senate leadership had been when the passage of legislation itself was threatened. For the Democratic party and for Lyndon Johnson there "had to be a bill."

[26] U.S. Senate, *Labor-Management Reporting and Disclosure Act of 1959*, 86th Cong., 1st Sess., 1959, S.1555 (as passed by the Senate), Section 101 (a) (11–12), pp. 3, 4.

V. THE GESTATION PERIOD

THE passage of the Kennedy bill in the Senate marked the beginning of a lull in the formal consideration of labor reform legislation. The only apparent activity was the leisurely hearings of the House Committee on Education and Labor. Behind the scenes, however, very significant actions and inactions which profoundly affected the course of legislation were taking place within the interest groups and in the official sphere. The span of seven weeks from the time a bill passed the Senate until the House committee began in earnest to write its own bill was a gestation period during which the positions of the major protagonists gradually hardened. It represented the last real opportunity for compromise. Later developments followed relentlessly from the policy choices made during this apparent lull.

In this chapter we shall trace a number of these important developments and become acquainted with some of the key participants. (Biographical information on the major participants is presented in Appendix C.) In the next chapter we will follow the legislative tactics of labor, management, the Democratic leadership, and the conservative coalition of Republicans and Southern Democrats in anticipation of the legislative climax which took place on the floor of the House.

The AFL-CIO

In April of 1959 the leaders of the AFL-CIO were in a difficult position. Their approval of the principle of regulation of internal union affairs had led to a great deal more than that to which they had originally agreed. The McClellan bill of rights, even in its

modified form, was considered less than ideal. Yet, union lawyers
had collaborated closely in its preparation; the federation had expressed its approval of the passage of compromise and had not opposed the passage of the bill in which it was contained.

Some members of some unions found the law satisfactory, but
in other unions there was violent opposition. Within the AFL-CIO
the International Association of Machinists (IAM), the United
Steelworkers, and the Communications Workers of America felt
that passage of the bill should be blocked. Their position was supported by the independent United Mine Workers and Teamsters
unions. The building trades unions were ambivalent. They strongly
supported, indeed insisted, on Title VII, which included their
sweeteners, but they did not like Title I, the bill of rights (although
we have seen that their legal representatives were active in the
revision of Title I). Many other internationals, including the United
Auto Workers (UAW), felt that legislation was essential and could
not be delayed.

President Meany, especially in the wake of the February meeting
of the Executive Council, did not feel free to decide the course of
the federation without consultation with others. The precariousness
of his seat as arbiter and spokesman for conflicting groups caused
him to look long and hard within his own organization before
acting. His commitment to attend the conference of the International
Labor Organization in Europe was a further complication. The net
result was that Meany let the situation ride until the next regular
meeting of the Executive Council, the established organizational
forum through which difficult policies are hammered out, scheduled
for less than a month in the future. Since House action would be
delayed for several weeks, there was apparently little need for
immediate decision on the future attitude of labor toward reform.
The interim period would allow time for the federation and its
affiliated unions to digest the provisions of the Kennedy bill and
their implications. This decision, though seemingly appropriate for
the loosely knit, democratically structured AFL-CIO, was to prove
embarrassing because of the actions of rival union groups.

Meany did discuss the progress of labor legislation with the
leadership of the Congress. Senator Johnson and Speaker Rayburn

gave him assurance that all their influence would be used to bring about a bill that would be acceptable to the AFL-CIO. This provided further salve to those who felt that a public stand on the bill was not necessary at that time.[1]

By now the formal organization of the AFL-CIO for liaison with Congress was functioning somewhat more smoothly. Coordination in the Senate had not been completely effective. The dangers of disorganization became obvious in the voting of that body. Steps had to be, and were, taken to remedy the matter.

It should be recognized that a greater degree of control over the affairs of the united labor movement than is actually possible has been imputed to labor leaders. A symptom of the decentralized power structure within the federation was the manner in which it organized to meet the needs of legislation. A group of vice-presidents was assigned the job of overseeing labor's efforts in relation to reform legislation. The members of this group were: George Meany, president of the AFL-CIO; Walter Reuther, president of the United Auto Workers; Al J. Hayes, president of the International Association of Machinists; George Harrison, president of the Brotherhood of Railway and Steamship Clerks. Their job was to determine policy for the labor side during the period when events would be moving at a rapid pace. This was an organizational adjustment to cover the periods between quarterly meetings of the Executive Council. The reader will note the differences of opinion among the unions represented in this group as the law progressed through Congress. The Railway Brotherhoods stuck generally with the AFL-CIO president. The IAM split widely, often working closely with the Teamsters. The UAW wanted a consistent public stand, well differentiated from that of the Teamsters Union and strongly in favor of internal reform.

On an intermediate level a similar committee, known as the Operations Committee, was established among the legislative representatives of various unions. It was under the direction and supervision of Andy Biemiller, head of the Legislative Department of the AFL-CIO and a former congressman. This committee had the

[1] What such a stand would have been at this stage is open to question. Even with the advantage of hindsight there is great disagreement within the federation on this question.

following members: Andrew J. Biemiller, chairman; Cy Anderson, Railway Labor Executive Association; Nordy Hoffman, United Steelworkers Union; George Nelson, International Association of Machinists. The legislative representative from the Steelworkers Union was closely associated with the negotiations in New York City over the pending and actual steel strike and, thus, did not participate fully in the activities of the committee. The legislative representative of the IAM did not participate fully either. The Operations Committee for labor legislation was the parallel of similar committees on other legislative problems, such as the Joint Minimum Wage Committee. Information was disseminated by the special committees to legislative representatives at the monthly legislative meetings and at special meetings called to discuss particularly pressing problems.

The committee of vice-presidents settled policy questions within the framework laid down by the Executive Council of the federation. The Operations Committee laid out the procedures and practices to be followed to implement the policy, and individual legislative representatives carried out particular assignments. At least, this was the theoretical chain of command. Many deviations and aberrations will be noted in the pages to follow.

This statement of organization does not cover some factors very important to the activities of the labor movement. Individual legislative representatives were (and are) directly responsible to their own international unions, not to the AFL-CIO. The "conventional wisdom" of the labor movement has exalted "business unionism," with its emphasis on economic gain for the particular union in collective bargaining. Traditions and loyalties have been primarily directed to the international or the local unions. Thus the absence, approved by the federation, of the Steelworkers' representative. And thus the month's vacation authorized by the international union and taken by a member of the committee of vice-presidents commencing at the end of July, 1959, one of the most crucial periods for the legislation.

The second loyalties of various officials were devoted to the federation (either the AFL or the CIO, not the AFL-CIO) to which the international had originally belonged. Jurisdictional disputes between unions of the old rival federations were still flaring. The staff people of the two federations were, and are, at least in some cases, still jealous of each other. Those who were members of the AFL still recognized their old associates as friends, while sometimes looking with suspicion on the "new" colleagues from the CIO. The two groups retained their identity even though their staffs were physically merged.

Outside the federation the Teamsters and the United Mine Workers were ardent opponents of legislation to regulate the internal affairs of unions. Each of these unions was very influential in the election of a sizable number of congressmen and thus influential in the voting decisions of these men. The Teamsters also had great influence at the local level with AFL-CIO local leaders who had long known them as friends and associates.

Teamsters Denounce S.1555

Within a few days after the Senate action on the Kennedy bill the Teamsters Union denounced it as an "antilabor" bill.[2] This denunciation was followed by vigorous action to make known to the Congress specific objections and by a direct campaign of propaganda within many local unions.

Although the Teamsters had been expelled from the AFL-CIO on the national level, close contact was maintained with many AFL-CIO locals by local Teamster bodies. Many personal friendships had been developed over years of joint meetings. The public reputation of the Teamsters did not extend to these men, who were known as individuals and friends. An "educational" campaign was conducted by the Teamsters through local representatives.[3] These men visited locals of AFL-CIO unions and spread the word that the Kennedy bill was antilabor and was designed to destroy the labor movement. They urged that the members make their opinions

[2] Washington *Post*, April 30, 1959, p. 1.

[3] There is evidence of this in the testimony of Sidney Zagri before the joint subcommittee of the House. See U.S. House of Representatives, Joint Subcommittee on Labor-Management Reform Legislation, *Hearings on Labor-Management Reform*, 86th Cong., 1st Sess., 1959, Part 5, p. 2,003.

known both to their congressmen and to the leaders of their national unions. The message was delivered in true demagogic fashion: anything that wasn't all white must surely be all black.

With the issues in question so complex that leading legal experts were in grave disagreement over their merits, and with the uncertainty about judicial interpretation inherent in legal phrasing, it is not surprising that the "educational" campaign did not attempt to discuss the legislative provisions directly. Members of local unions (as well as the public at large) can be more easily swayed by slogans than moved by ambiguous issues.

An important theme expressed and implied by Teamsters was that the leadership of the AFL-CIO was "going soft." They were not fighting for the interests of the members. They were not willing to stand and be counted, to fight against antilabor legislation. Meany had become a Pollyanna.

Such charges are hard to fight under any circumstances. With the issues involved here, the complications of congressional procedures, and the conflict within the AFL-CIO, they were virtually impossible to overcome.

The Impact of Labor's Action

The Teamsters' Washington representatives conducted a series of breakfasts for members of the House of Representatives to acquaint them with the objections of their union to the Kennedy bill. These were presided over by International Vice-President Harold Gibbons and his chief legislative advisor, Sidney Zagri. Groups of about twenty members of Congress were invited to each of several such gatherings. Union members from individual congressmen's districts were brought to Washington to express their views personally. The program included a detailed discussion of the Senate bill's undesirable features (from the Teamster viewpoint) and suggestions for their revision.[4] This presentation has been described as extremely well done and effective by several congressmen and their aides who attended.

While the formal presentation dealt with suggestions for im-

[4] These breakfast meetings were discussed in prominent news magazines. See *Time*, Vol. LXXIV, No. 4 (July 27, 1959), 12.

proving the bill in the House, the discussion at individual tables usually centered on postponing action till the next year. The atmosphere was too inflamed for "responsible" legislation to be enacted in 1959. "Why not put this off till next year so that this thing can blow over?" was an inquiry reported by several who attended.

These breakfast meetings showed a surprising degree of sophistication on the part of the Teamsters' representatives. They contrast sharply with the activities at the local union level and, unfortunately for supporters of the general position of labor, with the tactics employed toward the Congress at a later stage.

Confronted with an invitation to one of these gatherings, individual congressmen faced a tough decision. The years of unfavorable publicity given to the Teamsters Union by the McClellan Committee made public association with them undesirable, but the political power of the Teamsters in many districts made it equally undesirable to offend them. Many a congressman solved his dilemma by sending his administrative assistant to the breakfast. The administrative assistant would not be as readily recognized by the public and is an acceptable stand-in in all but the most unusual circumstances.

The highly organized and articulate program of the Teamsters interacted with the lack of program and action by the AFL-CIO to produce the impression that labor opposed the Kennedy bill only a few days after the bill had passed the Senate in a vote which labor's friends had been told was an "approved" vote. It was during this period that House Minority Leader Charles Halleck issued his widely quoted statement: "It looks like we won't have a labor bill this session." [5] There is no question that the Teamsters were actively promoting this objective. There is no question that, at the weekly meetings of the AFL-CIO, legislative representatives openly discussed the possibility of killing the bill in the House. But there were other strong forces at work on the opposite side of the issue.

Management Groups

During the consideration of the Kennedy bill in the Senate some coordination of management's effort had been achieved by the so-

[5] New York *Times*, May 28, 1959, p. 16.

called "task group." Further coordination among management
groups was worked out through a special liaison with the White
House, Robert Gray. The organization of management and some
of its activities have already been discussed. For the program on
labor reform legislation Mr. Gray called together some of the
most important of the management groups. Since all those present
were interested in achieving the same objectives, he proposed that
they work together to avoid conflicting efforts and waste motion.
Gray asked for suggestions on how best to proceed. After discussion, a clearinghouse operation was decided on. This would apply
to the actions of associations toward the public in general, in other
words, a program of "consumer advertising." Gray would assess and
pass on suggestions for action, effective wording for advertisements,
and so forth. Timing of group action would be decided jointly. The
clearinghouse function performed by the White House made it
possible to avoid contradictory pressures by people on the same
side of the question and obviated possible questions of status and
prestige among the interest groups.

One White House spokesman indicated that the bill of rights
vote in the Senate had convinced backers of the Administration
program that, at some point in the legislative process, they would
be able to "write their own bill." From the Administration's view,
Robert Gray's job was to muster public support and channel it to
a substitute bill when such a bill might emerge.

The Legislative Subcommittee of the National Chamber of Commerce's Secondary Boycott Committee performed a coordinating
function directed toward the Congress itself. This group included
the following members: [6]

    Charles Tower, National Association Broadcasters, *chairman.*
    Robert T. Borth, General Electric Company.
    Lucius P. Chase, Kohler Company.
    Arthur Erwin, National Lumber Manufacturers.
    Andrew Murphy, Jr., National Association of Home Builders.
    Ellison D. Smith, Jr., attorney, Columbia, N.C.
    M. Maynard Smith, attorney, Smith and Swift.

The historical development of the parent committee was traced in
Chapter III.

[6] See also Appendix B.

The Legislative Subcommittee arranged for meetings of management representatives, several of which were held on the top floor of the National Association of Broadcasters' Building. The over-all strategy toward legislation and the implementation of specific tactics were determined in these sessions. The most important discussions took place during the later stages of House consideration of the bill.

The usual support functions had been carried out by this group all along: preparation of speeches, suggestion of language for inclusion in bills, briefing of legislators on the questions at issue, appearances before congressional committees, and so on. (There was a very close correlation between the wording and order of presentation in the Senate of McClellan's secondary boycott amendment, on the one hand, and the National Chamber's pamphlet *Employer Rights in Secondary Boycotts*, on the other.) As mentioned earlier, this group prepared the bill, S.76, dealing with secondary boycotts, which was introduced by Senator Curtis in 1959.[7] Similar bills had been introduced over the years to keep the question before the Congress as a part of the educational campaign.

In addition to these coordinated activities, most of the individual associations were pursuing their own projects. One group, the General Contractors of America, shunned coordinated action (much as their counterparts in the labor organization did), but nonetheless were considered quite effective in making their influence felt.

Speaker Rayburn's Role

Sam Rayburn was in his forty-sixth year in the Congress of the United States. Since his election as Speaker of the House of Representatives in September of 1940, he had been undisputed leader of the Democratic Party in the House.

Born in Tennessee in 1882, a 1903 graduate of East Texas Normal College in Commerce, Texas, a student of law at the University of Texas, and a member of the bar in that state in 1908, Rayburn was first elected to the Congress in 1913, after serving six years in the Texas state legislature (the last two years as speaker).

Though he came to the House as a states' righter, he soon developed into a liberal thinker, supporting Presidents Wilson, Roose-

---

[7] U.S. Senate, *To Amend the Labor Management Relations Act of 1947, as Amended, and for other Purposes*, 86th Cong., 1st Sess., 1959, S.76.

velt, and Truman, and later, John Kennedy. Rayburn never let his sectional interests deter him from his broader responsibilities as a national leader of his party. During the New Deal he was chairman of the House Commerce Committee and sponsored bills which created the Securities and Exchange Commission, the Rural Electrification Administration, and the Federal Communications Commission and expanded the authority of the Federal Power Commission. As Speaker he had thrown his weight behind civil rights legislation, reciprocal trade measures, and the whole gamut of foreign aid bills.

The press has described the "stumpy Texan" as one of the legislative greats of his day. His manner was one of lovable irascibility and friendly grumpiness. He was widely esteemed and admired, but he could not be termed a beloved leader. In his later years his testiness, lack of communication with the membership, and power-wielding tactics caused grumbling on both sides of the House aisle.[8]

As Speaker of the House "Mr. Sam" set in motion machinery to ensure that there would be labor legislation in 1959. He convinced Graham Barden of North Carolina that he should hold hearings on the labor question, something Barden had resisted the year before. The Speaker's strategists, Representatives Lee Metcalf and Richard Bolling, were given the assignment of shepherding the bill through the committee and the House itself. The Speaker had also contacted a group of liberal Democratic congressmen on the Committee on Education and Labor and requested their assistance in getting a bill out of the committee.

The activities of the committee in writing its version of the Labor-Management Reporting and Disclosure Act, H.R.8342, are discussed in detail in the pages to follow. Let us now trace the factors which led up to the rewriting of the bill.

First, the role of the Speaker's representatives should be explained. To begin with, such men—in this case Bolling and Metcalf—cannot bind their principal in a contractual way. They cannot guarantee action by the Rules Committee (though Bolling was the Speaker's representative on the committee) or by the standing committees on

[8] This section, including certain phrasing, relies heavily on an article by Paul Duke in *Wall Street Journal,* Aug. 27, 1962, p. 8.

a given question. Obviously, they cannot state what the House itself will do. They can, and do, represent the views of the Speaker to others, represent the views of others to the Speaker, and help shape his perception of the particular legislative problem. They are, in effect, an extension of his eyes and ears but, except in specific instances, not of his decision making. Perhaps this is an overstatement, though technically correct. The Speaker usually agrees with the thinking of his "boys" and vice versa. By influencing the Speaker's knowledge and perception of a problem, they do supply stimuli to his decision processes.

In the case of the labor bill, the roles of Metcalf and Bolling supplemented each other. Their duties were similar, the only differentiation being along geographic lines (with House delegations). It should be noted that neither of these men were members of the House Committee on Education and Labor, although Metcalf had been in previous years. During the evolution of the labor reform battle in the House of Representatives they met formally with representatives of the AFL-CIO to discuss perceived differences of opinion with them. There were four such gatherings. The changes which they reflect form an interesting pattern of thinking and action. The evolution of the position of the House Democratic leadership is the best evidence of the influence of the public on Congress. It is the role of congressional leaders to mold and to measure the attitudes of their colleagues on important questions. It was through the attitudes of the members of Congress that the congressional leaders were able to measure the views of the public.

Strategy Meeting Number One

When the Executive Council of the AFL-CIO met for its spring session, its agenda was as crowded as it had been in February. The general tone was less acrimonious, but labor-managment legislation enjoyed a position of only slightly greater importance. As a result of internal pressures, especially those generated by the Teamsters and unions of similar persuasion, the decision was made not to give further support to the Senate version of the Kennedy bill.

In late May, following the meeting of the AFL-CIO Executive Council which denounced the Kennedy bill, the first strategy meeting took place in the dining room of Washington's Carlton Hotel. Among those present were the AFL-CIO Vice-Presidents George Harrison, Al Hayes, and Walter Reuther, plus President Meany and the key legislative representatives, Andy Biemiller and Cy Anderson. The Speaker himself accompanied Metcalf and Bolling. The atmosphere of the meeting was described as that of a collective bargaining session rather than a gathering of people seeking a common goal. The Democratic strategists repeated advice the union representatives had heard earlier: drop the sweeteners in Title VII and support a straight reform bill. The answer was also a familiar one. The federation would insist on the inclusion of the Taft-Hartley changes it desired. It would also demand sweeping changes in the new Title I, the bill of rights.

It is hard to see how the AFL-CIO could expect a less stringent bill from the House than it had been able to get from the Senate. The more conservative nature of the House, with its many "safe," one-party districts and the powerful leadership positions held by archconservatives, were well appreciated. Yet, if the reader puts himself in the position of the hard-pressed President Meany, attempting to unite divergent groups within his federation and fighting the well-organized campaign of the Teamsters and others from without (with its internal repercussions for him), such a stand is not hard to comprehend. It would be possible to view the bill of rights episode in the Senate as a temporary aberration produced by unusual circumstances. It would be possible to look back to the 1958 election as a source of renewed confidence and as the wellspring of changes which brought about the "friendly-to-labor" majority in the Committee on Education and Labor. But this view is one which looks inward at the problems of the labor federation, not outward to the realities of the situation in the Congress.

Politicians are artists who seek to scrutinize the inscrutable, who seek to weigh the mood of the public on various issues. On certain important issues Congress becomes the focal point of aroused public perception. The Democratic House leadership was attempting to assess what was necessary and what was possible both in the Congress and also in light of the variables that might effect future elections, especially the crucial presidential election of 1960. The Speaker and his strategists were looking ahead to the coming battle in the House. They were looking to the general public and its growing pressure for labor reform legislation. Despite any thoughts about the origins of the conditions which were felt to exist, the conditions themselves could not be ignored. The Democratic Party had to demonstrate its responsibility, its ability to pass needed reform legislation.

The strategy meeting ended with little agreement, but the views of each group were well aired. Apparently, the federation felt it could block any legislation of which it disapproved, despite the statements by the Speaker that a bill would have to be passed by the overwhelmingly Democratic Congress.

A Second Look at the Position of Labor

The Kennedy bill was admittedly "more than the AFL-CIO had bargained for," but the damage was more to pride than to the legitimate interests of the AFL-CIO. Essentially, there were three major areas in which the Kennedy bill exceeded the bounds which labor had hoped to enforce. First was the bill of rights. This represented an extensive invasion of the internal affairs of unions. It had provisions which threatened to be unworkable. But experience in the Senate had demonstrated that, when these problems were clearly and forcefully pointed out, the Congress was prepared to act in a reasonable way. If reflection and analysis showed that further difficulties were present in the Kuchel compromise language, these could most probably be removed. Of course, it is always possible to view with alarm most provisions of complex legislation. For alarm to be justified in this case, however, would have required a determination by federal courts to destroy legitimate unions in this country.

Second was a ban on organizational picketing under specified conditions. But what were the conditions? They were: (1) where the employer had already recognized another labor organization, or (2) where, in the preceding nine months, a valid representation election had been held (and the union not certified). In addition, if a union were charged with an unfair labor practice under this section, it would be a defense to show that the employer had himself committed an unfair labor practice. In what way could this be deemed inimical to the legitimate rights of labor?

Third was a provision making hot cargo agreements unfair labor practices for certain employers and unions. Who were the employers? Motor carriers subject to the Interstate Commerce Act (who constituted only a small portion of all motor carriers). Who were the affected unions? Mainly the Teamsters, who were now outside the AFL-CIO.

A major difficulty which the labor movement had experienced from the start had resulted from its failure to recognize the major "pay-off" from reform legislation. That pay-off would be the ability of the union man to raise his head in honor once again in the society in which he lived. The McClellan Committee and the press had not invented or imagined the problems which they publicized. The problems existed and were in need of rectification. The labor movement had proven its inability to achieve the rectification and thus needed the aid of the federal government to bring about action to make possible once again a favorable public image of labor. That this objective was a powerful stimulus is attested to by the support given to legislation by unions from the start. But all unions did not recognize this major benefit from reform legislation. Some unions could not look with equanimity on reform legislation.

In a number of public statements many legislators charged with responsibility for developing and passing a reform bill had stated or implied that a law was necessary to curb certain activities of Jimmie Hoffa and the Teamsters Union. Hoffa had been built into the personification of the need for change, and change was (supposedly) directed at him. Thus, change was an immediate and direct threat to the Teamsters Union.

Social scientists have documented what laymen have long observed: that an organization (or an individual) subjected to outside threat draws inward, takes on certain rigidities of thought and action, and strikes out at its antagonist in ruthless fashion.[9] This is clearly

[9] See Ronald Lippitt, Jeanne Watson, and Bruce Westley, *Dynamics of Planned Change: A Comparative Study of Principles and Techniques* (New York, Harcourt Brace, 1958) for an elaboration of this thesis in a slightly altered but directly relevant context.

what the Teamsters did and should have been expected to do. Their antagonists had set out to frame a law that would "get" them. Clearly, the prohibition of hot cargo agreements would deprive the Teamsters Union of one very powerful weapon it had used with great effect in the past. Even less desirable provisions might still be forthcoming.

The leaders of the AFL-CIO failed to make clear to their members (and perhaps themselves to understand) the fundamental fact that the action necessary to bring about a changed image for labor in general would most probably bring changes to the Teamsters Union which its leaders would strongly oppose. The greatest sweetener which the labor movement as a whole could desire would be one which purified the public perception of its collective moral aroma. Without such purification it would be only a matter of time before more and more regulation and proscription would be inflicted on labor in general. The insistence of certain unions on specific desired provisions of law in return for what should have been perceived as beneficial fumigation demonstrated a less than clear awareness of self-interest.

The AFL-CIO had itself expelled the Teamsters from its ranks. It had attempted in its literature to make clear the distinction between the Teamsters and the "legitimate" labor unions. An intelligent program of action would have been for the AFL-CIO to continue to differentiate itself clearly from the Teamsters Union, the public whipping boy of 1959.

It appears that President Meany found himself under attack and thus became preoccupied with demonstrating that he was a good union man fighting the good fight against labor's enemies. Perhaps with a greater degree of preplanning he could have avoided being placed in this position.

The Kearns Bill

On May 20, 1959, Representative Kearns, the senior minority member of the House Committee on Education and labor, introduced what came to be known as the second Kearns bill, H.R.7265.[10]

[10] U.S. House of Representatives, *Strengthening the Protection to Employees in the Exercise of Their Rights of Full Freedom of Association, Self-Organization, etc.*, 86th Cong., 1st Sess., 1959, H.R.7265.

This bill was significant for several reasons, and thus its background will be traced at least in outline.

The minority had retained a labor consultant, Kenneth C. McGuiness, a member of a law firm which represents a number of conservative clients. McGuiness had been appointed on the recommendation of Edward McCabe, of the White House staff. In fact, it was McCabe who sold Barden on the idea of providing the minority with a consultant. As is typical under such conditions, McGuiness worked closely with Kearns, the ranking minority member. The idea for H.R.7265 grew out of the relationship of the two men. McGuiness, former staff member of the NLRB, was the chief salesman of the bill's ideas and chief draftsman of its provisions, which would channel reform through the NLRB.

Kearns had earlier introduced the Administration's bill, H.R.3540,[11] the House parallel to the "Goldwater" bill, S.748. His new bill was introduced on his own responsibility, to the chagrin of the Administration. He was very pleased with the new bill and attempted to gain bipartisan support for its introduction in the House. He contacted a congressman friendly to labor and attempted to enlist his support. Although this congressman appeared to favor the provisions of the bill, he withheld his support until he could determine how the AFL-CIO felt about the position he might take. The AFL-CIO met his overtures on the question with statements of confidence in its ability to prevent any undesirable provisions in the bills then under consideration. The AFL-CIO position was apparently that there was no need to try a new approach.

Graham Barden and Judge Smith

Graham Barden, along with Rules Committee Chairman Howard Smith, is a prototype of the regional Southern politician. Both men are known to their constituents as "Judge," Smith's title carrying over to the public at large. It is through men like Barden and Smith that the South has sustained its veto over legislation since Calhoun first proposed his doctrine of the "concurrent majority." Utilizing every vantage point for the exercise of power, they have capitalized

[11] U.S. House of Representatives, *Requiring Disclosure of Certain Financial Transactions and Administrative Practices of Labor Organizations and Their Officers and Agents, etc.*, 86th Cong., 1st Sess., 1959, H.R.3540.

on the conservative bias of the seniority system for selection of committee chairmen to fortify their hold on the Congress. Barden had represented the third district of North Carolina for twenty-six years. Smith represented the eighth congressional district of Virginia, from which he first served in the Seventy-second Congress in March, 1931. Each man had a reputation for skilled legislative infighting which each richly deserved.

Graham Barden is about six feet tall, a Southern gentleman who wears glasses. He is a former football captain from the University of North Carolina. He earned a law degree from the same institution. His nickname to his wife and other intimates is "Hap," short for "Happy." He appears to be just that, a very happy man, at least in his home environment in New Bern, North Carolina, a clean, easy-going Southern town of about 22,000 people, with many small shops, two or three motels, a Sears Roebuck, and a J. C. Penney store, chain five-and-ten-cent stores, and so on. The major point of interest in the town is the residence of the last British governor of North Carolina.

Congressman Barden lives out on the edge of town on Country Club Road, in a rambling, one-story brick home that he built about 1957 or 1958 on a lot he had owned for some time. The land is lightly wooded and well landscaped, with a patio and several gardens. There is always a cool breeze blowing in from the river. Mr. Barden has a Chris-Craft in a small boathouse that he built and a smaller boat that he uses for his fishing, an occupation he thoroughly enjoys. He has two children: a boy who is a doctor and a girl who is married to a neurosurgeon. He has five grandchildren and a lovely wife named Agnes.

In conversation Barden's countenance is animated and cherubic, especially when he is telling a story. He is a pleasant person to be with, a person very easy to like and a person with a flair for mimicry. He is said to do a take-off on John L. Lewis which is superb. His imitations of Judge Smith are an equal delight.

Barden had strong opinions about the members of his committee. He sometimes showed a virtual physical reaction when he discussed the committee. "Oh, what a bunch of people to work with! Oh, you can't imagine what it is to try to deal with a group of people like that! Have you met those people on my committee? Have you talked with them? Do you know them?"

He commented about individual members: about one member who could never be relied upon; another who "is just not straight! That man is crooked!"; another who "can cause more trouble, can think of more ways and more subterfuges for slowing up discussion, for messing up a meeting"; and one who is "someone who I just can't understand. That person, I just don't understand that person!" Clearly, these things are deeply and emotionally felt. They may help explain the retirement of Barden at the end of the Eighty-sixth Congress.

To many of his committee members Barden was a "tyrant." Often he achieved his goals merely by force of personality. If he felt sure of an advantage, he would invariably press it to the utmost. On occasion the chairman is reported to have mimeographed the result of his committee's action even before the committee had met. One participant told of occasions when the committee met with an avowed purpose, agreed on in advance by a caucus among its more liberal members, only to dissolve, in confrontation with the full committee, into minor wrangles (fanned by the chairman) obviating the stated objective.

Barden was also a master of the tactical delay, usually utilizing a colorful homespun yarn: "That reminds me of the fellow back home . . . ," the story would usually start, and friends and staff members would recognize that they had several minutes to rethink an argument, patch up differences, or rewrite a provision.

Recent History of the House Committee on Education and Labor

Graham Barden became the chairman of the House Committee on Education and Labor in 1950, following the death of the former chairman, Democratic Representative John Lesinski, in May of that year. During Barden's early reign the committee and its agenda were at the whim of the chairman. In 1953 and 1954 the House was organized by the Republicans. Representative Samuel McConnell of Pennsylvania became chairman and carried on in the tradition of his predecessor. Though the party label had changed, the economic philosophy of the chairman remained as conservative as before. A number of labor people have commented, however, that they found the Republican more responsible and easier to deal with than Democrat Barden, who resumed his chairmanship as a result of the Democratic majority in 1955.

Total membership of the committee was twenty-five in 1948. It was increased to twenty-seven in 1953, to twenty-eight in 1954, and then, in 1955, to thirty. This "packing" of the Committee had bipartisan backing. In addition, Speaker Rayburn had been using his influence to dilute the power of the chairman by making Democratic appointment of liberals to the committee. In 1957, with thirty members on the committee, of which a majority were Democrats, the opposition to Barden at last had enough votes to demand a showdown. It was the intention of the more liberal members to strip the chairman of his powers. Barden apparently learned of the intention of the opposition before the showdown meeting. The New York *Times* [12] reports the fateful occasion. In face of the demand that he end his "one-man-rule," Barden introduced a package of proposed reforms. These included a regular meeting day and time, the creation of standing subcommittees to deal with specified substantive issues, and the proposed assignment of members to the subcommittee. The proposals were accepted by the committee members. Thus, Barden was able to blunt the thrust of the opposition and retain a good degree of control over most matters. He made a strategic retreat before his opponents, who had the votes to neutralize his power completely. As a result, he remained a powerful figure as committee chairman. This will be demonstrated in the pages to follow.

The Hearings in the House

The hearings of the House Committee on Education and Labor are illustrative of several interesting points on the tactics employed in the legislative process. Little important substantive contribution was made by these hearings, however.

As an example of the canny ways of Graham Barden, the mere organization of the hearings is of interest. Representative Carl

[12] New York *Times*, Jan. 16, 1957, p. 21.

Perkins of Kentucky had been chairman of the Subcommittee on Labor-Management Relations since the formation of the standing subcommittee in 1957. His subcommittee would appear to have been the logical one to handle labor-management legislation. Rather than put Perkins in such a powerful position, Barden took an imaginative tack and referred labor legislation to a joint subcommittee made up of members of the Labor-Management Relations and Labor Standards subcommittees. No chairman of the joint group was named, no doubt because Representative Perkins was senior to Representative Phil Landrum of Georgia, chairman of the Labor Standards Subcommittee.

In the combined grouping Landrum, a fellow Southern Democrat, would be able to represent the conservative viewpoint without raising too much ire. The make-up of the Joint Subcommittee on Labor-Management Reform Legislation then stood as follows: [13]

Joint Subcommittee on Labor-Management Reform Legislation

LABOR-MANAGEMENT RELATIONS SUBCOMMITTEE
Carl D. Perkins, Ky., *chairman* (9 - 3)

Roy W. Wier, Minn. (11 - 2)	Robert P. Griffin, Mich. (5 - 7)
Elmer J. Holland, Pa. (13 - 0)	Clare E. Hoffman, Mich. (0 - 13)
Ludwig Teller, N.Y. (11 - 0)	

LABOR STANDARDS SUBCOMMITTEE
Phil M. Landrum, Ga., *chairman* (4 - 9)

James Roosevelt, Calif. (13 - 0)	William H. Ayres, Ohio (7 - 6)
John H. Dent, Pa. (3 - 1)	Edgar W. Hiestand, Calif. (0 - 13)
Roman C. Pucinski, Ill. (Freshman)	

The cochairman arrangement ensured that there would be strong conservative representation at the hearings. Disagreement between the cochairmen could only be resolved by the chairman of the full committee. In this situation Perkins saw that it would be useless to have direct clashes.

Actual hearings before this joint subcommittee had begun on March 4 and continued through June 10. A large number of witnesses were paraded before the group. The stated objective of the

[13] U.S. House of Representatives, Joint Subcommittee, *Hearings,* Part 1, p. ii. The numbers in parentheses again represent the COPE evaluation of the voting record of the congressmen.

lengthy public hearings was to lay the groundwork for the legislation to come. This proved true in several senses. The hearings did acquaint the congressmen with the issues involved. They did provide volumes of information. They served as a forum for various interest groups to air their opinions before the public, they served the function of legitimizing propaganda by including it in public documents, and they made propaganda readily available to the Congress for use in the coming debate on the floor.

Hearing Highlights

Secretary Mitchell was the first witness to appear. His reception was a good deal more cordial than it had been in the Senate. He strongly endorsed the Administration bill, H.R.3540. His presentation was more polished than in his Senate appearance. He stated that the Administration took no stand on the question of the so-called two package approach to legislation. That question he left to the Congress to decide.

Representatives of management groups continued to hammer away at the necessity for closing loopholes in the laws on secondary boycotts and organizational picketing. They usually demanded more than this, with the better-known associations continuing to advocate the extension of the antitrust laws to combat the "monopoly power" of labor and the passage of a national right-to-work law to make unions truly voluntary associations. There were variations of emphasis, but the theme was constant throughout the hearings.

A relatively new departure was the inclusion of "plain folks" and their stories of abuse through denial of internal democracy in their unions, through the imposition of secondary boycotts, through the workings or organizational picketing, and so forth. Such witnesses were produced by representatives of chambers of commerce, labor lawyers, the Retail Federation and others.

In one early skirmish over the appearance of witnesses Representative Perkins found the schedule filled with people whom he considered "antilabor." Representative Landrum had gone ahead and laid out his plans without consultation. This led to a strong reaction by Perkins and his fellow liberal Democrats. The witnesses were subjected to long cross-examination and other tactics bordering on harassment when they appeared.[14] The minority continued its attempts to bring in individual union members who had had unpleasant experiences with unions. Many of these were people whose histories had been gathered by the Secondary Boycott Committee of the Chamber of Commerce in its four-year hunt for "atrocity cases." After the initial barrage such attempts were usually frustrated by the majority members before they could be scheduled.

The appearance of John L. Lewis marked a real change of pace and raised some interesting historical questions. With the exception of Clare Hoffman of Michigan, who brought forth questions about the United Mine Workers from a file dating back to the 1920s, the congressmen treated Lewis with great admiration and respect. His contributions to the labor movement were highly praised; his statesmanlike vision in disputes in the industry was lauded; the honesty and efficiency of his union were noted. The attitude was bipartisan, though the degree of warmth was noticeably greater among the majority members. One comment by Representative Kearns will give the flavor of the reception:

Mr. Lewis, I want to say at the outset that you are the Lionel Barrymore of the labor movement, with this beautiful presentation this morning. . . . In my time I think Samuel Gompers and you have done more for the labor movement, than any two men I have ever known. I congratulate you.

The discussion with Representative Dent, who represents a coal-mining district in Pennsylvania, is especially instructive:

Mr. Dent: . . . I was pleased to hear certain members of this committee hold the Mine Workers' Union up as a sort of model union.

Tell me, Mr. Lewis, if you care to, was it always held up as a model union in the eyes of the public?

Mr. Lewis: Was what?

Mr. Dent: Was the United Mine Workers always held up to the public as a model union?

Mr. Lewis: Congressman Dent, I am glad you asked that question. I think it is a fair statement for nearly a quarter of a century that I was the whipping boy of the editors of the *Post*, quoted by the famous Congressman from Minnesota [Mr. Hoffman].

Mr. Perkins: Michigan.

[14] *Ibid.*, Parts 1 and 2.

Mr. Lewis: Michigan. I stand corrected. That was wholly uninten-
tional. And during all of those years I occupied the proud position that
Jimmy Hoffa now occupies.

Now, strange to say, I feel lost, sometimes when I rise in the morning
and can't find an editorial of denunciation because I had got used to
them. I knew that they were wrong and someday the writers thereof
would come to recognize it. But, of course, there was a long painful
period of waiting. But now, as you gentlemen have noticed, every once
in a while I am treated by some public body or public representatives
with some consideration, and made to feel that I am as other men now.
In other words, I have achieved some degree of respectability, chiefly
because, I suppose, the public found somebody else whom they could
enjoy more greatly being mad at—if the public has to have a whipping
boy, or if the editors, again espousing the interests of property against
human values, always want to find some scapegoat in labor. But I will
say this. Mr. Hoffa seems to be flourishing like a green bay tree. His
members support him because he brings home the bacon to them, and
they are interested in the bacon.[15]

In 1947, when the Taft-Hartley Act was being considered, John
L. Lewis had appeared before the Senate Committee of Labor and
Public Welfare. The contrast in conditions was striking. The coal
mines had been seized by the government under wartime emergency powers to prevent an industry-wide strike. They were being
run by the government through the regular managers of the mines.
The atmosphere of those hearings and the tone of the questioning
was as acrimonious as any faced by Jimmy Hoffa before the Mc-
Clellan Committee.

Senator Ellender: But that common sense, Mr. Lewis, was not apparent, surely, in November when you and your miners refused to go to
work, and the only way by which they returned to work was because
the courts stepped in and operated its—
Mr. Lewis: There were 76,000,000 tons of coal on hand at that time,
and there was no harm that could befall anyone.
Senator Ellender: That may be so and that short supply would not
have lasted long. Many industries had curtailed production, and the rail-
roads were hard pressed. Suppose you had persisted, in short, if you had
persisted in striking then certainly there would have been damage to the
national economy for lack of coal?
Mr. Lewis: That is purely hypothetical. My word, I do not know how
I could answer a question of that character.

[15] *Ibid.*, p. 1,121.

"What would you do in 1944 if you were an evil man?"

I cannot answer a question like that.[16]

Where the revisions to the Wagner Act were directed against John L. Lewis as the personification of evil among labor "bosses" and the focal point of public wrath, the 1959 legislation was directed against the current public image of labor, Jimmie Hoffa. The passage of time had placed a halo where horns had previously grown above the bushy brows of the great John L. Just as Taft-Hartley dealt with a great number of issues in addition to the nation-wide strike, so the legislation of 1959 dealt with many issues in addition to union corruption. The parallel is indeed striking.

Several witnesses testified in the early part of the hearings and then again after the Kennedy bill passed the Senate. Among these was President Meany of the AFL-CIO. In light of the analysis of events in the Senate as presented in the preceding chapters, this testimony is most interesting.

Meany's testimony covered three things: (1) the position of the AFL-CIO favoring some legislation, in particular legislation along the lines of S.505 (the form of the Kennedy-Ervin bill initially referred to the Senate subcommittee); (2) the federation's reasons for opposing S.1555 (the Kennedy bill as passed by the Senate); and (3) provisions of the second Kearns bill, H.R.7265. The first point was virtually lost in press comment on Meany's appearance. This is not surprising, since the second point was the first expression to Congress of reaction by the AFL-CIO to the Kennedy bill which had passed the Senate six weeks before and was, thus, the real "news" made by Meany. The particular provisions of the so-called second Kearns bill were not important to the final development of legislation; therefore, they will not be discussed further.

Meany's comments on S.1555 included a detailed technical discussion of the bill. The amendments included in the bill from the floor of the Senate came in for special criticism. The bill of rights provisions, even in their modified form, were criticized for being either so vague as to require litigation or so precise as to put unions into a strait jacket. Many of these objections could have been met by the inclusion of specific modifying phrases or the acceptance of

[16] U.S. Senate, Committee on Labor and Public Welfare, *Hearings, Labor Relations Program,* 80th Cong., 1st Sess., 1947, Part 4, pp. 1,991, 1,992.

the possibility that certain questions are important enough to be settled in court. Several of the suggestions made by Meany were later included as modifications to the Kennedy bill by the House committee. An example was the modification of fiduciary requirements to take account of the special conditions faced by a labor union. Meany also made the point that

There are times in any union when discipline is all-important. When a union is engaged in collective bargaining, it ought not be compelled by law to conduct its deliberations and actions in town-meeting fashion. If it is weak and endeavoring to function in predominately nonunion or antiunion segments of an industry it ought not be required by law to allow company agents who have wormed their way into membership to have free access to the courts or administrative bodies for disruptive proceedings designed to harass or hamper its activities or be restrained by law from punishing or otherwise disciplining members whose conduct threatens the very existence of the union. There are circumstances when the union members by majority vote may properly decide that their bill of rights must yield to the necessities of the situation in which a union finds itself at a given time. But neither the union nor its members could administer a federally legislated members' bill of rights with the flexibility which might be needed.[17]

This touches on a question which was more directly and forcefully put by James Carey in his testimony a few days after the appearance of Meany.[18] In essence, Carey's point was that unions face powerful oligarchies in the large corporations which control the major industries in this country. In their struggles with their far-from-democratic adversaries, unions cannot afford the luxury of complete democracy. Perhaps the statement of the issue in such blunt terms would have ruffled the public relations image that both management and labor work so hard to maintain and would thus have been inappropriate to the president of the AFL-CIO; however, it appears to have been a reasonable ground on which to oppose the inclusion of Title I and a ground which approaches the question more nearly "on the merits."

Meany did criticize the manner in which the bill of rights had been included in S.1555 because it had not been subject to analysis in committee. We have seen the intimate acquaintanceship of the

[17] U.S. House of Representatives, Joint Subcommittee, *Hearings*, Part 4, p. 1,480.
[18] *Ibid.*, Part 5, pp. 2,200–203.

AFL-CIO attorneys with the provisions of this amendment when
it was first introduced as a part of the McClellan bill and the
important role they had played in its modification on the floor
of the Senate. Its provisions could hardly be called a surprise to
them.

The statements of labor spokesmen all amounted to the same
general conclusion: if it was possible to return to a bill like the
original Kennedy-Ervin bill, their organizations would support
legislation in the field. The mass media had stressed the fact that
the AFL-CIO and its component unions opposed S.1555, the Senate-
passed version of the bill. Thus, the general picture was that unions
opposed labor reform legislation in the House. This was a dangerous (though in some respects accurate) posture for the AFL-CIO
to accept. It represented an unrealistic appraisal of the Congress and
the "art of the possible."

Los Angeles Junket

The difficulty experienced by the minority members in getting
the desired number and kind of witnesses to appear at the hearings
of the joint subcommittee led to the gambit of a special subcommittee to hear testimony in Los Angeles. This was not a difficult project
to sell to the members who were asked to serve on the subcommittee,
Representatives Roosevelt and Hiestand.[19] These congressmen are
both from California and welcomed the opportunity to be in the
spotlight in their home area. Representative Landrum served as
chairman of the subcommittee and made the necessary arrangements.

May 28 and 29 were the dates of the hearings. The presence of
Roosevelt assured those friendly to labor that they would have
effective representation. This is borne out by the record. But an
impressive documentation of abuses in all the desired areas was
achieved. There was particular emphasis on violation of rights
which would be guaranteed by bill of rights provisions. The fact
that violence had occurred in a labor dispute greatly overshadowed
a rejoinder that adequate laws exist for the punishment of such acts

[19] Representative Hiestand was one of the first members of Congress to
profess openly his membership in the far-right John Birch Society.

if local and state officials would exercise the authority they already possessed. The courage of an independent restaurateur in standing up to 925 days of organizational pickets backed by secondary boycotts and harassment by local governmental officials pointed up the great odds against which he toiled and the unfairness of the battle. That he (1) was and would be too small to come under federal (NLRB) jurisdiction under past or present law, and (2) was saved by a ruling of the state supreme court which had, and would continue to have, jurisdiction in the case and his testimony was therefore irrelevant to the matter before the special subcommittee—these facts are somehow lost in the poignancy of his case and sincerity of his presentation. To sum up: these special hearings were a miniature McClellan Committee operation, exposing some grievous (though sometimes irrelevant) wrongs along with developing a great human interest record.

There was a good deal of pressure within the committee to end the hearings following the trip of the special subcommittee to Los Angeles, but it was decided that hearings should continue for an additional week. The deadline for completing hearings was set by the full committee for Friday, June 10, at 6 p.m.

The Teamsters Are Heard

The Teamsters Union availed itself of an opportunity to present its views before the joint subcommittee on June 9, the next to last day of the hearings. Two representatives of that union, Sidney Zagri and lawyer David Previant, discussed their attitude toward the proposed legislation. The statement included their twelve principal objections to the Kennedy-Ervin bill and ten objections to the amendments approved on the Senate floor. The reaction to these gentlemen was indeed surprising:

Mr. Hoffman: . . . I appreciate the effort you have made, and it is wonderful, but now if you would just come along, with all your ability, you two gentlemen, and give us a bill. . . .

Mr. Barden: . . . I think you two gentlemen have given about the finest illustration of just how versatile the human mind can be when you are looking for a way to do something that you want to do or to avoid something that you do not want to be bothered with. . . .

Mr. Hiestand: Mr. Chairman, I believe these two witnesses have been

about as effective witnesses as we have had before us. It is obvious that
they have not only thought deeply on the matter but have studied this
from the legal and the legislative point of view, and I join with my
colleague from Michigan in complimenting them certainly to that extent. . . .

Mr. Roosevelt: May I say you certainly are to be congratulated, because you received the congratulations of people I did not think would
ever be willing to congratulate you. So that is a step in the right direction.[20]

They were reminded of the record developed by the McClellan
Committee in regard to their union, but the atmosphere of the
session was restrained and almost friendly. Senator McClellan himself appeared on the final day, followed by Judge Boyd Leedom. It
is interesting to note that McClellan and Goldwater were the only
two senators to appear before the House committee.

Representative Pucinski had requested that Leedom, chairman
of the NLRB, appear before the committee prior to the closing
date. Earlier, Pucinski had requested and received from the NLRB
a copy of the McKinsey and Company report on its internal administration. He wished to interrogate Judge Leedom about the
findings of the report. Apparently, it wasn't a coincidence that this
witness was the last to appear and that Pucinski was the last member
to question him. The deadline was a convenient way of limiting
the questioning of Leedom, which did become practically insulting
at times.

Throughout the hearings and later in the deliberation over the
bill itself, Pucinski's conduct failed to follow the norms of his congressional society governing acceptable conduct of a freshman member. The reaction of his seniors is exemplified in the following two
comments:

Chairman Barden: There was supposed to be a 5-minute rule, and
he [Pucinski] has already used 15, but that is all right. . . .

Mr. Landrum: Let the record show that Mr. Pucinski has had the
floor for 1 hour and 15 minutes and the rare privilege of interrogating
the witness for that length of time with a minimum of interference. I
hope, sir, that you do not feel that we are foreclosing you from anything
but I feel constrained now to say that the committee session is adjourned.[21]

[20] U.S. House of Representatives, Joint Subcommittee, *Hearings,* Part 5, pp.
1,996, 2,005, 2,008.
[21] *Ibid.,* Part 5, pp. 2,283, 2,323.

Representatives Pucinski and Dent tended to speak more than is deemed appropriate for such junior members in the committee. Their effectiveness was greatly impaired as the sessions progressed. Statements to this effect were heard from many congressmen on both sides of the table. Codes of acceptable conduct played a significant role in the handling of the reform legislation at many levels. Some of these will be mentioned in the next chapter.

At this point the AFL-CIO was on record in opposition to anything more stringent than the program it had approved four months earlier. It was facing internal dissension resulting from Teamsters' pressure and public pressure, both channeled through the rank and file of its component unions. The Democratic House leadership was determined that some legislation would pass the House in this session to meet public demand. The management groups and the Administration were fanning the public pressure and preparing to capitalize on it at some stage with their own bill. The Teamsters were geared for large-scale participation in the legislative process. Clearly, the interaction of such forces would be less than harmonious.

In the pages to follow, the reader will be struck by the reaction of the AFL-CIO to the people who gave them such wholehearted support in the earlier sessions of Congress and who were to continue to show voting records in accord with votes "approved" by labor.

VI. THE COMMITTEE ON EDUCATION AND LABOR WRITES A BILL

IN 1959 the House Committee on Education and Labor had thirty members, twenty Democrats and ten Republicans. The members and their voting records as evaluated by COPE were as follows: [1]

Democrats		Republicans	
Graham A. Barden	(4 - 9)	Carroll D. Kearns	(6 - 6)
chairman		Clare E. Hoffman	(0 - 13)
Adam C. Powell	(12 - 0)	Joe Holt	(4 - 9)
Cleveland M. Bailey	(7 - 4)	Stuyvesant Wainwright	(7 - 6)
Carl D. Perkins	(9 - 3)	Peter Frelinghuysen, Jr.	(8 - 5)
Roy W. Wier	(11 - 2)	William H. Ayres	(7 - 6)
Carl Elliott	(11 - 2)	Robert P. Griffin	(5 - 7)
Phil M. Landrum	(4 - 9)	John A. Lafore, Jr.	(1 - 3)
Edith Green	(12 - 1)	Edgar W. Hiestand	(0 - 13)
James Roosevelt	(13 - 0)	Albert H. Quie	(0 - 2)
Herbert Zelenko	(12 - 0)		
Frank Thompson, Jr.	(13 - 0)		
Stewart L. Udall	(13 - 0)		
Elmer J. Holland	(13 - 0)		
Ludwig Teller	(11 - 0)		
John H. Dent	(3 - 1)		

[1] U.S. House of Representatives, Joint Subcommittee on Labor-Management Reform Legislation, *Hearings on Labor-Management Reform*, 86th Cong., 1st Sess., 1959, Part 1, p. ii. Fr. = freshman. Numbers in parentheses indicate COPE evaluation of 1957–58 voting record. First number indicates "right" votes, second "wrong."

Democrats (cont.)

Roman C. Pucinski   (Fr.)
Dominick V. Daniels   (Fr.)
John Brademas   (Fr.)
Robert N. Giaimo   (Fr.)
James G. O'Hara   (Fr.)

The voting records of some of the other major actors, as evaluated by COPE, were as follows:

Richard Bolling	(13 - 0)
Lee Metcalf	(13 - 0)
Homer Thornberry	(6 - 5)
Charles Halleck	(2 - 7)
Howard Smith	(2 - 11)

It should be remembered that the particular issues used in evaluation were chosen by the AFL-CIO Committee on Political Education (COPE) and that the "'proper" vote was determined by them. On many issues the interests of management and labor were not directly opposed, and it is not a necessary conclusion that an "approved" vote for a measure (a "right" vote) was actually a vote against the interests of management (one which would be evaluated as "wrong" by management).

Early Action of the Committee

Until the consideration of the labor bill in 1959 these men were grouped by competent observers of the Congress in the following way: eighteen liberal Democrats, two Southern Democrats,[2] and ten Republicans.[3] Among the Republicans some, Representative Robert Griffin, for example, had the endorsement of certain labor unions in the 1958 election. The joint subcommittee discussed in the last chapter had shown itself incapable of resolving major problems which occasionally confronted it. In all important votes the two ex officio members (Chairman Barden and Representative

---

[2] Representative Elliott of Alabama is more appropriately listed with the liberals, though geographically he is a Southerner.
[3] The COPE ratings clearly support such an evaluation.

Kearns) joined the minority members plus Representative Landrum to balance the voting power of the remaining Democratic members, producing a 7 to 7 deadlock. Some committee members who were friendly to labor came to the view that a bill was necessary in 1959 and that it should follow the general form of the Kennedy bill from the Senate. They discussed this with Andy Biemiller while President Meany was in Europe, but they were unable to get a clear answer to the question of what the federation really had to have in the way of amendments to make the Kennedy bill "livable." Biemiller vacillated, apparently waiting for Meany to make a final pronouncement.

In a memorandum to Representative Udall dated June 8, 1959, Senator Kennedy jotted down what he called "random thoughts" on the situation in the House. These are paraphrased below:

1. Representative Teller wants to report out S.505 under a closed rule. But this would be opposed by the United Mine Workers and the Republicans and attacked by the press, which would call it weak. The result would be neither a bill nor a political asset.

2. A comparison of S.505 with S.1555 as it came from committee.

3. It is necessary to get Speaker Rayburn to get a commitment to protect a bill from amendment on the floor. A bill that could do this would require the Senate bill provisions with a rewritten bill of rights to attract Southern votes.

4. If this is not possible, then it is necessary to control the House conferees. In this case the later a bill is presented the better. It would then be possible to say that if the House goes wild, the result might be no bill at all.

Random though the thoughts may have been, this quick outline is quite prophetic of the problems to come, if not of their solution.

The Speaker's representatives, Metcalf and Bolling, saw the futility of leaving the writing of the law to the subcommittee. The result would be interminable wrangling. In addition, the subcommittee membership did not include the legislators on whom the House leadership could depend most strongly. These two men, therefore, worked through those members of the full committee who had expressed their willingness to act for the Speaker, and they arranged for a motion to transfer consideration of the bill to the full committee at the completion of the hearings. This was opposed by Representative Wier, who introduced a motion to return responsibility for the writing of legislation to the subcommittee. Since there were a number of accusations that this was a delaying tactic to bottle up legislation for this session, Representative Pucinski offered an amendment limiting the time allowed the joint subcommittee to ten days. The discussion of these motions took place in a very stormy four-and-one-half-hour committee session in which tempers ran high. On a roll-call vote the Wier-Pucinski motion was defeated, 20 to 10.[4]

This vote came as a great shock to labor's legislative representatives. Not only had Barden and Landrum joined the Republicans, but eight other Democrats had done so as well. These included five who were to hold the balance of power throughout these sessions—Carl Elliott, Edith Green, Frank Thompson, Stewart Udall, and freshman James O'Hara—plus three other freshmen—Dominick Daniels, John Brademas, and Robert Giaimo. All of these were staunch liberals, and, as shown above, all (except the freshmen) had voting records highly favorable to labor.

Behind the Explosion

In light of the deadlock in the joint subcommittee, the reaction of the leaders of labor would seem to be hard to understand. But, if developments during the last days of the hearings are noted closely, there is an obvious reason for the reaction. Pucinski and Dent were developing a basis for "further study" of the questions before the committee. Labor people frankly state that at this point in the history of the law there was an attempt, though not public or official, to bottle up legislation in the committee. The motion to return the bill to the subcommittee was a definite delaying tactic. The members of the committee were aware of the position of the AFL-CIO and the way its legislative representatives would like them to vote, but they had voted to "get on with the show" and consider the bill in the full committee.

The political fortunes of the Democratic Party were dependent

---

[4] The outline facts of the House committee consideration of labor legislation were carried in "Summary of Developments," *Labor Relations Reporter*, Vol. XLIV (Washington, Bureau of National Affairs, 1959). The events and votes reported in this study can be verified in that publication.

on reform legislation in the Eighty-sixth Congress. The ambitions of two potential presidential candidates were also directly affected. The public mood required that there "had to be a bill." Against this tide the AFL-CIO had, at least in this instance, been unable to stand.

The preoccupation of the Democratic leaders was that of the artist with his craft. They were keenly aware of obstacles to the passage of a bill which would remain after committee action. The Rules Committee would set the conditions under which the bill would reach the floor and assign the floor managers for the bill. Judge Smith's skill would be directed toward providing the conditions necessary for "strengthening" amendments to take hold. The temper and mood of the House, as modified by the influence the leadership could bring to bear (in interaction with the influence of the opposition), would determine the fate of such amendments.

The Democratic leadership wanted to face the House with a bill which would attract as much support as possible, especially the support of labor. It was clear that the opposition would be determined. It was known that they were skilled.

The Significance of the Vote

The period following the first crucial vote of the full committee was one of great consternation. Within hours after this vote was taken, Teamster representative Sidney Zagri [5] was on the phone to unions in the districts of the congressmen who had voted "wrong" on the motion, telling the unions to get in touch with their congressmen and get them in line.[6] The AFL-CIO acted in a similar way. They, too, exerted pressure against those who had voted "wrong." This will be discussed at greater length in the pages to follow.

The Committee on Education and Labor, which had been gradually packed with a prolabor majority, had rebelled against those who had felt that they could at last command performance with the wave of a hand. It became obvious that there might be enough individuals

[5] For a substantiating summary of this event see *Time*, Vol. LXXIV, No. 4 (July 27, 1959), 13.

[6] *Life*, Vol. XLVII, No. 4 (July 27, 1959), 30. *Life* carried a slightly modified version of this story, but both magazines limited their statements to the actions of the Teamsters Union.

on the committee to vote out a bill in spite of the feelings of the federation. The "rampaging political combine" had been unable to command its "minions," either at the leadership or at the committee level.

Speaker Rayburn had thrown his great weight behind the need for action. The conservative forces also recognized the need for action by the committee, since the procedures for consideration of legislation outside of committee channels would most probably work to the benefit of the Kennedy bill supporters, in which case the pressure which the conservatives were building for the passage of a law would then backfire and aid the Kennedy bill. Though the labor movement was now officially opposed to the Kennedy bill, management groups could still see little to recommend it from their point of view. They recognized that passage of the labor sweeteners it contained would cut off the bargaining lever necessary to bring about the passage of management-backed changes in the Taft-Hartley Act through mutually beneficial compromise. To achieve these changes at all, they would have to append them to the reform bill which would face the House in this session.

The labor movement had done all it could to bottle up the bill and had failed. Management groups could muster at most twelve votes. It was the Democratic Party leadership of the House, with its eight votes, that decided the issue. The AFL-CIO found itself beyond the point of no return; it had committed itself to reform legislation and was unable now to back out. The only question remaining was: what would be the form of the law—or perhaps, what issues would ride on the coattails of reform? In the Senate labor itself had pinned Taft-Hartley changes onto that coattail and had refused to let them be removed.

On with the Show

The blowup in the committee was on a personal as well as an ideological basis. Metcalf and Bolling had to bring about a new working relationship among the committee members if any law was to emerge. Through a good deal of persuasion and "head knocking" this was achieved.

At the next scheduled meeting of the committee, June 16, there was further heat generated. If the committee was to work on a bill, it had to start somewhere. Each congressman had his own ideas, and there was a great number of bills which might serve as a convenient vehicle. The logical suggestion that the committee start with the bill passed by the Senate was objected to violently at the outset. A compromise was suggested and tried. This was the preparation of a comparative print of five bills, the Barden, Administration, Kennedy, McClellan, and second Kearns bills, for a starter. But with thirty committee members attempting to read, understand, remember, and discuss the provisions of all five measures simultaneously, the result was chaos. After two and one-quarter hours of wrangling, the procedure was dropped. The Kennedy bill was adopted as the basic form from which argument would proceed.

Strategy Meeting Number Two

The second of the meetings between the Democratic strategists and the AFL-CIO leadership took place shortly after the House Committee on Education and Labor went into executive session to work on its version of labor reform. George Meany was still overseas at the conference of the International Labor Organization, but Vice-Presidents Reuther and Curran and chief legislative representative Andy Biemiller, plus a few others, met with Bolling and Metcalf. The discussion was charged with ill feeling.

Stung by developments in the committee, the federation had come around to a position backing a "clean" six-title bill.[7] But now the congressmen stated their belief that they were "overrun" on a clean bill and would have to include at least token measures on secondary boycotts and organizational picketing in a seventh title (even if no sweeteners at all were included). Political soundings by these Democrats indicated that their colleagues were a good deal more aware of the issues than they had been the year before. It would have been extremely difficult, if not impossible, to gain their support for a bill with no Taft-Hartley changes. There was sufficient awareness of secondary boycotts, hot cargo clauses, and "blackmail picketing," inspired in great measure by the attention given these

[7] Here the words "clean bill" are not used in the technical sense, but merely indicate a bill exclusive of Taft-Hartley amendments.

issues by the McClellan Committee in the previous six months, so that many congressmen were at least uneasy about facing their constituents with a reform bill which did not include provisions directed at the problems. The Republican Administration and the President continued to specify that these issues required attention in any reform law. The political climate had shifted. The Democratic leaders were recommending a shift in strategy to adjust to the change.

Reuther's attitude was reasonable. He attempted to explore the reasons for the advice of the strategists, but several of the other labor representatives were adamant in their demands. The demands themselves represented a considerable concession from the earlier stand of the AFL-CIO. The Building and Construction Trades Department had agreed to sacrifice its sweeteners to forestall those Taft-Hartley amendments which the federation considered harmful to all. Once again, the meeting achieved minimal tangible results beyond an airing of views, but there appears to have been some feeling that more was accomplished. Reuther is reported to have gained the impression that the Democratic leadership was committed to a clean bill. The House Democrats did not share this impression. A leadership spokesman specifically and emphatically denied that such was the case. In 1963 an active labor spokesman forcefully restated his position that the commitment had been given.

Labor vs. the Democratic Party: The Legislative Process

The mechanics of the committee consideration of this bill were rather elaborate. There was extensive interaction with the technicians made available by those interest groups which played a part in the development of the bill. The entire process represented a power struggle between the Democratic House leadership and the leaders of the labor movement, who were unwilling to accept the possibility that their wishes might not prevail and thus, in effect, assured their own defeat. The chronical of events clearly demonstrates the degree to which the Democratic congressional leaders had to modify their program and strategy if labor legislation was to pass the Eighty-sixth Congress. Each modification had its cost in anguish and reaction from the labor movement. It seems clear that the adjustments would not have been made had they not been necessary. The attitude of the public and the mood of the House of Representatives made them necessary.

Subsequent events were to prove that the assessment of the situation by the House leaders had been correct. The tactical decisions of the AFL-CIO were consistently one step behind what was necessary to capture the initiative and lead, rather than follow, the developing situation.

The Committee Begins to Function

Although there was no agreement on over-all considerations, some working arrangements were set up on the liberal side. Apparently, each group felt that it could achieve its will on the tactical level of committee voting and that there was no need to resolve points of view.

Biemiller recommended that Representative Teller be the "lead man" for those friendly to labor. Teller would maintain liaison with union representatives and call the signals for the liberals during the executive sessions of the committee. Recognizing that the staff of the committee could not be relied on for technical support, since it was responsible to Chairman Barden (and there was no provision for a labor consultant to the majority of the committee), Biemiller suggested, "let Teller be your lawyer." This arrangement was agreed to, but with reluctance on the part of some, including Representative Bolling. No one questioned the technical competence of Teller, who had been professor, scholar, and writer in the labor law field, but there were misgivings about his part in the Welfare Fund Reporting Act of the year before and about his personal relations with other members of the committee.

On June 17 work began in earnest on what would become the committee bill. The major labor reform bills which came before the House in 1959 are shown in Table 4. The Kennedy bill, S.1555, as it came from the Senate, was used as the basis for committee discussion and action. To avoid initial controversy, the committee decided to go through it section by section, starting with Title II, making changes as necessary, then returning to anything which ap-

Table 4. Major House Bills on Labor-Management Reform
(Eighty-sixth Congress, First Session)

Bill	Sponsor	Some Identifying Features
H.R.3302	Representative Green	Essentially, S.505, the original Kennedy-Ervin bill.
H.R.4473	Representative Barden	A bill setting forth very detailed licensing requirements for unions and their activities.
H.R.4474	Representative Barden	The counterpart of the Curtis bill of the Senate (S.76), dealing with boycotts.
H.R.3540	Representative Kearns	The counterpart of the Administration bill introduced in the Senate by Senator Goldwater (S.748)
H.R.7265	Representative Kearns	The second Kearns bill, which never received serious consideration, but almost achieved bipartisan support when first introduced. Would have provided individual union members with opportunity to bring reform through NLRB procedures.
H.R.7811	Representative Teller	A bill generally comparable to the Kennedy bill, but without Taft-Hartley changes.
S.1555	Senator Kennedy	The Senate-passed bill. Included seven titles, from the bill of rights (compromise) to Taft-Hartley changes.
H.R.8342	Representative Elliott	The seven-title bill developed by the House committee, embodying 102 amendments to the Kennedy bill, S.1555.
H.R.8400, (8401)	Representative Landrum (and Griffin)	The substitute of the coalition group. Made up of Title I of the Kennedy bill, Titles II–VI of the Elliott bill. with important though minimal changes, and a new Title VII embodying changes to the Taft-Hartley Act desired by management.
H.R.8490	Representative Shelley	A bill similar to the Elliott bill but considered an "all-labor" version of the bill; had no hot cargo or organizational picketing provisions.

peared to need further attention in what was referred to as the "second go-round."

This session lasted two and one-quarter hours. No voting on the bill itself was accomplished. The meeting the following day, June 18, was a short one, lasting only one and one-quarter hours, at which Representative Teller introduced his own bill. Union lobbyists prepared a comparative print of the Kennedy bill and the Teller bill as their official tally sheet on which to trace the progress of the committee. The first voting began the following week. In the three days, from June 23 to June 25, five sessions were held, lasting a total of approximately eleven hours. Twenty-four changes were made in S.1555, and the lines were drawn for the battles that continued to rage in the committee during the remainder of its consideration of labor reform legislation. Many events lay behind the amendments included by the committee.

Lobbyists and Legislators

It has been intimated that the Committee on Education and Labor was expected by the AFL-CIO to be a rubber-stamp committee. When some members, the five mentioned earlier plus Representatives Daniels, Brademas, and Giaimo, showed a mind of their own, they were immediately subjected to considerable pressure. Representative Udall (COPE score 13-0), a Mormon, and an athletic and fiery young Congressman, is given credit for an effective explosion in the face of Teamster Zagri's statement that "I am going to get you in line." Udall, making reference to his state's lack of strong unions, the fact that it had a right-to-work law, and its increasingly conservative climate of opinion, said: "Barry Goldwater sets the tone in my state." His intent was to demonstrate that threats of Teamster opposition were relatively ineffective on him. Zagri translated Udall's statement into "Goldwater calls the tune in my state" and used it to rally other unionists against the congressman. In the propaganda campaign which followed, this was carried another step to: "Udall's afraid of Goldwater, so he's voting antilabor."

On June 18 Udall issued a statement to the press emphasizing that the committee could report out a bill "despite the Hoffas and the Lewises." This statement included reference to hot cargo prohibitions and the outlawing of extortion picketing as necessary provisions for a committee bill. It gained him the animosity of the AFL-CIO, which had come to oppose such measures. The AFL-CIO joined the Teamsters in a campaign to change the congressman's mind.

Representative Thompson (COPE score 13-0), who was a tall, handsome, slightly graying man, was accused by the Teamsters of "buckling under to the Chamber of Commerce" and voting "wrong" on the committee. This was because of alleged ambitions to run for governor of New Jersey in order to bring the state's delegation to Kennedy at the Democratic convention. Thompson received threatening phone calls and eventually asked the FBI to have his wife and three daughters put under guard. At some point direct AFL-CIO pressure was also brought to bear on Thompson. In the final week of consideration of the committee bill Thompson expressed his reaction to the pressure from the federation directly to Andy Biemiller in very colorful language. This will be discussed later in the chapter.

Edith Green, a very pleasant woman of middle age, had had, like the others just mentioned, a virtually spotless voting record from the point of view of the labor movement up to this time (COPE score 12-1). Her district in Oregon is a strong labor district representing large numbers of Teamsters Union members and building tradesmen. The latter are now dominant politically, but this was not always the case. Teamster Zagri contacted local unionists in Mrs. Green's district and intimated that she was trying to repudiate her old relationships with the Teamsters by her actions on the bill. On behalf of the AFL-CIO, legislative representative Walter Mason personally called on Mrs. Green on several occasions. He was attempting to enlist her support for the lead of Representative Teller within the committee. One of his calls happened to come on June 25.

During the committee session on that day, Teller had done something that had confused the other Democratic Representatives. He had introduced Chairman Barden's proposals on employer reporting instead of the similar sections of his own bill. Just the evening before, in discussion with other Democrats, Teller had scoffed when he read the proposals circulated by Barden, and commented: "Well, look at what [he] is trying to do!"

With the aid of Ken Meikeljohn of the Industrial Union Department and his own administrative assistant, Donald Baker, freshman Representative O'Hara had spent a good part of the evening preparing modifications to the language of the Teller bill. Teller's actions came as a complete surprise to him the next day. He exclaimed in a whisper in the committee room: "No, introduce your own language!" Teller replied: "This is what our friends (the AFL-

CIO) want. We'll humor [Barden]. We can come back to it and change it later." O'Hara voted against Barden's language, but it was carried by the committee. O'Hara then introduced language from the Teller bill as an amendment to Barden's amendment. Teller voted with a majority against it.

Mason's urging of Mrs. Green to "follow Ludwig Teller" was more than the ladylike Mrs. Green could stand on this afternoon. She exploded with "You can go to hell!" [8] Mason dutifully reported his reception by the lady from Oregon at the next meeting of legislative representatives.

The AFL-CIO flew members of Mrs. Green's campaign committee down to Washington to "camp on her doorstep" and convince her that she was doing the wrong thing. A Mr. Roberts, the chairman of her labor committee during the campaign, was one of these people.

The federation also contacted Michigan's politically powerful Gus Scholle to inform him that O'Hara was "going wrong." Rather than call O'Hara directly, Scholle called some people he knew in Washington, told them of the calls from the AFL-CIO, and asked what was wrong with O'Hara. He was told that there was nothing wrong with O'Hara except that he was working night and day with a group of other congressmen to try to determine just what the labor movement wanted and had to have in the way of legislation. And he wasn't getting any help from labor's representatives in the Capitol.

The Teamsters did contact O'Hara directly. They notified him that they had one million dollars that they could use in a campaign against him and that "they would put a Teamster on every corner" of his district, if necessary, to defeat him at the polls if he persisted in his activities.

Representative Carl Elliott of Alabama (COPE score 11-2) was the fifth to bear the brunt of labor's wrath. As a Southerner, with relatively weak union representation in his district, Elliott was not very susceptible to direct union pressure, but he was open to pressure from his conservative colleagues for being "too liberal" in his

[8] It is interesting to note that both *Time* and *Life* report Mrs. Green's words, but refer them to Teamster Zagri instead of Mason.

thinking. Yet, he appears to have been able to maintain the respect of both groups.

When Sidney Zagri visited the offices of various congressmen, he was usually accompanied by a group of union people from AFL-CIO locals in the man's district. Zagri did most of the talking in such interviews, usually demonstrating a great deal of information about the bills under consideration and misinformation about the degree of support among Democrats and labor groups for his own thinking about them. An example of this was his visit to the office of Representative Brademas. Zagri entered with his troupe and began a discussion with the congressman. In the course of his conversation he stated, among other things, that the Speaker backed his position on a clean bill and other matters. Brademas lifted the phone and called the Speaker to question this. The reply came back unmistakably: "That's a damn lie!" This cleared the air of misunderstanding for the union representatives who had come along with Zagri, but it did not relieve the pressure on Brademas.

The group which held the balance of power in the committee consisted of the five members mentioned above—Elliott, Thompson, Udall, Green, and freshman O'Hara—plus three other freshmen, Daniels, Brademas, and Giaimo. The role of the last three was not as well publicized as that of the first group, who gained fame under the title given them by William Whyte, the "faithful five" (translated by the Teamsters into the "faithless five"). This is because the three freshmen were especially susceptible to pressure from their districts. The violence of the reaction of union representatives to the 20 to 10 vote showed that the path to a House labor bill would not be an easy one. The three were advised by the House leadership to "lay low" and go along with the AFL-CIO as far as they could. "There is no need in your continuing to lacerate yourselves," they were told.

On crucial votes the committee usually divided into three groups. Moving figuratively from left to right: thirteen Democrats generally voted in accordance with the wishes of labor representatives, five Democrats held the balance of power (the "faithful five," who were also known as the "swing group"), and ten Republicans plus Barden

and Landrum voted in general accord with the wishes of management groups. The middle group was thus able to decide most controversial issues even without the support of its "reserves" (who are
included above among the Democrats).

The Role of Whipping Boy

Newspaper and magazine articles showed the influence of the
McClellan Committee hearings in many ways. One effect, the legitimizing of attacks on the Teamsters Union, is significant from
several points of view. Politically, it was not merely "O.K." to oppose the Teamsters and have your strong stand against them publicized, it was highly desirable. The AFL-CIO, however, had been
able to maintain, and was striving to improve, its public image of
respectability. In most districts it was neither desirable nor proper
to have this group publicly against you, or vice versa. A campaign
against you by the Teamsters, especially if you were known as a
"labor supporter," might lose you some Teamster votes and perhaps
some other union votes, but it was almost certain to bring you the
sympathy and support of the local press and the public at large.
Such a benefit would not accrue if AFL-CIO unions were to campaign against you. Thus, in the articles which appeared, it was
always the Teamsters and not the AFL-CIO against whom righteous
wrath was directed, even though the actual situation might have
been otherwise.[9]

Headquarters at the Congressional Hotel

After it was abundantly clear that the committee would go ahead
with consideration of the bill in spite of the wishes of the AFL-

---

[9] The same was true of personal interviews with various congressmen and their
staffs. They were extremely reluctant to discuss any disagreements they may
have had with the AFL-CIO or its affiliated unions, but they were more than
willing to discuss the tactics and threats of the Teamsters. It was only from
other sources, including representatives of the AFL-CIO itself, that the activities
of the federation were disclosed. These could often be documentd with the
congressman once they were known, but even when well-documented accounts
of events were presented to some of these men they denied their part in the
events. For some this was an aversion to opening old wounds which were beginning to heal; for others it was a fear that their participation in interviews might
become known, with the attendant repercussions and straining of relationships.
However, the participation of so many people at various stages did make it
possible, with few exceptions, to confirm events.

CIO, the federation decided to use its influence to make the bill as good as possible.

It was generally agreed that the efforts of the federation in the Senate had not been well coordinated. The same senator was often given conflicting information by different representatives of the AFL-CIO. This resulted in confusion, exasperation, and inefficiency. Then, too, there was the problem of the lack of technical advice for the numerical majority of the congressmen on the House committee. The majority staff was controlled by, and loyal to, Chairman Barden. Thus, the two Southern Democrats had ample technical support. The minority staff, augmented with a legal consultant, was under the control of Representative Kearns. The eighteen liberal Democratic members—the majority of the committee—had no staff support at all.

To rectify the situation, the AFL-CIO set up lobbying headquarters in the Congressional Hotel, a short distance from the Capitol. Its staff would coordinate the lobbying effort and make the services of competent lawyers available to the liberal committee members. A "drafting group," consisting of lawyers for the various interested unions, was organized to prepare amendments to S.1555. Lawyers from the union most directly affected were given over-all responsibility for the section of the bill most important to them.

The drafting group operated from the downtown headquarters of the federation, had a shifting membership over time, and numbered from five to seven in all. Under the initial working arrangements, proposed amendments were prepared, mimeographed, and distributed to friendly members of the committee. The suggestions would be discussed (in caucus) and a decision on the general Democratic position would be made.

Time magazine indicated that the Teamsters were also submitting proposed amendments to the committee through certain Democratic Representatives and were receiving regular reports on the progress made at each of the meetings.[10] The men named by *Time* are Representatives Roosevelt and Pucinski. It should be noted that roll-call votes of committee members were known to representatives of all interest groups, as reported by members sympa-

[10] *Time,* Vol. LXXIV, No. 4 (July 27, 1959), 36.

thetic to the groups. They also appeared regularly in Drew Pearson's column and in the reports of the *Labor Relations Reporter* of the Bureau of National Affairs. Press reports imply that there is something sinister about the transmittal of such information. Perhaps the practice is sinister, but it was almost universal.

The "whipping boy" bias in press reporting was apparently applied by committee members to suggested amendments as well. If they had been suggested by the Teamsters, proposed amendments were automatically bad, and the person who suggested them was automatically tainted. Little attention was paid to the merits of such amendments.

The Opposition

From the point of view of the minority, the odds appeared overwhelming at this stage. A year earlier the best either side could do in a real test vote was a tie. This year there were eighteen liberal votes against the twelve that the conservatives could muster. Some of the actions of the majority appeared to be unusual and hard to understand, but there was little chance that the minority could include in a committee bill the type of reforms that the President was calling for at his press conferences. The minority faced an uphill fight all the way.

Management groups maintained close contact with Republicans, Southern Democrats, and the House committee staff, distributing proposed amendments and suggesting changes, but there just weren't enough votes to institute their desired program. In executive session of a committee it's the votes that count, despite the occasional wonders the chairman can perform. This is not to say that management representatives were ineffective. The manner in which they were organized and the broad scale of their operations were shown in earlier chapters.

In an article in the Washington *Post* correspondent Bernard D. Nossiter gave further evidence of management activities:

Sophisticated business lobbying, combined with conscious manipulation of a public mood, is being credited with a major role in the passage of the strong labor bill.

Details of the skilled operation began coming out this week.

The core of the technique, as spelled out by its practitioners, was to focus on uncommitted House members, particularly those in marginal districts. There a deliberate effort was made to translate public anger at the disclosures of union corruption by the McClellan committee into a barrage of letters urging the Congressmen to vote for a tough bill.

The major organizations involved were the National Association of Manufacturers and the United States Chamber of Commerce, aided by many of their state groups; the American Farm Bureau Federation; the American Retail Federation; and the little known National Small Business Men's Association.

The business group's first task was listing House members in marginal districts—those won by 55 per cent or less of the popular vote—who had never voted on a labor bill. About 120 were in this group.

The next step was to refine this list to those who favored a bill, but were not clearly committed to either a strict or a softer measure.

Left to their own devices, the Democrats in this group would have likely followed their leadership and backed a "moderate" bill; the Republicans, generally from industrial districts, also would have been in this camp. A few more Congressmen with similar viewpoints but from "Safe" districts were added. A final list of 54 was selected for the major effort, which began in June.

The problem then became one of arousing constituents in these districts to flood their Congressmen with mail. One important tool was a television drama, "Sound of Violence."

This hour-long show portraying union hoodlums in the jukebox field had run in April on Armstrong Cork Co's Circle Theater to an audience estimated at 25 million. It ends with an appeal from Sen. John L. Mc-Clellan (D–Ark.) urging the American people to do something about the evils shown.[11]

One representative of a management group gave an account of the work his group encountered trying to sponsor a rerun of this program in the key districts described above. This would have required a bond of one million dollars to cover possible claims for performers' salaries, and so forth. If there was mention of legislation by name in the introduction or the follow-up to the program itself, the expenses for the program would be "lobbying" expenses and not tax deductible. These and other problems made the project seem impossible. But it was solved in another way, as will be shown later.

[11] Bernard D. Nossiter, "The Labor Bill Lobby," Washington *Post*, Sept. 10, 1959.

No matter how effective the program of "consumer advertising" might be, it would not change the number of votes available on the House Committee on Education and Labor. The Republicans saw that it was not going to be possible to get a bill to their liking through the committee itself. This meant that they would have to do one of two things: amend the committee bill on the floor of the House or introduce a substitute for the committee bill in its entirety. The second course would not be at all unusual, but rather would be a repeat of a standard device. As one informant put it: "That's the strategy we used against the (Democratic) Administration's repeal of Taft-Hartley in 1949, the FEPC bill in 1950, and the Fair Labor Standards Act." For the success of such a strategy the program of "consumer advertising" would be essential.

Some Further Considerations

On June 24 Representative Dent proposed an amendment which, as it turned out, was taken verbatim from the Teamsters' bill submitted to the committee at the request of Representative Hoffman. His proposal was approved as amendment No. 8 to S.1555 and a few weeks later became a very convenient weapon for use against the committee bill, or "Elliott bill," as it was to be called. This provision exempted unions with fewer than two hundred members *or* less than $20,000 in gross receipts from the financial reporting requirements of the bill. It states that such a labor organization "shall be exempt . . . unless the Secretary determines, after due notice and opportunity for a hearing, that the exemption of such a labor organization should be withdrawn." [12] The Kennedy bill stated that "the Secretary may exempt . . . any labor organization having fewer than two hundred members *and* having gross annual receipts of less than $20,000 [italics added]." [13]

This provision was marked by the faithful five for change on the "next go-round."

The actions and attitude of Representative Teller up to this point

[12] U.S. House of Representatives, *To Provide for the Reporting and Disclosure of Certain Financial Transactions and Administrative Practices of Labor Organizations and Employers, etc.,* 86th Cong., 1st Sess., 1959, H.R.8342, p. 20.
[13] U.S. Senate, *Labor-Management Reporting and Disclosure Act of 1959,* 86th Cong., 1st Sess., 1959, S.1555, p. 8.

convinced even the representatives of the federation that, although he might lead, the committee would not follow. For a short period Representative Udall was asked to "handle our amendments" by the AFL-CIO, but his public stand on the issues referred to earlier and his brusque attitude made it "impossible for us to work with him." Thus, Representative Thompson was asked to handle the amendments. This he continued to do throughout the remainder of the consideration of the bill by the committee.

Back to the Committee

On June 30 the committee met in two sessions for five and one-half hours. This was a very productive day, in which amendments numbered 25 to 38 were adopted. It was followed by the first real pause in the deliberations. The committee members took time out over the fourth of July. During the interim Representative Udall sent a copy of the committee's amendments to Professor Cox in Cambridge for comments, which Cox supplied in detail. Interest groups, as well, submitted analyses of the first thirty-eight tentative amendments. Thus, the members of the committee had a pretty clear idea of the impact that their amendments to Title II (Reporting by Labor Organizations) and the first part of Title III (Trusteeships) would have.

On July 7 the committee again went into executive session, completing consideration of Title III and commencing its work on Title IV, which deals with union election procedures, during two meetings lasting a total of five hours. Fifteen amendments, numbered 39 to 53 were added. On July 8 work was completed on Title IV with the inclusion of amendments 54 to 61. Several of the provisions of the committee bill's Title V and Title VI had been shifted from other sections of S.1555 and thus had been dealt with previously. In place of the Kennedy bill's Title V, a statement of a code of ethical practices, the House committee included the following provisions in a new Title V:

501: Fiduciary responsibility of officers of labor organizations.
502: Bonding.
503: Loans to officers of labor organizations.
504: Prohibition against Communists, ex-Communists, and persons convicted of certain crimes holding certain offices and employment.

505: Amendment to Section 302, Labor Management Relations Act, 1947.

Title six now dealt with a number of controversial matters but was so drafted that the impact would be minimal. Title VI had the following sections:

601: Investigations.
602: Extortionate picketing.
603: Retention of rights under other federal and state laws.
604: Enactment and enforcement of state laws.
605: Service of process.
606: Administrative Procedure Act.
607: Other agencies and departments.
608: Criminal contempt.
609: Separability provisions.

With the addition of amendments 62 to 72 during five and one-half hours on July 9, the bulk of the work on the anticorruption section of the bill, Titles II through VI, was completed.

Throughout these sessions many committee members had been very puzzled by the actions of Representative Teller. The only explanation that some congressmen could find for his erratic behavior was that he was introducing provisions which would make the bill unpalatable to as many interest groups as possible. In a heated discussion with another union representative, Andy Biemiller defended Teller's action on the Barden management reporting section as "sound strategy." No further light was thrown on the question.

It came to the attention of some union lobbyists after investigation, however, that Representative Teller had served as Jimmie Hoffa's attorney-of-record during Hoffa's hearing on contempt of Congress charges. Publication of this fact could have been a devastating blow to the federation's position in the House. This was the clincher for those who had earlier expressed objection to lining "labor" up to follow Teller's lead, and it formalized the unseating which had already taken place informally within the committee.

A Committee Is People

The thirty individuals who made up the House Committee on Education and Labor differed from one another in many respects.

They ranged in years of congressional service from a quarter century to a few months, their backgrounds from labor law professor to coal miner, their ages from thirty-two to eighty-four, their political philosophies (if the word can be used) from far left to extreme right, and one of their number was a woman. At this point the thirty had worked together for over a month in long executive sessions augmented by longer hours of preparation, in addition to their regular duties as congressmen. The last thirty days had brought some of the strongest pressures from labor, management, and the public that a person could be asked to endure. It is not surprising that personal animosities began to grow and flourish. The garrulousness of one, the intellectual snobbery of another, the associations of another, the unreasonableness of others—these things began to wear and grate. Individual members were approaching hysteria under the pressure and strain, but the most controversial sections of the bill had not yet been considered.

Personal and situational considerations had to be taken into account if the work of the committee was to progress. For example, amendments were passed to "neutral" people to be introduced, personal animosities were anticipated to avoid losing votes, and those who had carried the discussion one day were "rested" so they would not wear out their welcome (as some of their colleagues had done). To bolster the morale of the four Democratic freshmen, the Speaker called them in for a chat. He commended them for the fine job they were doing in the committee and promised that he would campaign for them personally if it should become necessary. The encouragement was warmly received.

Strategy Meeting Number Three

At this crucial point in the deliberations of the committee the third strategy meeting took place. Representatives Metcalf, Bolling, Thompson, and Udall met with the AFL-CIO's Meany, Harrison, and Hayes, plus their aides, McDevitt, Wohl, Harris, and others. At this meeting Meany set forth the federation's desire that hot cargo and organizational picketing provisions not be included in the committee's bill. He also strongly objected to inclusion of the bill of rights title. He stated that the federation was willing to give in on all Taft-Hartley changes to get rid of these "provisions that labor can't live with."

Some of the pressures on Meany have been discussed. The demand that hot cargo provisions (whose application had specifically been limited to the Teamsters Union) be excluded from a bill further substantiates the conclusions reached. It appears that Meany's actions represented self-defense as much as anything.

For their part, the congressmen stated their belief that the House would not pass a bill without the provisions to which Meany objected; that, in fact, the exclusion of such language would lead to even stronger language in amendments from the floor. Meany was advised that, with all the public furor, his wisest course was to make the best of it. Representative Udall suggested that the AFL-CIO should "cut your losses, and get out" (of the legislative spotlight). Meany's reaction was violent. He let it be known that he would rather go down fighting with his friends than go along with such "antilabor" provisions. It is significant that Walter Reuther was not present at this meeting. Both the Auto Workers and the Steelworkers were "lying low" at this point. The industrial union leaders desired to maintain a consistent public position. They were in favor of internal union reforms. They were opposed to the excesses of the Teamsters Union and wanted to differentiate themselves clearly from Jimmie Hoffa. They did not agree with Meany's tactics at this stage because they felt that such tactics made it difficult to separate the AFL-CIO position from that of the Teamsters.

At the end of the third strategy session Meany demanded an immediate meeting with the Speaker. This was arranged, and a day or two later the two men met.

Meany and Rayburn

When he had a discussion with a man of Meany's position, Rayburn usually met on a man-to-man basis with no others present. This occasion, however, was an exception to the rule. Meany had aides with him, and D. B. Hardiman, the Speaker's assistant, was present. The discussion centered on the inclusion and content of Titles I and VII. Meany's position was that the bill of rights section and all Taft-

Hartley changes had to be excluded from the committee bill. Rayburn explained his conviction that the Congress would have to pass a bill this session. He told him that the committee bill would be a fair bill, but that it must contain provisions on boycotts, hot cargo contracts, and organizational picketing in order to pass the House. That was the temper of the country, and that was the way it would have to be. The discussion became heated. Meany slammed his fist on the desk and stormed: "I can't go back to my people and tell them a thing like that! I can't support antilabor provisions!"

Rayburn responded that he had had to go against the temporary tide of opinion many times in his own career, but that he had been vindicated with the passage of time, and the wisdom of his position had been upheld. He suggested that perhaps this was just such a time for Mr. Meany.[14] Unable to reach agreement with the Speaker, Meany proceeded to try at the next level.

This meeting and a meeting later that day between Meany and Majority Leader John McCormack who was more sympathetic to the wishes of labor, were reported in the press.[15] McCormack's role on the floor of the House will be discussed in a later chapter.

The Bill Takes Final Form

On July 14 work on the remaining sections of Titles V and VI were completed with the adoption of amendments 73 to 80. On the fifteenth changes to Title I, the bill of rights, were considered. Amendments 81 to 90 were adopted. Behind this flat statement, as behind many others, is the drama that is government in the United States.

Professor Cox had been asked by the faithful five if he could prepare a draft of a "workable" bill of rights section. This he did. The draft was delivered to them, and on the morning of July 14 it was in the possession of Representative Thompson, who discussed its provisions with Representative Udall. The offices of these two congressmen were on the fourth floor of the old House office building. Between them is a men's room. Whether by coincidence or design, this was the scene of an important meeting. Three AFL-CIO representatives, including Cy Anderson and Tom Harris, and the two Congress-

[14] Such remarks might be viewed as a double-edged sword.
[15] *Time*, Vol. LXXIV, No. 5 (Aug. 3, 1959), pp. 12, 13.

men were present. Thompson handed the federation men the draft of the bill of rights and said: "Here it is. You can make at most 5 percent changes, but bring it back tomorrow." The federation lawyers prepared a series of position papers giving their views on the bill of rights. The revised draft was presented to the committee the next day and was approved in the form in which it appeared in the committee bill.

The following day Andy Biemiller held a meeting at the Congressional Hotel with some congressmen, including members of the faithful five. He outlined his plan of action for the final days. In effect, the AFL-CIO was trying again to achieve its ends, this time at the committee level. This meeting preceded a gathering of seventeen Democratic congressmen in Representative Wier's office. There Biemiller "laid down the law" to the assembled congressmen, using a form of address which left no doubt about the implied relationship of the speaker to his audience. Biemiller was saying in essence that Titles I and VII must come out of the bill. He was reminded of the position papers prepared by lawyers for the federation, but he insisted that he had not authorized those and repeated his demand. He then glanced at Thompson and asked: "Well, aren't you going to say anything?" "Yes," replied Thompson, "you don't have the votes," with which he left the room. This signaled the end of the meeting.

From there the congressmen went into three sessions of the committee, lasting over eight and one-half hours. The key vote came rather early. On a motion by Teller to strike all Taft-Hartley amendments (Title VII), it was demonstrated that the AFL-CIO indeed did not have the votes. The motion was defeated, 17 to 13. The faithful five, by joining the two Southern Democrats and ten Republicans, again decided the issue.

With the decision firmly established that there would be provisions dealing with secondary boycotts and picketing, the committee was free to adopt another provision which had been consistently left out of all legislation because of the fear of opening the door to further boycott amendments. This was a repeal of the Denver building trades doctrine, to legitimize common situs picketing. This provision was the one the building trades really wanted, and at this point the committee could and did include it in the bill.

One objective of this provision was to split the building trades unions from the Teamsters. There were indications that these two groups were working more and more closely together in bringing pressure on members of the committee. That evening Professor Cox, who was again in Washington, called Lou Sherman (lawyer for the Building and Construction Trades Council) and informed him of the committee's action. This news brought forth pledges of support for the committee bill by leaders of the Building Trades Council. It also brought about cries of anguish from the Teamsters. One of their number exploded at a key congressman: "Do you realize what you have done? You have cut us off from seven million construction people!" No member of a construction union could believe that a bill which set out to solve its most pressing problem could be "antilabor." But the provision may have had an additional disfunctional result in stirring the ire of the large Texas contractors who operate on a nonunion basis and of the AFL-CIO, which itself was not pleased with the action. Labor's solid front of opposition to the committee bill (if such a thing existed) was definitely split. AFL-CIO pressure was brought on the building trades unions to reverse their stand in the name of labor harmony.

The following day, July 17, the "first go-round" of 102 amendments was completed during a four-hour meeting. The management reporting requirements were revised during the session.

Title VII of the committee bill had six sections, as follows:

Section 701 would change the membership of the NLRB from five to seven members, require the NLRB to assert jurisdiction over all cases in interstate commerce, and provide for the delegation of board powers under specified conditions to make this feasible.

Section 702 would retain sweeteners of the Kennedy bill, make picketing of a common site in the building and construction industry legal (reversal of Denver building trades doctrine), and legalize hot cargo clauses in this industry.

Section 703 would revise the Labor Management Relations Act of 1947, Section 9(c)(3) by striking out the sentence: "Employees on strike who are not entitled to reinstatement shall not be eligible to vote."

Section 704 would provide for the circumvention, under certain circumstances, of the requirements calling for a pre-election hearing and the holding of representation elections within thirty days of notice of filing a petition for an election.

Section 705 would prohibit hot cargo clauses and secondary boy-cotts, except in the building and construction trades, and organizational picketing where (a) another labor organization is legally rec-ognized, and (b) where there has been an election during the pre-ceeding nine months, except where employer unfair labor practice could also be shown.

Section 706 would require cases involving charges of unfair labor practices to have priority of consideration by the NLRB.

To the surprise of the exhausted committee members, Chairman Barden announced that there would be no further consideration of the bill. The committee would meet the following week, on July 23, vote the committee bill either up or down, and that would be that. This statement would have been open to cynical questioning were it not for the psychological state of the members and the unusual force of character of the chairman. On previous occasions Barden had insisted that certain provisions be included, for example, the management reporting section and the bonding provisions, and al-though he had no more power over the voters on these occasions than on any others, he had prevailed. This time the result was the same. Perhaps the desire "to be done with it" worked in his favor.

The Phantom Bill

On the evening of July 17 a great ordeal had ended, though a few formalities remained. Edith Green made plans to take a two-day vacation, the first in many weeks, to relax from the strain of events. Walter Mason from the AFL-CIO stopped by in the late afternoon with an envelope under his arm. Other legislative representatives were making similar calls at the offices of Democratic committee members. The envelope contained a proposed bill which the con-gressmen were being asked to consider as a substitute for the com-mittee bill when the committee began voting the following Thurs-day. Copies of the bill were handled with tight security precautions. Each was prenumbered, and the whereabouts of each was continu-ously noted. Mason made a sales presentation, and Mrs. Green agreed to consider the bill. This would be the only work she would take with her during her vacation.

After Andy Biemiller had called on Stewart Udall to discuss the federation's bill, he entered Frank Thompson's office. Thompson asked him to sit down and offered him some Scotch; Biemiller accepted and took a seat on the couch. Thompson opened his drawer and took out some letters. "Let me read you some of these," he said, as he flipped through them. It was clear that Thompson was angry. There was one from an influential backer who questioned Thompson's failure to go along with the AFL-CIO. "This guy is important to me," Thompson commented, in effect admitting the effectiveness of the pressure brought on him. "Now when I go home I'm going to have to call him up, and then go see him. I'm going to have to convince him that I've been doing the right thing." To convince his friend that he was right, Thompson would be forced to show that others were wrong. At this point he launched off into a discourse in very colorful language. The gist of the statement was that some people with whom he had associated had shown a lack of sagacity in their recommendations and in the pressure they had brought to bear on him.

Biemiller ignored personal references and indicated that the bill in his hand was the bill the federation "had to have." They wanted someone to sponsor the bill in the committee and to see that it was reported. Thompson adamantly refused "to read the stuff." Apparently, the reaction was similar at each stop made by the lobbyists. Had the proposal been made six weeks earlier, it might well have been cordially received.

Other union representatives heard about the new bill in various ways. When they asked for copies, they were told there were none available. The following Monday at least one union representative asked Biemiller for a copy of the bill. Biemiller's reply was that there wasn't, and never had been, any such bill. The New York *Times* carried an account of the proposed legislation in its edition that day.[16]

Because of its short history and early demise, the bill became known as the phantom bill. It was an "all-labor" bill with no bill of rights or Taft-Hartley changes. Its reporting and disclosure sections

[16] New York *Times,* July 21, 1959, p. 16.

were very much watered down. The comments passed privately among some liberals was that even Sid Zagri couldn't have done a better job of preparing a bill for defeat before the House. Though withdrawn from the battle, the phantom bill (also called the Meany bill) was not dead. It would later be returned to the halls of Congress in modified form.

An Agreement

There would be difficulty in reporting a bill out of the committee over the objections of the AFL-CIO, especially since both the United Mine Workers and the Teamsters also opposed the committee bill. The Democratic leadership had only eight votes it could count on on its side of the table. For reasons of their own (already suggested and to be discussed more fully in the next chapter), the Republicans and Southern Democrats also wanted a bill reported to the floor. Rayburn and Halleck agreed that they would join forces to see that a bill was reported. Halleck agreed to provide the votes needed to achieve a majority to report the bill. Barden and Landrum agreed to vote out the committee bill. Thus, it would require six from the Republican side to do the job. All ten Republicans were available if needed.

A Sponsor for the Committee Bill

Another question facing the Democratic strategists was the one of a sponsor for the committee bill. The Speaker still had some hope that Chairman Barden would lend his name to the bill, since this is the usual procedure for a bill which has been substantially amended by a committee.

Sam Rayburn asked Graham Barden, fellow Southerner and Democrat, to assume the sponsorship of the committee bill. The mere presence of Barden's name on the bill would have tied the hands of a number of proponents of stronger legislation and removed one of the most effective fighters from the conservative ranks. Barden indicated that he didn't believe it was right for the Speaker to ask him to do something that he did not believe in. To ask him to vote for the committee bill would be bad enough, but to ask him to sponsor it was too much. He couldn't do this. He was planning to introduce a bill that he could support, the Landrum-Griffin bill, and he couldn't go along with the Speaker.

The Speaker is reported to have replied to the effect: "Graham, if you do introduce a new bill, you're going to get hurt and you're going to lose." Barden replied: "Well, losing is not the worst thing that could happen as long as I know I have done all I can in the fight."

Under these circumstances it was decided that Representative Elliott would be the best choice to lead the floor fight. He had participated closely in the preparations, he was not strongly identified with unions, he was liked and respected by Southerners and Northern liberals alike, and his relatively senior position would help in attracting support. As a loyal supporter of the Speaker and a member of the faithful five, Elliott readily agreed to lend his name to the bill.

A Final Attempt at Modification

On the afternoon of Wednesday, July 22, Congressman Perkins called the House committee Democrats together to attempt to get agreement on tactical considerations and on certain specific amendments to improve the committee bill. The legislative committee of the AFL-CIO put out the word that "the eighth floor" couldn't support the committee bill in its present form. Perkins would try to get at least some of the objectionable language removed by the Democratic majority.

One of the considerations actually discussed by the Democrats was the possibility of preventing the reporting of the committee bill in any form. However, it was clear from the comments of several members that this possibility was foreclosed by their commitment to the Speaker; at least, the Democrats alone couldn't prevent the bill from reaching the House floor. If there was any agreement reached at this meeting, it was not clear from succeeding events what it was.

The meeting of the full committee on July 23 was marked by a flurry of activity and proposed substitutes for the bill that had occupied the group for six weeks.

Representative Frelinghuysen moved that the committee report the Administration bill, H.R.3540. The motion was defeated by a vote of 21 to 9 (all the Democrats plus one Republican).

Representative Teller moved that the committee report the Kennedy-Ervin bill, S.505, as it was submitted to the Senate committee. The motion was defeated by a vote of 19 to 10.

Representative Roosevelt proposed some amendments to the Elliott bill. These were defeated by a vote of 19 to 11.

Representative Kearns moved that the committee report the second Kearns bill, H.R.7265. The motion was defeated by a vote of 23 to 6.

Representative Teller moved that the committee report the Teller bill, H.R.7811. The motion was defeated by a vote of 19 to 9.

Representative Perkins moved that the committee report the committee bill with Title VII stricken. The motion was defeated by a vote of 19 to 11.

Representative Teller moved that the committee report the committee bill with a series of changes. The motion was defeated by a vote of 20 to 10.

After this series of motions the committee bill was approved by the vote of 16 to 14, with ten Democrats and six Republicans voting as agreed beforehand.[17] The six Republicans were Representatives Ayres, Frelinghuysen, Griffin, Holt, Lafore, and Quie. Immediately following the vote there were disclaimers of support for the bill provisions by all but the faithful (or "faithless") five. Representative Landrum announced to the committee that, although he had voted for the bill, he did not support it, and, in fact, he and Representative Griffin would introduce a substitute for it before Monday. There were chuckles throughout the room. The fact was already known or strongly suspected by his colleagues. We will see later what lay behind this remark.

The report of the committee is among the strangest that has ever come from the Congress. It included a "statement" by the chairman, "supplementary views" by the faithful five, "supplementary views" by eight other Democrats, "separate views" of Carl Perkins, and "additional statement" by Landrum and Griffin, "supplementary views" by eight Democrats on failure to include civil rights provisions, "supplementary views" by Ludwig Teller, and "additional views" by

[17] U.S. House of Representatives, *To Provide for the Reporting and Disclosure of Certain Financial Transactions and Administrative Practices of Labor Organizations and Employers, etc.*, 86th Cong., 1st Sess., 1959, H.R.8342.

Clare Hoffman.[18] As indicated earlier, only the second set of "views" approved of the bill as it was written.

A great many things were to happen before this bill finally reached the floor of the House for debate. They will be explored in the next chapter.

In spite of every effort of the labor movement, the bill reported by the House Committee on Education and Labor contained provisions on all subjects which the Senate-passed bill had covered. Also, virtually in spite of the efforts of the labor movement, the bill eliminated a number of possible snares from the language of the bill of rights and called for the legalization of common situs picketing. The content of the bill had been determined by the congressional leaders of the House of Representatives, based on their evaluation of what the public demanded. Despite every effort to the contrary, it was a strangely constitutional resolution of the issues before the committee.

[18] U.S. House of Representatives, *Labor-Management Reporting and Disclosure Act of 1959*, 86th Cong., 1st Sess., 1959, House Report No. 741 to accompany H.R.8342.

VII. PRELUDE TO THE HOUSE FLOOR ACTION

IN the hot summer of 1959 the issue of labor reform came to a boil. Television, radio, newspapers, and newsmagazines all featured accounts of the battle taking place in the Congress. Washington was the focal point of all pressures and the scene of action. The AFL-CIO and the Teamsters poured local union people into the city. The management groups and the Administration called on the grass roots to flood the offices of congressmen with letters and telegrams. The Congress would have to choose among three different forms of reform legislation. The choice would be a close one.

Myriad factors influenced the final choice. A number of these will be discussed in this chapter. A brief chronology of events is presented in Table 5 to help the reader. The most important factors turned out to be the address of President Eisenhower to the nation and the strategy decisions of various camps.

The Decision for a Substitute

We have seen that, from the point of view of the conservatives, the liberal Democrats, despite any parochial disagreements they might have been having, were in control of the committee. Occasionally, serious consideration would be given to the proposals of the minority, but certainly the Democrats wouldn't approve provisions to do what the conservatives felt "needed" to be done. By the week following the Independence Day recess the form of the bill which would emerge from the committee was clear. Since that bill "wouldn't do the job," the Administration decided to press for an alternative solution.

Table 5. Some Major Events: July 23–August 11, 1959

July 23	Committee voted to report Elliott bill (H.R.8342) favorably. Robert Kennedy appeared on Jack Paar "Tonight" show.
July 27	Landrum, Griffin bills (H.R.8400, H.R.8401) introduced in the House.
August 1	AFL-CIO President Meany stated opposition to Elliott bill in letter to all members of Congress. Republican members of House Committee on Education and Labor made public a letter to President Eisenhower urging him to support Landrum-Griffin bill over radio and television.
August 3	Shelley bill (H.R.8490) introduced in the House. Speaker Rayburn endorsed Elliott bill in press conference.
August 4	President announced that he would address nation on labor reform legislation.
August 6	House Committee on Rules reported H.R.8342, the Elliott bill, under an open rule allowing unlimited amendment from the floor. President Meany addressed nation over radio. President Eisenhower addressed nation over radio and television.
August 10	Speaker Rayburn addressed nation over Mutual network.
August 11	Debate opened in the House on H.R.8342 and proposed substitutes.

The first consideration was that the committee must report a bill favorably. If it did not, the alternative would be to face the Kennedy bill under a suspension of the rules procedure which allows no amendments (similar to the situation of 1958). If this situation were to develop, all the grass roots pressure that had been built up would backfire and force the passage of S.1555. A bill reported through regular channels and considered under an open rule from the Rules Committee would provide ample opportunity for key provisions or a substitute bill to be offered in amendment. A substitute bill would be the most desirable alternative. It was decided to press for such a bill.

In their planning for a substitute, certain factors were paramount in the minds of conservative strategists. In order to pass the House, a substitute would have to attract the votes of a large number of Southern Democrats. This meant that it could not be presented as an Administration bill or a Republican bill. Because of the complexity of the situation in the Congress (and the fewness of Republican votes), the bill would also have to win the support of the general public. This meant that its sponsors should be relatively attractive personalities, able to speak intelligently and forcefully on television and radio. It also meant that they could not be identified as anti-labor people, or there would be the risk of losing the sympathy of the public and unnecessarily raising the ire of union members. Another, longer-range consideration was the vulnerability of the potential sponsor to defeat in later elections. If labor could "purge" the sponsor or sponsors of the substitute (as they had failed to do with Senator Taft of Taft-Hartley), they would greatly strengthen their image of political power in future encounters.

To quote an Administration source:

The type of person needed to sponsor such a bill would be someone who was relatively neutral, or at least not a known and rabid "labor hater"; someone who could rally others to his support; someone who could understand the bill; and who would be capable of selling the bill both to the House in debate and to the public over radio and television. We would have gone outside the committee if necessary to get the right man.

On these criteria Representatives Landrum and Griffin were selected. The men doing the selection were "those who wanted to get a coalition together": [1] Rules Committee Chairman Howard Smith and Labor Committee Chairman Barden from the Southerners, and Minority Leader Halleck and Presidential Assistant Edward McCabe for the Administration. The bill did have bipartisan support and was always referred to as "bipartisan" or "nonpartisan." "We definitely didn't want this to be an Administration substitute," a spokesman said. "That's one reason why it was referred to as 'Landrum-Griffin' and not the other way around." The bipartisan sponsorship would also protect the substitute from purely partisan harassment.

The Campaign to the Public

The general campaign for public awareness of the evils requiring reform in the labor movement was continuing apace. While manage-

[1] This phrase was used by several confidential sources in the course of interviews.

ment groups found it difficult to arrange for a rerun of the television play *The Sound of Violence,* the problem was solved in another way, and the showing was exploited, as stated by Nossiter:

When Armstrong decided to run the drama . . . as a summer repeat, the business lobbyists latched on. Local NAM affiliates and other trade associations told their members when and where the show would be seen; they advised employer members to urge their workers to watch it; above all, they encouraged their members to get viewers to write their Congressmen on the bill.

The Texas Manufacturers Association, for example, advertised the viewing time and stations for Amarillo, Austin, Dallas, Houston, Galveston, Lubbock, Odessa and El Paso. The Lumbermen's Industrial Relations Committee did the same for Spokane and Seattle, Washington, and Portland, Medford and Klamath Falls, Oregon.

The strategists discovered that stations in 27 key Congressional districts would not carry the show. Arrangements were made to get eight of these stations to run it as a public service or under local sponsorship. Newspaper ads were taken in 20 of the important districts, urging people to watch and write.

An estimated 4.5 to 5 million mailings plugging both the show and letters to Congress were sent out. Between 15 and 20 million persons were said to have seen the re-run.[2]

As shown in Appendix B, a representative of the Armstrong Cork Company was a member of the Secondary Boycott Committee of the Chamber of Commerce.

There were other activities in which various groups were engaging. All the groups kept a steady stream of information flowing to their members; all urged that the congressmen be apprised of the feelings of the folks back home. These efforts are estimated to have resulted in 80,000 letters to Congress.

As another Administration spokesman put it, in discussing the image they were trying to create: "We wanted this to look like the people against the labor bosses and not Big Labor against Big Business or even against the Administration, because of the propaganda connotation given this Administration." To do this, the major effort of those who were seeking a strong bill was to the public at large

[2] Bernard D. Nossiter, "The Labor Bill Lobby," Washington *Post,* Sept. 10, 1959.

through the mass media and, where possible, through personal contact.

The Channels for Public Support

Nine days before the actual introduction of the Landrum-Griffin bill in the House, Cabinet Secretary Robert Gray was informed of the names of its sponsors. He set his organization in motion preparing an all-out campaign to support the substitute by name. Each of the management groups set in motion machinery to notify its members the minute the substitute was ready to be introduced. This was the general format for their communication: these are the facts, now is the time to act, notify your congressman! During the height of the preparations Gray was host to small groups of association representatives at two luncheons daily to ensure coordination.

The activities of the groups were varied. A newspaper chain prepared mats for advertisements to be distributed around the country in time for the introduction of the bill. This venture ran into a little difficulty. There was some question over the appropriate sponsorship for the ads. Some thought that they should be sponsored by individuals in each community; others thought that large associations should provide the funds. The National Chamber of Commerce did sponsor some of the ads at the last minute, but in the squabble over sponsorship some of them were never run. A thirty-minute television show (described by one spokesman as having the following content: comments by Victor Riesel, newsreels of labor violence, scenes of idle men on strike, statements by Landrum, Griffin, and McClellan) was presented by the National Association of Manufacturers on stations which would show it. This was one of the two programs distributed by the NAM. It also was arranged that Landrum and Griffin would appear on the "Today" Show—the major morning television program of the NBC-TV network—as well as on tape-recorded spot announcements to be used in the key areas.

The Substitute Takes Form

In the preparation of the language of the actual substitute bill many individuals and groups participated. The management groups, usually identified only as "those who wanted a stronger bill," wanted to introduce a completely new approach to the problem. The plan was rejected by top Administration strategists. To be successful, a substitute should differ from the main opposition proposal only in important areas; otherwise, it was argued, it would cause too much confusion for friends as well as foes. The substitute was conceived to be something that would achieve mutually contradictory goals. It should be attractive enough to gain wide support in the House, yet be "beefed up" to provide some provisions which could be given in trade at the conference with the Senate, with a final result embodying the original intent. The representative of the Secretary of Labor suggested that the committee bill's provision on the reversal of the Denver building trades doctrine be included in the substitute, partly to split the ranks of labor, but this was rejected by the coalition's Southern members and referred to as "transparent hypocrisy" by another participant (although the Department of Labor had repeatedly recommended such a provision). Among those who determined tactical provisions within this over-all policy framework were Smith, Barden, Landrum, Halleck, McCabe, and Griffin, plus group representatives.

The question of who had done the actual drafting of provisions to produce the conservative substitute bill presented to the House of Representatives was a point on which serious controversy developed. The answer which in the author's judgment is most probably correct will be discussed here. In Appendix D a brief analysis of the evidence from which the judgment derives is presented.

It should be pointed out that drafting was not an excessively difficult task. The sources of most of the language are clear: Title I was a slightly modified "Kuchel compromise" bill of rights; Titles II through VI, the reform sections of the bill, were taken from the committee bill with few (but sometimes important) changes; Title VII, the revisions to Taft-Hartley, had provisions from the Kearns bill of 1958 [3] and the Curtis bill of 1959 [4] and were management-backed changes known to the Congress for several years.

[3] U.S. House of Representatives, *To Provide for the Reporting and Disclosure of Certain Financial Transactions and Administrative Practices of Labor Organizations and Employers, etc.*, 85th Cong., 1st Sess., 1958, H.R.13739.
[4] U.S. Senate, *To Amend the Labor-Management Relations Act of 1947, as Amended, and for Other Purposes*, 86th Cong., 1st Sess., 1959, S.76.

Early Leads

The development of the evidence on the question of the drafters of Landrum-Griffin, which is minor in substance but major in emotional appeal, is itself instructive. During the early stages of the investigation many persons made suggestions about who the authors of the Landrum-Griffin bill in fact were. Those who admitted that they didn't actually know the answer indicated the people they felt must have had something to do with it. The group so-named grew as the investigation continued. Of course, in the Washington atmosphere Landrum and Griffin themselves were seldom, if ever, mentioned. Those who were mentioned included Deputy Assistant to the President Gerald Morgan, lawyer and Chamber of Commerce representative Gerard Reilly, committee counsel Charles Ryan, Senate committee minority counsel Michael Bernstein, Administrative Assistant to the President Edward McCabe, and a few others.

Further interviewing and investigation showed that Bernstein and Ryan had most probably not drafted the bill. Of those remaining, McCabe and Morgan certainly did affect policy making with respect to the law but probably did not do the drafting. We have seen that McCabe was probably the most active participant in the day-to-day direction of Administration policy on the labor bill. He was certainly technically qualified to perform the task, and he was on the spot to do the job. Morgan had been a legislative counsel in the House several years before and had just left the House when Taft-Hartley was under consideration. It was shown in Chapter III that he was paid by the Republican National Committee to assist in the drafting of the Taft-Hartley Act. The Majority Leader of the House at that time was Republican Charles Halleck. During the course of legislation in 1959 Morgan and Halleck were present at weekly legislative meetings held at the White House.

Gerard Reilly was an old hand in Washington. As a consultant to a member of the Senate Committee on Labor and Public Welfare in the Eightieth Congress, he was centrally concerned with the language of the Taft-Hartley Act. Morgan testified that Reilly was his chief assistant in the drafting of the 1947 law. It was alleged on the floor of Congress that Reilly was also under a $3,000 retainer from the Chrysler Corporation at the time.[5] Reilly had since served on the NLRB and in private practice of labor law. In 1959 he appeared before both the House and Senate committees, representing the United States Chamber of Commerce as chairman of its Labor Relations Committee. He was a member of the committee of experts convened by Senator Kennedy in 1958 to recommend labor reform legislation and of the 1959 blue ribbon committee to recommend revisions to the Taft-Hartley Act. There is no question that he prepared research memoranda, drafted proposed amendments, and assisted in the preparation of the Senate minority report.

It is evident that the associations and firms which retain lawyers such as Reilly do so on the assumption that these men have been, and will be, influential in the legislative process in the labor-management field. It is also a fact that there are literally hundreds of people who take credit for having written or, as the case may be, passed the Taft-Hartley Act. It is indiscreet for such persons to announce their part in this work, but it is highly desirable that the participation become known. This could be the key to attracting new clients and retaining present clients.

There are other important factors to be considered. Close, open association by legislators with management lobbyists is definitely disapproved of in this country today. Men like Barry Goldwater who take extreme positions can apparently defy this taboo. (Just as Wayne Morse, on the other extreme, openly discussed his association with Teamster representatives.) The general lay public is unaware of the many legitimate services and functions of interest group representatives. For this reason, any public suggestion that a congressman has not done his own drafting, of course with the exception of aid from the Legislative Drafting Service on highly technical matters, would be hotly denied for the record.

One additional person should now be added to the list of possible drafters. He is Tom Shroyer, another old Washington hand and "Hartley's Man" in 1947, who remained with the staff of the House Committee on Education and Labor until 1952. His name was not mentioned often, but when it was, it figured prominently.

[5] U.S. Congress, *Congressional Record*, 81st Cong., 1st Sess., 1949, Part 4, pp. 5,072, 5,073.

The Bill Is Born

The origin of the bill begins as described above with the formation of the coalition on the labor issue (an extension of the arrangement which had functioned on other legislation in this and earlier sessions of Congress).[6] When the coalition became a reality, meetings were held to determine policy for the substitute and to set general outlines of its provisions. It was necessary to include a good deal of familiar language so that the "important" changes would stand out. Within these general guidelines Gerard Reilly and Tom Shroyer were asked to put together a draft of a bill embodying the suggestions. The two lawyers returned to Reilly's office on 16th Street in downtown Washington and prepared a draft. They then returned to the Hill and discussed its language with the policy-makers—Barden, Smith, Landrum, Halleck, McCabe, and Griffin. Seldom were discussions held as formal meetings. Seldom did they take place in the same office twice. As one participant put it: "If you meet in the same place, people begin noticing that you are there."

Modifications in provisions were requested and included. After a few revisions the final bill in typewritten form was handed to Representatives Landrum and Griffin, along with an explanation of its terms and content. It was stated that this was the form of the bill and explanation that was placed in the *Congressional Record* upon official introduction of the bill.

The really significant points in this presentation are that the opinions of management groups were solicited and given consideration in the preparation of the bill and that the great number of factors influencing the content of the substitute made it impossible that any single faction could dictate its content. This account does not state that a finished bill was taken from a file and presented to anyone at the bidding of a special interest. Yet, the degree of emotion surrounding this issue and the importance given it by "inside dopesters" made it both necessary and impossible to resolve with certainty.

[6] See Daniel M. Berman, *A Bill Becomes a Law: The Civil Rights Act of 1960* (New York, Macmillan, 1962), pp. 74, 75, where evidence of the Republican participation in the civil rights coalition is set forth.

The preparation of the first two of the three major bills to face the House of Representatives have been discussed. The third bill bore the name of Representative Shelley of California.

The Shelley Bill

Throughout this crucial period there were staunch labor supporters who were urging the federation leaders to demonstrate their militant position and stand up and be counted. One such person was Representative Shelley from San Francisco. Virtually guaranteed support by the voters in his district, he could speak out—a fact he would be the first to admit. Shelley could afford to take such a stand since San Francisco is a strongly unionized town. It was Shelley's feeling that labor should close ranks against the enemy which had shown itself bent on destroying the bargaining position of the workingman. Both before and after the introduction of his bill he scored the disunity of the labor movement on the issues before Congress. The Teamsters and Teamster-inspired local unions were also demanding a stand-up-and-be-counted position from the friends of labor. Informants both within and without the labor movement commented on the impact of all of this on President Meany. Meany had to avoid appearing to be a Pollyanna in contrast to the "strong" stand of the Teamsters and, for that matter, of the Machinists (IAM) and, to some extent, the Steelworkers, at least as represented, within his own federation.[7]

The first substitute which the federation proposed, the phantom bill, had met an early demise before being considered in the committee. When the AFL-CIO strategists became aware of the true strength of congressional feeling (reflecting, as it did, the aroused public), they dropped their plan for an "all-labor" bill, and gradually came around to the idea of submitting a substitute embodying the Elliot bill's titles but in watered-down form. Thus, the bill would include a bill of rights and reform provisions but exclude provisions on organization picketing, hot cargo, and secondary boycotts. Ini-

[7] Seymour Lipset and others have documented the fact that the behavior of labor leaders is greatly influenced by the opinions and actions of their fellows—their peer group—to whom they look for approval and esteem. This phenomenon appears to have been operating in the case of Meany. See Seymour Martin Lipset and Martin Trow, "Reference Group Theory and Trade Union Wage Policy," in M. Komarovsky, ed., *Common Frontiers of the Social Sciences* (Glencoe, Ill., The Free Press, 1957), pp. 391–411.

tially, this was to be introduced by Representative Roosevelt, but Shelley was prominent in the discussions with Meany and others and became the major sponsor. When Tom Harris and Ken Meikeljohn completed their drafting efforts on the Shelley bill, its sponsors set out to attract support for it. Shelley (himself not a member of the House Committee on Education and labor) held a series of conferences in his office with some Democratic members of the committee and then, on July 30, held a larger meeting, after which he announced that forty-seven Democrats would join him in introducing identical bills in the near future.[8] Representative Roosevelt became the major cosponsor of the bill. Teamster Zagri was called in to express his opinion of the bill. He had several immediate suggestions for "improvement." "Well, Sid," commented Shelley, "you are really for no bill at all," to which Zagri smiled broadly. No changes were made for the Teamster spokesman.

On August 3 the new substitute was officially introduced in the House, and on August 6, in his public speech, President Meany announced the support of the AFL-CIO for the Shelley bill.

Looking at the tactical considerations introduced by Shelley's sponsorship of the federation proposal, some difficulties became evident. To begin with, Shelley was not a member of the Labor Committee. He was a staunch supporter of labor, a member in good standing of the Teamsters Union, and a former president of the California Labor Council. His bill could easily be typified as "prolabor" and thus "soft." On the positive side, it provided staunch labor supporters with something to be *for*, it put the AFL-CIO back on record as supporting reform legislation, and, in effect, it cast the Elliott bill in the role of a middle-of-the-road measure. But, realistically, it still had no chance of passage and siphoned off support from the Elliott bill, which was being opposed by management, labor, and the Administration. Had it been a tactical move to point up the relatively "strong" Elliott bill, it would have been a desirable maneuver. This could have been accomplished if the federation had provided genuine support for the Elliott bill after the introduction of the Shelley bill, but it would have involved swallowing considerable pride after

[8] This announcement is mentioned in the New York *Times,* July 31, 1959, p. 10.

such a strong fight had been waged against the Elliott bill as it evolved in committee. It would also have taken great courage in face of the pressures against that course within the labor movement.

Comparative Analysis of the Bills

The three bills before the House were by intention substantially the same in most of their provisions. It was only on especially "important" matters that they differed. The main direction of differences was as might be expected: the Landrum-Griffin bill tended to eliminate the changes to the Taft-Hartley Act desired by labor and to substitute those desired by management; the Shelley bill tended to apply any restrictions specified for union employees or officers also to their counterparts in management, and it eliminated any reference to hot cargo agreements and the more restrictive amendments to secondary boycott or organizational picketing provisions; the Elliott bill was quite similar to the Kennedy bill, except for some modifications to make the bill more palatable to labor and the inclusion of a provision stating that picketing of all contractors in a primary dispute at a common construction site was not an unfair labor practice (the reversal of the Denver building trades doctrine). The positions of the bills dealing with questions of "reform" were different only to a minor degree.

The substance of each title (Titles I-VI) will be briefly summarized, using the committee (Elliott) bill as the starting point and then specifying the major areas of difference among the House bills. A more detailed columnar comparison of the three House bills and the Senate bill is given for Title VII, the Taft-Hartley changes.

Title I. Rights of Members of Labor Organizations. The committee bill prescribed rights of union members in broad terms, subject to reasonable qualifications uniformly imposed. It included general provisions preserving union authority over the conduct of its internal affairs and restraining conduct by members which might interfere with the union's ability to carry out its legal or contractual obligations. The rights would be enforceable by members' suits in federal courts after exhaustion of reasonable remedies or after failure to receive a final decision following six months of invoking such remedies.

The Landrum-Griffin bill adopted what was the Kuchel compromise version of the McClellan bill of rights (and titled its section "Bill of rights . . . ," not simply "Rights . . ."). It did not include the general provisions on a union's authority over its internal affairs. It did adopt some of the committee bill changes (e.g., specified the procedure for "increasing," not "changing," dues and assessments). The Secretary of Labor could sue to enforce the rights and, under certain conditions, interfering with the rights was a federal crime, punishable by a fine of up to $10,000 and imprisonment for up to two years or both (much as was true of the Kuchel compromise provisions).

The Shelley bill followed the committee bill, but further specified the responsibility of union members not to abuse their rights and stated that their rights and remedies under their constitutions and bylaws were not limited except where expressly provided.

Title II. Reporting by Labor Organizations, Officers and Employees of Labor Organizations, and Employers. The committee bill required every labor union to adopt a constitution and bylaws and to file a copy thereof and of certain information and reports concerning their administrative practices with the Secretary of Labor. It required every labor union, except small unions having fewer than two hundred members or gross annual receipts of less than $20,000, to file reports concerning their financial operations with the Secretary of Labor, similar to information and reports presently required under Section 9 (f) and (g) of the Taft-Hartley Act, except that filing would not be a condition of access to the procedures of the NLRB. It required union officers and employees to file reports with the Secretary of Labor on specified conflict-of-interest transactions in which they engage. It required employers to report on certain payments or loans made by them to unions or to union officers or employees and on payments to employees or labor relations consultants, who would themselves be required to report, for engaging in certain antilabor activities, but these reports by employers and labor relations consultants would be limited to expenditures for activities that are already made illegal or defined as unfair labor practices under the Taft-Hartley Act. It provided criminal penalties for failure to file reports, false reporting, and false record keeping or destruction of records. Injunction actions by the Secretary of Labor in federal courts to enforce the reporting requirement were provided for. Reports filed under the bill would be public information.

The Landrum-Griffin provisions were the same as in the committee bill, except that Landrum-Griffin did not eliminate small unions. The Shelley bill was also the same, except that in Section 3 it adopted the Senate employer-reporting requirement while eliminating some of its exceptions.

Title III. Trusteeships. The committee bill stated that reports must be filed, subject to criminal penalty, by international unions regarding subordinate unions placed in trusteeship. Trusteeships might be established only for legitimate union objectives and other stated purposes. Status of trusteeship might be litigated in a federal district court suit by the Secretary of Labor or by any affected union member or subordinate union body. In such proceedings trusteeships would be presumed valid for eighteen months and thereafter presumed invalid. All other rights and remedies would be preserved, except that suit by the Secretary would give district courts sole jurisdiction.

The Landrum-Griffin bill was the same, as was the Shelley bill, with the exception that the Shelley bill made no express provision preserving rights and remedies from other sources.

Title IV. Elections. The committee bill required that union officers be selected by secret ballot or by delegates chosen by secret ballot. Maximum terms were established. Adequate safeguards for fair elections were to be maintained. Removal procedures were to be provided for local officers. Candidates for union office were to be allowed to copy membership lists. An aggrieved member might sue in federal district court to enforce these provisions.

The Landrum-Griffin bill was the same, as was the Shelley bill, except that the Shelley bill would not have permitted the copying of membership lists but would have required the union to mail campaign literature to members at the candidate's expense.

Title V. Safeguards for Labor Organizations. This title of the committee bill specified the fiduciary responsibilities of union officers; required their bonding under specified conditions through an acceptable surety on federal bonds; prohibited loans of more than

$2,500 total to officers or employees of unions or union payment of fines of an employee convicted of willfully violating the act; prohibited Communists or persons convicted of specified crimes from holding office or being an employee of a union, of a labor relations consultant, or of a management association for five years after conviction; and amended Section 302 of Taft-Hartley to prohibit certain management payments to employee representatives (except those specified).

The Landrum-Griffin bill was the same as the committee bill, except that it provided criminal penalties for violation of the bonding section. The Shelley bill would have substantially amended the fiduciary section, applied bonding and employment disqualifications to employers' personnel departments, limited the bonding requirements, and allowed blanket bonds.

Title VI. Miscellaneous. According to the committee bill, picketing for "extortionate" purposes was a criminal offense. Also, express provision was made for retention of all rights and remedies under federal and state law, except as explicitly provided to the contrary. No general provisions were made on union discipline or criminal penalties for use or threat of force.

Landrum-Griffin outlawed picketing for "personal enrichment" (except bona fide employment benefits) and provided that the Secretary of Labor might sue to prevent the union from disciplining a member for exercising rights under the act. Use or threat of force to interfere with rights under the act would be a criminal offense.

The Shelley bill was substantially the same as the Landrum-Griffin bill on picketing for "personal enrichment." It had no other provisions in this title.

Between the Elliott (committee) bill and the Landrum-Griffin bill there were some differences in language in the first title and substantial differences in Title VI. Otherwise, the major difference was the Elliott bill's exclusion of small unions from the reporting requirements.

Title VII, Taft-Hartley Amendments. The detailed comparison of Title VII provisions for four bills is presented on pp. 190–191. In general terms Title VII of the Elliott bill called for the minimum "necessary" on the questions of hot cargo contracts and boycotts, while resolving other issues in accord with the desires of the AFL-

CIO. It represented a detailed reworking of the Kennedy bill from the Senate. Landrum-Griffin would have resolved the no man's land issue by allowing state courts to settle cases declined by the NLRB, made hot cargo contracts with any employers an unfair labor practice, closed all the loopholes in the Taft-Hartley prohibition of secondary boycotts, and further restricted organizational picketing. Whether by accident or design, the boycott language of Landrum-Griffin could also be interpreted to prohibit primary strikes under certain conditions (the section making it unlawful to "threaten" any person could include the threat to strike).

It can be seen that the Shelley bill resolved all questions in the interests of labor. It is interesting to note, however, that it did have a Title I and a Title VII which were contrary to what President Meany had demanded.

Around these bills strategies would be formed and battles waged. Great energy and wealth would be expended to achieve and prevent the inclusion of a few sentences in a seventy-page document. Let us return now and view the development of strategy and of the law.

Strategy Meeting Number Four

The identity of all participants in the fourth strategy meeting is not clear. The important thing is that men empowered by the House Democratic leadership met with authorized representatives of the AFL-CIO just after the committee reported its bill. Bolling and Metcalf were among those from the House. While carefully stating that they had no desire to contradict the federation's policy of opposition to both the Elliott and Landrum-Griffin bills, they wished to establish a joint operations group to determine and influence the support each proposed bill had in the House. They wished to work as a team to eliminate double counting and other potentially annoying problems.

The AFL-CIO agreed to the plan, and it was set in motion. When the first survey of opinion was completed, many labor lobbyists were taken aback. They had not been fully aware of the temper of the House on the issue. The labor strategists began to re-evaluate their stand on the committee action. It was clear that the Shelley bill had no chance of passage, but this was not a complete surprise. What was now also clear was that the Elliott bill was in real trouble. A

Title VII. Taft-Hartley Amendments

Committee Bill	Landrum-Griffin Bill	Shelley Bill	Kennedy Bill
No man's land. NLRB must handle all cases over which it has jurisdiction. Board increased from 5 to 7 members and would have to delegate certain powers to the general counsel. Regional directors given final authority in representation cases, subject to review on request by board.	State courts and agencies may handle cases over which NLRB declines to assert jurisdiction. No requirement that federal law be applied. Composition of board not affected.	Same as committee bill, except no provision that board must delegate certain administrative powers to general counsel.	State agencies but not courts may handle cases over which NLRB has declined to assert jurisdiction. Federal law must be applied, and enforcement and appeal would be through federal courts. Composition of NLRB not affected.
Construction industry. Prehire contracts in construction industry permitted and might require union membership after 7 days' instead of 30 days' employment. Picketing of fellow contractor in primary labor dispute allowed at common construction site.	Prehire contracts allowed only where there is prior history of collective bargaining. No provision on reducing time limit from 30 days to 7 days in construction industry. No provision on picketing at common construction site.	Same as committee bill.	Same as committee bill regarding prehire contracts. No provision on picketing at common construction site.
Strikers' voting rights. Economic strikers may vote in representation elections at struck firm.	No provision for voting by economic strikers. However, during a strike where recognition was not originally an issue, there can be no election for 6 months if the petition is filed by someone other than the bargaining representative (or for 12 months if the petition is filed by the employer).	Same as committee bill.	Economic strikers may vote, subject to regulations prescribed by NLRB.
Supervisors. No provision.	No provision.	No provision.	Service assistants in communications industry excluded from the term "supervisor" and thus made eligible for union membership.

Committee Bill	Landrum-Griffin Bill	Shelley Bill	Kennedy Bill
Hot cargo and secondary boycotts. Making hot cargo contract with common carrier subject to Part II of Interstate Commerce Act (motor carriers) is unfair labor practice, but employees may contract for right not to cross primary picket line.	Making hot cargo contract with any employer is unfair labor practice. It is also unfair labor practice for union to induce individuals employed by any person (including farm workers and those subject to Railway Labor Act) to refuse to handle goods so as to force any person to cease doing business with another person. Also unlawful for union to "threaten" (e.g., threaten to strike) any person to force any person to cease doing business with another.	No provision. Left unchanged Taft-Hartley's prohibition of inducement of concerted activity by "employees of an employer" (excluding farm and domestic workers and those subject to Railway Labor Act) to force any person to cease doing business with another person.	Same as committee bill, without provision regarding employee's right not to cross primary picket line.
Picketing. Organizational or recognitional picketing would be unfair labor practice if (1) another union has been recognized by employer, or (2) a valid representation election has been held in preceding 9 months without certification of picketing union or without its subsequently being chosen as bargaining representative by a majority of employees. Employer's unfair labor practice would be defense for union against charge of illegal picketing.	Organizational or recognitional picketing by an uncertified union would be unfair labor practice if (1) another union has been recognized by employer, or (2) a valid election has been held in preceding 12 months, or (3) union cannot demonstrate "sufficient showing of interest" on part of employees, or (4) picketing has continued "reasonable time" (up to 30 days) and no election petition has been filed. No provision making employer's unfair labor practice a defense against charge of illegal picketing.	No provision.	Same as committee bill.

large number of Congressmen had not made up their minds, and the men who could usually be counted on to support the leadership —those from neutral and marginal districts—were showing unusual resistance to overtures of leadership representatives.[9] The mood of the House provided sobering perspective to the labor people.

The Management Approach

A large number of representatives of management, including Ford Motor, General Electric, General Motors, and Reynolds Metals, met at a luncheon in a Washington hotel the Friday before the substitute bill was supposed to be introduced (this would have been July 24, 1959). The content of the proposed bill was announced by Edward McCabe. McCabe gave the provisions and strategy of the bill and indicated what the management people could do to support its passage. A number from the audience suggested changes in specific details of the bill. McCabe suggested that the "professionals on the Hill" had decided what could get through the House. They were going to push for the "possible," not the ideal. Therefore, it would not be worth while to discuss specific phrasing at the meeting.

The management people also wanted to know what the President was going to do. McCabe's answer was that he was going to do his part and that he would do it fully and well. McCabe went on to make several major points to his audience. First, leave the infighting to the professionals. They knew the climate of opinion; it was not up to the management groups to try to control particular raindrops. Second, the way management people could be most effective was by going to the public to bring pressure back on the Congress.

At this point former Representative Carter Menesko, who was then with the coal industry but had once been a member of the Rules Committee, stood up and seconded McCabe. He said, in effect: "Now don't fool around with those detailed things. You have to rely on the 'pros' on the Hill to do all that can be done and to make the tactical decisions."

McCabe's third point was that the management people should

[9] One of these representatives commented: "I have read of the way the management people concentrated their efforts on men from marginal districts. I can tell you that I was aware of it by the unexpected resistance I met in lining up support for the Elliott bill."

avoid becoming conspicuous on the Hill. Of course, they should not refrain from using their influence, but they should do it as subtlely as possible. This would involve a substitution of mail, telephone, and telegraphic channels for personal contact. The experience of Representative H. Erwin Mitchell of Georgia will be discussed later to demonstrate the extent and effect of the telephone campaign (conducted by the Atlanta Chamber of Commerce in that case). Similar pressure was applied to others. The refrain which supporters of Landrum-Griffin were repeating was "The *people* are demanding a strong labor reform law."

The contrast in the approaches of the two sides became striking as the legislative process approached a climax. Union representatives were thronging the halls of the office buildings and the Capital. With the pressure from all sides building up within the closed social unit of the House, there were bound to be sparks which could ignite fires of animosity. Since the union people were present, they were convenient targets for steam-blowing, or at least finger-pointing. Most management lobbyists remained in the background or telephoned. Local representatives of the Associated General Contractors were known to be in town. When they did meet with congressmen, it was often in downtown offices or in restaurants.

The President Addresses the Nation

The Republicans on the House Committee on Education and Labor also wanted to know what the President was going to do. In the weekly legislative sessions at the White House they had urged him to "go to the people" to back the Landrum-Griffin Bill. The suggestion received a cool welcome. These congressmen were sure that the President had made a policy decision and would not make a special address to the nation on the labor problem. They then decided to put themselves publicly on record calling for the intervention and support of the President in an effort to get him to change his mind. A letter signed by all ten Republicans of the House committee was sent to President Eisenhower and then released to the press.

This move upset the Administration strategists, who were concerned with the "public image" of Landrum-Griffin. Great pains had been taken to establish it as a bipartisan measure. The letter was clearly calling the substitute a partisan issue. The incident was upsetting, but not crucial.

The congressmen and a group of management representatives took another step as well. They set out, in the words of one informant, "to put some pressure on the President." They organized a campaign to get state and local Republican leaders to phone, telegraph, or visit the White House to inform the President of the importance of the Landrum-Griffin bill to them in their localities. The efforts were rewarded, and a wave of grass roots opinion in support of Landrum-Griffin broke over the White House. The question here was not whether or not the White House would support Landrum-Griffin but whether or not the President himself would directly support a particular bill by name—something he had not done in the past.

Despite his pride in the campaign, one management spokesman stated that the President would not have consented to taking to the airwaves had it not been for the earlier occurrence of an unusual event. Robert Kennedy, as chief counsel on McClellan's Rackets Committee, was close to inside information. He was distressed by the rumblings in the AFL-CIO inner circles during the week before the reporting of the committee bill, rumblings which he feared would grow into labor efforts to block all legislation. Arrangements were made for him to appear on the "Tonight" show on the NBC television network, a show better known as the "Jack Paar Show," in an attempt to counteract any such plans. The program began shortly after 11 p.m. in the East and proceeded at a leisurely pace through its usual informal format of comment, entertainment, and discussion. The host, Jack Paar, then introduced his guest, Robert Kennedy. Kennedy spoke informally, sincerely, and directly to his audience. He delivered a moving plea for the public to support labor reform legislation. Although he pointed out that management as well as labor practices required reform, this comment apparently failed to strike any resonant chords in his audience.

Kennedy's talk was extremely effective in motivating latent resentment against the labor practices he spoke of. The viewers on that evening were the "people." One might speculate that the most hardened devotees of what was soon to be called the vast "wasteland" were among them. They were people who had been conditioned by two and one-half years of exposure to and by the McClellan Committee. It is probable that many of them who had given their periodic, fleeting attention to the political-economic controversy of labor-management corruption had mistaken revelations for reform. A few years before they had made this error in evaluating the exposure of organized crime by Senator Kefauver in the first major use of the televised congressional hearing (Senator McClellan had been a prominent member and student of that committee, too). After all, how could "they" (those who had the power to govern) fail to act once the problems were so forcefully made known? Yet, no legislation had resulted then, and now this clean-cut, earnest young man from one of America's prominent families was telling them that it was possible, even likely, that nothing would be done about "labor rackets." He was asking for their support. The appeal closed the gap between awareness and political action for many viewers.

Within three days after Robert Kennedy's appearance, a flood of mail engulfed the Congress. There were some interesting qualitative as well as quantitative changes in the communications. Up until this time the mail received by many members of Congress was easily identified as "inspired" mail: form letters, or mail from one area using the same phrasing. But now the letters were coming from those of the "people" who had happened to be watching television on that evening. And the mail was calling for strong labor legislation. Though it could hardly have been his intent, Kennedy's plea had led to a response which was interpreted by congressmen as a call to support the Landrum-Griffin bill against the "weak" committee bill. Bobby Kennedy's appearance produced evidence that, in addition to the special-interest public, at least a portion of the general public could be aroused and had indeed been aroused.

At the legislative meeting the Tuesday following the Congressmen's letter and the televised appeal of Robert Kennedy, President Eisenhower announced that he would make an address over radio and television in support of the Landrum-Griffin bill.[10]

[10] It should be noted that an Administration spokesman denies this version of the process. He stated that Eisenhower's policy was to "go to the people" whenever necessary in support of his legislative program. "The only question," he said, "was over the timing of his speech." He added: "The Congressmen

Once this decision was made, it was up to the presidential staff to assist in the preparation of the speech. Major responsibility was given to Ed McCabe. Gerald Morgan assisted to some extent. As is typical of such speeches, this one was the product of extensive co-operation. First, there was a general discussion of length, format, and content with the President. Then came the outline from this discussion, as modified by the President. A draft was prepared from the outline and revised by the President. After several such revisions the speech was ready to go. Final modifications were made just before speech time and also in the actual presentation by the President.

The address was made on August 6 over all the major radio and television networks. It has been called the "most political" speech made by President Eisenhower. All estimates indicate that it produced a volume of mail more than double the response to Bob Kennedy. Like Kennedy, Eisenhower had activated the general public. But carrying Kennedy one step further, the President had specified his bill by name. The people responded to the call with mail requesting "strong" labor reform legislation in the package of the Landrum-Griffin bill. This was an extremely important factor. As an Administration official put it, rather cynically but perhaps quite accurately: "When the people demand just 'strong' labor legislation you could pass a tariff act and they wouldn't know the difference, but when they call for a bill by name there is no way for a Congressman to get around it."

Apparently, the President's speech did some other things as well. In his position as "lame duck," Eisenhower effectively presented himself as a man with no political motivations. As the man elected by all the people, he was one person who could speak for the interests of all the people. Thus, his strong stand gave legitimacy to the fight for the Landrum-Griffin bill and made it hard for opponents to resist. The man in the street had been called upon to express himself; he had been asked by his President to lend support. The public was aware of the problem. Now it took action.

concerned may feel that they were instrumental, but they were not. The questioning in the press over the President's intentions was just a public relations device to stimulate interest." The concern of this informant with public relations led me to believe that his version was colored for this purpose.

The backers of the Elliott bill were truly in difficulty when the major networks refused them equal time to reply to the President. This was done on the basis that Eisenhower's appeal was a "non-partisan" one for a bill which had "bipartisan" support. The Mutual network, least influential of the major radio networks, did offer Speaker Rayburn an opportunity to reply.[11] This he accepted; his speech, on the evening of August 10, was heard by only a fraction of those who heard the President. There was little public response to Rayburn's speech, which ran into technical problems during delivery. Besides, there was no interest group backing for the Elliott bill.

It is interesting at this point to note some of the points cited by the President and some informed comments on them. One outspoken reaction came from an unexpected source. In the New York *Times* on the Sunday before the labor bill reached the decisive stage in the House, Joseph Loftus discussed the President's speech and the three areas which distinguished the reform bills which were before the Congress (secondary boycotts, organization picketing, and federal-state jurisdiction over small—in dollar volume—labor-management disputes). The article states:

The curious thing about all three of these is that they are Taft-Hartley law matters. They figured in the McClellan Committee disclosures of power abuses in a secondary way, but they were not the spectaculars which brought the committee its fame or aroused the public clamor for a law. The Committee's twenty-one point "indictment of Hoffa" this week contains no mention of these three points.

It then goes on to spotlight the real meaning of the McClellan Committee hearings (which was also the message of the Kefauver Crime Committee hearings which, as already stated, resulted in no legislation at all):

If the states had enforced their own laws and applied their exclusive police powers competently and incorruptibly, the McClellan hearings might never have been held or, at most, they would have been gone and nearly forgotten by now. . . .

All three issues—boycotts, picketing, and federal-state jurisdiction (no man's land) figure in the union-management *power struggle* [italics added]. In this sense they are traveling as reform measures.

[11] News reports indicated that Mutual was in receivership at about this time.

It has been shown how the AFL-CIO opened the gates to this type of "fellow traveler" with its earlier insistence on the sweeteners. The management side had responded as expected.

The article then goes on to discuss an example of a secondary boycott used by the President to show the difference in the impact of Landrum-Griffin and the Elliott bills and to which he had said: "I want this sort of thing stopped! America wants it stopped!" Loftus concludes: "This practice is already outlawed by the Taft-Hartley Act, so much so that where it occurs the National Labor Relations Board *must* seek a court injunction [italics added]." [12] This is very strong language for a paper which usually supported the President. It flatly stated that the President had misinformed the people about the issues involved. The remainder of the article clearly presented the two sides to the problem in each of the other areas of controversy.

The President's speech was the deciding factor for a number of congressmen who were perplexed by the labor reform issue. First, it stimulated mail from the type of constituent who is ordinarily disinterested in political matters and who is likely, therefore, to remember his Representative's vote on the issue which stirs him. And second, the prestige of the President—a nonpolitical President—itself carried weight with a number of congressmen, especially some of those newly elected. [13]

The congressmen were subjected to enormous pressure during the final days before a vote on the labor reform law. The pressure took varying forms.

Labor Lobbying Strategy

The Congressional Hotel headquarters of the AFL-CIO was more active after the committee bill had been reported than before. Pro-

---

[12] Joseph E. Loftus, New York *Times*, Aug. 9, 1959, p. E-7. As indicated in earlier sections of the present study, court rulings have established specific exceptions to the Taft-Hartley prohibition of secondary boycotts. Often there is room for difference of opinion on the applicability of law to a certain fact-situation.

[13] This necessarily represents the judgment of the author, based on extensive interviews with labor, management, congressional, and Administration participants. It is in agreement with the common perception of individuals and groups on all sides of the question that the President's speech was a true turning point. From a scientific point of view it must be stated as an hypothesis, the complete testing of which would require resources not available to the author (including, perhaps, the ability to move backward in time).

fessor Cox arrived in town to work as a member of the operations group, serving as adviser to Representative Elliott and as working head of the drafting group. A large-scale organization was set in motion to coordinate the importation of labor people from all parts of the country. Regular union representatives served as "directors" for specified regions. They advised and briefed the local delegations called into town to influence their congressmen. The delegations were informed of the federation policy on the bills before Congress and conducted on visits to congressmen from their areas whom they knew, many on a first-name basis. Reports of conversations were closely followed, and a running record of the probable voting tendency of each congressman was kept. The "amateur status" of many of these local men sometimes made their estimates less than reliable. The union people, however, apparently believed strongly in the personal approach in lobbying.

At the same time the Teamsters also brought in a large number of people from various districts. They conducted daily tours to the offices of congressmen, but they had nowhere near the "professional" support for their importees that the federation had. The New York *Times* quotes President Hoffa as stating at a dinner meeting on August 4 that he had two hundred local Teamsters in Washington to call on their congressmen.[14] All reports, both public and private, indicate that these men caused a good deal of damage to labor's cause by their lack of appreciation for the finer points of lobbying techniques. They often antagonized staff people in the outer offices of congressmen as well as the congressmen themselves. The Teamster representatives had a single purpose: to prevent legislation. They were well organized (if not well schooled), and they made their presence known. They had a real impact, but apparently produced reverse "English."

It is interesting to note Representative Frank Thompson's statements made at Princeton University several weeks after the Congress recessed. He said that, in addition to threats from both management and labor groups in his district, there were also promises of reward from both groups. He indicated that it was made clear to him that large sums of money would become available if a congressman voted

[14] New York *Times,* Aug. 6, 1959, p. 17.

"properly." [15] There is little question that both sides were playing this one for keeps.

A House Divided

The official policy of the AFL-CIO was not receiving whole-hearted support from its affiliated unions. Although the official position of the Building Trades Council had been reversed and the building trades were again opposing the Elliott bill, they could hardly be expected to oppose it enthusiastically. The switch in position imposed on them by federation pressure greatly impaired their effectiveness. Some unions from the Industrial Union Department, the UAW and Steelworkers for instance, were both lukewarm to the official policy, but for opposite reasons. The UAW wanted to stress its opposition to corruption and make its stand against the Teamsters Union emphatic and clear. They felt that the public should be aware of the difference between the level of conduct required of officers of the Auto Workers as opposed to the Teamsters. The Steelworkers, through Nordy Hoffman, their legislative representative, were more in sympathy with the Teamsters than with the AFL-CIO itself.

In dealing with congressmen most union legislative representatives were confronted with a very difficult and perplexing question. "All right," the congressman would say, "so I'll back the Shelley bill, but you know as well as I do that it isn't going to pass. What do I do then? You fellows say that both the Elliott and Landrum-Griffin bills are antilabor, but with all the feeling in my district I have to vote for something."

As was pointed out earlier, the AFL-CIO was in the position of being against all available alternatives from the time that the Landrum-Griffin bill was introduced on July 27 until the Shelley bill was put forth on August 3. The Shelley bill was an apologia, but there was so little chance of its passage that its congressional advocates would still be essentially in the position of supporting no bill. In answer to the question "What do I do then?" the official policy of the federation was silent. The operational result was hemming and

[15] The *Daily Princetonian,* reported in the *Courier-Post,* Camden, N.J., Oct. 29, 1959, p. 24. Thompson's statements about threats from both sides appear in the New York *Times,* July 28, 1959, p. 16.

hawing and double talk on the part of many legislative representatives.

Local AFL-CIO unions were equally hamstrung. An example was the Texas AFL-CIO. Tremendous pressure was being put on all the state's Representatives by management groups. What union pressure did exist was directed to backing the Shelley bill. The Speaker's assistant, D. B. Hardiman, asked the Texas AFL-CIO president to round up some support for the Elliott bill, but he was told that such action would violate official policy. Support would first have to come from the parent body.

One state AFL-CIO group was first told to oppose the Elliott bill as antilabor, then told not to oppose it but to stand by for further instructions. Periodically they wired AFL-CIO headquarters in Washington for instructions. They were still standing by two weeks after a bill had passed the House.

The Speaker's Role

Speaker Rayburn had given unusual support to the Elliott bill. In fact, for a good portion of the time his was the only voice raised in support of the measure. He had ensured its birth and existence and aided in its growth. The faithful five had conducted a series of meetings—"seminars"—to explain the provisions of their bill to other congressmen, with special emphasis on the freshmen and the uncommitted. Rayburn personally came to two or three of these meetings to lend his prestige and support. Invitations were often sent in his name. He told assembled representatives that the bill was necessary and "a good bill." He told them how it had been put together in the committee. He said it was of primary interest to the Party; he supported it, and he hoped that they could do likewise. The meeting would then be turned over to one of the faithful five, often Representative Udall, who would make a detailed presentation of the substance of the measure and answer questions.

The Speaker announced his support of the bill in a press conference on August 3, his statement was read on the House floor on August 10, and he supported the bill in a speech over the Mutual network on the evening of August 10.[16]

[16] *Daily Congressional Record*, 86th Cong., 1st Sess., Aug. 10, 1959, p. 14,049.

What he did not do was to speak to individuals in person or by phone and insist that they support the bill. From all indications he did not work this way. He had achieved a great degree of success in the past by using his own methods.

Another thing the Speaker did not do was to take the floor personally in support of the Elliott bill. An Administration spokesman explained this as the result of the Speaker's agreement with Minority Leader Halleck that neither of them would make floor speeches on the issue. This was stated to be attractive to the Speaker because of Halleck's relatively greater knowledge of labor matters, a factor which could become embarrassing to the Speaker in debate. It also complemented Halleck's and the Administration's desire to keep Landrum-Griffin nonpartisan.

The Leader of the Opposition: Charles Halleck

The election of Charles Halleck as Minority Leader of the House of Representatives early in 1959 brought about a series of changes in the operations of the Republican Party in the House. Representative Joseph Martin of Massachusetts had not been a hard-driving leader. Halleck operated in a manner which contrasted strongly with that of his predecessor. In his own words: "I am a gut fighter." [17]

Halleck admitted that more than one Representative had been forced into line by a threat to cut off his campaign funds. "Some guys say I drive too hard. You've got to know when to let up. You can go too far though, and I have a few times on fellows in this session."

The Minority Leader did a great deal to improve the liaison of the lower house with the White House. Eisenhower had referred to him as a "political genius" and usually took his advice on legislative strategy in the House.

The Civil Rights Deal

The traditional position of House Republicans in support of civil rights legislation was suddenly reversed in the summer of 1959. Emanuel Celler, Chairman of the Committee on the Judiciary, had

---

[17] This section is based on articles on Halleck in *Time*, Vol. LXXIII, No. 14 (April 6, 1959), and No. 23 (June 8, 1959).

expressed himself as very hopeful that his committee would take effective action on civil rights legislation in that session of Congress. Later he indicated his surprise at a sudden loss of Republican support within his committee for the most meaningful provisions of the bill. On August 5, when the civil rights measure was finally reported, Celler stated that an "unholy alliance" of Republicans and (Southern) Democrats had emasculated the bill in the committee.[18] A few weeks later, after the House had considered the labor bill, Cellar remarked about the fact that the civil rights measure was apparently stalled for the session in the Rules Committee. He stated that he was "firmly convinced" that votes had been mustered for the labor bill on the basis of a civil rights "deal." [19] Representative Lester Holtzman of New York stated on August 23 that four Republicans had voted with Chairman Smith to block clearance of the civil rights measure from the Rules Committee.[20]

An article on the role of Representative Smith of Virginia in the passage of Landrum-Griffin states:

The labor battle prompted whisperings of a civil rights "deal" wherein Mr. Smith supposedly wrung a promise from Republican leaders not to push civil rights legislation this session. Rumors aside, the beetle-browed lawmaker has worked closely with Minority Leader Halleck and the two are warm personal friends.[21]

An Administration source who dealt personally with Halleck quotes him as denying a civil rights deal but stating: "I wouldn't be above such a thing." The second session of the Eighty-sixth Congress rang with accusations of a "pay-off" for Southern Democratic support of the Landrum-Griffin bill by Republican refusal to support a petition to discharge the Rules Committee of responsibility for the civil rights bill—this was the civil rights deal.

These are but a few samples of the symptoms of the agreement by the House Republicans and Southern Democrats. There are few people who were interviewed who doubt the "deal," but there were none who would provide direct knowledge of it.

[18] New York *Times*, Aug. 6, 1959, p. 1. See also Berman, *A Bill Becomes a Law*.
[19] New York *Times*, Aug. 20, 1959, p. 26.
[20] *Ibid.*, Aug. 24, 1959, p. 9.
[21] Paul Duke, "How Virginia's Quiet Congressman Wields His Powerful and Conservative Hammer," *Wall Street Journal*, Sept. 16, 1959, p. 12.

Floor Tactical Considerations

Experience in the Senate had convinced the AFL-CIO that opening the bill to amendment on the floor could be very dangerous. Both Bolling and the AFL-CIO agreed that, if possible, they wanted a vote on the Elliott bill unamended. Both felt that it was vulnerable to single-shot "strengthening" amendments which could make the bill even worse than Landrum-Griffin. Another tactical consideration was to keep Landrum-Griffin unmodified. It would be desirable to prevent the accommodation to minor objections which might win it further support. Elliott bill backers were foregoing such support-gathering as being too risky. The Democrats' objective was to freeze the situation and decide the question on the merits of the bills as they appeared on the floor.

One reason for this was the discovery of a chink in the Landrum-Griffin armor. Apparently through inadvertence, Landrum-Griffin drafters had included a provision which was open to civil rights interpretation similar to that given in Lyndon Johnson's "memorandum" discussed in an earlier chapter. This could prove very embarrassing to the Southern supporters of the bill. Several hundred copies of an analysis of the provision had been prepared and were sitting in Bolling's office, awaiting distribution at the last minute before a vote on Landrum-Griffin. It was entitled "Griffin-Landrum Analysis in Terms of Civil Rights." (The interchange in order of sponsors' names was common but may also be significant.) It stated that the bill: (1) incorporated by reference the equal rights provisions of the Fourteenth Amendment; (2) would require integrated union locals in the South, with integrated social activities; (3) included a Fair Employment Practices Committee program in construction, maritime, and longshore trades; and (4) provided a two-year and $10,000 risk for interference with Negro rights in an integrated union. In short, it would be a damaging precedent for the South.

Arrangements were made that, on signal from the Speaker at the last minute before the vote, when amendment would be impossible, Jimmie Roosevelt would make reference to this provision and the analysis would be distributed.

Introduction of the Shelley bill made it possible to cast the Elliott bill in the role of the compromise measure between the two extremes.

This was the image which its supporters tried to convey. Support by Speaker Rayburn aided in this plan, since he had a reputation for achieving workable compromises among warring factions.

There were parliamentary bars to the Democrats' tactical goals. First, there was no way of preventing modification of Landrum-Griffin other than by majority vote. Then, according to the rule for consideration of the labor bill (discussed more fully in the next chapter), the only way to prevent the amendment of the Elliott bill would be first to allow Landrum-Griffin to be substituted for Elliott by winning the teller vote in the Committee of the Whole House, and then to be beaten on the roll-call vote,[22] thus leaving the Elliott bill unmodified as the only alternative available. This would be a complex and risky procedure, requiring a nice degree of coordination and control.

From the point of view of the coalition (Landrum-Griffin) strategists, at least in the opening stages, any move to modify their bill might be seized on as an admission of weakness and thus should be avoided. They would rely on the grass roots pressure being generated by their supporters and on the persuasive ability of top Administration officials making personal contact among those with whom they might have some influence.

The image desired for Landrum-Griffin was that of a moderate, effective, bipartisan bill. It was cast as a "fair bill" intended to "punish" no one.

The Stage Is Set

The House had before it three approaches to labor reform which we have seen were similar in major part. In Title I each had a bill of rights. The Shelley bill was watered down from the Elliott bill,

---

[22] For the conduct of approximately 90 percent of its business the House of Representatives sits as a committee of the whole. Detailed discussion and amendment of legislation is conducted in this manner. A quorum of one hundred is required (instead of the majority required for the House itself to do business), and roll-call votes are eliminated. Technically, debate is limited to one speaker per amendment and five minutes per speaker. When the Committee of the Whole House dissolves and the House reconvenes, the legislation considered and amended in detail by the committee is either accepted or rejected by the House on roll-call (recorded) vote. On the nonrecord votes in the Committee of the Whole House two Representatives are appointed as tellers to count their colleagues as they file by one or the other to express their vote on the question. Only the total teller vote is recorded.

which, in turn, was watered down from the Kuchel compromise (the Senate version), which was included in Landrum-Griffin. The reform sections in Titles II-VI were virtually identical, based on Elliott bill language except for minor changes in expected directions. It was in Title VII that the bills were different—that is, in their approach to Taft-Hartley Act changes. The Shelley bill excluded the management-desired changes. The Elliott bill had those changes which the Democratic leadership felt were necessary to get the bill through the House in a form which they thought labor could "live with," balanced by reversal of the Denver building trades doctrine and the other sweeteners from the Kennedy bill. Landrum-Griffin excluded all labor sweeteners and included provisions "beefed up" for trading. One provision could have been interpreted to bar primary picketing, namely, the strike itself!

VIII. THE HOUSE PASSES
A BILL

THE House of Representatives began formal consideration of a labor bill on August 11, 1959. A few days before, the backers of H.R.8342 had suffered a grievous blow when Carl Elliott of Alabama became ill and was hospitalized for an abdominal operation. This was especially important in view of the need to attract Southern votes if the opposition substitute was to be resisted. Elliott's illness also caused a last-minute shift in assignments for other supporters. Representative Udall was called on to pinch-hit for Elliott, the choice between Udall and Thompson apparently being decided on the basis of previous identification with labor, or rather, lack of such identification.

The Rules Committee

Chairman Smith of the Committee on Rules was clearly an important actor in the drama on labor legislation. His key position provided him with great leverage in developing a bill to his liking and in affecting its passage. There were delays in acting on a rule for the Elliott bill, but, in comparison with many other measures, it was given expeditious treatment. During the delay the Landrum-Griffin bill had been introduced. The great number of Representatives who wished to appear before the committee during the hearings caused further delays.

The Rules Committee is charged with the responsibility for passing a rule to govern the debate for each piece of legislation which comes to the floor of the House. (Until recently no committee chairman could even consider a bill until it had been assigned to his committee by the Rules Committee.) The committee decides whether a bill may be amended on the floor of the House and the length of the debate to be permitted on the bill. A closed rule is one prohibiting amendment; an open rule is one permitting free amendment within the time limit for the debate.

After all the fanfare and speculation, the committee reported a rule which would be "wide open":

Resolved, That upon the adoption of this resolution it shall be in order to move that the House resolve itself into the Committee of the Whole House on the State of the Union for the consideration of the bill, H.R.8342 [the Elliott bill], a bill to provide for the reporting and disclosure of certain financial transactions and administrative practices of labor organizations and employers, to prevent abuses in the administration of trusteeships by labor organizations, to provide standards with respect to the election of officers of labor organizations, and for other purposes, and all points of order against said bill are hereby waived. After general debate, which shall be confined to the bill and shall continue not to exceed six hours, to be equally divided and controlled by the chairman and ranking minority member of the Committee on Education and Labor, the bill shall be read for amendment under the five-minute rule. At the conclusion of the consideration of the bill for amendment, the Committee shall rise and report the bill to the House with such amendments as may have been adopted and the previous question shall be considered as ordered on the bill and amendments thereto to final passage without instructions.

That after the passage of H.R.8342, the Committee on Education and Labor shall be discharged from the further consideration of the bill, S.1555; that it shall then be in order in the House to move to strike out all after the enacting clause of said Senate bill and insert in lieu thereof the provisions contained in H.R.8342 as passed; that it shall then be in order to move that the House insist upon its amendment to said Senate bill S.1555 and request a conference with the Senate; and that the Seaker [sic] shall thereupon appoint the conferees on the part of the House.[1]

By these provisions there would be no limitation on the number of substitutes or amendments which could be offered. The bill could

[1] U.S. Congress, *Daily Congressional Record*, 86th Cong., 1st Sess., Aug. 6, 1959, p. 13,981. This five-minute rule "limits debate on any amendment to one speaker and five minutes for each side." The rule is circumvented as a limit to debate by proposal of a *pro forma* amendment "to strike the last word" of the amendment under debate and thus be eligible for an additional five minutes. *Pro forma* amendments are not voted on.

be sent back to committee with or without instructions. These provisions were in the interests of everyone except the Elliott bill supporters and thus had little trouble in being cleared by the Rules Committee. Chairman Smith explained his rule:

Mr. Speaker, We have a very remarkable situation here today. We have a rule for the consideration of a labor bill. We have two proposed substitutes to the labor bill. And to be as brief as I can about the rule, it is, I will say, a wide open rule under the rules of the House. The so-called committee bill will first be considered. When it is read for amendment, at the conclusion of the first section, the gentleman from Georgia will offer the so-called Landrum-Griffin bill as an amendment. It will then be in order to offer the so-called Shelley-Roosevelt bill as a substitute for the Landrum amendment. Then it will be in order to have one amendment each to the Shelley-Roosevelt substitute and the Landrum-Griffin amendment pending at the same time. The Landrum-Griffin amendment will be perfected by whatever amendment may be offered before any vote is taken on amendments to the Shelley-Roosevelt substitute. Then that amendment will be perfected. Then the Roosevelt substitute will be, I hope, voted down. Then the Landrum-Griffin bill will, I hope, be voted up. If that occurs, we will then be at the end of the road. That would then be reported back to the House and the House would vote on the Landrum-Griffin amendment. If that is defeated, in the Committee of the Whole, of course, the committee bill will be open to the much-needed amendments to make it a good labor-management bill.

When all that is done in order to get it to conference, it will be necessary to substitute [it for] the Senate bill. The provisions of the Senate bill will be stricken out and whatever the result of the House deliberations is will be inserted in Senate bill, S.1555. Then, the Speaker will appoint conferees. So much for the rule.[2]

The coalition would have an opportunity to pass the Landrum-Griffin substitute. If this failed, they would still be able to amend the Elliott bill by including particular provisions from Landrum-Griffin. For Elliott bill supporters to get their bill without any amendments, the Landrum-Griffin bill would have to be adopted by the Committee of the Whole. This would end amendment to Elliott. Then, when the House took its record vote, if the substitute could be defeated, the only alternative available would be the Elliott bill as proposed.

Since control of time was fully in the hands of the coalition, the cards were further stacked against the Democratic leadership group.

[2] *Ibid.*, Aug. 10, 1959, p. 14,175.

Barden allotted his three hours equitably among Democrats: one hour to Elliott supporters, one hour to Shelley supporters, and one hour to Landrum supporters. Representative Kearns allotted all three hours to Griffin supporters. The result was four times as much time for Landrum-Griffin supporters as for either the Elliott or Shelley supporters. Some writers have said that congressional debate is of little meaning or effect, but in a complex situation such as this there is little doubt of its importance. Representative Ray Madden pointed to the reason: "I venture to say that more than half of the Members in this House have not read or mentally digested en toto any of the three long and complex bills now under consideration by this body." [3] The feeling of those on the short end of the time arrangement were well illustrated later in the debate. Congressman Neal Smith of Iowa made a very biting comparison:

Mr. Chairman, I just want to call attention to section 101 [of the Landrum-Griffin bill] which provides, as the gentleman from Georgia read, that every member of a labor organization shall have equal rights and privileges to participate in deliberations. Take out the words 'a labor organization,' substitute the word 'Congress,' and apply that provision to the fact that the proponents of the Landrum bill received 4 hours of the time for debate while the supporters of the committee bill received only 1 hour, and under the Landrum bill those Members of Congress responsible for allocation of time would be subject to 1 year in the penitentiary.[4]

Lobbying Intensity

The AFL-CIO lobbying effort was continuing in a manner unchanged from before. Unity was found only in opposition to the "killer" Landrum-Griffin bill (so characterized by the Teamsters). The Elliott bill was more or less ignored both by management and the unions, except for some building trades representatives and legislative representatives from certain other unions. It was still officially opposed by the AFL-CIO. The United Auto Workers, among others, continued to try to create a more positive stand within the AFL-CIO but grudgingly accepted the official position. One legislative representative expressed his feeling toward the official stand in this way: "It's awfully hard to line up support behind an idiotic strategy."

The federation made no change in its effort except to increase its

[3] *Ibid.*, Aug. 11, 1959, p. 14,178   [4] *Ibid.*, Aug. 12, 1959, p. 14,391.

intensity. Union people from various districts were shepherded to the offices of their congressmen with increasing frequency. This led one member of Congress, who had been under almost constant pressure for many weeks, to remark: "The thing these people seem to forget is that I don't *have* to be a Congressman!" This is quite a departure from the stereotype of congressional behavior. Apparently, there are some things which a politician will not do, no matter how much pressure is put on him.

The Teamsters Union continued its organized visitations to congressional offices. The visitors continued to antagonize the legislators and to threaten them with certain election defeat for voting "wrong." Teamster tactics caused a heightened antagonism and an impact the opposite of the intention. As the bill headed for a vote, congressmen spent more and more time on the floor of the House as the only refuge from the visitors of one side and the phone calls and telegrams of the other. The relative calm of the debate was a soothing balm to these weary men.[5]

The Administration-coordinated effort of the management associations had reached its peak in the first full week in August. About ten days to two weeks was the time considered necessary for a successful public campaign. Unlike the case of Pavlov's dog, the lag between stimulus and response is two to three days, making efforts during the debate itself useless. It was thus intended that the campaign end a few days prior to the floor consideration of the bill. As the situation developed, the unexpected delays in the Rules Committee meant that the cutoff date fell somewhat over a week prior to the final vote on the bill.

The group had done its work well. Again referring to the article by Nossiter:

After the Griffin-Landrum bill, strongest of the measures proposed, was introduced in late July, the strategists continued to pour on the heat.

Brief tape recordings were made for radio and television, featuring Reps. Phil M. Landrum (D–Ga.) and Robert P. Griffin (R–Mich.). Beginning in August, these were run frequently, again as public-service features or under local sponsorship in 35 of the crucial districts.

[5] See Sar A. Levitan, "Union Lobbyists' Contribution to Tough Labor Legislation," *Labor Law Journal*, Oct., 1959, pp. 675–82, for a detailed discussion of the impact of union lobbyists.

In one swing area, an experiment was tried. A good-sized corporation sent its foremen out to ring neighbor's doorbells. This tactic, it is claimed, produced 3000 letters in one week, urging a stiff bill.[6]

One member of Congress reported that mail had been received within two days after Landrum-Griffin was introduced, mail that was inspired by ads placed in the local paper by the state "Landrum-Griffin Committee." Another congressman stated that he had had calls and telegrams from his district asking if he would vote for the Landrum-Griffin bill. He had been forced to reply that he did not know because the bill hadn't been printed as yet! A congressman who favored the Elliott bill mailed out copies of the Elliott and Landrum-Griffin bills to those who asked his intentions. He soon gave this up, for it did no good. People weren't interested in what the bill said or how it compared with another bill; they were interested in whether the congressman was going to vote for the Landrum-Griffin bill.[7]

Undecided Southern congressmen were being subjected to telephone and telegraphic pressure from management groups in their local districts, stressing the theme that "Labor is keeping industry out of the South" and therefore it was necessary to pass the Landrum-Griffin bill to keep unions out of the South. The NAM, Chamber of Commerce, American Farm Bureau Federation, and smaller agricultural associations were the main supporters of this campaign. *Business and Opportunity*, the official publication of the Associated Industries of Florida, stated:

When southern lawmakers teamed up on the labor bill vote with Republicans in the House, they had more to gain than meets the eye. Stiff reform measures would make it very difficult for labor to organize in states such as Florida. This would maintain the attractive climate for drawing industry from the north.

Another reason reportedly was that the Republican Leadership in the House agreed to help block any civil rights legislation this year if the southern lawmakers would join in supporting the strict labor bill.[8]

[6] Bernard D. Nossiter, "The Labor Bill Lobby," Washington *Post*, Sept. 10, 1959.

[7] Senator Goldwater is quoted as saying: "To the people of the country, Landrum-Griffin is the bill they want, even if they don't know what's in it." Washington *Evening Star*, Aug. 29, 1959, p. 1.

[8] *Business and Opportunity*, Vol. I, No. 3 (Tallahassee, Associated Industries of Florida, Sept., 1959).

Representative Mitchell of Georgia notified his constituents that he planned to vote for the Elliott bill as a reform measure which would accomplish the goals set forth by the McClellan Committee. Mitchell told a reporter for the Atlanta *Journal-Constitution* of the reaction which this brought from business groups and former supporters in his state. Excerpts from the article are quoted at length, since it documents a side of this story which has not received much coverage in the news media and which is extremely difficult to document through interviews:

Listen to this letter from E. T. (Gene) Barwick, a big manufacturer who runs E. T. Barwick Mills in Dalton and LaFayette. It was the fifth communication Mr. Mitchell received from Barwick, about the Landrum Bill, and was in response to a letter explaining his position:

"I personally spent time, money and energy getting you elected, hoping that we had a man who would be above the ordinary. I can assure you that I will devote one hundred-fold more energy, time and money in getting you out, if you support the kind of legislation you announce in your letter."

Here is a telegraph from another manufacturer in the Northern end of Mr. Mitchell's district:

"Received your two pages of hogwash . . . We along with many others are very disappointed that you are so confused in your thinking on this matter. . . ."

The first call came from a member of a local Chamber of Commerce in the district before the Landrum bill had even been introduced.

Mr. Mitchell said, "That was apparently the start. I told him I didn't know what was in the bill, that it had not even been printed, and that I didn't think he knew what was in it either.

"He was just buying a 'label' that the Landrum bill was a strong labor bill."

The word then darted around the Seventh District that Mr. Mitchell was "wavering" on the Landrum bill.

"From then on," said the Congressman, "the tempo began to pick up day by day and night by night. All day Tuesday, Wednesday, Thursday and Friday, I was taking call after call and was doing nothing else.

"Almost without exception," said the Congressman, "the telephone pressure was from manufacturers or somebody representing manufacturers." (The Seventh District has more than 100 manufacturing plants in the tufted textile group alone.)

"I either knew every one of them personally or had had dealings with them over the telephone or by mail. Most of them were supporters of mine. . . ."

One of the wealthiest and most influential businessmen in the district called and said: "Don't make it difficult for us to support you, Erwin." Then he added, "Campaigns are expensive, you know. . . ."

"One of my friends who was very active and prominent in my campaign called me at least a dozen times over the whole period," said Mr. Mitchell. "He said pressure was being applied to him in the manufacturing end of his textile business."

"He said he was going to stay with me politically but that he wondered if I wasn't hurting myself."

Another long time friend said: "They have been after me all week. I've had eight or 10 calls coming mostly from Atlanta. I've just about given up working and am trying to protect you from getting lynched. I am spending all my time on the telephone. . . ."

The *Atlanta Journal-Constitution* called the Georgia State Chamber of Commerce in the Forsyth Building in Atlanta, to inquire if the state chamber were responsible.

"We are not trying to put the heat on (Mr. Mitchell)," said Walter Cates of the state chamber in a telephone interview.

"We just want him to know that he's got some constituents down here who support the Landrum bill."

Cates said the state chamber enlisted the aid of the Associated Industries of Georgia and the Cotton Manufacturers Group in getting a stream of telephone calls directed toward the Congressman and his friends.[9]

Charlie Halleck and Les Arends, the Republican whip, were canvassing the Republican members of Congress for support. Their efforts were very thorough and quite pointed. The factors they used in persuasion of their colleagues became clear from the nickname that was given to the labor bill—"The Congressional Retirement Act of 1959."

For this bill the Administration was prepared to go all out to deliver the votes of members of both parties. The *Congressional Record* refers to Postmaster General Arthur Summerfield and Attorney General William Rogers being present in the offices of some congressmen and even just off the floor of the House.[10] Comment was also made about the activities of Budget Director Maurice Stans. As an Administration spokesman put it: "All cabinet members who had even remote connections with Congressmen who were in doubt did what they could to convince them to support Landrum-Griffin. That in-

[9] Atlanta *Journal-Constitution*, Aug. 15, 1959.
[10] *Daily Congressional Record*, 86th Cong., 1st Sess., Aug. 13, 1959, p. 14,494.

cluded everyone except McElroy, Herter, and Flemming," he said. Though the coalition "in-person" lobbying effort was not as visible, it made up for any lack of numerical strength with pressure from sources of great prestige.

There was one strategic stone which was considered by some to have been unturned. A representative of the Chamber of Commerce remarked: "We made a mistake in not introducing a bill to balance the Shelley bill"; he then added: "But you never know when something like that will confuse the people you are sure of." The afterthought would appear from the experience of the AFL-CIO to outweigh possible advantage.

The Elliott Bill Image

Supporters of the Elliott bill agreed that the Landrum-Griffin bill could probably do what management groups said it would do. They felt that the battle was really a North-South struggle over the new industry of the nation. It was their feeling that Republicans were joining a coalition program both facets of which were contrary to their own interest. The coalition, by preventing unionization of the South and by slowing the Negro's rise from second-class citizenship, would ensure an unorganized pool of low-cost labor to attract Northern industry, or at least new industry, to the South.

The argument was never introduced into the struggle over the law. Elliott bill supporters felt that they needed the votes of Southern Democrats and thus could not afford to offend them by informing them that the Elliott bill would be less successful in achieving their goals. These goals would be economically beneficial in the short run, even if they might not be morally or spiritually beneficial—or beneficial at all—in the long run. The Elliott bill, then, was still put forth on the basis that it was the compromise solution to a difficult problem.

Potentially, the South-vs.-North argument could have won enough Northern Republican votes to offset the loss of Southern Democratic votes. "Potentially" is used in recognition of the fact that rational argument alone does not decide issues such as this. Yet, in retrospect, it would appear that the Elliott bill supporters who were also Democratic leadership supporters and Kennedy supporters were unrealis-

tic in their hopes of attracting Southern votes. They were opposed
by two of the most skilled and effective high priests of Southern
conservatism, Howard Smith and Graham Barden. And in some
ways congressmen from the one-party South are more vulnerable to
pressure from influential men in their districts, who may influence or
control nominations, than are men who must face open competition
between the two parties for election. We will see later that only a
handful of Southerners did vote against Landrum-Griffin—and, more
striking, only three or four congressmen from border states.

By the time the issue had reached the boiling point, both sides
recognized its deeper social and economic meaning, yet neither side
openly met the issue head on. The coalition was happy to press its
campaign for "reform of union corruption" with the public while
pursuing its private campaign among Southerners for continuing industrial growth. Elliott bill supporters were counting on shifting the
issue from the public one of reform to the private one of racial integration, as we shall see. The vote on the matter, however, was to
indicate that they had nothing to lose by calling the Landrum bill
what they saw it to be, and perhaps they had much to gain. Curbs
on organizational picketing, on secondary boycotts, on hot cargo
clauses, combined with conservative state laws interpreted by conservative state courts, would be effective tools against the wedges
used by unions to pry open hostile territory for unionization.

Barred from this issue, and having suffered a debacle in losing
AFL-CIO support and a further debacle in the loss of the floor leadership of Carl Elliott, the bill's supporters still looked to the chink
in the Landrum-Griffin armor, which appeared more and more decisive as the struggle became heated. But they were not to be
granted even this as an effective tool.

The Schooling Group

Before the floor debate, a number of lawyers were active in the
role of tutor. On the coalition side, Ted Iserman (who represented
the American Small Business Association in Senate and House hearings) worked closely with Graham Barden and Charlie Halleck.
Gerard Reilly worked with a number of congressmen, explaining the
impact of various provisions of the various bills. Michael Bernstein,

from the Senate committee, also worked with a number of the members of the House committee, including Representatives Robert Griffin, Edgar Hiestand, Albert Quie, Joe Holt, and William Ayres. One of the major tools used was the critical analysis of the Senate bill prepared for Senator Goldwater by the Senate minority staff. In addition to the men just mentioned, Dr. Sar A. Levitan, the labor expert of the Legislative Reference Service of the Library of Congress (a service available to and utilized by men of both parties), worked several hours one Saturday morning with an important Democratic figure. Professor Cox of Harvard was also active in educational efforts on the Democratic side.

The Debate

The debate itself established the similarity among the three bills. As we have already noted, they were substantially the same in the first six titles, the bill of rights and reform titles. The Elliott and Landrum-Griffin bills differed in their coverage of three major points in Title VII: secondary boycotts, organizational (blackmail) picketing, and federal-state jurisdiction. Landrum-Griffin was "stronger" in these three areas. The Shelley bill had no provisions on the first two subjects and would have applied federal law on the third. Beyond these general comments the issues became very complex. Because both federal courts and NLRB cases have interpreted previous statutes, the facts of any situation have to be thoroughly spelled out before the applicability of present or proposed legislation can be determined. With but a single hour at their disposal, backers of the Elliott bill were hard pressed to explain their bill fully. The unfortunate inclusion of the "Teamster" amendment, which exempted 70 percent of all unions from the reporting requirements of the act, made it necessary to spend much of the time explaining the facts behind the percentage.[11] Thus, some "objectionable" features of the Landrum-

[11] While it was agreed that by the provisions of the Elliott bill 70 percent of the unions would be exempted from financial reporting requirements, it was pointed out that these unions represented only about 10 percent of all membership in unions. Also, the exemption applied only to requirements of a single page in a seventy-two-page bill, and even this could be revoked by the Secretary of Labor. The argument that the exemption would free paper locals from reporting was answered by the fact that such locals would not be covered by this section in any case, since they would have no assets or financial transactions. They would

Griffin bill were not firmly established by the debate. Informal bulletins, seminars, and lobbying had to be used to strike at these issues. The training of the men charged with the lobbying effort was not ideal for their educational task.

Shelley bill supporters had attacked the Elliott bill from the day that it was reported out of committee. Representative Roosevelt said in the debate:

> As will quickly appear when the House and Committee of the Whole considers the bill, it is full of mistakes, inaccuracies and, in the opinion of at least a majority on the Democratic side, wholly indefensible provisions.
>
> It can be flatly stated that the bill, in its present form, is antilegitimate union in many of its important provisions, even though containing some excellent provisions, and the warning has clearly been given that attempts will be made to make it even more antilegitimate union.[12]

Representative Dent used the old McClellan-Ervin argument:

> Mr. Speaker, I am opposing the so-called labor reform bill now before us. I do so only after very serious consideration of all of its provisions.
>
> If this legislation had been confined to the first six titles dealing with the rights of members, the safeguards against racket control, the reporting of all union finances, elections, contract negotiations, the cleaning up of the no man's land in the Taft-Hartley Act, widening the powers of both the Secretary of Labor and the NLRB in keeping with the intent of the act, no Member could find too much ground for opposition.
>
> It is my sincere belief that most of the proponents of this legislation at one time or another felt the same way about it.[13]

For their part, supporters of the Elliott bill made, at most, passing reference to the Shelley bill.

Each side made a point of the similarities among the bills. Elliott supporters were "flattered" that so much of the coalition substitute came from their bill. On the other hand, coalition supporters used this to bolster their contention that their substitute was "the mini-

---

not be exempted from the other relevant sections of the bill. If argued "on the merits," the question would seem to come down to whether the procedures allowing the Secretary of Labor to remove the exemption were adequate and whether it would be possible to prevent present unions from splitting into smaller units merely to qualify for exemption. As argued, this was a "Teamster amendment" (which it has been seen to be) that would exempt seven out of ten unions from the bill's reporting requirements.

[12] *Daily Congressional Record,* 86th Cong., 1st Sess., July 23, 1959, p. 12,858.
[13] *Ibid.,* July 29, 1959, p. 13,371.

mum necessary" for a moderate and fair bill. Shelley supporters claimed their bill was a "pure" reform bill without extraneous provisions. There were several clear, well-reasoned statements of the issues on each side of this debate. There were also many slogan-statements and statements designed as much to cloud as to illuminate issues.

Over-all floor leadership of the legislation was in the hands of Chairman Graham Barden. He conducted himself forcefully, attempting to move proceedings along as rapidly as possible and also keeping the other groups on the defensive as much as possible.

Barden and Judge Smith were seeking support for the coalition bill among Southern congressmen. Early in their campaign they became aware that their backers were few. In the Texas delegation, where Speaker Rayburn's influence was supposed to be strong, they felt that, at most, they had two or three votes, among them Bruce Alger's. As the two Southern gentlemen talked, explained, and cajoled, they began to feel their backing grow. "Judge, I do believe there has been considerable accretion, especially from the Texas delegation," Barden is reported to have said to Smith at one point. They continued to talk and explain while the public campaign continued to yield letters, telephone calls, and telegrams. The pressure mounted on all sides.

The floor tactics of the coalition group included continual reference to the bill as "moderate." The execution of this tactic produced a rather staged appearance, however. Landrum had led off with a general discussion of the intent of the coalition measure (including comment on several of the witnesses heard in Los Angeles), followed by Griffin, who gave a more detailed account of its provisions. Representative Alger of Texas was then recognized. He demanded that the labor movement be put under the antitrust laws, referring to his proposed legislation to accomplish this goal. When Alger had finished, Griffin commented:

Mr. Chairman, I thank the gentleman from Texas and say that the gentleman's statement, I believe, serves to point out that the substitute is a minimum bill. It might be well at this point to mention some provisions that are not in it.
There is no antitrust law provision in this bill.

There is nothing dealing directly with the use of union dues for political activities.

There is no national right-to-work law in any of these bills.

There is not a secret strike ballot provision in this substitute bill.[14]

The bipartisanship of the bill was also stressed. There was a good deal of anxiety that it might be identified as a "Republican" measure or a "politically motivated" measure.

August 11 was devoted to speechmaking by the three sides in the issue; no voting took place. By the twelfth the Elliott bill had the support of such men as Representatives Ludwig Teller and Cleveland Bailey, as well as those men who had been among the leadership's "reserves" in the committee. This was the first tangible evidence of de facto support by the labor movement for the Elliott bill. Both Representatives Bolling and Metcalf spoke briefly for the Elliott side. Shortly after the debate opened, Bolling read a portion of the speech Elliott would have made had he been present, and Bolling expressed his own support for the measure. Metcalf introduced a letter from Robert Kennedy, expressing the view that the Elliott bill best met the requirements for legislation demonstrated by the Senate select committee's two and one-half years of hearings and investigations. This letter was answered shortly by members of the coalition, who quoted Senator McClellan as disagreeing with what McClellan called "Kennedy's personal opinion" on the legislation.

The supporters of the committee bill began to stress the probability that passage of the Landrum-Griffin substitute would lead to no legislation at all, since it would be completely unpalatable to the Senate. There was also much speculation in the corridors of the House and in the press that, if a bill were passed and sent to a joint conference with the Senate, Barden would prevent the emergence of any legislation. This rumor was apparently of sufficient effect to cause Barden to issue a specific denial on the floor.[15] The six hours of debate ended on the afternoon of the twelfth, and the Landrum-Griffin bill was proposed as a substitute for H.R.8342. Representative Perkins then offered the Shelley-Roosevelt bill as a substitute for the first substitute. The two substitutes were then opened to perfecting amendment.

[14] *Ibid.*, Aug. 11, 1959, pp. 14,198, 14,199.
[15] *Ibid.*, Aug. 13, 1959, p. 14,484.

Adam Clayton Powell offered an amendment to the Landrum-Griffin bill to incorporate civil rights provisions therein. Landrum opposed the amendment. James Roosevelt then rose in support of the Powell amendment. He made the following statement:

I am not going to completely belabor the Griffin-Landrum bill. I have tried to find some good points in it and I think I have found at least one thing which shows that we are making some progress. You will find, for instance, on page 58 of the Griffin-Landrum bill in title IV a statement which applies to the entire act and says that a union which attempts to suspend, expel or otherwise discipline any of its members for exercising any right to which he is entitled under the provisions of the act—that is the whole bill—then the enforcement shall be found in section 210, and in section 210 which is on page 29 we find that we have given the power to the Secretary of Labor under the Griffin-Landrum bill to bring an action for such relief, as may be appropriate, including injunctions to restrain any such violation and to compel compliance with the title; and that the action may be brought in the district court of the United States where the violation occurred or, at the option of the parties, in the U.S. District Court for the District of Columbia.

This is the very thing which the gentlemen from the South, up to this time, in other bills of rights have fought with all their hearts to eliminate from civil rights procedures and have told us is wrong. I am happy to see it in the Griffin-Landrum bill. It means that there will be a precedent, because I have heard no one get up, Judge Smith or anybody else, to say that this was wrong. And so, while I think it would be a dark day if the Griffin-Landrum bill were adopted I would have to say that there is at least that silver lining, that there seems to be some beginning of the understanding of the necessity for civil rights to be employed in a proper way in order to have them enforced as the law of the land and not just of any one particular section of it.

We will now see whether our Republican colleagues will vote against civil rights for the sake of preserving the coalition that fights real progress and protection for all, not some, Americans.[16]

This was the end of the civil rights question as a weapon of the anti-coalition forces. The question of premeditation or accident in the premature unveiling of this issue by Roosevelt remains unresolved. Motivation for premeditation would be difficult to understand. In any case, the premature action gave the Landrum-Griffin group an opportunity to eliminate the issue.

Just how they accomplished this is indicative of the very close

[16] *Ibid.*, Aug. 12, 1959, p. 14,389.

situation which both sides sensed at the climax. Representative William Cramer of Florida rose to point out a very significant fact:

Mr. Cramer: Mr. Chairman, I take this time solely for the purpose of clarifying the Record to some extent in regard to the remarks of the distinguished gentleman from California (Mr. Roosevelt) concerning an attempted comparison of this bill, the Landrum-Griffin bill, with the so-called title III of the civil rights provision. The gentleman from California very adroitly failed to mention and apparently purposely overlooked the matter which clarifies the matter that was an issue in the civil rights bill, that is, the issue of trial by jury. The Landrum-Griffin bill provides fair trial by jury in any criminal contempt as is provided in section 608, page 57, of the Landrum-Griffin bill, which was the real issue in that civil rights fight and right of trial by jury in criminal contempt cases is specifically protected under the Landrum-Griffin bill as it was provided for on the floor of the Senate in the Kennedy-Ervin bill.

Mr. Roosevelt: Mr. Chairman, will the gentleman yield?

Mr. Cramer: I yield to the gentleman from California.

Mr. Roosevelt: What I referred to is not a criminal case; it is a civil action.

Mr. Cramer: Contempt in the form of criminal contempt is the means of enforcing a court order in a civil action of injunction as I am sure the gentleman realizes and as was successfully argued, at least in the Senate, for the civil rights bill and those objections have been overcome in H.R.8400 by section 608 and I am glad to see that the majority as well accepts the doctrine now in that it is also included in the committee bill and was unanimously made a part of the Senate bill.

Section 608 of the Landrum-Griffin bill provides, in this connection, the following:

Criminal Contempt

Sec. 608. No person shall be punished for any criminal contempt allegedly committed outside the immediate presence of the court in connection with any civil action prosecuted by the Secretary or any other person in any district court of the United States under the provisions of this act unless the facts constituting such criminal contempt are established by the verdict of the jury in a proceeding in the district court of the United States, which jury shall be chosen and empaneled in the manner prescribed by the law governing trial juries in criminal prosecutions in the district courts of the United States.[17]

This debate shows that the issue was somewhat overplayed, especially in the statement prepared for distribution from Representative

[17] *Ibid.*, Aug. 12, 1959, p. 14,391.

Bolling's office. When the vote came, the Powell amendment to H.R.8400 was rejected, 215 to 160.[18]

After some further debate the Shelley substitute was put to a vote. It was defeated, 245 to 132.[19] Following this vote the Committee of the Whole House rose.

Several people in the labor movement have focused on this vote as the one giving the real measure of labor support in the House. The 132 votes did represent die-hard labor supporters, but these are not the people who decide issues.

Now the showdown had arrived. The defeat of the Shelley bill had been expected, but here it was, and the federation was faced with two bills which it had officially opposed. There was little time to reverse the official position, though growing support for the Elliott bill by Democratic committee members indicated that the change had taken place.

There had been unanimity in the labor movement in opposition to the Landrum-Griffin bill, but the important factor for many congressmen in an issue on which the public is truly stirred is that they be *for* something. Many had, therefore, made a decision to support Landrum-Griffin. They would be for a bill which had a chance. The management groups would be pleased, and, if it were defeated, there would still be the Elliott bill before the House for consideration. All-out support by a congressman for the Elliott bill would have pleased almost no one.

At this point the AFL-CIO did make it clear that the vote on which it would judge the "friendliness" or "unfriendliness" of congressmen toward labor would be on the Landrum-Griffin substitution vote. As a last-minute change in the official criterion for support, the effectiveness of this maneuver was greatly undercut. Several legislative representatives, however, had been advocating such a position unofficially to the members of Congress from the beginning.

The Final Hours

The joint operations group of the Democratic leadership and the AFL-CIO had tabulated its estimate of votes over and over, to the

[18] *Ibid.*, Aug. 12, 1959, p. 14,391.   [19] *Ibid.*, Aug. 12, 1959, p. 14,395.

point where the key strategists could recite the name and voting intention of each member alphabetically from memory. At no time did
they have a majority of "definite" votes. The upper limit broke at
about two hundred. It appeared that the addition of "probables"
and "possibles" would make the difference. Any manipulation of the
voting would be very dangerous in such a fluid situation.

The AFL-CIO had the services of a special representative, Bob
Oliver, during this final stage of consideration of the bill. Oliver
knew the Speaker well and was close to members of the Texas delegation. His job was that of federation tactician with authority to
make some of the on-the-spot decisions.

The situation was both tense and intense. Lobbying efforts had
reached a white heat.

For the coalition, Smith and Barden, aided by Landrum, continued soliciting support among the Democrats; Halleck, Arends, and
Griffin did so among the Republicans. There was no member left to
chance. The intention of each was solicited. If it were "wrong," last-
minute pressure was applied.

Each legislative expert had his own estimate of outcome of the
key vote. Discounting those on each side who "knew" they would
win by one, two, or six votes, as the case might be, the situation was
in real doubt up to the last minute. The eleventh-hour maneuvers
of the Landrum-Griffin supporters demonstrated their anxiety.

On the other side, Udall and Thompson were pleading with the
AFL-CIO for the flexibility to allow amendment to the Elliott bill.
They cited the congressmen who had come to them requesting minor
changes in provisions in exchange for their support. "You draft the
change yourself," these congressmen had said. "Even introduce it
yourself, but we can't vote with you as the bill stands." The experience in the other house was still too fresh to allow the AFL-CIO to
agree to take the chance on sustaining undesired changes by opening Elliott to amendment. There is some indication of a change in
approach at the opening of debate on August 13, at least as a maneuver to help against the substitute:

Mr. Machrowicz: I wonder if the gentleman will agree with me that
the parliamentary situation at this moment is such that if the motion to
substitute the Landrum bill is adopted, this Committee will have no

possible chance of going through the Landrum bill section by section but will have to accept it in whole. On the other hand, if the Landrum bill is defeated, we will then be able to go into the committee bill section by section in an orderly fashion and amend it in every way possible.

Mr. Udall: The gentleman has stated the parliamentary situation correctly.[20]

But Udall's position is made clear by the inquiry which followed immediately:

Mr. Jones of Missouri: I want to ask this question. Suppose that would happen. Would you as one of the sponsors of this committee bill agree to an amendment removing the amendment which you have put in the bill which weakens the hot cargo section? With one or two small amendments I will vote for it. I would like to have the gentleman's view on it.

Mr. Udall: I appreciate very much the honest statement of the gentleman. As I regard this provision, it is a harmless disclaimer which does not add or subtract a thing from the significance of the section.[21]

The liberals would not agree to perfecting amendments to Elliott before the Landrum-Griffin vote. If the substitute were rejected in the Committee of the Whole, then the Elliott bill would be open to amendment. The parliamentary situation was clarified a few moments later by Representative Barden, who pointed out that Landrum-Griffin was, and would be, open to amendment.

The coalition ranks were split by a dissenting voice. Representative Clare Hoffman of Michigan made an attack on the coalition leaders.[22] He stated that the coalition had had pledges for enough votes to pass the Landrum-Griffin bill since the afternoon before, and continued:

I cannot see any reason why other Members of the House who may agree with the general purposes of that bill should be treated so arbitrarily—as though they were spies or thieves or something similar. . . .

For myself, I never knew what they were up to, although I suspected, and I understood who was writing the bill. Someone was objecting over here on this side or the charge was made in the Committee on Rules that the NAM wrote it. Of course, they had a finger in the pie, and why should they not? And, of course, the Chamber of Commerce had a hand and foot in it as was their right and duty. I have gone along with those two groups. They are fine. . . .

[20] *Ibid.*, Aug. 13, 1959, p. 14,484.   [21] *Ibid.*, Aug. 13, 1959, p. 14,484.
[22] The motivation for Hoffman's attack can be inferred from his statement. It will be further discussed later in the chapter.

But, I can see no reason, absolutely none, why the committee should not give us a chance to see what the Republican—my leader is not here— he did not speak on this—so there is nothing partisanship [sic] about this—to see the substitute before it is bottled. They act as though they were possessed of all wisdom. Just get that in your head and keep it there —oh no there is nothing political about this proceeding—there is no partisanship at all in this matter. Just how dumb do we think our home people are?

The Republicans do not want it, the Democrats do not want it. At least some of them, I mean. Some in both parties do and some do not. So we have this little coalition which I will be glad to go along with in the effort to make it law, although I do not like the roughshod, the unfair Hoffa way, in which they kick their opposition around and outlaw me.[23]

Hoffman, who was eighty-four at the time, was known to become emotional on occasion, and his outburst was generally ignored. Nonetheless, he was one of the most colorful members of Congress in his day.

Shortly afterwards, in the debate, Dale Alford of Arkansas rose to make a spirited condemnation of the civil rights implications of the substitute measure. Representative Cramer again explained that the interpretation had been taken care of by the guarantee of jury trial in contempt cases arising from injustices. He then went on:

It is my understanding that an amendment will be offered to section 609 which will have the effect of permitting a union member to bring an action himself in his own name pursuant to section 102, and I believe that this will overcome the second objection suggested, which is that of an unnecessary injection of the executive branch on the Federal level into law enforcement matters, which would result if the Secretary could bring an action in behalf of a union member.[24]

This is partially an admission of substance to the attack made on the bill, and, perhaps equally, an admission of the emotional appeal of the issue.

On this third day of the debate Majority Leader McCormack joined the Elliott forces. He baited Minority Leader Halleck with his blast at Administration lobbying:

Mr. McCormack: Mr. Chairman, we have now come to what might well be termed the "nutcracking" stage of this legislation. I saw it coming.

[23] *Daily Congressional Record*, 86th Cong., 1st Sess., Aug. 13, 1959, p. 14,485.
[24] *Ibid.*, Aug. 13, 1959, p. 14,490.

We have come to that point. There is no question that from all sides there are persons and groups interested for or against certain bills. That pressure is upon the Members of the House.

For example, the National Association of Manufacturers is very strong for this bill, the Landrum bill. In fact, the bill is not strong enough for the NAM. The NAM has opposed labor legislation during my 31 years as a Member of the House. They opposed every progressive piece of legislation—social security, minimum wage, farm legislation. Everything the NAM opposed. The Chamber of Commerce has also opposed every progressive piece of legislation.

I imagine there may be 25 or 30 Members of this House who still have their minds open. I imagine most of them are on the Republican side, from what I hear. They come from close districts.

May I say that last year Postmaster General Summerfield pressured them on several bills, as he is today on this bill now.[25]

This invitation to polarize the struggle on party lines was not accepted by Halleck. Still, the support of the Democratic floor leader was welcome to the hard-pressed Elliott forces.

At one point during the House floor battle the Speaker is reported to have come to chat with Graham Barden, who, as we have seen, controlled the time for the Democrats. He asked Barden if he had decided who was going to speak last. Barden replied: "Yes, I've decided! I am!"

The clear implication of the question was a request by the Speaker that Barden allow him to make the final statement on the bill (in favor of the Elliott bill). This Barden said he wouldn't do. It was like asking a lawyer to give up his natural advantage in a courtroom. By custom the defense is allowed to speak last in the final summary. This is done purposely so that the jury will have the summary in their minds during their deliberations on a verdict. Barden told the Speaker that he would certainly allow him time to speak, but that he, Barden, would make the closing statement.

The floor fight raged on. Orrin Harris, chairman of the Committee on Interstate and Foreign Commerce, proposed an amendment to "strike out the words 'or the Railway Labor Act, as amended' and insert 'but does not include any industry or activity consisting solely of any employer or employers subject to the Railway Act, as amended.' " [26] The Subcommittee on Transportation and Aeronautics

<hr>

[25] *Ibid.*, Aug. 13, 1959, p. 14,494.   [26] *Ibid.*, Aug. 13, 1959, p. 14,505.

had been hastily called into morning session to approve this amendment. The sudden nature of the move was documented by committee members who spoke shortly after Harris. The amendment, which proposed the exemption of the unions covered by the Railway Labor Act from the requirements of the Landrum-Griffin bill, was an attempt to gain the votes of six Republican congressmen who were under great pressure from railroad unionists in their districts. If it passed, it would clear the way for the congressmen to vote in favor of the substitute; if it lost, the congressmen could always say to their union constituents that they "did their best." The introduction of the Harris amendment showed that the situation was not viewed with rose glasses on the coalition side.

Representative Udall jumped on the issue:

Mr. Udall: This amendment very plainly let the cat out of the bag. The Landrum-Griffin people do not have the votes, and this is an attempt to get them. Let me give you some facts, and these are the facts. First, the railway labor people have not asked to be exempted from this act. I talked to their chief counsel only this morning, and he said to me he did not even know how to draft an amendment to exempt his unions.[27]

Other representatives reported the opposition of the railway unions to the exemption. Many speakers called it a cynical attempt to gain votes, a means to divide and conquer. Representative John Dingell was the final speaker. "This is a bad amendment. It reveals bad faith. . . . This amendment is a transparent favoritism, so obviously calculated to purchase votes in a cynical hypocritical way that it should be voted down unanimously." [28] The amendment was voted down, 183 to 179, a mere four-vote margin.

There is still a great deal of controversy over the amendment. One representative of the Chamber of Commerce said: "The Harris amendment was a real blunder. We should never have introduced it." A key congressman said: "The Harris amendment was a mistake, but we couldn't have stopped it if we wanted to." An Administration spokesman said: "We had the votes and there was no question about it. If we needed those other six, we would have passed the amendment." In a later interview, however, the same man admitted that

[27] Ibid., Aug. 13, 1959, p. 14,506.   [28] Ibid., Aug. 13, 1959, p. 14,508.

the real reason these Republicans didn't vote for Landrum-Griffin was that they didn't like its provisions. They used the most convenient excuse they had—pressure from their districts—as a rationalization to their leaders. Even after the Harris amendment, they remained firm. The defeat of the Harris amendment was a small boost to the Elliott forces, but the size of the majority showed real reason for concern.

Representative Teller was the first speaker recognized after the flurry over the Harris amendment. He raised the question of applicability of the secondary boycott provision to the International Ladies Garment Workers Union. Both Landrum and Griffin replied that their intent was that it should not apply. Griffin's statement was that "the amendments to Taft-Hartley Act proposed in our bill, H.R.8400, would in no way affect the existing law concerning the allied employer doctrine, and there is no intent to do so." [29] Thus, by this bit of legislative history the way was cleared for further support for the Landrum-Griffin bill.

Graham Barden proposed, at about 3 p.m., that debate on all amendments close in thirty minutes. There was objection to this arbitrary speed-up, so he modified his request and made a motion to cut off debate at 4 p.m. There were four amendments to the Landrum-Griffin substitute at the desk, two of them proposed by Representative Hoffman. Representative Paul Jones of Missouri demanded a division on Barden's motion. It was approved, 278 to 26. Jones then got the floor on a preferential motion and expressed his exasperation at not being recognized during the whole afternoon. He made a suggestion and a statement. The Barden motion had closed any possibility of modifying the Elliott bill prior to the vote on Landrum-Griffin, he said.

My suggestion here today is that the committee bill be amended in those respects where it has weakened the present law, and to eliminate some of the features of the committee bill that have been advocated by the Hoffa interests. . . .

Furthermore, since we convened here today, I have talked with some of the sponsors of the committee bill, and was unable to secure any assurance of support for the amendments which I think are needed to perfect

[29] *Ibid.*, Aug. 13, 1959, p. 14,509.

and improve the committee bill. This should explain my decision to vote for the Landrum bill.[30]

Hoffman's first amendment to eliminate strikes in public utilities was rejected. Then Representative John Dowdy of Texas offered an amendment: "Amendment offered by Mr. Dowdy to the amendment offered by Mr. Landrum: On page 58, line 11, strike out '210' and insert '102.'" He stated that he was "inclined to believe that it was a misprint or a transposition of figures that make the amendment necessary." [31] Landrum and Griffin announced that they would accept the amendment. This is the amendment referred to earlier by Representative Cramer. It would apply the individual remedies available in Section 102 in place of remedies brought in the name of the Secretary of Labor in Section 210 to violation of the rights specified in Title I of the bill; the reader can judge the accuracy of Mr. Dowdy's statement of the need for the amendment. It was voted on anyway and approved, 207 to 158. Thus, the civil rights loophole was closed.

The difficulty of their position and the loss of the ace-in-the-hole civil rights issue convinced the leadership strategists for the Elliott bill that they could not afford to take the psychological setback of losing the teller vote, the step necessary if the Elliott bill was to be voted on unamended. This meant that, even if they were successful in fighting off the Landrum-Griffin substitute, they would face individual amendments to "strengthen" the Elliott bill.

Representative J. Carlton Loser proposed an amendment to Landrum-Griffin to reduce the penalty for force or violence or any disorder in a union hall from $10,000 to $1,000.[32] The amendment was agreed to.

Representative Hoffman then introduced his second amendment, designed to bring unions under the antitrust laws. There were but few minutes left for debate, a fact which Hoffman took as a personal gag rule. The amendment was rejected. Hoffman grew more angry. Representative Basil Whitener offered a minor amendment which was accepted. A few last-minute speeches were made. Four o'clock was reached, and the tellers were ordered on the amendment of the gentleman from Georgia.

[30] *Ibid.*, Aug. 13, 1959, pp. 14,510, 14,511.
[31] *Ibid.*, Aug. 13, 1959, p. 14,513.   [32] *Ibid.*, Aug. 13, 1959, p. 14,513.

Many of the congressmen were undecided on the issue even as they rose from their seats to head toward the tellers. The floor of the House was crowded; the galleries were full; the pressure had reached its maximum. Walking down the aisle, congressmen could see labor and management representatives watching them from above. More important to those from marginal areas who had not yet made their decision were the correspondents from the hometown newspapers who were watching and who could report their unrecorded vote to the people back home. Some in the Texas delegation were considering the Speaker's last request, relayed by one of their number: "If you can't vote with us, would you consider not going through the tellers on either side?" Other representatives were holding back to watch their colleagues in hopes that a trend might be revealed to help them pick the winner.

In the gallery a muffled cry went up when Texas Representative W. Homer Thornberry went through the tellers on the "aye" side. "Look, Thornberry has voted wrong!" commented one union representative. Bob Oliver, himself one step behind, confided: "No, that's part of the strategy." On the floor some congressmen, noting this and other key votes, made a last-minute decision to join those who were voting in favor of substituting the Landrum-Griffin bill for the Elliott bill.

A few Elliott supporters had remained in the cloakroom, not aware of the switch from the earlier proposed strategy. But, when the votes were counted, it would have made no difference. They were beaten! The tellers announced their totals: ayes, 215, noes, 200.[33] A change of eight votes could have made the difference.

If it had been possible to defeat the Landrum-Griffin substitute when the House itself took a record vote on the question, the Elliott bill would have been the only bill still remaining for consideration and, under the rule, would not have been open for amendment. This was the situation that the Elliott strategists had originally hoped for —with one exception. They did not have the votes to reverse the tide. If, however, the civil rights issue had been introduced at this point, might not the situation have been quite different?

When the Committee of the Whole rose, it reported its acceptance

[33] *Ibid.*, Aug. 13, 1959, p. 14,519.

of the Landrum substitute. The question was referred to the House for a record vote. By the vote the House would accept or reject the Landrum-Griffin amendment, as amended, as a substitute for the Elliott bill. The House faced the following parliamentary inquiries:

Mr. Thompson of New Jersey: Is it my understanding that the vote about to be taken is on whether or not the substitute will be accepted, and that it is not a vote on final passage?

The Speaker: It will be a vote on the amendment adopted in the Committee of the Whole. . . .

Mr. O'Neill: Will a vote to recommit then be in order?

The Speaker: After the third reading.

Mr. O'Neill: And then a vote would be in order on the final passage?

The Speaker: That is correct.

Mr. Halleck: At this juncture, then, if this substitute is voted down, no further amendments could be had to the so-called committee bill?

The Speaker: That is correct. . . .

Mr. Hoffman of Michigan: When will I get an opportunity to ask for the engrossment of the bill?

The Speaker: After it is ordered to be engrossed and read a third time.[34]

Representative Hoffman indicated his intention to delay proceedings. This may have influenced certain congressmen, such as three Maryland representatives who, seeing the majority against them, decided to shift their support to Landrum-Griffin on the record vote. Or perhaps these three were among those looking at the hometown correspondents who were ready to write local headlines.

When the vote was taken, the total represented a near record percentage of eligible House members. Only four of those eligible did not vote. Out of 434, 430 cast their votes on the labor reform issue. On this, the decisive ballot, Landrum-Griffin was substituted for the Elliott bill by a vote of 229 to 201.[35] The vote, though not unexpected, was still a shock. In opposition to the entire labor movement and the official commitment of the Democratic leadership of the House, the coalition group had pressed to victory. The Nossiter article provides some evidence for the cause:

Of the 54 target Congressmen, 23 voted for the bill, or more than the 14 whose votes decided the issue.

Since the entire group of 54 had originally been selected on the premise

[34] *Ibid.*, Aug. 13, 1959, p. 14,519.   [35] *Ibid.*, Aug. 13, 1959, p. 14,519.

that they leaned towards a softer bill, the lobbyists claim their missionary work helped produce the margin of victory.

Business lobbyists, pleased with their efforts, expect to use these techniques with more success in the future.[36]

But the battle would not be officially over until the following day.

This was the climax. It represented an apparent stinging defeat for the Democratic leaders and for labor. Before we analyze it further, let us look at a few sidelights, including Clare Hoffman's parliamentary maneuver that led to an anticlimax.

The Role of Lyndon Johnson

When the votes were counted, the supporters of the Elliott bill found that they had lost every one of the votes which they had listed as "doubtful." Nowhere did this appear more striking than in the Texas delegation, where only four of twenty-two members voted with the leader of the delegation, Speaker Rayburn. The support given by Rayburn to H.R.8342 has already been stated. There is little doubt that the vote was a setback to his personal prestige, since he had so clearly laid it on the line. The question was, how did this come about?

Many people point to fellow Texan, Senate Majority Leader Johnson, to help explain this. The actions of business lobbyists could not explain all problems, especially that of the Speaker's delegation in Texas. Before continuing the inquiry, one of the institutions of the House, "the board of education," must be explained.

"The board of education" met in a small room on the first floor of the House-side of the Capitol building. Each day at about 5:30 or 6 p.m. Speaker Rayburn repaired to this room with a few regular or invited guests for relaxation and a quiet discussion of politics. Individual congressmen were often invited to participate in the ceremony, but there were several who were usually present and some who had a standing invitation. Among the regulars were Majority Leader McCormack, Representative Bolling, Texas Representatives Olin Teague and Frank Ikard, and the Speaker's assistant, D. B. Hardiman. Among those who had standing invitations were Lyndon

[36] Nossiter, "The Labor Bill Lobby."

Johnson, who frequently stopped by after the day in the Senate, and Charlie Halleck, who often made an appearance, although he himself was host to a similar institution. The discussions usually took place over highballs.

Johnson was often present when members of the House Texas delegation were there. Representative Thornberry is an especially close protégé of Johnson. On several occasions the discussion got around to the great pressure on the congressmen from home districts. Johnson is reported to have stated in casual conversation that the men could not afford to go against such pressure. They should vote to protect themselves in their districts.

These words may sound innocuous, but the classic phrase used by a group representative or a leadership person when he wishes to release a congressman from obligation is "Vote your district." In other words, forget any obligation to me and vote as you feel would be politically most beneficial to you.

The Texas delegation was the key to the loss on the vote to substitute Landrum-Griffin. When Thornberry and others went through the tellers on the "wrong side," several Maryland votes also changed sides, as we have seen. The Senator from Texas had been in conversation with members of his state's delegation on several occasions. He was a candidate for the Presidency of the United States, and his major rival was closely identified with the Elliott bill and stood to lose most if the Landrum-Griffin bill passed. Add to this private statements by several other representatives that "We can't prove it, but we're sure that Lyndon Johnson ruined support for the Elliott bill among members of the Texas delegation," and the implication is hard to avoid. The fact that the Speaker must necessarily have been present during such conversation does raise a further question.

Several members of the Texas delegation stated that they had attended the seminars with the Speaker and Representative Udall and others, that the Speaker had indicated his preference for the Elliott bill on several occasions, but that in their view they felt he would "have done more" if he had really wanted to ensure the passage of the committee bill. They also stated that there had been no reprisals against them for their vote and no change in their personal relationships with the Speaker after the vote.

One reprisal move was attempted against a Texas congressman by a group of Northern liberal congressmen when his pet pork-barrel project came up. The reprisal failed to carry, apparently because of lack of organization.[37]

The Background of Clare Hoffman's Move

When Administration officials selected Robert Griffin as the Republican whose name would appear on the substitute bill and in subsequent headlines, they did so without prior notification of or consultation with two congressmen who were senior to him, Carol Kearns and Clare Hoffman. Kearns had already introduced two bills, and Administration people had reason to feel that he might not be completely reliable. Hoffman had been an outspoken "labor baiter" but also possessed a burning ambition to sponsor a major labor bill from the time he had first introduced one in 1937. Hoffman, an erratic, fiery, white-haired congressman, eighty-four years of age at the time, was one of the most colorful men of the House. We saw some of his tactics during the appearance of John L. Lewis in the hearings of the House committee.

Ordinarily, the senior member of a committee is given an opportunity to sponsor major bills. When the two congressmen learned that they had been bypassed, both were angered by the implied affront. Hoffman made many statements in the *Congressional Record* which show his feelings.

After the floor vote to substitute the Landrum-Griffin bill, Congressman Hoffman was recognized. He utilized the antiquated parliamentary device of requesting an engrossed copy [38] of the bill prior to a final vote on the issue. This is a privileged motion taking precedence over other business. It introduced a full day's delay before the vote could be made final. Minority Leader Halleck was outraged. He had just tasted sweet success in an all-out struggle, and his victory could now be jeopardized. Red-faced, he intercepted Hoffman, who

[37] A reliable source states that Representative Jim Wright was refused labor backing in the 1961 Texas Senate primary elections solely because he voted for Landrum-Griffin (and then Republican "Rip" Tower beat Blakely for the seat).

[38] In essence, an engrossed copy is a copy of the bill which embodies all the amendments adopted during consideration of the bill. It can usually be prepared overnight.

was striding up the aisle by his desk. Before he could unleash his own anger, Halleck was stopped short by Hoffman's outburst. In his drive toward success Halleck had violated the "rules of the game" and thus brought about the situation he now faced. Hoffman, himself still smarting, unleashed a colorful blast and then continued up the aisle. Halleck had not had a chance to open his mouth.

Significance of Delay

The vote on the substitute had been a close one, achieved with all the power the coalition could bring to bear. The vote had come this day because the coalition feared the effect that labor lobbying might have if allowed to run much longer. Although the apparent result of the massive importation of unionists had been virtually negative, the approach was a traditional one, indicated the degree of commitment of the labor people, and was not discounted by the coalition side. The scale of the effort frightened them a bit. The margin of victory had come from several members who had been undecided and from last minute change-overs. It was clear from the rule for considering the bill that there could be one motion to recommit with or without instruction. The delay provided the labor supporters an opportunity to rally their forces and perhaps use the opening to recommit the Landrum-Griffin bill to the committee.[39]

From the point of view of the Elliott bill supporters, while they recognized the opportunity available to them, they also were aware of the power of the local newspaper. The delay allowed the papers free rein to headline the names of those who were opposed to "strong" labor legislation. These men would be fidgeting in the unfavorable light for twenty-four hours. The vote the next day would more than likely continue the trend of eroding strength which had been developing. The crystallizing effect of key votes has been discussed earlier. Since the real test was lost, a congressman might just as well vote his district at this point.

After worried conversation, Charlie Halleck and Ed McCabe saw that it would be possible to forestall any Democratic moves, but it would require the help of another man they had bypassed. A motion

---

[39] After all, the labor people had been able to do just this on the McClellan bill of rights in the Senate several weeks earlier.

to recommit must be made by one opposed to the bill in question. On a motion to recommit, the senior man from the committee with jurisdiction who desires recognition is recognized by the chair. Carol Kearns was thus in a pivotal position. He would be recognized above all others except Barden himself, but Barden could hardly be called a man in opposition to Landrum-Griffin. Nor could Kearns, for that matter, unless some gimmick could be worked out.

Halleck went to Kearns to court his motion. At first Kearns was not receptive, but then he thought of the possibility of bringing out the so-called "second Kearns bill." After saying all the things that a man in his position would and could say, Halleck enlisted Kearns's support for the Party with no strings attached.

The Final Vote

The next morning the House resumed discussion of the labor bill. At the appointed moment Kearns sprang to his feet. In another part of the Chamber Representative Roosevelt had risen simultaneously. The chair recognized the senior man, Kearns, and he made the following motion:

> Mr. Kearns: Mr. Speaker, I offer a motion to recommit.
> The Speaker: Is the gentleman opposed to the bill?
> Mr. Kearns: Mr. Speaker, speaking to the motion, the reason I am making this motion to recommit is because I have a bill of my own, H.R.7265, which I thoroughly believe in and which was not considered. Therefore, I am opposed to the bill.[40]

As anticipated, and especially since no one had heard of this bill, the motion was defeated, 280 to 148.[41] Kearns strode up the aisle to the applause of the Republican side of the House, the man who was willing to forget insult for the good of the Party. As he left the floor, he was met by a tearful, if not overly sophisticated, labor representative, who expressed a deep gratitude for the attempt Kearns had made to recommit the "antilabor" Landrum-Griffin bill.

Shortly thereafter, the Landrum-Griffin bill passed the House by the lopsided margin of 303 to 125.[42]

This final vote on the bill has been the subject of much contro-

[40] *Daily Congressional Record*, 86th Cong., 1st Sess., Aug. 14, 1959, p. 14,540.
[41] *Ibid.*, Aug. 14, 1959, p. 14,540.
[42] *Ibid.*, Aug. 14, 1959, pp. 14,540, 14,541.

versy. The Teamsters Union threatened to use it as an indication of antilabor sentiment on the part of congressmen. Yet, it was a vote taken after the battle was lost. There was some talk about "holding the vote" to strengthen the hand of the liberal conferees when the Senate and House Conference Committee met to resolve the differences in the bills, but this implied a degree of control which neither the liberal forces nor the AFL-CIO possessed. Some union legislative representatives frankly told their friends to vote their districts. It is no use having friends who are not re-elected! [43] Perhaps the real significance of this vote is an indication of the pressure in favor of the Landrum-Griffin measure.

The Conferees

Once the vote was settled, the next question was that of appointing conferees from the House. Technically, this is done by the Speaker, but usually he accepts the recommendation of the committee chairman. Apparently, the usual procedure was followed in this instance. Four Democrats—Barden, Landrum, Perkins, and Thompson—and three Republicans—Kearns, Ayres, and Griffin—were named.[44]

The reaction of the AFL-CIO was immediate and agonized. Five of the seven House conferees were charter members of the coalition. Had the Speaker been a passionate advocate of his cause, he could have used the power which was nominally his, just as his opponents had done with such telling effect at every point throughout the history of the bill, and appointed a conference committee more favorable to a "moderate" approach. But the fact that the split was four Democrats to three Republicans and that Barden himself could hardly be left off any conference committee makes this view seem rather hopeless. In the conference voting is by houses, not by individuals. A four-to-three margin is as effective as a five-to-two margin (if all votes can be counted on, and at least one might not have been). It is clear that the Conference Committee, though lopsided, did represent the majority view of the House of Representatives, if not of the House Committee on Education and Labor.

[43] One of these legislative representatives indicated that his statement was for quotation and attribution if that was felt to be necessary.

[44] *Daily Congressional Record*, 86th Cong., 1st Sess., Aug. 14, 1959, p. 14,555.

IX. TWO BILLS BECOME A LAW

AT this point the balance of power between labor and management in the overwhelmingly Democratic Eighty-sixth Congress has been forcefully made clear. In the face of vote after vote in the friendly environment of the House Committee on Education and Labor, the union leaders had steadfastly refused to recognize that they could not command the content of legislation. Rather, they clung to the belief—repeatedly demonstrated to be false—that the Eighty-sixth Congress would do their bidding, that the election of 1958 had placed them in command of a congressional majority, that they had the power management propagandists told them (and the nation) that they had. Finally, after there were no more votes to be taken and the House of Representatives had passed a law to which all unions were unalterably opposed, there was no further room for illusion. Even if the actions of the AFL-CIO had sprung from the desire to fight the good fight in spite of a realistic appraisal of their position, the fight was now lost. The next problem was one of using the absolute strength of the labor movement to salvage some order from the impending chaos. And there was no question that the labor movement had great political strength and that it could be amplified by realistic strategy and effective interaction with congressional leaders.

Now the overoptimism began to appear in the other camp. Some conservative leaders themselves began to look through rose glasses at inappropriate criteria to assess their own position. A vote of 303 to 125 seemed to them an impressive victory indeed.

But the 303 to 125 vote to pass the Landrum-Griffin bill in the House was no more an endorsement of the provisions of the bill than had been the 90 to 1 vote for the Kennedy bill in the Senate. Each reflected the fact that the particular House had gone as far as it could with its proposed law; the bill which emerged was the best on which concensus could be reached. Individual legislators were endorsing the principle of labor reform legislation with their vote.

Many conservatives viewed the lopsided victory as an indication of a trend that had swept the country. They pointed to the gradual build-up of strength that had coincided with the campaign for public support. Senator Mundt was a leader of the group which wanted to bypass the normal conference procedure and take the House-passed bill to the floor of the Senate for a direct vote. The public had demonstrated its naïveté about matters congressional by pouring mail into the offices of senators as well as representatives while the lower chamber was considering the bill and thus had softened up the more liberal upper chamber. By striking while there was sufficient momentum, Mundt reasoned, it would be possible to take the unmodified Landrum-Griffin bill through the Senate. This attitude is in great contrast to the reaction to the Landrum-Griffin bill that Elliott bill supporters had predicted a few days earlier during the House debate.

Conference Committee Procedures

Before proceding further, it may be helpful to set forth here the procedures of the conference committee in broad outline. The conference committee device is used to reconcile the differences between the House and Senate when each has passed a bill on the same subject. Each house appoints managers to represent it. The power of appointment technically rests with the presiding officer of each house, but in fact he usually accepts the recommendation of the chairman of the committee which had jurisdiction, and the senior members of the committee from each party are ordinarily appointed. The number of appointees differs from time to time and need not be the same for each house, since action is taken only by approval of managers from both houses, each house indicating its approval by majority vote of its own managers.

Often it is possible to compromise the two bills only with the inclusion of new language. Although this is technically forbidden, it is often practiced. The managers for each house agree only to those provisions which they feel their house will honor. If differences cannot be compromised, the bill may die in conference. On some occasions the managers of one house may go back and request instructions on matters which have led to deadlock. When they do so, the house may "recede and concur" with the proposals of the other house managers, or it may "insist on its amendment" to the bill.

The deliberations of the conference committee are secret except as the members of the committee make them known. The managers do prepare a conference report, acceptance or rejection of which constitutes passage or defeat of the compromise bill. The managers for the House of Representatives prepare a report which is always printed. The reports of the Senate managers are often made orally. The chamber which asks for the conference allows the other chamber to vote first on the report.

The Cooler Heads

A combination of Republican and Democratic congressional leaders blocked the effort to present the House bill directly to the Senate for vote on the floor after a more "realistic" appraisal of the situation. It was difficult to get senators to commit themselves on their possible reaction to the Landrum-Griffin bill on the Senate floor. There were strong factors of tradition which said that one house should not be a rubber stamp for the other, that pointed to the conference committee as the time-honored means of resolving differences. The effect of such traditions was difficult to gauge and was thus the cause of uncertainty.

There were also political considerations. If the conservatives took the House bill to the Senate floor and a combination of factors conspired to prevent its passage, the momentum which had been built up would be broken. In such a situation the hand of the Senate conferees would be immeasurably strengthened. Thus, it was decided that the simple threat of going to the Senate would be of much greater value than the action itself. No doubt there were also those who wanted to put Senator Kennedy on the spot.

Senate Conferees

The Senate appointed the members of its Subcommittee on Labor
to be its conferees. The line-up was again four Democrats—Kennedy, Morse, McNamara, and Randolph—and three Republicans—
Goldwater, Dirksen, and Prouty. Control rested with the four-man
Democratic majority. The conservative forces had powerful representation in the persons of the Senate Minority Leader and the Senator from Arizona. Senator Prouty, as a representative of the liberal
wing of the Republican Party in the Senate, would play an important
role. Throughout the conference there would be rumblings about going to the floor of the Senate. It was important that many voting
blocs were represented within the Conference Committee. The original instructions to the conferees set a seven-day limit to their deliberations.

The AFL-CIO Position

The AFL-CIO had suffered a resounding defeat. They knew it.
They also realized at this stage that it would be necessary to salvage
what they could from the ruins. They had a number of genuine fears
about certain provisions of the House bill which they hoped the conference could eliminate, but the most they could anticipate from the
conference was a strong "rear guard" action. Their hopes rode on
Senator Kennedy and his fellow Senate Democratic conferees.

This was a period of soul-searching and name-calling in the labor
movement. Many labor people felt that the House leadership had
betrayed them, that friendly congressmen had deserted them, that
management groups had hoodwinked the public, or that the Teamsters had been the extra cook who had spoiled the broth. The famous
letter of James Carey, president of the International Union of Electrical, Radio, and Machine Workers (IUE) to the 229 congressmen
who had voted for the Landrum-Griffin substitute, promising the
efforts of his union to defeat them in the next election, was one manifestation of the feeling. A great deal was made of the letter in the
press and in the Congress. It has been shown in this study that the
letter was no more than these men had received from various constituents during the battle, but it was a dramatic gesture which

could be, and was, used to show the "arrogance" of "labor bosses." To the extent that the reaction could have been anticipated, it was a mistake politically. It certainly did not help the cause of the supporters of labor in the Conference Committee.

There were some in the labor movement who worried about the failure of rank-and-file union members to understand and support the federation and about their readiness to accept the views of the Teamsters or their local press. Yet, these labor people recognized that their unions had employed their best people in Washington and had not emphasized communications with local members. There were others who questioned the ability of the federation to adjust rapidly to changing conditions or even to gauge change.[1] This was a question which was difficult to deal with openly without becoming concerned with personalities.

Anyone reviewing the newspapers of the union movement during the period that legislation was being considered by the House (by the Senate, too, for that matter) would be struck by the general absence of reference to the legislation. There are some obvious explanations for this. In the first place, most union papers are monthlies. Often they are published and distributed after national news is "old." Often, too, the local unions do not meet during one month of the summer, and interest in union affairs tends to lag at that time.

When a union's president appeared before a committee of Congress or when some other event of particular interest to the international occurred, there would be coverage. The device of the union paper, however, does not appear to lend itself to mobilization of opinion in a fast-moving context. (How could any paper mobilize opinion behind the actions of the AFL-CIO during the last four weeks of consideration of legislation in the House? The last ten

[1] Some representatives of the AFL-CIO are extremely defensive about their part in the passage of this bill. On the author's first visit to the AFL-CIO headquarters, he was introduced to one person as a "fellow who is trying to find out who is to *blame* for the Landrum-Griffin bill." It took an hour of rapid talking to convince the person interviewed that these were the words of his colleague and not of the author. It is fair to note that many management people were at least equally defensive. One official of the NAM indicated that he was not willing to discuss various questions because: "We have been burned in the past. Everything management does is made to look sinister in the press—like that Nossiter article." (Bernard D. Nossiter, "The Labor Bill Lobby," Washington *Post*, Sept. 10, 1959.)

days? The last two days?). Studies have shown that some union papers are valued by their readers as sources of news alternative to the regular mass media. But this is a judgment on criteria other than those used here.

The union papers were much more effective in interpreting events which had already occurred. These can often be oversimplified in familiar terms. Certain union papers did this more responsibly than others. The better presentations were from *Solidarity*, of the UAW, and *Labor*, of the Railway Brotherhoods, among others. But even *Labor* adhered to the "devil theory" of politics. Management "bad guys" had twisted the arm of the Congress, and Landrum-Griffin was the result. There was much more to the problem than this, as has been shown.

To be fully understood, the complications of organization and interaction of the Congress and its environment and the complexities of labor law would have to be understood by a reader. Often, the interest and education, even of the upper intellectual stratum of a union, would not allow such presentations—even if the time and resources were made available for them. The familiar slogan is much more effective with busy men of anti-intellectual bent, in any case. The Teamsters used such slogans. The McClellan Committee used the saturation approach. Both proved effective.

The Conference Committee

The fact that there was a conference at all demonstrated that neither side was certain about its voting support. The conservatives weren't sure they could put through the Landrum-Griffin bill, and the liberals weren't sure they could stop its passage at this time. In the glare of publicity and under the pressure the two sides brought to bear, the Conference Committee held its first meeting on Tuesday, August 18, 1959, in the Foreign Relations Room of the Capitol.

Procedural matters were considered first. It was decided that each conferee might have one advisor to assist him during the deliberations of the committee. Senator Kennedy introduced Professor Cox, who would be his assistant during the sessions. The next matter was a decision on a chairman for the conference. This question had been discussed at meetings of the conservative coalition members. The coalition felt that it would be fitting to have Senator Kennedy preside over the meeting which would spell finis to his presidential hopes. With the momentum which had been built up, the "strong" House bill in their hands, and firm control of the vote of the House conferees, the coalition was in a position of strength. It was clear that the labor movement would not be pleased with the bill to emerge from the committee, and thus it might abandon Kennedy. Without the backing of labor, Kennedy had little chance as a candidate. When the question was brought up, Representative Barden deferred to Kennedy for the chairmanship.

Several other issues were decided by compromise. In summary, the proceedings went as follows: Representative Thompson moved that the committee commence at the beginning of the bill and work through it, this in direct opposition to a motion made by Senator Dirksen to start with the "big problems." Each house had a majority in favor of Thompson's motion. Individual votes were recorded. Senator Kennedy, apparently as a reflex conditioned by his chairmanship of the Senate Subcommittee on Labor, had asked the clerk to call the roll. This is not usually done, since the voting is by houses, agreement depending on a majority of each in support of a motion. In any case, all individuals votes were recorded throughout the conference.

Senator Goldwater felt that the committee could improve on Titles I-V, the bill of rights and reform sections of the House amendment. In a discussion Senator Dirksen and Representative Perkins got their colleagues to agree that language on which both versions were in agreement would not be changed by the committee. This agreement brought discussion of Title I to an end. With the exception of a few minor differences (on which the Senate receded), each bill had the Kuchel compromise as Title I.

It was also agreed that the staffs of the two committees would go over the minor differences in language in the definitions section to recommend a consolidated draft to the Conference Committee. The House receded on one provision in the labor reporting title, Title II. With that the first meeting came to a close.[2]

_____

[2] The decisions of the Conference Committee were well covered in the press. The account presented here was developed from interviews, except where other-

Interest Group Representatives

Outside the room there were approximately one hundred labor lobbyists, a large number of management lobbyists, and representatives of the press. They swarmed around the conferees as they left the room. Senate Democrats conversed freely with union representatives, but the same was not true of conservative representatives and their management friends. Only Senator Goldwater had no qualms about public discussion with management people. Representatives of the International Ladies Garment Workers Union (ILGWU) were among the labor representatives. They had established liaison with the federation headquarters and were authorized to work to ensure exemption for all integrated industries from the secondary boycott provisions of the Landrum-Griffin bill. Building trades representatives were also prominent among the union people.

AFL-CIO special counsel Arthur Goldberg was authorized to represent the federation itself, and thus the ILGWU as well. Though busy in New York with the issues of the steel strike, he maintained contact with developments by telephone and flew back to Washington on specific occasions. Legislative representative Cy Anderson was performing the task of liaison between Democratic leadership and conference personnel and the building trades unions. The fact that the president of the Building and Construction Trades Department of the AFL-CIO was a Republican complicated direct dealings with Kennedy and Johnson.

Drafting support was provided for liberal conferees. Ken Meikeljohn and a special consultant, Bernard Dunau, were on hand to draft proposed language for compromises and suggested revisions. It was arranged that they be given working space near the scene of the discussions. Their dealings were generally with Professor Cox.

Management group representatives were working quietly with the members of the coalition. They were in a position of strength. They had their bill and were content to await developments. As one person put it: "Our approach was to sit tight till things got 'sticky' in the conference, then decide what we would give on." More will be said about the activities and functions of these groups later.

wise noted. Verification of this account is possible through the New York *Times,* the New York *Herald Tribune,* the Washington *Post,* and the *Wall Street Journal* for the period.

The Second Conference Meeting

The second conference committee meeting convened at 10 a.m. in the Old Supreme Court Chamber in the center portion of the Capitol building. It was fitting that the conference between the two houses of Congress take place on this middle ground in the Capitol itself. The chamber made a suitable setting for the committee deliberations. In the place where the great justices of the past had seasoned and displayed their talents, a young senator from Massachusetts, who was later to become President of the United States, pitted his wit, stamina, and judgment against the wisdom, cunning, and experience of the chairman of the House Committee on Education and Labor, a committee on which the younger man had served as a member of the House. The match developed slowly.

One of the important issues discussed in the morning session of the meeting was Section 201 of the Kennedy bill, that prescribing an exemption to certain unions.[3] Senator Dirksen moved that the Senate recede from its language. Representative Perkins proposed an amendment to Dirksen's motion, suggesting the provision of the Elliott bill exempting unions with gross annual receipts of $20,000 or less or two hundred members or less. This was defeated; Senator Kennedy and Representative Thompson were among those voting against it. Senator McNamara then made a motion to amend the Dirksen motion by substituting the Senate language for that of the House. This was not acceptable to the House. The Senate then receded from its language.

This series of votes confirmed the expected. The House conferees were voting as a coalition block to defend the language of the Landrum-Griffin bill in all important issues. Flexibility in the voting pattern had come with shifts in the votes of the liberals.

The Power Relationships

Each side controlled the vote in one house, a situation which could easily lead to stalemate. Such a possibility was far from unpalatable

[3] For the full significance of the conference proceedings, the reader should make reference to either of the two bills (S.1555 or H.R.8342) or to the Act as passed (U.S. Congress, *The Labor-Management Reporting and Disclosure Act*, 86th Cong., 1st Sess., 1959, Public Law 86-257). The text of the Act appears in Appendix E.

to Republicans, who could then point to the continuing inability of a Democratically controlled Congress to pass meaningful labor legislation. It would "demonstrate" the control exercised by "labor bosses" over the Congress and would reflect on the ability of Senator Kennedy. From the viewpoint of Southern Democrats, the possibility of a direct vote on the House bill in the Senate would still be open. If all failed, the blame could be put on "Northern liberals," who had "obviously" caused the impasse. Yet, the conservatives had far exceeded their expectations in gaining the bill which passed the House. They would be reluctant to let it die at this stage.

The Democratic leadership had a real stake in passing a bill. This was especially true of Lyndon Johnson, who would be running for the Presidency on the basis of the record of the Congress. But a bill which would please labor clearly would strengthen the hand of one of his rivals, Senator John Kennedy.

The individual who most needed to achieve a workable bill acceptable to the AFL-CIO was Kennedy. Since he was chairman of the Conference Committee, a failure would reflect directly on him and on his legislative ability. It might lead to the passage of the Landrum-Griffin bill in the Senate, something neither he nor the AFL-CIO would relish. Such a calamity would leave Kennedy denuded of credit for "major legislation," with no prospect for a name bill in the next session of Congress. It would leave the labor movement saddled with a bill it regarded as totally unacceptable—the result of a process set in motion and presided over by Kennedy. It is clear, then, where the real pressure lay.

In his fight Kennedy had the assistance of an excellent staff. The services of Professor Archibald Cox cannot be overestimated. Though Kennedy had become a competent student of labor law in his own right, he could rely on this man, whose knowledge, loyalty, and integrity were unquestioned. In a situation where the issues are so complex and abstruse, a relatively disinterested observer is an invaluable aid. Cox's presence was not an unmixed blessing, however. Graham Barden made it clear from the outset that staff people were present "at the sufferance" of the committee members. It became obvious that the professor symbolized the "fast-talking Yankee" to the Southerners present, who cast themselves in the contrasting (and equally misleading) role of "Southern country boys." There were occasional eruptions of feeling against the presence or actions of Cox. Landrum clearly took a great dislike to him, and Barden was known to express similar feelings. Cox's role was considerably altered from the one he played during the Senate committee sessions. Now he was the staff assistant to one committee member, not the final arbiter of legal matters for the committee.

Further Sessions of the First Week

The afternoon meeting of the second session essentially covered the remainder of Title II, Title III, and part of Title IV. It should be remembered that in the Landrum-Griffin bill the provisions of these titles had been taken directly from the Elliott bill, which contained, with minor modifications, the language of the Senate bill. It is not surprising that the consideration of these sections went smoothly. For example, the Senate receded from its language in all of Title III. Thus, Title III is entirely from the Elliott bill. With no fight the Senate dropped its provisions for a commissioner of labor reports and for non-Communist affidavits for employers. There was some discussion and disagreement over the provision in Title IV for inspection of membership lists. Representative Perkins wanted the adoption of the Senate language, Senator Goldwater that of the House. Each motion was objected to by a majority of one house, with individual votes exactly reversed on the two motions. On this note of disagreement the meeting recessed.

The pattern of voting during the sessions remained essentially the same.

On the third day the meeting opened at 10 a.m. The conferees were considering the various sections of Titles IV, V, and VI. The only significant section was that on bonding.

It is a little surprising that the Senate conferees did not follow up on an opening offered by Representative Griffin to allow firms such as Lloyd's of London to serve as bonding companies under the Act. (This provision on strict bonding regulations has been one of the most troublesome and expensive to unions of all the provisions of the Act.) The discussion continued over relatively minor matters for the remainder of the afternoon, but no decision was reached.

The conferees moved rapidly through the provisions of Title VI, with Professor Cox playing a major role in clarifying the proposals and issues. Agreement was reached, although Senators Morse and McNamara were not going along with Senator Kennedy. Following the adoption of Title VI changes the committee recessed and agreed not to meet until the afternoon of the twenty-first to allow the staffs time in the morning to adjust any differences in the first six titles.

At 1:30 p.m. on the twenty-first the committee went back into session in the Old Supreme Court Chamber. The staff reported its recommendations on the employer reporting section, 203 (a). After discussion and amendment, suggested by Senator Goldwater, the section was finally approved. The Senate Section 611 on attorney-client relationships was agreed to. The bonding company issue was raised again. Should mutual companies be authorized as bonding agents or not? Barden thought they should, but no decision was reached. Senator Kennedy proposed an upper limit for the amount of the bond. Representative Thompson suggested that it be fixed at $500,000. This suggestion was agreed to.

The next question to be tackled was the time limit for the exhaustion of internal remedies by a union member before availing himself of the remedies of the Act. The Senate conferees suggested the limit of six months (as provided in the Senate bill), then five months. They finally settled for the House provision of four months.

Senator Prouty suggested that the House manager's report include the statement that the intent of the conferees was to allow a union to be able to suspend an officer who was guilty of an offense. This marked the second time the manager's report was suggested as a means of clarifying language capable of more than one interpretation. Representative Griffin had earlier asked that the report be used to clarify Section 505. Then Senators Dirksen and Kennedy proposed that the provisions agreed to in Titles I-VI be closed, except where opened by unanimous consent.

In a little more than three days the conferees had come to agreement on the reform sections of the "labor reform" bill. We have seen that they never were far apart on the bulk of the questions. Throughout the discussions Senator Goldwater was the staunchest advocate of the Senate language. His Democratic colleagues were ready and willing to compromise in favor of the often less stringent House language. The way was now clear for discussion of the riders on the reform issue, Taft-Hartley changes.[4]

The expeditious treatment of fifty-eight of the bill's sixty-eight pages was definitely not an indication of the speed with which the conference would proceed. These pages dealt with the internal reform of labor unions, and on this issue—the issue of the McClellan Committee and the public furor—there was little controversy. The real battle, the battle to determine future economic power relations between management and labor, was yet to be waged.

By the middle of this first week the Senate Democrats had a bit of information which helped them to brace for the real struggle to come. It was reported that a nose count showed enough votes in the Senate to stop a straight Landrum-Griffin bill (subject, of course, to all the normal vicissitudes of such counts).

The remainder of the week was taken up with initial skirmishes over Title VII.

The conferees agreed to put the no man's land question over until the following Monday. Senator Kennedy stated that he would not insist on the Senate language on this. Senator Morse indicated that he would propose: (1) departmentalization of the NLRB; (2) ceding jurisdiction to the states if they agree to apply federal law; and (3) a provision that state law not be allowed to govern interstate commerce.

The committee then began discussion of the problems of the building and construction industry. The differences in the approach of the two bills before them were in line with the differences between labor and management on this question.

The Second Week

The morning session of August 24 lasted for somewhat over an hour in a discussion of the no man's land. All proposed compromises were defeated. The only development of note was the change in the posi-

---

[4] The reader can use the comparative analysis of the various bills presented in Chapter VII to help him follow the developments on Title VII.

tion of Senator Prouty, the proponent of the major compromises, who
was now voting with the Democratic senators. Each house was now
split, 5 to 2.

The afternoon session was devoted to the issues of the building
trades and of economic strikers. After Senator Prouty's amendment,
which limited an economic striker's right to vote in union elections
to a period of one year, the Senate language on this provision was
adopted.

This was followed by a discussion of the garment industry. Senator Kennedy asked Professor Cox to inquire into the meaning of
some of the language of the House provision.

For some reason the request sparked a violent reaction. Representative Landrum, who clearly showed his dislike for the professor,
exploded at Cox; "You are always making loopholes through which
the rascals could slip!" he stormed. "You don't have to take the result
and go back to your constituents to face them in an election!" Landrum's face was red with anger. Cox was somewhat taken aback.
Senator Morse intervened. He suggested that the committee adjourn
to allow tempers to cool. It was already late afternoon; his colleagues
accepted his suggestion.

A development of significance the next day came when Kennedy
mentioned a package substitute that he would prepare to break the
obvious impasse. Graham Barden expressed concern. "The House
came over with a bill it was satisfied with," he said. "I can't see any
use in further discussion!"

In the face of House unwillingness to suggest compromises, the
Senate Democrats suggested that the meeting adjourn until 4 p.m.
the same afternoon. They would be ready with their package plan
by that time. This was agreed to.

During the recess key Senators Johnson, Kennedy, Dirksen, and
Goldwater discussed the scheduling of possible Senate action.[5] Apparently during this session, the seven-day limit placed on Senate
conferees was lifted.

At approximately the appointed time Senator Kennedy distributed
copies of his "package," which had been discussed with his colleagues and approved by Arthur Goldberg for the AFL-CIO. There

[5] Washington *Post*, Aug. 26, 1959, p. 1.

was little discussion. Twenty minutes later the committee adjourned
to allow the conferees an opportunity to study the package proposal.
In its major features the compromise would have modified House
language on secondary boycotts and organizational picketing and
proposed limitations on the House no man's land provision, including delegation of authority to regional directors of the NLRB as
previously proposed by Representative Kearns. If there was no
agreement on the construction industry, both sides were to drop
their provisions. The package involved some sweeping concessions.[6]

The Caucuses

At various points the formal session of the conference would dis-
band and the conferees would assemble in working groups. Small
knots of people would gather and attempt to devise compromise language or smooth over personal antagonisms. Individuals would drift
from group to group, supplying bits and pieces of information. The
staff personnel present were performing an invaluable service in
keeping the line between fact and fancy as clear as possible. These
sessions could be called working sessions within the meeting itself.
There were also times when a "caucus" would be called. The line-up
in these cases was interesting. It was never one house meeting to
discuss the proposals of the other house; it was not a gathering of
Democrats to discuss strategy against the Republicans; it was a gathering of the five House coalition members with the three (and sometimes two) Senate Republicans discussing strategy or proposals for
meeting the Senate Democrats, who were usually joined by Representatives Perkins and Thompson. Gradually, the staff people became more and more prominent in informal discussion and in formal
debate. Michael Bernstein was the key staff member for the coalition, ably supported by Charles Ryan and Ken McGuiness from the
House side. Professor Cox and Ralph Dungan were key Kennedy
staff men. Sam Merrick worked with Senator Morse. There were
many others present, in most cases the administrative assistants of
the individuals involved. On one or two occasions the conferees
cleared the room of staff people for important debate. It wasn't long,

[6] It is not clear whether at any point provisions were suggested for the reversal
of the Denver building trades doctrine during discussion of the compromise.

however, before they were called back in to untangle resulting confusion.

The Conference Itself

The conferees reconvened on Wednesday, August 26, at about 2 p.m. Kennedy presented amended language on boycotts and picketing which the staff had prepared to replace provisions considered legally and technically deficient.

Despite Kennedy's urging, particularly for an exemption from the boycott provisions for the garment industry, the House was not disposed to accept his substitute.

Goldwater, Barden, and Dirksen continued to press for agreement on the concessions offered by Kennedy, for splitting the package by dropping the issue of the building and construction trades, and by voting on the no man's land. Kennedy resisted these attempts, pointing out that his concessions were made only in return for concessions in other parts of the package. After some discussion and wrangling one agreement was reached. A motion to drop all reference to the construction industry was approved unanimously by the Senate and 5 to 2 by the House. With that the session adjourned. The construction industry problem was settled—for a moment. Almost immediately, the union people reacted strongly and demanded that the problems of their industry be resolved. Kennedy had to backtrack.

Against the intransigence of the House conferees, the Kennedy compromise package had burst apart practically on delivery. It tipped his hand on the issues on which he was willing to give ground, while making not the slightest headway on the others. Yet, faced with the opposition power, the public pressure, the private pressure, and the need to achieve something, Kennedy had little choice. It would be hard to regain the ground he had indicated his willingness to give, but even this fact was not all bad.

Public Relations and Interest Group Relations

As chairman of the conference, Kennedy dealt directly with the representatives of all the news media. It became clear to the coalition people, on advice from management representatives and in other ways, that, although Kennedy was in a precarious position within the committee, he was winning the battle in the eyes of the public. He was able to convey the fact that the initiative was his, and he was carrying the battle against great odds. One prominent management representative forcefully made this point to Bob Griffin. Early in the second week the conservative side resolved to redress the balance. Both Griffin and Goldwater began making their own statements to the press. They stressed that the conference had accepted language that was 90 percent Landrum-Griffin and that Kennedy was being forced to eat crow. The tide began to swing back toward even coverage.

Outside the conference room representatives of the ILGWU ("Lady Garment Workers" to the movement) and Amalgamated Clothing Workers Union were engaging in earnest discussion with Democratic and Republican senators alike. Even Senator Goldwater listened intently to their statements.

The building trades unions were not idle either. An account of some developments was given to the convention of these unions in September, 1959. General counsel Louis Sherman said:

Now on Thursday, August 27, there was presented to the President of the Department in one of the historic rooms of the Capitol, a proposal or offer of compromise in which some of the things we were seeking would be attained and there would be some kind of a postponement of the on-site picketing issue until the beginning of the next year.

I happened to be there along with others and I think I should state my own personal views with respect to the matter.

It was a hard decision to make and the President of the Department in a way which I am sure you are all familiar with, gave the offer of the compromise a very firm negative response, even though that response meant that everything might go by the board. . . .

Now on Friday Senator Prouty of Vermont, a member on the Republican side swung over and offered an amendment in conference which would have given us the on-job-site picketing relief.[7]

August 28

The morning of August 28 was taken up with technical discussions. Senator Morse clarified three technical questions which had been brought to his attention by Teamsters' representatives at break-

---

[7] Building and Construction Trades Department, AFL-CIO, *Proceedings of the Fiftieth Convention,* San Francisco, Sept. 9, 10, 11, 1959, p. 31.

fast that day. The hard issue under discussion was informational picketing, which would not prevent employees or delivery people from entering the picketed premises.

Late in the afternoon it was Barden's turn to tangle with Cox. "You're always trying to confuse everybody and prevent action," he roared. But this time Kennedy, usually relaxed and unemotional, returned Barden's remarks in kind. "I'm tired of your attacks on Professor Cox," he shouted. "He will speak whenever he is asked or this conference will come to an end!" It was quite a display, but Cox remained as a working member of the conference.

Some participants explain these periodic outbursts against Cox as a definite part of the psychological warfare of the conference. Though this might not be true of the volatile Phil Landrum, it would be characteristic for Barden, who seldom did anything the effect of which had not been carefully weighed in advance. Gradually, the conference settled down and returned to indecisive voting.

Shortly after 3 p.m. the staff was cleared from the room on request of Senator Dirksen. Forty minutes later the staff and the press were called in to hear a statement read by Dirksen. The highlights of the statement were that the minority would take two issues to the floor of the Senate for instructions. His motion would request that the Senate recede and accept the language of the House on Sections 701, the no man's land, and 705, the organizational picketing and boycott section. He said the conferees were essentially agreed on language on prehire agreements in the construction industry. Despite the motion to go to the floor, the conferees decided to meet again the following Monday.

Senator Kennedy then issued a statement of his own. He would introduce an amendment to Dirksen's motion on the floor of the Senate, recommending that Senate conferees be instructed to:

1. Accept Republican Senator Prouty's compromise on the no man's land.
2. Accept Republican Senator Prouty's compromise on situs picketing in the construction industry.
3. Insist on an exemption from the secondary boycott provisions for the garment industry.
4. Permit picketing of employers selling goods produced in a plant engaged in a labor dispute.

5. Permit unions to publicize their views on the organization of employees in nonorganized industries.

There was a good deal of discussion about the wisdom of going to the Senate. Dirksen then stressed that the forty-two changes in Titles I-VI were closed and not openable except by unanimous consent.

Political Considerations in Going to the Floor

No politician would publicly advocate anything which would be interpreted as favoring sweatshops. If issues could be shifted to fit these labels, they would be lost no matter what their merits. Nor would anyone openly oppose legitimate unionism. Thus, the threat of going to the floor of the Senate for open debate of some issues was a two-edged sword. "If you go to the floor with something like this," an Administration spokesman stated, "you have to have a reasonable position to defend." He indicated that the Dirksen move was a part of the war of nerves to keep pressure on Kennedy. At no time did the Senate Minority Leader make a real nose count to see if his proposals would carry. The minority prepared an amendment (a very "reasonable" one) to Kennedy's amendment, to be introduced if it did become necessary to vote on the issues on the floor.

From the foregoing, it appears that Kennedy's position in facing the Senate was the more advantageous as of that Friday afternoon. He was backing two Republican proposals; he was against sweatshops and for free speech and free unionism. He also turned Goldwater-Griffin statements against them by "admitting" that the Senate conferees had accepted 90 percent Landrum-Griffin already, but that he would not accept "101 percent Landrum-Griffin." [8] This could well stimulate the natural jealousy of the Senate to stiffen its conferees and insist on its amendment.

The Weekend

The weekend was filled with conferences and maneuvering by both sides. Kennedy's position appeared fairly strong on the issues before the Senate. The coalition saw that it was beaten on the exemption for the ILGWU and the Amalgamated Clothing Workers

[8] U.S. Congress, *Daily Congressional Record*, 86th Cong., 1st Sess., Aug. 28, 1959, p. 15,900.

Unions, since the emotional tag of "sweatshop supporter" would be irresistible in floor debate. The effectiveness of the lobbying effort was clear. One staff member came up with the idea of taking credit for the exemption for the clothing and apparel unions by attributing it to the initiative of six Republican senators who had indeed been active behind the scenes. He prepared a news release to this effect, to be issued the moment the concession was made in the conference.

Monday, August 31

The coalition had an important discussion at a Monday breakfast meeting, one of several such that had taken place. Senator Dirksen had invited Senate minority whip Kuchel to the breakfast. The Senate and House coalition conferees were present, along with two others, one a representative of a management association who was also affiliated with the Chamber of Commerce, the second apparently Edward McCabe. Newspaper reports indicate Kuchel was present to explain the potential difficulties and dangers of debating the labor bill issues before the Senate at this late stage in the legislative calendar.[9]

On Monday the Senate did not debate the instructions to be given to its conferees. The Conference Committee met informally for two hours in the morning, long enough to establish that bargaining would be continued. Both sides were very busy behind the scenes. A scheduled afternoon meeting was postponed until Tuesday. It apparently became clear to the Republicans that there were not enough votes to back their position. Kennedy's willingness to compromise (mainly on the reform sections) had cut the ground from under the Landrum-Griffin bill supporters. He had demonstrated his "reasonableness." It was now necessary for the coalition to compromise the outstanding issues if a bill was to result. The Washington *Post* quotes Representative Griffin, whom it calls the leader of the coalition group, as saying that, if the heated issues go back to the Senate, "we feel the chances of a bill are not so good."[10]

There was another development of importance. President Richard Grey of the Building and Construction Trades Department of the

[9] Donald Erwin in the New York *Herald Tribune*, Sept. 11, 1959, p. 1.
[10] Washington Post, Sept. 1, 1959, p. A-2.

AFL-CIO had sent an urgent telegram to Secretary Mitchell, asking the Administration's position on the Denver building trades doctrine, the reversal of which Mitchell had recommended on several occasions. The Secretary's answer was unequivocal. The position of the Administration was unchanged from previous statements. At this crucial point the statement was of great importance. Senator Goldwater showed his annoyance with the comment "the Administration is overseas," referring to the fact that the President was in Europe.

The Last Two Days

The conferees came together on Tuesday, September 1, at about 10:30 a.m. in the Old Supreme Court Chamber. This meeting was one of very hard bargaining. Senator Kennedy made a proposed solution to the outstanding issues. The major points were:

1. Exemption of the existing practices in apparel and clothing industries from the secondary boycott provisions, since the industries are integrated industries.
2. Overruling of the Denver building trades doctrine, except in cases which resulted from competitive bidding in public works or which involved a mere grievance under a collective bargaining agreement.
3. Legalizing publicity to consumers without picketing.
4. Making an unfair labor practice by the employer a defense for organizational picketing under certain conditions.

The morning was taken up with discussion and caucusing. Then, later, at the suggestion of Senator Morse, the conference recessed until 3 p.m.

When the conference reconvened, the coalition presented its counterproposals:

1. An exemption for the ILGWU would be all right.
2. Publicity other than picketing was agreed to.
3. Organizational picketing would be legal if it could be shown that the employer had unlawfully recognized the present union or had made a "sweetheart" contract in violation of Section 8 (a)(2) of the Taft-Hartley Act.
4. The common situs picketing question was not in either bill and so should be dropped from consideration.

Senator Kennedy objected to the language of the first proposal because it did not cover unions such as the Amalgamated Clothing
Workers. The conference recessed for two more hours of caucuses
and discussion. In the late afternoon the conference was called back
to order.

Bob Griffin offered modified language on the clothing industry,
whereby "a jobber, manufacturer, contractor or subcontractor working on the goods or premises of a jobber or a manufacturer or performing parts of an integrated process of production in the apparel
or clothing industry" would be exempted.

In return for the House language on the clothing industry, Griffin
proposed that the House drop its provision allowing an employer to
file suit for damages which might result from organizational picketing. There would be one defense against an injunction; if an unfair
labor practice were filed under Section 8 (a) (2) of the Taft-Hartley
Act and the general counsel had reasonable cause to believe that
such had been committed and would issue a complaint, then he
wouldn't seek an injunction against picketing. Mike Bernstein indicated that, although the precise language on picketing wasn't
drafted, it would be along the lines of the Prouty amendment.

The section on consumer picketing would remain as in the earlier
proposal.

Kennedy urged that the conference come to an agreement on situs
picketing before recessing. This keyed a long discussion of the very
important issue. Graham Barden pointed out that the House rules
would prevent the acceptance of any provision which was not in
either bill. Thompson countered that, when he had discussed this
point with the House Parliamentarian on Monday and again in the
morning, he was given the "horseback" opinion that the provision
would be germane. He also reminded the conferees that any ruling
on a point of order was reversible by majority vote of the House.
The first indication of a break in the coalition ranks came when
Representative Ayres indicated his support for the Prouty amendment on the question. Representative Kearns was known to feel the
same way. The votes were there to pass the Prouty amendment on
the construction industry.

Kennedy pointed out that the conferees were writing entirely new language on secondary boycotts and hot cargo and thus should be able to provide an exemption for the building trades without being subject to a point of order. Barden reiterated his position. Senator Goldwater queried whether the choice were between "situs picketing and no bill." Landrum indicated that the House was not willing to face that alternative.

Senator Kennedy was willing to take the question of situs picketing to the Senate floor if the conference could not agree on it. With this, he suggested that the press be told that there was no agreement and no policy as yet.

A Pilgrimage to the Parliamentarian

During the afternoon caucus of the conference, several members went to discuss the controversial question of the point of order with the House Parliamentarian, Lewis Deschler. This group included Lyndon Johnson, who had played an important behind-the-scenes role in the proceedings. Two others are identified in the *Congressional Record* as Senator Dirksen and Representative Landrum.[11] There were others as well, Johnson being the only one who was not avowedly a member of the coalition.

During this visit the Parliamentarian reversed his earlier "horseback" decision, stating that he probably would rule the reversal of the Denver building trades doctrine out of order. The next morning this was formalized, and it was alleged that, if such a ruling were made, the Speaker would sustain it. The inability of liberals to achieve a majority in the House in opposition to the Landrum-Griffin bill, even with the formal support of the Speaker, was evidence of the position in which this placed Kennedy. Again quoting from the speech of Louis Sherman at the Building Trades Convention:

It was at this time, late Tuesday, that the Conference adjourned to Wednesday morning and we heard about "Point of Order." . . .

Our position, of course, was that it [the reversal of the Denver building trades doctrine] came in as a qualification, of the new restrictions in the House bill.[12]

[11] *Daily Congressional Record,* 86th Cong., 1st Sess., Sept. 2, 1959, p. 16,263.
[12] Building and Construction Trades Department, *Proceedings,* p. 32.

September 2

At about 11:30 a.m. the conference convened. A Conference Committee print of language proposed to resolve the outstanding issues was distributed to the conferees and its first two sections approved.

The conferees turned to the question of the exemption of the building and construction trades unions from the secondary boycott provisions. The question of the point of order came up again. Senator Morse suggested that the question be taken to the Senate floor for separate vote so that there would be no question that it was germane. The Parliamentarian's "ruling" was brought up. Senator Prouty showed his surprise with a remark that this was the first time in his life he had heard of a presiding officer ruling on a motion *before* it had been made. Representative Thompson questioned whether either the Parliamentarian or the Speaker had made the statements attributed to them and reiterated the possibility of overruling the chair by majority vote of the House. Senator Prouty asked the very practical question of whether such a point of order would be raised. Barden said he felt it would be his "duty" to raise it. Senator Dirksen backed him by saying he would be remiss in his duty if he did not raise it. Yet in private interviews even an Administration spokesman referred to the point of order as "that ridiculous ruling made before a question was raised." Ridiculous or not, it was to be the crucial influence on the issue.

Senator Kennedy asked about the exemption for the garment industry, which was technically a parallel provision. Barden felt that no member of the conference would raise that question in a point of order. Landrum and Griffin stated that they would resist such a point of order should it be raised. The inconsistency of the two positions did not seem to bother anyone.

Over Morse's objection, Kennedy commented that he would raise the Denver building trades question in January as a separate bill. At about 12:30 the conference recessed until 2 p.m., later changed to 3 p.m. Again quoting Louis Sherman:

The fact is that at that moment on Wednesday the question was whether this very firm negative which had been asserted on [the previous] Thursday was at its end in return for the concessions which were to be offered, or whether the President of the Department should run the locomotive off the tracks.[13]

During the recess Thompson discussed compromise language on the construction industry question with Rayburn. Over the objection of Lyndon Johnson (who was present), the Speaker agreed to support the compromise. Thompson returned to the conference with the backing of the Speaker. A solution was worked out, as indicated in the remarks of President Grey (of the Building and Construction Trades Department of the AFL-CIO).

President Grey: We were forced to yield on this crucial issue. But in return for yielding, we got some important concessions to the building trades written into the final bill. They were:
1. Validation of the legality of employer contributions to joint apprenticeship training programs and pooled vacation funds.
2. Legalization of pre-hire contracts in the building trades in an effective form.
3. Exemption for the building trades from the hot-cargo prohibitions in the law. This means that building trades unions will be able to write into their contracts with prime contractors the provision that only union subcontractors will be used on the jobs.
4. Assurance from leaders of both parties that Congress will consider and act, early in the next session that begins in January, on the issue of on-site picketing. This will give us our long-sought opportunity to upset the disastrous Denver Building Trades decision of the United States Supreme Court.[14]

This version is confirmed in the *Congressional Record.*

Senator Dirksen: Mr. President, I believe the chairman of the conference will agree with me when I say that if we have not completed the necessary action, in the sense that something still remains to be done in connection with the construction field, certainly the majority leader has given his word, and the chairman of the conference committee has given his word, and distinguished junior Senator from Arizona (Mr. Goldwater) concurs, and I concur, that when we come back here in January, if there is something to be done in that field, we will do it, so that nobody will feel aggrieved or feel that he has been forgotten in the process. . . .[15]

Mr. Kennedy: When I have concluded my remarks I will introduce a bill dealing with the Denver case. It will be introduced by the Senator

[13] *Ibid.*, p. 33.   [14] *Ibid.*, p. 18.
[15] *Daily Congressional Record*, 86th Cong., 1st Sess., Sept. 2, 1959, p. 16,264.

from California (Mr. Kuchel) and myself and will lie on the desk for several days in the hope that other Senators will cosponsor it. I have received the assurances of the majority leader and the minority leader that if the Committee on Labor and Public Welfare reports the bill, they will schedule it. Likewise, both the Speaker of the House and Representative Halleck have said that they will use their influence to secure a rule for the consideration of the bill if the House Committee on Education and Labor reports it.[16]

In midafternoon the conferees returned to the Old Supreme Court Chamber, and the final language on the remaining issues was agreed to. A motion was approved that the staff should perfect the language on technical grounds if there was unanimous consent to the change. The requirement for unanimity protected some ambiguities which had been intentionally included.

Senator Dirksen's motion that the conference result should be reported to both houses was approved, and the conference came to a close. Compliments were passed out to the staff and to the conferees themselves, and Representative Barden went so far as to state that he "loved everybody." Senator Morse and Representative Perkins stated that they would not approve the conference report. At 4:10 Senator Dirksen emerged from the chamber and announced: "We've got a bill." [17]

The coalition group had a press release prepared and duplicated for distribution at this time. The release had been prepared by a number of people, including at least one management representative. "That release was the basis for the stories of the wire services and all the newspapers I saw," stated one participant. This was another part of the effective public relations counteroffensive by the coalition supporters.

On September 3, 1959, the Senate agreed to the report of the Conference Committee on S.1555 by a vote of 95 to 2. On September 4, 1959, the House agreed to the report by a roll call of 352 to 52. The President signed the Act on September 14, 1959, as Public Law 86-257.

When he was asked what name the bill should bear, Senator Kennedy stressed the changes that the conferees had included in the

[16] *Ibid.*, Sept. 2, 1959, p. 16,416.
[17] Bernard D. Nossiter, Washington *Post*, Sept. 3, 1959, p. 10.

Table 6. Major Changes Made in Landrum-Griffin Bill by Conference Committee

1. *Subcontracting.* The legality of restricting subcontracting in the garment industry in order to keep out sweat shops was established.
2. *Consumer Appeals.* The right to publicize non-union goods to consumers, without causing a secondary work stoppage, is recognized in the Conference agreement. Employees will also be entitled to publicize, without picketing, the fact that a wholesaler or retailer sells goods of a company involved in a labor dispute. All appeals for a consumer boycott would have been barred by House bill.
3. *Organizational Picketing.* The Conference report preserves the right to engage in organizational picketing provided that a petition for an election is filed within a reasonable time not to exceed 30 days. Unless the union won the election, the picketing would have to cease.
4. *Informational Picketing.* The right to engage in purely informational picketing without filing a petition for an election is secured provided that the picketing does not halt the pick-up or delivery of goods or the rendition of services by the employees of other employers.
5. *Primary Strikes.* The Conference report recognizes the right to engage in primary strikes and primary picketing, thereby eliminating the danger that the House bill would sometimes invalidate such picketing.
6. *Defense to Picketing.* Although the Conference agreement contains a prohibition upon picketing an employer who has a contract with another union, language was added to the House bill which would make it a defense to show that the General Counsel had issued a complaint charging the employer with unlawfully dominating, maintaining, or assisting the other union.
7. *Union Liability for Damage Suits.* The section imposing liability on labor unions for damages in the case of unlawful organizational picketing was eliminated.
8. *Federal-State Jurisdiction (No-Man's Land).* The Conference report permits the State to take jurisdiction over labor cases over which the Board currently refuses to assume jurisdiction. Under the House bill the NLRB could have refused jurisdiction over additional cases. The Board's present jurisdictional standards are broader than they have ever been, thus insuring more unions and employers protection of the Act.
9. *Economic Strikers.* The House bill contained no provision permitting economic strikers to vote in representation elections. The Conference provision permits strikers to vote in representation elections within one year after the commencement of a strike.
10. *Struck Work.* The Conference report preserves existing law on the question of the right of labor to refuse to work on struck goods. The House bill would have limited this right.
11. *Pre-Hire Contracts in the Construction Industry.* Conference report permits pre-hire contracts in construction industry accepting Senate provision on this subject. Conference report also permits unions and prime contractors in construction industry to enter into agreements by which contractor refuses to subcontract to non-union operators.
12. *Bonding.* Conference report places a $500,000 limitation on amount of bond required to be taken by a union officer; the House bill had no such limitation.
13. *Elections.* Conference report makes the Secretary of Labor responsible for bringing suits in a Federal Court to remedy improper elections. The House

Table 6 (cont.)

bill would have provided that individual members could bring suits in
U.S. District Courts to overturn improper elections.
14. *Membership Lists.* House bill gave candidates for union office the right to
inspect and copy from membership lists in union shops. Conference report
restricts this to *one* inspection 30 days prior to an election *without* right
to copy.
15. *Employer Reporting.* Conference strengthened immeasurably employer reporting section 203 which was meaningless in the House bill.

SOURCE: Handout by Senate Subcommittee on Labor.

House bill. They are shown in Table 6. He then suggested that the
law should probably be called the "Labor-Management Reform
Bill." [18]

[18] *Ibid.*, p. 1.

X. CONCLUSION

THE law was passed. The "worst" of Landrum-Griffin had been removed and the Landrum-Griffin bill itself was more moderate by several light-years than the monstrosity which had passed the House twelve years before in the form of the Hartley bill, but the leaders of labor did not perceive it to be so. The law as passed in 1959 was a good deal more moderate in intent, content, and tone than had been Taft-Hartley. The labor movement demonstrated the strength which it still could exercise; indeed, individual unions demonstrated their ability to hold up negotiations between the two houses of Congress and even to imperil passage of any reform legislation. The conference brought about a law which the unions could probably find "livable." The outcome was a far cry from total defeat or surrender.

The analyst should now find himself able to answer the questions: Why had this law—so far from the desires and expectations of the labor movement—been passed? How had the congressional election of 1958 been misread?

The Election of '58 Revisited

The labor papers had shouted long and hard to their readers about labor's triumph in that 1958 election. There is every indication that the leaders of labor believed they had achieved a great victory and would be in command of the Eighty-sixth Congress. Even after the repeated rebuffs and outright defeats they continued to act as if they had the power to achieve their will, especially in the House of Representatives. Their assumptions about their power were so fixed that the evidence of repeated tests was ineffective in dislodging them. The drama of 1949 and the misreading of Truman's election victory had been reenacted.

What is a proper explanation of the 1958 election? In the first place, it should be recognized that providing election support to candidates is something certain unions do very effectively. (In the literature printed and distributed by the NAM, the pamphlets on increasing voter registration and getting out the vote are reprints of labor pamphlets on the subjects.) But aiding the election of a representative is not the same thing as owning his vote, as the labor people discovered in the repeated tests in the House Committee on Education and Labor. Individual congressmen recognize that there are many issues of interest to the AFL-CIO and other unions, that they will be evaluated on balance, that no one vote is all-controlling. The labor people were engaged in so many lobbying gymnastics that it would be difficult for the unions themselves to decide which vote on the labor bill was the crucial one. (The Teamsters and others have utilized the meaningless vote of 303 to 125 on final passage of Landrum-Griffin as the test; some unions have used the vote on the Shelley bill; some have used the vote for the Conference Committee report; the AFL-CIO has advocated the use of the 229 to 201 vote to substitute Landrum-Griffin for Elliott as the measure in the House and the original vote on the McClellan bill of rights as the measure in the Senate.) Thus, it would not necessarily be a contradiction for the 1958 election and the passage of the Landrum-Griffin bill in the House to stand side by side.

But the more plausible explanation would be that labor had relatively little to do with the outcome of the 1958 election. This was a congressional election in a nonpresidential year. The prior history of such elections had been that, with one exception, the party of the President had lost seats in the Congress in such years. Probably the most important factor in determining the unusual size of the loss of seats was the 1957–58 recession, a real bogey for the party of Hoover. The McClellan Committee had had its impact on the voters, but this impact was not measurable in the selection between people to represent congressional districts. In any case, the issue of labor reform was one which struck more at the conscience of the public, while the issue of recession struck at its pocketbook. The impact of the bread-and-butter issue appears to have been sufficient to mask the impact of the moral issue. The reading of public reaction had been taken on a scale inappropriate to the task, at a time when opinion was disturbed, but not crystallized, when other issues were decisive in the choice expressed. The result in the election of congressmen backed by labor was a bit of evidence which was misinterpreted (with tenacity) and distorted the calculations of labor people during the important months which followed.

When, in the cold light of defeat, the labor movement analyzed what had happened—by use of data available to them all along—they realized (at least the more perceptive of them realized) that they had miscalculated from the start. Their friends had stayed with them, but the Congress contained too few of their friends. Out of 174 Democratic representatives from Northern and Western states, only three had voted for substitution of Landrum-Griffin at the crucial vote. Of the 95 Democrats voting for the Landrum-Griffin substitute, 92 were from Southern and border states. Of the 153 Republicans in the House, only 17, or 11 percent, had voted against the Landrum-Griffin substitute. Thirty Democrats from Southern and border states had voted against the Landrum-Griffin substitute. The public campaign and the efforts of the Republican Administration and congressional coalition leadership had mustered the basically conservative votes of the House of Representatives. Even with the efforts of Speaker Rayburn, only one quarter of the Southern votes were cast with the party leadership. On this evidence, one could say that the AFL-CIO had done surprisingly well in spite of inept handling. The difference from earlier interpretations would result merely from a shift in expectations.

But the coalition had not been so effective on most other issues. And the vote of the House of Representatives had reflected the enormity of the pressure exerted on the Congress. Massive effort had been required to bring the coalition to the point of majority—and a slim majority at that.

The Groups

The interest groups themselves were important, as the body of the study has amply indicated. But the significance of their actions and, indeed, the impact of their actions was overshadowed by other factors. Without the intervention of the interest groups this legislation would never have developed in the way it did. But the legislation under study was designed to tinker with the internal mechanism of one of the major interest groups, labor. It would be hard to envision legislation of this character without important participation by interest groups.

The most striking thing about the labor interest group was its very lack of power, its inability to achieve its will once it became committed to reform legislation. It would appear that, on an issue in which opposition from the start was possible, the labor movement's power might prove more formidable. Here, however, the analyst is struck with labor's weakness. The (false) perception of the labor leaders of their great strength in the Eighty-sixth Congress itself contributed to the weakness. It appeared that excessive caution and internal coordination were not really necessary. The labor side had become intoxicated by the heady liquor of management propaganda.

The resulting disunity within the labor movement was not the open rivalry of old between the AFL seeking legislative advantage over the CIO in retaliation against the alleged favoritism of the NLRB for the CIO unions. But much of the internal animosity was between the old AFL and CIO unions. The industrial unions were opposed to the inclusion of sweeteners for the building trades of the old AFL. The industrial unions were much more anxious for the passage of anticorruption measures than were their friends in the craft unions. At no time did the unions really work in harmony.

The structure of the AFL-CIO itself, while apparently quite functional (for the predecessor organizations) in the earlier days of the labor movement, appears to be one of the major impediments to effective labor action in today's political environment. The increasing degree of socialization of conflicts has placed new demands on the federation for which the old structure has proven inadequate. Conflict is built into its internal system. Autonomy and jealousy ensure the perpetuation of conflict. The labor movement might well question whether it can afford the luxury of more defeats of the type it sustained in 1959.

It is quite clear that both general and specific resistances to change grew within the AFL-CIO as the legislation progressed in Congress. Increasingly, the labor movement, especially certain of the internationals, felt threatened. It is clear that President Meany himself, especially in light of his sharp and bitter clashes with the leaders of the CIO and the personal demogogic attacks on him by the Teamsters through AFL-CIO local unions, felt threatened. Seated atop the organizational rug which covered the bouncing, shifting heads of internally squabbling international unions, he could hardly have been comfortable or secure. The psychological reaction to threat was evident in the behavior of the AFL-CIO (in addition to the Teamsters) at certain points. Part of the feeling of threat was generated by the inability of the labor movement to trust in the Democratic political leadership. At no point did they, the unions, appear secure in the belief that the Democratic leadership (especially in the House) would do its best for them. Lyndon Johnson had written a letter to management people which would clearly lend credence to the apparent fears of the leaders of the AFL-CIO.[1] This problem was not of single or simple origin.

The interrelations of various unions at the local level should be stressed. In some localities and states—Arkansas, for example—the local leader of the Teamsters Union was the most responsible, honorable, and effective leader of the labor movement of that region. Yet, the Teamsters were in disrepute at the national level. The local people found it extremely difficult, if not impossible, to disassociate themselves from the men who were their friends of long standing merely because they were Teamsters. When the Teamsters, the avowed target of the legislation, were threatened, they themselves felt threatened.[2]

The labor movement manifested several specific resistances to change. Some leaders reacted strongly to Kennedy, feeling that he was more interested in his presidential candidacy than in the problems of the labor movement (a suspicion which may have been well founded, but which ignored the fact that Kennedy could not achieve the one without successfully dealing with the other). The IAM pro-

[1] The letter reprinted in the New York *Times,* Jan. 6, 1960, pointed to Johnson's support for Taft-Hartley over Truman's veto and to his support for much of Landrum-Griffin.

[2] A reliable source in the labor movement stated that the Arkansas leader resigned as president of the state AFL-CIO but still functioned as effective leader of the organization on an ad hoc basis.

duced and showed to every local union which would permit it a movie of Senator Morse clearly and logically expounding on the "betrayal" of labor by its liberal friends. Morse pointed to problems in the legislation which "demonstrated" this.

Clearly, the resistance to change grew as the change progressed. Equally clearly, the forces for change in the country as a whole grew in even greater measure. It was this fact that the AFL-CIO did not or could not bring itself to understand until too late. It would have taken such recognition for the federation to be truly effective. It would have taken recognition of its relative weakness for the federation to have realized its potential strength. Its change in identity —resulting from effective reform legislation—might have been achieved at considerably lower cost, but, once set in motion, the process of change could not be stopped.

The distinctive feature of the management side of the labor reform battle was the degree of participation by the White House. The direct coordination of the management groups by the Administration made possible working relationships which were smoother than had ever been achieved before among usually widely ranging groups. The management side worked more closely *without* formal organizational ties than did the labor movement with its "united" federation.

Differences in the positions of the two groups make such direct comparison difficult, however. First, legislation is passed by votes of congressmen. Management was clearly outvoted in the committees of both houses. Management had been able to count on the support of a coalition of Republicans and Southern Democrats for a number of years, but the coalition would not work automatically or on all questions. It operated after some negotiation on some issues. The odds against an "all-management bill" in such a Congress were astronomically high. In fact, the prevention of a "giveaway" to labor would have been considered a major victory in the perspective of the early months of 1959. This put a premium on optimal use of all legislative resources. It made unity of effort essential. The recognition of certain basic weaknesses and the possible remedy to such weaknesses was a source of great strength to the management side.

There were natural advantages for the conservative side in a labor issue. It was easiest for management groups to achieve emotional consensus, even if there might be disagreement on certain substantive problems. The willingness or eagerness of the White House to take an active role helped solve some of the potentially embarrassing status problems among independent associations.

The management side practiced what had been demonstrated earlier to be effective tactics. It capitalized on the public mood of indignation at evidence of corruption in some unions (and managements) to bring about changes in labor-management power relations. The legislation resulted from an evil which was widely publicized and skillfully manipulated.

The public exposure of evil brought pain to a major group—the labor unions—and resulted in their commitment to change. Once there was commitment to change, the battle raged over the substance of this change. Management sought—by tying its objective to the issue of reform and phrasing public discussion in terms of this issue alone—the achievement of an objective only indirectly related to the issue on which there was such strong public reaction.

The Crucial Factor

The most crucial factor in the total picture was the reaction of the public to the issue of labor corruption.

The Select Committee on Improper Activities in Labor-Management Affairs had publicized the issue. It brought about the original painful change in the identity of the labor movement. It set the climate of opinion in which public and congressional discussion of labor matters took place. The hearings of the committee and the publicity they received made it possible for the conservative forces to advocate openly the revision of the power balance between management and labor, although they never stated their case in these blunt terms. The question was always one of effective reform (as had been the February statements of the AFL-CIO Executive Council demanding sweeteners) and a "strong" measure necessary to achieve reform.

The existence of corruption in some unions had not led to a "house cleaning" by the AFL-CIO. True, the CIO had stipulated as one of its conditions for merger with the AFL the necessity for the elimination of corrupt unions. But it was the actual public exposure of existing corruption which stung the AFL-CIO into action. The changed image of the labor movement required strong action. After the expulsion of more than 10 percent of its membership and the adoption of a code of ethical practices for the conduct of union affairs, the AFL-CIO recognized that it had not and could not achieve the goal of "purification" on its own. It could not expect to have influence on unions no longer a part of its organization. The recommendations for legislation prepared by the McClellan Committee suggested the obvious avenue for such purification. The Republicans in the Senate prodded the Democratic congressional leadership for action on the recommendations. The 1958 Kennedy-Ives bill, given the blessing of the AFL-CIO, was the result. These three acts committed labor to a change in identity through legislation on the issue of internal union reform.

Chairmanship of the Rackets Committee made McClellan a center of power in the Senate in 1959, able to rival the bill's floor manager, Senator Kennedy, for leadership on the floor. Passage of his bill of rights, even though by a single vote, was the first indication of the character of legislation which would finally emerge. The signal was dismissed by the AFL-CIO as a temporary aberration which had been quickly reversed, but it was to prove a closer measure of the sentiment of the Congress and the country than any other Senate vote.

When the bill reached the House of Representatives and the conservative side called to the general public for support, it was to the information supplied him by the McClellan Committee that the citizen looked for the basis for his decisions. President Eisenhower's appeal for support of "strong" reform legislation was the catalyst, along with the earlier plea by Robert Kennedy, which activated the private citizen and brought him to commit his personal resources to political influence, to take up the slack in his political impact. The people responded to the President on the basis of their evaluation made from McClellan Committee data.

Once activated, the public had its impact on the political professional and on his subjective evaluation of the mood of the voters in his district. Dahl has pointed to the usual manner in which private citizens go about making decisions on questions referred to them by the political professionals. He has also clearly analyzed the radical change in the character of a problem after it has been referred to the people by the "dissenters," those who feel they can't win at the political level: [3]

If the dissenters succeed in forcing the issue out beyond the political stratum, and the dissenters and legitimists begin making appeals to the populace, then the nature of the debate begins to change. Technical questions, subtle distinctions, fine matters of degree are shed. The appeal is now shaped to the simple democratic creed which nearly every citizen believes in. Because the creed does not constitute a tightly logical system, it is possible for the legitimist to demonstrate that the existing norms are necessarily consequences of the creed, and for the dissenters to show that existing norms run counter to the creed. Because the creed is deeply laden with tradition and sentiment, emotion rises and reasoned discussion declines.[4]

When the ordinary citizen perceives that the professionals are turning to him for a decision when usually he has relied on them to interpret his over-all democratic ideals, he is faced with a dilemma.

Management people felt themselves beaten at the congressional level, so they socialized the resolution of the issue. With a simplified issue supported and attacked through slogans, the deck was stacked against the AFL-CIO.

The bill the labor people backed in the House, the Shelley bill, was introduced merely as "something to support." The bill labor should have been backing (if it were to achieve its objective), the Elliott bill, was presented by its major proponents as a "compromise bill," a "middle-of-the-road bill." The bill presented by the conservative coalition had been characterized by the President of the United States as the "strong" labor reform measure. The man in the street could easily surmise that to control "corrupt" unions and their "arrogant" leaders, especially James Hoffa, strong measures were both necessary and desirable. The President had said that strong reform required prohibition of secondary boycotts and organizational picketing, and the application of state laws to labor disputes shunned by

[3] Here again, note the parallel to Schattsneider (see Chapter I, footnote 5); the weak seek the socialization of the issue.

[4] Robert A. Dahl, *Who Governs?: Democracy and Power in an American City* (New Haven, Yale University Press, 1961), p. 322.

the NLRB. How would the untutored be made to understand and differentiate justifiable secondary boycotts from reprehensible ones? Or the application of federal law in state courts for no man's land cases instead of federal law in state agencies (or federal courts) or state law in state courts? It could not be done with slogans. Nor could rapid shifts from opposition to support of complex measures on short notice aid in such understanding. The delay in mail delivery alone was too great to allow effective support for the type of shift the AFL-CIO made in August of 1959.

A Matter of "If"

The best ally the management groups had was the AFL-CIO. The obstinate refusal of the federation to see beyond its own problems made life miserable for its closest supporters while achieving nothing for the federation itself. The unwillingness to accept the advice of the professionals, especially Speaker Rayburn and Representatives Bolling and Metcalf, caused the unnecessary splintering and dissipation of the power of the liberal side. The closeness of the crucial vote indicated that victory was within reach of the liberals—even with their lack of coordination, their disunity, debacles, and blunders. It seems highly likely that consistent AFL-CIO support for the Elliott bill could have brought the whole-hearted backing of the UAW and other industrial unions as well as of the Building Trades Council and lost only the "ultras" who thought along the same lines as the Teamsters. A consistent position could have avoided much of the personal animosity of the course selected—and would probably have meant the passage of the Elliott bill. From the point of view of labor it was clear that the Elliott bill would have been preferable to the Kennedy bill (we have seen that the Senate conferees receded on most matters which offered them essentially this choice). The final outcome could have been less restrictive of unions had this been done.

If the leaders of the labor movement had perceived their problem as one of social change through change in identity (minus the jargon and scholastic trappings), they could have anticipated the resistances and interferences which in fact developed. A statesmanlike attitude could have resulted in a winning position. Effective slogans to differentiate the AFL-CIO from the Teamsters could have been developed early, since it should have been clear that the Teamsters would be unable to support any legislation at all. Cooperation with the Democratic leadership in the House—at least in recognition that the leadership did have effective control of the House committee and that there was no alternative—would have greatly improved the atmosphere in the House, a closed system in which atmosphere is of great importance.

Even at a much earlier stage, when the labor people saw the strength of the management reaction to the Taft-Hartley changes included in the proposed legislation to "buy" the cooperation of particular unions, they could easily have anticipated an all-out effort to push management-backed provisions through under the guise of reform (the same guise adopted for the labor sweeteners). It was labor opposition which had prevented modification of Taft-Hartley to the mutual benefit of management and labor. It would appear to have been better strategy to allow a "reform" measure through the Congress to take the steam and sting from the issues fanned by the McClellan Committee, and then to harness management enthusiasm to a reasonable and equitable shift in Taft-Hartley provisions. Of course, these suggestions are made after a large dose of that potent elixir, hindsight, but analysis of the past can often provide lessons for the future. Over the years the labor movement has shown substantial immunity to that usually great educator, experience. When tactics have failed in the past, the AFL-CIO and other unions have apparently reasoned that the fault could be overcome through more energetic application of the same tactic in the future. Each international has felt free to pursue its own narrow ends during a legislative battle while blaming the parent federation for the failure of the broader, over-all effort. The fact is, there is not, and perhaps never has been, a labor "movement" in this country. There is—and has been, at least since the days of the Depression—an inharmonious group of autonomous unions capped with a purposely weak and ineffective superstructure, the parent federation.

Political Parties

The Democratic leadership of the Congress operated in a way which supports the statement that "interest groups are more a captive of the party than the party of the group." [5] It consistently defied the wishes of the labor movement, although it did so in an attempt to do minimum harm to the labor movement while at the same time assuring that labor reform legislation would be passed by the Congress. The experience must have been an excruciating one for the leaders of labor, especially if the labor leaders had begun to believe the press notices about "unbridled union power." The labor movement fiddled, but the Congress would not dance to its tune. The Party and its presidential candidates needed a labor bill to demonstrate their responsibility and their concern for the public interest.

There were no alternatives open to the labor people. They could extol Jacob Javits and curse Graham Barden, but their only avenue of effective action was still through the Democratic Party. Their best hope of preventing a recurrence of the defeat they had just suffered was to support John F. Kennedy for the Presidency. They would certainly not be better served with Richard Nixon as President and Barry Goldwater as chairman of the Senate Subcommittee on Labor.

There is evidence that the same phenomenon existed on the conservative-management side of the issue. Technical decisions were being made by the experts, political decisions by the professionals. Suggestions were entertained, the positions and expectations of various groups understood, but the political leaders appeared to be making the decisions on what was possible of achievement. Consultation was often after the fact, leading the management people to complain of their lot in perceived contrast to the actions of the liberal Democrats with labor groups.

There is no question that the presidential candidacy of a number of persons in the Senate interfered with the passage of the labor reform law on its merits. It is doubtful if the Senate Republicans would have closed ranks so solidly in favor of the McClellan bill of rights if there had been no Democratic presidential candidate to be embarrassed by their actions. It is probable that the Majority Leader in the Senate would have given greater support to the bill on the Senate floor if such actions would not have given direct support to a rival for the presidency. But the attraction of a personality who

[5] See E. E. Schattsneider, *The Semisovereign People: A Realist's View of Democracy in America* (New York, Holt, Rinehart, and Winston, 1960).

might one day be President of the United States in need of a Cabinet, skilled advisors, and trusted supporters is a great advantage, a bonus for the backers of a bill. On balance, however, it would appear that the interference worked to the disadvantage of the liberal side.

The Public Influence

The statement has been made that the public exerted the crucial influence in the passage of labor reform legislation. Yet, the study which has been presented indicates a vast array of personalities, forces, and events, all of which did impinge directly or indirectly on the outcome. In the face of this evidence, one might say that the conclusion "the people demanded a labor reform law" is a mere recitation of the management propaganda, or, more damning, irrepressible idealism worthy only of a high school civics class.

Despite these potential evaluations, the judgment has nonetheless been stated. It was reached because of the evidence and not in spite of it; it was reached even after the repeated inhalation of the vapors of scholastic cynicism.

It was to change their public image, hopefully through changes of substance, that the labor movement agreed to back reform legislation of any kind. The Democratic Party had to demonstrate to the public that it was a responsible party—this was why there "had to be a bill."

There are more specific manifestations of the influence of the public which support the conclusion as well. The clearest evidence was presented in the analysis of the treatment of the bill by the House Committee on Education and Labor. The actions of the Democratic leadership and their agents, the faithful five, were undertaken at great cost. Their efforts to develop a reasonable bill which would do minimum harm to the labor movement and still have a chance of passage in the House were met only with pressure and pain. Their legislative product was not designed to please management people or the Administration. At the same time, there must have been a good reason for the liberal Democrats to displease their closest political allies so thoroughly.

The concentration of the House Democratic leadership on, first, passing a bill and, second, passing a bill which would be a political asset demonstrates their preoccupation with the reaction of the public. The Democratic leadership could not have been swayed by direct pressure from the Eisenhower Administration or by the direct pressure of management groups (indeed they refused to be swayed by pressure from one of their allies, the labor movement). They were directly influenced by the actions and reactions of the public as reflected through the normal political channels. The leadership did adjust its strategy to the "reality" of the political climate. It has been recognized, however, that at the same time the Administration and the management groups were devoting their resources to long- and intermediate-range political meteorology.

The coalition groups recognized the necessity to bring a bill to the floor of the House through the regular channels because they were also aware that public pressure for a bill would have forced the passage of the Kennedy bill under suspension of the rules procedures if it had not.

The recognition of congressmen from all but the solidly union districts that they had to be *for* something (supporting the Shelley bill was equivalent to being against reform) indicated their perception of political necessity. Poignant statements of such concern were made to more than one labor lobbyist by congressmen with whom they had grown quite friendly. The statements were not designed to mislead. These congressmen were not stating that they had to be for a particular form of reform, merely that they had to support reform of some kind—because "the people demanded a labor reform law."

A few congressmen who were interviewed several months after the passage of the law still showed strong emotional conflict when they told of facing the tellers on the showdown vote and at the same time glancing at the reporters from their home-district newspapers who were ready to inform constituents of the decision that their congressman made. One congressman flatly stated that he would have voted for the Elliott bill except for the fact that his constituents would have learned of his decision in the next day's paper.

After the crucial teller vote had been lost, the numbers of the Elliott bill supporters began to shrink. The consecutive votes went 215 to 201, 229 to 205, and then, when it was certain that Landrum-

Griffin could not be defeated, 303 to 125. The size of the first record vote has been remarked; legislators could not fail to be recorded on this issue in 1959. When they were "released," an additional seventy-three congressmen found it expedient to be recorded on the positive side of the issue.

It has also been stated in an earlier section of this chapter that, with a modified strategy, labor could have ensured the passage of the Elliott bill. This statement in no way detracts from the conclusion that the public was the crucial influence on legislation, because the Elliott bill embodied those provisions which the House leadership felt were necessary to generate favorable public reaction.

The situation in the Senate is not as easily analyzed because there was an interaction of two important variables: the pressure from the public (resulting from disclosures of corruption through committee investigations) and the influence of the man who had gained great stature and prestige through the conduct of the investigations, Senator McClellan. The near unanimity of the final vote supports the conclusion, however, that, as with the support of motherhood and the American flag, a senator could not go wrong with a vote for labor reform. The public demanded it.

The influence of the public was more subtle in the Conference Committee. Everyone wanted reform, and some conferees would have supported "punitive" provisions behind closed doors, but on any issue which would be aired in public (such as by being referred back to the floor of either House) each side hoped to present itself as being "fair," "reasonable," and in support of legitimate unions. (Reform, *si*; sweatshops, *no!*) But even here a continued pressure was recognized. If they were to delay too long, the situation might become explosive, because a bill had to be passed.

It has been pointed out that the McClellan Committee informed the public of improper activities in labor-management affairs. We have now seen the degree to which management groups were able to capitalize on this awareness and channel it even to particular congressional districts. This factor, then, must be included along with the legitimizing and activating function of President Eisenhower when striking the balance in determining causation in the defeat of labor which had been so totally unexpected a few months before.

Impact of the Act

The impact of the law has not been as extreme as expected or at least as predicted in the propaganda of the two sides. There are several reasons for this:

(1) The participants perceived the law in its worst form—not the form in which it was finally passed. The union people were often outraged at what "management tried to do," while failing to understand clearly what the content of the act was as passed.

(2) A given provision may often, under extreme circumstances, be interpreted in a very detrimental way. Extreme circumstances are sometimes encountered in some district courts, but not in appeals courts or the Supreme Court.

(3) The laws may be effectively amended through administration. In today's environment both the interpretation and the administration of the laws have been in a "reasonable" direction.

(4) The impact of the law on existing unions has not been nearly so great as the impact on the establishment or expansion of unions in hostile environments. The law has been more of a "contraceptive" than of a "killer."

(5) Perhaps the reform portions of the law have had less impact than expected because management was not really interested in them. Perhaps management never intended to use them as wedges for the destruction of unions.

The law "to get Jimmie Hoffa" did not "get Jimmie Hoffa." It freed Hoffa from court-appointed monitors because he scrupulously followed the election procedures outlined in the act and thus became undisputed president of the Teamsters Union.

Yet, this was labor reform legislation. It was a modification of the strongest version of reform legislation which had been seriously considered. The Select Committee on Improper Activities in Labor-Management Affairs (the Rackets Committee) has been dissolved. The AFL-CIO has not readmitted the Teamsters Union. Dave Beck continues to serve his prison sentence for misuse of Teamster funds (convicted under laws in existence for many years prior to the activities of the McClellan Committee and still available for the prosecution of criminal acts).

The labor movement has achieved a change in identity. Social change has been accomplished through the medium of labor legislation.

Management has achieved an adjustment in its power relations with the labor movement. Additional barriers to the unionization of the industrialized South have been raised and old barriers strengthened.

Yet, the issues and, perhaps more important, the symbols over which the fight took place still exist. The thorniest problems of labor-management relations and of economic-government relations still plague our society. Automation, unemployment, inflation, recession, and the balance of payments are issues which have not been attacked in a direct assault by the government. In these areas a potential for strife exists which may rekindle public animosity to unions. The public can be reactivated on the same old issue by the injection of new and sustained publicity. Jimmie Hoffa remains as able and co-operative an antagonist as before. It is true that the avenues of access to political power have shifted considerably with the change in Administrations, but the experience of teamwork and the fruits it brought may make management dependence on Administration co-ordination less of a requirement than before.

The law has imposed a financial and administrative burden on the unions, especially the smaller unions, which now have an incentive to join together into larger unions. The bonding provisions have been especially burdensome. The law has led, in particular cases, to the unseating of unpopular and autocratic presidents of local unions. Even Caesar Petrillo has been dethroned. But, after a brief flurry of compliance, the law has been ignored by several large unions.

The law was passed. The "worst" of Landrum-Griffin had been removed. Other plans could now proceed. For John Fitzgerald Kennedy, the junior Senator from Massachusetts, the presidential campaign was to carry to victory. Each obstacle had been overcome in turn, but the closeness to defeat had been breathtaking. The labor law of 1959 had almost proved to be the barrier to success even before the campaign had been fully launched.

APPENDIX A

BIOGRAPHICAL DATA ON MEMBERS OF ADVISORY PANEL
ON LABOR-MANAGEMENT LAW REVISION

David Cole: Practicing attorney and arbitrator, active as labor relations counsel to textile employers; chairman of War Labor Board iron and steel panels; chairman, Presidential Inquiry in Bituminous Coal Industry and other presidential boards; president, National Academy of Arbitrators; past director, Federal Mediation and Conciliation Service.

Archibald Cox: Professor of law, Harvard University; formerly practiced law in Boston; formerly Associate Solicitor, Department of Labor; chairman, Wage Stabilization Board; cochairman, Construction Industry Stabilization Committee.

Guy Farmer: Practicing attorney specializing in labor law and representing management; formerly associate general counsel of the National Labor Relations Board and former chairman of the National Labor Relations Board under the Eisenhower Administration.

Arthur Goldberg: Practicing attorney, counsel to various labor organizations, including Steelworkers Union and Industrial Union Department, AFL-CIO; special counsel to AFL-CIO.

Charles Gregory: Professor of law, University of Virginia; former professor of law at the University of Wisconsin and University of Chicago; formerly practiced law in New York; formerly Solicitor of Labor.

Clark Kerr: President, University of California; arbitrator; author of numerous works on labor matters; chairman, UAW impartial review board.

Denison Kitchel: Practicing attorney from Phoenix, Arizona, representing management in labor matters; counsel, American Mining Congress.

Plato E. Papps: Counsel, International Association of Machinists; chairman, American Bar Association panel on NLRB practices and procedures.

Gerald [sic] Reilly: Practicing attorney, representing management; practiced law in Boston and later in Washington, D.C.; formerly Assistant Solicitor and Solicitor of Department of Labor; member, National Labor Relations Board; former counsel, Senate Committee on Labor and Public Welfare.

Louis Sherman: Practicing attorney, representing labor organizations, including the Building and Construction Trades Department, AFL-CIO; general counsel, IBEW (AFL-CIO); former chairman of the ABA Committee on the Labor-Management Relations Act of 1947; Assistant Solicitor of Labor.

Russell Smith: Professor of law, University of Michigan; arbitrator; former industry member, National War Labor Board; served on various public fact-finding bodies.

W. Willard Wirtz: Practicing attorney; professor of law, Northwestern University; arbitrator; former chairman, National Wage Stabilization Board; General Counsel and later public member of the War Labor Board.

SOURCE: *Daily Congressional Record,* Feb. 16, 1959, p. 2,108.

APPENDIX B

SECONDARY BOYCOTT COMMITTEE,
UNITED STATES CHAMBER OF COMMERCE

C. Boydd Mahin, *chairman,* attorney, Chicago.
H. E. Aldrich, American Bosche Company.
M. V. Barnhill, Jr., general solicitor, Atlantic Coast Railroad.
Robert Barrett, Deere and Company.*
Desmond Barry, Galveston Truck Lines.
A. R. Borden, president, Borden Metal Products.
Robert T. Borth, General Electric Company.†
S. J. Campbell, Harry T. Campbell and Sons.*
Lucius P. Chase, Kohler Company.†
Robert Clark, Atcheson, Topeka and Santa Fe Railroad.
Arthur Erwin, National Lumber Manufacturers.† ‡
Parker M. Holt, Holt Brothers, Stockton.
Paul R. Karer, president, Tasty Baking Company.
Gilbert L. Klein, Falk Corporation.
O. C. Lance, manager, National Woodwork Manufacturer's Association.
Irving L. Malcolm, J. L. Hudson Company.
Henry J. Marshall, director of employee relations, Armstrong Cork Company.
William L. McGrath, president, The Williamson Company.*
A. F. Metz, chairman of the board, Okonite Company.* ᵃ
Ben Miller, American Trade Association.‡
Morgan R. Mooney, United Aircraft.
Andrew Murphy, Jr., National Association of Home Builders.†
Erwin Nachaus, Great Western Sugar.
Frank R. Pitt, DeVilbiss Company.
Herbert M. Ramel, president, Precision Auto Company.*
F. C. Sawyer, executive vice-president, The Burt Manufacturing Company.*
Ellison D. Smith, Jr., attorney, Columbia, N.C.†
M. Maynard Smith, attorney, Smith and Swift.†

E. C. Swanson, vice-president, Andersen Corporation.
W. B. Thomas, Thomas Associates.*
Charles Tower, National Association of Broadcasters.† b
John T. Tuttle, Oneida Daily Dispatch.*
T. E. Veltfort, Copper and Brass Research Association.
H. Leigh Whitelow, Gas Appliance Manufacturers.

* Member of Publicity Subcommittee.
† Member of Legislative Subcommittee.
‡ It is possible that there are minor errors in indicated title.
ᵃ Chairman, Publicity Subcommittee.
ᵇ Chairman, Legislative Subcommittee.

APPENDIX C

BIOGRAPHICAL DATA ON SOME PARTICIPANTS IN
LANDRUM-GRIFFIN

THE HOUSE OF REPRESENTATIVES

Barden, Graham Arthur, Democratic Representative from N.C.; born in Turkey Township, Sampson Co., N.C., 1896; attended the public schools; during World War I served as a seaman in the U.S. Navy, 1918–19; was graduated from law department of University of North Carolina at Chapel Hill, 1920; admitted to bar, 1920, and commenced practice in New Bern, N.C., judge of county court of Craven Co., N.C., 1920–24; member of state house of representatives, 1933; served in Seventy-fourth and twelve succeeding Congresses, 1935–60, retired 1960; one of the Southern leaders of the House, Chairman of the Committee on Education and Labor.

Bolling, Richard Walker, Democratic Representative from Mo.; born in New York City, N.Y., 1916; attended Phillips-Exeter Academy, N.H.; was graduated from University of the South, Sewanee, Tenn., 1937, graduate work at University of the South and Vanderbilt University; educational administrator by profession; during World War II served in U.S. Army, 1941–46, discharged as a lieutenant colonel, overseas service as assistant chief of staff to Gen. MacArthur, awarded Legion of Merit and Bronze Star; Midwest director of Americans for Democratic Action, May–July, 1947; served in Eighty-first and six succeeding Congresses (Jan., 1949—); for several years a member of the informal Democratic leadership of the House, serving on the Rules Committee and the Joint Economic Committee.

Dent, John Herman, Democratic Representative from Pa.; born in Johnetta, Armstrong Co., Pa., 1908; educated in the public schools, the Great Lakes Naval Aviation Academy, and through correspondence school courses; member of local council of United Rubber Workers, 1923–37, served as president of Local 18759 and on executive council, also member of the international council; served in U.S. Marine Air Corps, 1924–28; member of state house of representatives, 1935–37; elected to state senate,

1936, re-elected 1940, 1944, 1948, 1952, and 1956, Democratic floor leader in state senate, 1939–58; operated Keldon Coal and Coke Co. of Hunkers, Pa., and Building and Transportation Co. of Trafford and Jeannette, Pa.; elected to Eighty-fifth Congress to fill vacancy caused by the death of Augustine B. Kelly, re-elected to Eighty-sixth and Eighty-seventh Congresses (Jan., 1958—), representing coal-mining district; served on Education and Labor Committee.

Elliott, Carl Atwood, Democratic Representative from Ala.; born in Vina, Franklin Co., Ala., 1913; attended the public schools, was graduated from University of Alabama at Tuscaloosa, 1933, and from its law school, 1936; admitted to bar, 1936, and commenced practice in Russellville, Ala., judge of recorders court, Jasper, Ala., 1942 and 1946, city attorney for various Ala. cities; during World War II served with U.S. Army, 1942–44; member of Alabama state Democratic executive committee, 1942–50; compiler of Annals of Northwest Alabama, Vol. I (1958) and Vol. II (1959); served in Eighty-first and six succeeding Congresses (Jan., 1949—); member of the Education and Labor Committee and (since 1961) of Rules Committee, one of the "faithful five" and sponsor of the committee (Elliott) bill.

Green, Edith, Democratic Representative from Ore.; born in Trent, Moody Co., S.D., 1910; attended Ore. schools and Willamette University, was graduated from University of Oregon at Eugene, 1939, graduate work at Stanford University, 1944; taught school in Salem, Ore., 1930–41, staff member of Portland Radio Station KPOJ and with station KALE, 1943–47; legislative representative of state Parent-Teachers Association to state legislature, 1951, director of public relations and legislative representative of Oregon Education Association for 1953 legislature, Democratic candidate for state secretary of state, 1952, delegate to Democratic national convention, 1956; U.S. delegate to Interparliamentary Conference in Switzerland, 1958, congressional delegate to NATO conference in London, 1959; served in Eighty-fourth and three succeeding Congresses (Jan., 1955—), representing a unionized industrial district; served on the Education and Labor Committee, one of the "faithful five."

Griffin, Robert Paul, Republican Representative from Mich.; born in Detroit, Mich., 1923; attended the public schools; during World War II served in U.S. Army as an enlisted man, awarded two battle stars; graduated from Central Michigan College at Mount Pleasant, 1947, attended The Citadel, Charleston, S.C., and Shrivenham University, England, graduated from University of Michigan Law School, 1950; admitted to bar, 1950, and commenced practice in Traverse, Mich.; served in Eighty-fifth and two succeeding Congresses (Jan., 1957—), representing an industrial and suburban district; member of the Education and Labor Committee and cosponsor of the Landrum-Griffin bill.

Halleck, Charles Abraham, Republican Representative from Ind.; born in Demotte, Jasper Co., Ind., 1900; attended the public schools; during World War I served in U.S. Army; was graduated from Indiana University at Bloomington, 1922, and from law department of same university, 1924; admitted to bar, 1924, and commenced practice in Rensselaer, Ind.; prosecuting attorney for thirtieth judicial circuit, 1924–34; elected to Seventy-fourth Congress to fill vacancy caused by the death of Congressman-elect Frederick Landis; re-elected to Seventy-fifth and to the twelve succeeding Congresses (Jan. 1935—); Majority Leader in Eightieth and Eighty-third Congresses, Minority Leader Eighty-sixth and Eighty-seventh Congresses, a key member of the conservative coalition in the House.

Harris, Oren, Democratic Representative from Ark.; born in Belton, Hempstead Co., Ark., 1903; attended the public schools, was graduated from Henderson College, Arkadelphia, Ark., 1929, and from the Cumberland University Law School, Lebanon, Tenn., 1930; admitted to bar, 1930, and commenced practice in El Dorado, Ark., deputy prosecuting attorney of Union Co., Ark., 1933–36, prosecuting attorney of the thirteenth judicial circuit of Ark., 1936–40; delegate to Democratic state conventions, 1936 and 1940, and to Democratic national convention at Chicago, 1944; served in Seventy-seventh and ten succeeding Congresses (Jan., 1941—), representing a rural, agricultural district; chairman of the Interstate and Foreign Commerce Committee and Subcommittee on Regulatory Agencies.

Landrum, Phillip Mitchell, Democratic Representative from Ga.; born in Martin, Stephens Co., Ga., 1909; attended the public schools and Mercer University, Macon, Ga., was graduated from Piedmont College, Demorest, Ga., 1939, and from the Atlanta Law School, 1941; admitted to bar, 1941, and commenced practice in Canton, Ga.; an unsuccessful candidate for nomination to Seventy-eighth Congress, 1942; during World War II served in U.S. Air Force, 1942–45; assistant attorney general of Ga., 1946 and 1947, executive secretary to governor of Ga., 1947 and 1948; served in Eighty-third and four succeeding Congresses (Jan., 1953—), representing a staunchly nonunion district; Chairman of the Labor Standards Subcommittee of the Education and Labor Committee, cosponsor of Landrum-Griffin bill.

Metcalf, Lee, Democratic Representative (later Senator) from Mont.; born in Stevensville, Ravalli Co., Mont., 1911; attended the public schools, was graduated from Stanford University, 1936, received law degree from Montana State University Law School; admitted to bar, 1936, and commenced practice of law; member of state house of representatives, 1937, assistant attorney general of Mont., 1937–41; during World War II served in U.S. Army; associate justice of state supreme court, 1946–52, delegate to state Democratic conventions, 1936, 1940, 1952–58, delegate to Democratic national convention, 1956; served in Eighty-third and three succeeding Congresses, 1953–60; member of the informal Democratic leadership of the House, member of the Ways and Means Committee and former member of the Committee on Education and labor; elected to Senate for term commencing Jan., 1961.

O'Hara, James Grant, Democratic Representative from Mich.; born in Washington, D.C., 1925; during World War II served in U.S. Army; was graduated from University of Michigan, 1954, and from law department of same university; admitted to bar, 1955, and commenced practice in Detroit; delegate to Democratic national convention, 1960; served in Eighty-sixth and Eighty-seventh Congresses (Jan., 1959—), representing a strongly unionized industrial district; member of the Education and Labor Committee and of the "faithful five."

Perkins, Carl Dewey, Democratic Representative from Ky.; born in Hindman, Knott Co., Ky., 1912; attended the public schools and Caney Junior College, was graduated from Jefferson School of Law, Louisville, 1935; admitted to bar, 1935, and commenced practice in Hindman, Ky.; in 1939 served out an unexpired term as commonwealth attorney from the thirty-first judicial district; member of Ky. general assembly, 1940; elected Knott Co. attorney, 1941, re-elected in 1945, resigned 1948 to become counsel for state department of highways; during World War II enlisted in U.S. Army and served in Europe; served in Eighty-first and six succeeding Congresses (Jan., 1949—), representing a coal-mining district; served on Labor Subcommittee of Committee on Education and Labor.

Powell, Adam Clayton, Jr., Democratic Representative from N.Y.; a Negro, born in New Haven, Conn., 1908; attended the public schools of New York City, was graduated from Colgate University, Hamilton, N.Y., 1930, from Columbia University, 1932, and from the theological department of Shaw University, Raleigh, N.C., 1934; studied four months in Europe, North Africa, and Asia Minor; was ordained to the ministry and has officiated in New York City since 1931; member of New York City Council, 1941, publisher and editor of a newspaper in New York City, 1941–45, instructor at Columbia University Extension School, Department of Religious Education, 1932–40, editorial writer for a New York City daily newspaper, 1934, cofounder of National Negro Congress, member of consumer division, state Office of Price Administration, 1942–44; served in Seventy-ninth and eight succeeding Congresses (Jan., 1945—), representing Harlem; member (and since 1961 chairman) of the Education and Labor Committee.

Pucinski, Roman Conrad, Democratic Representative from Ill.; born in Buffalo, N.Y., 1919; attended the public schools in Chicago, Northwestern University, 1938–41, and John Marshall Law School, 1945–49; staff reporter and writer for the Chicago Sun-Times, 1939–59; enlisted in U.S. Air Force, 1940, led his bomber group on the first B-29 bombing raid over Tokyo, 1944, discharged as a captain, 1945, awarded Distinguished

Flying Cross and Air Medal with Clusters; served as chief investigator for a select committee of Congress investigating the mass murder by the Communists of fifteen thousand Polish army officers in World War II; served in Eighty-sixth and Eighty-seventh Congresses (Jan., 1959—), representing a strongly unionized district; member of the Education and Labor Committee.

Rayburn, Sam, Democratic Representative from Tex.; born near Kingston, Roane Co., Tenn., 1882; attended rural schools in Tex. and was graduated from East Texas Normal College, Commerce, Tex., 1903, studied law at University of Texas at Austin; admitted to bar, 1908, and commenced practice in Bonham, Tex.; member of state house of representatives, 1907–13, served as speaker, 1911–13; served in Sixty-third and twenty-four succeeding Congresses, 1913–61; Majority Leader in Seventy-fifth and Seventy-sixth Congresses, Minority Leader in Eightieth and Eighty-third Congresses, elected Speaker, 1940, to fill vacancy caused by the death of William B. Bankhead, re-elected Speaker in Seventy-seventh, Seventy-eighth, Seventy-ninth, Eighty-first, Eighty-second, Eighty-fourth, Eighty-fifth, Eighty-sixth, and Eighty-seventh Congresses; died 1961.

Smith, Howard W., Democratic Representative from Va.; born in Broad Run, Fauquier Co., Va., 1883; attended the public schools, was graduated from Bethel Military Academy, Warrenton, Va., 1901, and from the law department of the University of Virginia at Charlottesville, 1903; admitted to bar, 1904, and commenced practice in Alexandria, Va.; assistant general counsel to Alien Property Custodian, 1917 and 1918; served as commonwealth attorney of Alexandria, Va., 1918–22, judge of corporation court of Alexandria, 1922–28, judge of sixteenth judicial circuit of Va., 1928–30; also engaged in banking, farming, and dairying; served in Seventy-second and fifteen succeeding Congresses (March, 1931—), representing rural, agricultural district; chairman of the Rules Committee and thus one of the most powerful men in Congress, has special interest in labor matters.

Thompson, Frank, Jr., Democratic Representative from N.J.; born in Trenton, N.J., 1918; attended parochial and public schools, was graduated from Wake Forest (N.C.) College, 1941, and from Wake Forest Law School, 1948; served in U.S. Navy, 1941–48, received three combat decorations for action at Iwo Jima and Okinawa, commanded naval reserve battalion, 1950–52; admitted to bar, 1948, and commenced practice in Trenton; member of state house of assembly, 1950–54, serving as assistant minority leader in 1950 and minority leader in 1954; served in Eighty-fourth and three succeeding Congresses (Jan., 1955—), representing strongly unionized industrial district; member of the Education and Labor Committee and a key member of the "faithful five."

Udall, Stewart Lee, Democratic Representative from Ariz.; born in St. John, Apache Co., Ariz., 1920; attended the public schools and Eastern

Arizona Junior College; during World War II served in U.S. Air Force; was graduated from the law school of University of Arizona at Tucson, 1948; admitted to bar, 1948, and commenced practice in Tucson, Ariz.; trustee of school district, 1954; served in Eighty-fourth and three succeeding Congresses, 1955–61, representing an urban district where unions are not strong; member of the Education and Labor Committee and a key member of the "faithful five"; became Secretary of the Interior to President John F. Kennedy, 1961.

THE SENATE

Church, Frank Forrester, Democratic Senator from Idaho; born in Boise, Idaho, 1954; attended the public schools, was graduated from Stanford University, 1947, and from Stanford Law School, 1950; during World War II served in U.S. Army; admitted to bar, 1950, and commenced practice in Boise, Idaho; selected as temporary chairman and keynoter of Democratic national convention and elected chairman of Idaho delegation, 1960; elected to Senate for terms commencing 1957 and 1963; a liberal Democrat, member of the Interior and Insular Relations Committee (Indian Affairs) and Foreign Relations Committee (International Organization Affairs).

Clark, Joseph Sill, Democratic Senator from Pa.; born in Philadelphia, Pa., 1901; attended Chestnut Hill Academy, was graduated from Middlesex School, 1919, Harvard University, 1923, and University of Pennsylvania Law School, 1926; admitted to bar, 1926, and commenced practice in Philadelphia; during World War II served with U.S. Army Air Force; city controller of Philadelphia, 1950–52; mayor of Philadelphia, 1952–56; member of board of overseers of Harvard University since 1953; elected to Senate for terms commencing 1957 and 1963; a liberal Democrat, member of the Banking and Currency Committee (International Finance), Labor and Public Welfare Committee (Employment and Manpower), Post Office and Civil Service Committee (Retirement), and Special Committee on Aging (Housing for the Elderly).

Dirksen, Everett McKinley, Republican Senator from Ill.; born in Pekin, Tazewell Co., Ill., 1896; attended the public schools and the University of Minnesota College of Law at Minneapolis; during World War I served overseas in U.S. Army, 1918–19; general manager of a dredging company, 1922–25; commissioner of finance of Pekin, Ill., 1927–31; admitted to bar, 1936, and commenced practice in Pekin, Ill.; served as a Representative in the Seventy-third and seven succeeding Congresses, 1933–49; elected to Senate for terms commencing 1951, 1957, and 1963; member of the Subcommittee on Labor of the Committee on Labor and Public Welfare, since 1959 Senate Minority Leader, a major force among conservatives of both parties.

Ervin, Samuel James, Jr., Democratic Senator from N.C.; born in Morganton, Burke Co., N.C., 1896; attended the public schools, was graduated from University of North Carolina at Chapel Hill, 1917, and from the law school of Harvard University, 1922; during World War I served in U.S. Army in France, awarded the French Fourragère, the Purple Heart with Oak Leaf Cluster, the Silver Star, and the Distinguished Service Cross; admitted to bar, 1919, and commenced practice in Morganton, N.C., 1922; member of the state general assemblies of 1923, 1925, and 1931, member of the state Democratic executive committee, 1930–37, judge of Burke Co. criminal court, 1935–37, judge of N.C. superior court, 1937–43, member of state board of law examiners, 1944–46; elected as Representative to Seventy-ninth Congress to fill vacancy caused by the death of his brother, Joseph W. Ervin, and served 1946–47; resumed practice of law, associate justice of state supreme court, 1948–50; elected to Senate to fill vacancy caused by the death of Clyde R. Hoey and served 1954–57, re-elected for terms commencing 1957 and 1963; a Southern member of the conservative coalition, member of the Armed Services Committee (Status of Forces), Judiciary Committee (Revision and Codification, Constitutional Rights), and Select Committee on Labor-Management Relations, nominal cosponsor of Kennedy-Ervin bill.

Goldwater, Barry Morris, Republican Senator from Ariz.; born in Phoenix, Ariz., 1909; attended the public schools, Staunton Military Academy, and University of Arizona at Tucson, 1928; began merchandising career in 1929 in family mercantile business, partner in Rainbow Lodge and Trading Post on Navajo Indian Reservation, Tonalea, Ariz.; during World War II served in U.S. Air Force; served with Ariz. National Guard, 1945–52, chief of staff, Ariz. Air National Guard, 1946–52, brigadier general in Air Force Reserve, 1959; member of advisory committee on Indian affairs, Department of Interior, 1948–50; member of city council of Phoenix, 1949–52; elected to Senate for terms commencing 1953 and 1959, a staunch conservative; member of Labor Subcommittee of Committee on Labor and Public Welfare, sponsor of Eisenhower Administration labor bills.

Javits, Jacob Koppel, Republican Senator from N.Y.; born in New York City, 1904; attended the public schools and night classes at Columbia University, was graduated from New York University Law School, 1926; admitted to bar, 1927, and commenced practice in New York City, lecturer and author of articles on economic problems; during World War II served with Chemical Warfare Service, awarded Legion of Merit and Army Commendation Ribbon; served as Representative in Eightieth and three succeeding Congresses, 1947–54; attorney general of N.Y., 1954–57; elected to Senate for terms commencing 1957 to 1963, a liberal Republican.

Johnson, Lyndon Baines, Democratic Senator from Tex. (later Vice-President of U.S.); born on a farm near Stonewall, Gillespie Co., Tex.,

1908; attended the public schools, was graduated from Southwest Texas State Teachers College at San Marcos, 1930, attended Georgetown University Law School, Washington, D.C.; teacher in Houston, Tex., public schools, 1930–32; served as secretary to Congressman Richard M. Kleberg 1932–35; state director of National Youth Administration, 1935–37; elected as Representative to Seventy-fifth Congress to fill vacancy caused by the death of James P. Buchanan, re-elected to Seventy-sixth and four succeeding Congresses and served 1937–49; lieutenant commander in U.S. Navy, 1941–42; delegate to Democratic national conventions in 1940, 1944, and 1948; unsuccessful candidate for election to Senate, 1941, elected to Senate for terms commencing 1949, 1955, and 1961, Majority Leader, 1953–61; elected U.S. Vice-President for term commencing 1961.

Kennedy, John Fitzgerald, Democratic Senator from Mass. (later President of U.S.); born in Brookline, Suffolk Co., Mass., 1917; attended Choate School, Wallingford, Conn., London School of Economics, London, England, 1935 and 1936, and Stanford University, was graduated from Harvard University, 1940; during World War II served as a lieutenant in U.S. Navy, 1941–45, awarded Navy and Marine Corps Medal and Purple Heart; wrote several books, engaged as correspondent for a news service and covered the San Francisco Conference, the British elections in 1945, and the Potsdam meeting in 1945; served as Representative in Eightieth and two succeeding Congresses, 1947–53; elected to Senate for terms commencing 1953 and 1959, chairman of the Subcommittee on Labor of the Committee on Labor and Public Welfare, sponsor of the Kennedy-Ives bill of 1958 and the Kennedy-Ervin bill of 1959; elected U.S. President for term commencing 1961.

McClellan, John Little, Democratic Senator from Ark.; born in Sheridan, Grant Co., Ark., 1896; attended the public schools; admitted to bar, 1913, and commenced practice in Sheridan, Ark.; during World War I served in U.S. Army; prosecuting attorney of seventieth judicial district of Ark., 1927–30; served as Representative in Seventy-fourth and Seventy-fifth Congresses, 1935–39; unsuccessful candidate for Democratic nomination for Senator, 1938; elected to Senate for terms commencing 1943, 1949, 1955, and 1961; member of Appropriations Committee (Department of State), Justice and Commerce Committee, chairman of Committee on Government Operations (and of its Permanent Subcommittee on Investigations), chairman of Labor Rackets Committee; leader of conservative coalition on labor legislation.

McNamara, Patrick Vincent, Democratic Senator from Mich.; born in North Weymouth, Mass., 1894; attended the public schools; labor leader in construction industry in Detroit, 1921–55, director, Detroit area of Office of Price Administration, rent division, 1942–45, vice-president of Stanley-Carter Co., Detroit, 1946–54, member of Detroit city council,

1946 and 1947, and Detroit board of education, 1949–55; elected to Senate for terms commencing 1955 and 1961; member of Labor Subcommittee of Labor and Public Welfare Committee, Public Works Committee (Public Roads), and Special Committee on Aging.

Morse, Wayne Lyman, Senator from Ore.; born near Madison, Dane Co., Wis., 1900; attended the public schools, was graduated from University of Wisconsin at Madison, 1923, from the law department of University of Minnesota at Minneapolis, 1928, and from Columbia University, 1932; taught argumentation at universities of Wisconsin and Minnesota, taught law at University of Oregon at Eugene, 1929–30 and served as dean and professor of law, 1931–44; member of state crime commission, administrative director of U.S. Attorney General's Survey of Release Procedures, 1936–39, Pacific Coast arbitrator for U.S. Department of Labor (maritime industry), 1938–42, chairman of President's Railway Emergency Board, 1941, alternate public member of National Defense Mediation Board, 1941, public member of National War Labor Board, 1942–44; elected to Senate as a Republican for terms commencing 1945 and 1951, elected to Senate as a Democrat for term commencing 1957, known as a "loner" and spokesman for some unpopular causes; member of District of Columbia Committee, Foreign Relations Committee (American Republic Affairs), Labor and Public Welfare Committee, Select Committee on Small Business.

Prouty, Winston Lewis, Republican Senator from Vt.; born in Newport, Orleans Co., Vt., 1906; attended the public schools, Bordentown (N.J) Military Institute, and Lafayette College, Easton, Pa.; mayor of Newport, 1938–41, member of the state house of representatives in 1941, 1945, and 1947, serving as speaker, 1948–50; officer and director of family-owned lumber and building material enterprises, director of bank in Newport; elected as a Representative to Eighty-second and three succeeding Congresses, 1951–59; elected to Senate for term commencing 1959, a liberal Republican; member of Labor Subcommittee of Committee on Labor and Public Welfare.

Randolph, Jennings, Democratic Senator from W. Va.; born in Salem, Harrison Co., W. Va., 1902; attended the public schools, was graduated from Salem (W. Va.) Academy, 1920, and Salem (W. Va.) College, 1924; associate editor of West Virginia Review at Charleston, 1925, head of department of public speaking and journalism at Davis and Elkins College, W. Va., 1926–32; unsuccessful candidate for election to Seventy-second Congress, 1930; served in Seventy-third and six succeeding Congresses, 1933–47; unsuccessful candidate for re-election to Eightieth Congress, 1946; professor of public speaking at Southeastern University, Washington, D.C., 1935–53, and dean of its School of Business Administration, 1952–58; assistant to president and director of public relations, Capital Airlines, Washington, D.C., 1947–58; delegate to Democratic national conventions in 1948, 1952, 1956, and 1960; elected to Senate to fill vacancy caused by the death of Matthew M. Neely and served 1958–61, re-elected for term commencing 1961, representing a state in which the United Mine Workers Union is politically very powerful; member of Public Works Committee, Select Committee on Small Business, Special Committee on Aging, and Labor Subcommittee of Committee on Labor and Public Welfare.

THE ADMINISTRATION

Gray, Robert Keith, Republican from Neb.; born 1922; among public offices: special assistant in the White House, 1956–57, acting secretary to the President, 1957–58, secretary of the cabinet, 1958–60; liaison man with management interest groups during 1959 labor reform legislation.

McCabe, Edward Aeneas, Republican from Washington, D.C.; born 1917; among public offices: general counsel to Committee on Education and Labor of House of Representatives, 1953–55, associate counsel to President, 1956–58, administrative assistant to the President, 1958; White House liaison with Congress for labor reform in 1959.

Morgan, Gerald Demuth, Republican from Md.; born 1908; among public offices: assistant legislative counsel to House of Representatives, 1935–45, special assistant in the White House, 1953, administrative assistant to the President, 1953–55, special counsel to the President, 1955–58, deputy assistant to the President, 1958–60.

APPENDIX D

THE DRAFTERS OF LANDRUM-GRIFFIN

The details of the participation of Gerard Reilly and Tom Shroyer were given by the same sources who detailed the participation of other persons at other stages in the development of this legislation. All details of participation, with the exception of the drafting of Landrum-Griffin, were substantiated in interviews with direct participants.

On the drafting of Landrum-Griffin, however, no two accounts were alike. One group of sources was consistent in stating that only a few persons (who turned out to be authorized, elected, or appointed officials) had participated. But each individual account conflicted with the others. "No Administration personnel participated," or "No Republican leadership personnel participated," or "The only technical assistance was provided by personnel of the Legislative Drafting Service." These sources insisted that no management representatives participated at all. Yet, other sources insisted that no management representatives participated with Republicans while General Electric's Bob Borth had Graham Barden "locked up."

For their part, certain management representatives gave detailed accounts of bringing about particular phrasing in sections of the final bill. Also, a representative of the Chamber of Commerce said: "We almost introduced a bill stronger than Landrum-Griffin, so that Landrum-Griffin could have been cast more easily as a middle-of-the-road measure. I still think we should have done so." He also spoke of the detailed strategy in introducing the Harris amendment to the bill (see Chapter VIII), referring to the whole episode as a "blunder." Yet, management group representatives were supposed not to have participated in any way.

The evolution of one version of the drafting of Landrum-Griffin was that Edward McCabe, although intimately acquainted with labor legislation, did not consider himself expert in the drafting of such legislation. Therefore, he had not participated in the drafting of the Landrum-Griffin substitute. When the account of the drafting which appears in the body of Chapter VII was sketched to a number of interviewees, it was specifically denied. Under this provocation, however, Edward McCabe's participation was gradually upgraded. He was then said to have participated actively in the drafting. In a series of reinterviews and follow-up interviews, McCabe's role became more central still and the participation of interest group representatives almost nonexistent. The bill had grown from the ground swell of public reaction to labor excesses, not from private interests. (Then, one might ask, why all the money and effort to amplify and direct the public reaction?) This version was put forth with such force and such a degree of internal contradiction that the author concluded that it was a cover story for the facts of the case.

If the accounts of the largest group of informants had been totally accurate, this legislation would have been as free of interest group participation at the working level as any in history, while at the same time involving extensive innovations in the interaction between the executive branch and interest groups in the development of public support. It would have involved the same cast of characters who wallowed in the detail of reference, punctuation, and phrase in earlier legislation but had somehow become cleansed and were "above all that" on this bill. It would also have been in stark contrast with the freely discussed drafting support provided at various levels on the other side of the issue.

The account presented in the body of Chapter VII represents the most plausible explanation of the origin of the bill, although the qualification that it was one among many explanations is necessary. It has since been confirmed by an additional well-informed management source.

APPENDIX E

THE LABOR-MANAGEMENT REPORTING AND
DISCLOSURE ACT OF 1959

Public Law 86-257
86th Congress, S.1555
September 14, 1959

AN ACT to provide for the reporting and disclosure of certain financial
transactions and administrative practices of labor organizations and
employers, to prevent abuses in the administration of trusteeships by
labor organizations, to provide standards with respect to the election
of officers of labor organizations, and for other purposes.

*Be it enacted by the Senate and House of Representatives of the United
States of America in Congress assembled,*

SHORT TITLE

SECTION 1. This Act may be cited as the "Labor-Management Reporting and Disclosure Act of 1959."

DECLARATION OF FINDINGS, PURPOSES, AND POLICY

SEC. 2. (a) The Congress finds that, in the public interest, it continues
to be the responsibility of the Federal Government to protect employees'
rights to organize, choose their own representatives, bargain collectively,
and otherwise engage in concerted activities for their mutual aid or protection; that the relations between employers and labor organizations and
the millions of workers they represent have a substantial impact on the
commerce of the Nation; and that in order to accomplish the objective of
a free flow of commerce it is essential that labor organizations, employers,
and their officials adhere to the highest standards of responsibility and

ethical conduct in administering the affairs of their organizations, particularly as they affect labor-management relations.

(b) The Congress further finds, from recent investigations in the labor and management fields, that there have been a number of instances of breach of trust, corruption, disregard of the rights of individual employees, and other failures to observe high standards of responsibility and ethical conduct which require further and supplementary legislation that will afford necessary protection of the rights and interests of employees and the public generally as they relate to the activities of labor organizations, employers, labor relations consultants, and their officers and representatives.

(c) The Congress, therefore, further finds and declares that the enactment of this Act is necessary to eliminate or prevent improper practices on the part of labor organizations, employers, labor relations consultants, and their officers and representatives which distort and defeat the policies of the Labor Management Relations Act, 1947, as amended, and the Railway Labor Act, as amended, and have the tendency or necessary effect of burdening or obstructing commerce by (1) impairing the efficiency, safety, or operation of the instrumentalities of commerce; (2) occurring in the current of commerce; (3) materially affecting, restraining, or controlling the flow of raw materials or manufactured or processed goods into or from the channels of commerce, or the prices of such materials or goods in commerce; or (4) causing diminution of employment and wages in such volume as substantially to impair or disrupt the market for goods flowing into or from the channels of commerce.

DEFINITIONS

SEC. 3. For the purposes of titles I, II, III, IV, V (except section 505), and VI of this Act—

(a) "Commerce" means trade, traffic, commerce, transportation, transmission, or communication among the several States or between any State and any place outside thereof.

(b) "State" includes any State of the United States, the District of Columbia, Puerto Rico, the Virgin Islands, American Samoa, Guam, Wake Island, the Canal Zone, and Outer Continental Shelf lands defined in the Outer Continental Shelf Lands Act (43 U.S.C. 1331–1343).

(c) "Industry affecting commerce" means any activity, business, or industry in commerce or in which a labor dispute would hinder or obstruct commerce or the free flow of commerce and includes any activity or industry "affecting commerce" within the meaning of the Labor Management Relations Act, 1947, as amended, or the Railway Labor Act, as amended.

(d) "Person" includes one or more individuals, labor organizations, partnerships, associations, corporations, legal representatives, mutual companies, joint-stock companies, trusts, unincorporated organizations, trustees, trustees in bankruptcy, or receivers.

(e) "Employer" means any employer or any group or association of employers engaged in an industry affecting commerce (1) which is, with respect to employees engaged in an industry affecting commerce, an employer within the meaning of any law of the United States relating to the employment of any employees or (2) which may deal with any labor organization concerning grievances, labor disputes, wages, rates of pay, hours of employment, or conditions of work, and includes any person acting directly or indirectly as an employer or as an agent of an employer in relation to an employee but does not include the United States or any corporation wholly owned by the Government of the United States or any State or political subdivision thereof.

(f) "Employee" means any individual employed by an employer, and includes any individual whose work has ceased as a consequence of, or in connection with, any current labor dispute or because of any unfair labor practice or because of exclusion or expulsion from a labor organization in any manner or for any reason inconsistent with the requirements of this Act.

(g) "Labor dispute" includes any controversy concerning terms, tenure, or conditions of employment, or concerning the association or representation of persons in negotiating, fixing, maintaining, changing, or seeking to arrange terms or conditions of employment, regardless of whether the disputants stand in the proximate relation of employer and employee.

(h) "Trusteeship" means any receivership, trusteeship, or other method of supervision or control whereby a labor organization suspends the autonomy otherwise available to a subordinate body under its constitution or bylaws.

(i) "Labor organization" means a labor organization engaged in an industry affecting commerce and includes any organization of any kind, any agency, or employee representation committee, group, association, or plan so engaged in which employees participate and which exists for the purpose, in whole or in part, of dealing with employers concerning grievances, labor disputes, wages, rates of pay, hours, or other terms or conditions of employment, and any conference, general committee, joint or system board, or joint council so engaged which is subordinate to a national or international labor organization, other than a State or local central body.

(j) A labor organization shall be deemed to be engaged in an industry affecting commerce if it—

(1) is the certified representative of employees under the provisions of the National Labor Relations Act, as amended, or the Railway Labor Act, as amended; or

(2) although not certified, is a national or international labor organiza-

tion or a local labor organization recognized or acting as the representative of employees of an employer or employers engaged in an industry affecting commerce; or

(3) has chartered a local labor organization or subsidiary body which is representing or actively seeking to represent employees of employers within the meaning of paragraph (1) or (2); or

(4) has been chartered by a labor organization representing or actively seeking to represent employees within the meaning of paragraph (1) or (2) as the local or subordinate body through which such employees may enjoy membership or become affiliated with such labor organization; or

(5) is a conference, general committee, joint or system board, or joint council, subordinate to a national or international labor organization, which includes a labor organization engaged in an industry affecting commerce within the meaning of any of the preceding paragraphs of this subsection, other than a State or local central body.

(k) "Secret ballot" means the expression by ballot, voting machine, or otherwise, but in no event by proxy, of a choice with respect to any election or vote taken upon any matter, which is cast in such a manner that the person expressing such choice cannot be identified with the choice expressed.

(l) "Trust in which a labor organization is interested" means a trust or other fund or organization (1) which was created or established by a labor organization, or one or more of the trustees or one or more members of the governing body of which is selected or appointed by a labor organization, and (2) a primary purpose of which is to provide benefits for the members of such labor organization or their beneficiaries.

(m) "Labor relations consultant" means any person who, for compensation, advises or represents an employer, employer organization, or labor organization concerning employee organizing, concerted activities, or collective bargaining activities.

(n) "Officer" means any constitutional officer, any person authorized to perform the functions of president, vice president, secretary, treasurer, or other executive functions of a labor organization, and any member of its executive board or similar governing body.

(o) "Member" or "member in good standing," when used in reference to a labor organization, includes any person who has fulfilled the requirements for membership in such organization, and who neither has voluntarily withdrawn from membership nor has been expelled or suspended from membership after appropriate proceedings consistent with lawful provisions of the constitution and bylaws of such organization.

(p) "Secretary" means the Secretary of Labor.

(q) "Officer, agent, shop steward, or other representative," when used with respect to a labor organization, includes elected officials and key administrative personnel, whether elected or appointed (such as business agents, heads of departments or major units, and organizers who exercise substantial independent authority), but does not include salaried non-supervisory professional staff, stenographic, and service personnel.

(r) "District court of the United States" means a United States district court and a United States court of any place subject to the jurisdiction of the United States.

Title I—Bill of Rights of Members of Labor Organizations

BILL OF RIGHTS

SEC. 101. (a) (1) EQUAL RIGHTS.—Every member of a labor organization shall have equal rights and privileges within such organization to nominate candidates, to vote in elections or referendums of the labor organization, to attend membership meetings, and to participate in the deliberations and voting upon the business of such meetings, subject to reasonable rules and regulations in such organization's constitution and by-laws.

(2) FREEDOM OF SPEECH AND ASSEMBLY.—Every member of any labor organization shall have the right to meet and assemble freely with other members; and to express any views, arguments, or opinions; and to express at meetings of the labor organization his views, upon candidates in an election of the labor organization or upon any business properly before the meeting, subject to the organization's established and reasonable rules pertaining to the conduct of meetings: *Provided,* That nothing herein shall be construed to impair the right of a labor organization to adopt and enforce reasonable rules as to the responsibility of every member toward the organization as an institution and to his refraining from conduct that would interfere with its performance of its legal or contractual obligations.

(3) DUES, INITIATION FEES, AND ASSESSMENTS.—Except in the case of a federation of national or international labor organizations, the rates of dues and initiation fees payable by members of any labor organization in effect on the date of enactment of this Act shall not be increased, and no general or special assessment shall be levied upon such members, except—

(A) in the case of a local labor organization, (i) by majority vote by secret ballot of the members in good standing voting at a general or special membership meeting, after reasonable notice of the intention to vote upon such question, or (ii) by majority vote of the members in good standing voting in a membership referendum conducted by secret ballot; or

(B) in the case of a labor organization, other than a local labor organization or a federation of national or international labor organizations, (i)

by majority vote of the delegates voting at a regular convention, or at a special convention of such labor organization held upon not less than thirty days' written notice to the principal office of each local or constituent labor organization entitled to such notice, or (ii) by majority vote of the members in good standing of such labor organization voting in a membership referendum conducted by secret ballot, or (iii) by majority vote of the members of the executive board or similar governing body of such labor organization, pursuant to express authority contained in the constitution and bylaws of such labor organization: *Provided,* That such action on the part of the executive board or similar governing body shall be effective only until the next regular convention of such labor organization.

(4) PROTECTION OF THE RIGHT TO SUE.—No labor organization shall limit the right of any member thereof to institute an action in any court, or in a proceeding before any administrative agency, irrespective of whether or not the labor organization or its officers are named as defendants or respondents in such action or proceeding, or the right of any member of a labor organization to appear as a witness in any judicial, administrative, or legislative proceeding, or to petition any legislature or to communicate with any legislator: *Provided,* That any such member may be required to exhaust reasonable hearing procedures (but not to exceed a four-month lapse of time) within such organization, before instituting legal or administrative proceedings against such organizations or any officer thereof: *And provided further,* That no interested employer or employer association shall directly or indirectly finance, encourage, or participate in, except as a party, any such action, proceeding, appearance, or petition.

(5) SAFEGUARDS AGAINST IMPROPER DISCIPLINARY ACTION.—No member of any labor organization may be fined, suspended, expelled, or otherwise disciplined except for nonpayment of dues by such organization or by any officer thereof unless such member has been (A) served with written specific charges; (B) given a reasonable time to prepare his defense; (C) afforded a full and fair hearing.

(b) Any provision of the constitution and bylaws of any labor organization which is inconsistent with the provisions of this section shall be of no force or effect.

CIVIL ENFORCEMENT

SEC. 102. Any person whose rights secured by the provisions of this title have been infringed by any violation of this title may bring a civil action in a district court of the United States for such relief (including injunctions) as may be appropriate. Any such action against a labor organization shall be brought in the district court of the United States for the district where the alleged violation occurred, or where the principal office of such labor organization is located.

RETENTION OF EXISTING RIGHTS

SEC. 103. Nothing contained in this title shall limit the rights and remedies of any member of a labor organization under any State or Federal law or before any court or other tribunal, or under the constitution and bylaws of any labor organization.

RIGHT TO COPIES OF COLLECTIVE BARGAINING AGREEMENTS

SEC. 104. It shall be the duty of the secretary or corresponding principal officer of each labor organization, in the case of a local labor organization, to forward a copy of each collective bargaining agreement made by such labor organization with any employer to any employee who requests such a copy and whose rights as such employee are directly affected by such agreement, and in the case of a labor organization other than a local labor organization, to forward a copy of any such agreement to each constituent unit which has members directly affected by such agreement; and such officer shall maintain at the principal office of the labor organization of which he is an officer copies of any such agreement made or received by such labor organization, which copies shall be available for inspection by any member or by any employee whose rights are affected by such agreement. The provisions of section 210 shall be applicable in the enforcement of this section.

INFORMATION AS TO ACT

SEC. 105. Every labor organization shall inform its members concerning the provisions of this Act.

Title II—Reporting by Labor Organizations, Officers and Employees of Labor Organizations, and Employers

REPORT OF LABOR ORGANIZATIONS

SEC. 201. (a) Every labor organization shall adopt a constitution and bylaws and shall file a copy thereof with the Secretary, together with a report, signed by its president and secretary or corresponding principal officers, containing the following information—

(1) the name of the labor organization, its mailing address, and any other address at which it maintains its principal office or at which it keeps the records referred to in this title;

(2) the name and title of each of its officers;

(3) the initiation fee or fees required from a new or transferred member and fees for work permits required by the reporting labor organization;

(4) the regular dues or fees or other periodic payments required to remain a member of the reporting labor organization; and

(5) detailed statements, or references to specific provisions of documents filed under this subsection which contain such statements, showing the provision made and procedures followed with respect to each of the following: (A) qualifications for or restrictions on membership, (B) levying of assessments, (C) participation in insurance or other benefit plans, (D) authorization for disbursement of funds of the labor organization, (E) audit of financial transactions of the labor organization, (F) the calling of regular and special meetings, (G) the selection of officers and stewards and of any representatives to other bodies composed of labor organizations' representatives, with a specific statement of the manner in which each officer was elected, appointed, or otherwise selected, (H) discipline or removal of officers or agents for breaches of their trust, (I) imposition of fines, suspensions, and expulsions of members, including the grounds for such action and any provision made for notice, hearing, judgment on the evidence, and appeal procedures, (J) authorization for bargaining demands, (K) ratification of contract terms, (L) authorization for strikes, and (M) issuance of work permits. Any change in the information required by this subsection shall be reported to the Secretary at the time the reporting labor organization files with the Secretary the annual financial report required by subsection (b).

(b) Every labor organization shall file annually with the Secretary a financial report signed by its president and treasurer or corresponding principal officers containing the following information in such detail as may be necessary accurately to disclose its financial condition and operations for its preceding fiscal year—

(1) assets and liabilities at the beginning and end of the fiscal year;

(2) receipts of any kind and the sources thereof;

(3) salary, allowances, and other direct or indirect disbursements (including reimbursed expenses) to each officer and also to each employee who, during such fiscal year, received more than $10,000 in the aggregate from such labor organization and any other labor organization affiliated with it or with which it is affiliated, or which is affiliated with the same national or international labor organization;

(4) direct and indirect loans made to any officer, employee, or member, which aggregated more than $250 during the fiscal year, together with a statement of the purpose, security, if any, and arrangements for repayment;

(5) direct and indirect loans to any business enterprise, together with

a statement of the purpose, security, if any, and arrangements for repayment; and

(6) other disbursements made by it including the purposes thereof; all in such categories as the Secretary may prescribe.

(c) Every labor organization required to submit a report under this title shall make available the information required to be contained in such report to all of its members, and every such labor organization and its officers shall be under a duty enforceable at the suit of any member of such organization in any State court of competent jurisdiction or in the district court of the United States for the district in which such labor organization maintains its principal office, to permit such member for just cause to examine any books, records, and accounts necessary to verify such report. The court in such action may, in its discretion, in addition to any judgment awarded to the plaintiff or plaintiffs, allow a reasonable attorney's fee to be paid by the defendant, and costs of the action.

(d) Subsections (f), (g), and (h) of section 9 of the National Labor Relations Act, as amended, are hereby repealed.

(e) Clause (i) of section 8 (a) (3) of the National Labor Relations Act, as amended, is amended by striking out the following: "and has at the time the agreement was made or within the preceding twelve months received from the Board a notice of compliance with sections 9 (f), (g), (h)."

REPORT OF OFFICERS AND EMPLOYEES OF LABOR ORGANIZATIONS

SEC. 202. (a) Every officer of a labor organization and every employee of a labor organization (other than an employee performing exclusively clerical or custodial services) shall file with the Secretary a signed report listing and describing for his preceding fiscal year—

(1) any stock, bond, security, or other interest, legal or equitable, which he or his spouse or minor child directly or indirectly held in, and any income or any other benefit with monetary value (including reimbursed expenses) which he or his spouse or minor child derived directly or indirectly from, an employer whose employees such labor organization represents or is actively seeking to represent, except payments and other benefits received as a bona fide employee of such employer;

(2) any transaction in which he or his spouse or minor child engaged, directly or indirectly, involving any stock, bond, security, or loan to or from, or other legal or equitable interest in the business of an employer whose employees such labor organization represents or is actively seeking to represent;

(3) any stock, bond, security, or other interest, legal or equitable, which he or his spouse or minor child directly or indirectly held in, and any income or any other benefit with monetary value (including reim-

bursed expenses) which he or his spouse or minor child directly or indirectly derived from, any business a substantial part of which consists
of buying from, selling or leasing to, or otherwise dealing with, the business of an employer whose employees such labor organization represents
or is actively seeking to represent;

(4) any stock, bond, security, or other interest, legal or equitable,
which he or his spouse or minor child directly or indirectly held in, and
any income or any other benefit with monetary value (including reimbursed expenses) which he or his spouse or minor child directly or indirectly derived from, a business any part of which consists of buying
from, or selling or leasing directly or indirectly to, or otherwise dealing
with such labor organization;

(5) any direct or indirect business transaction or arrangement between
him or his spouse or minor child and any employer whose employees his
organization represents or is actively seeking to represent, except work
performed and payments and benefits received as a bona fide employee
of such employer and except purchases and sales of goods or services in
the regular course of business at prices generally available to any employee of such employer; and

(6) any payment of money or other thing of value (including reimbursed expenses) which he or his spouse or minor child received directly
or indirectly from any employer or any person who acts as a labor relations consultant to an employer, except payments of the kinds referred to
in section 302(c) of the Labor Management Relations Act, 1947, as
amended.

(b) The provisions of paragraphs (1), (2), (3), (4), and (5) of subsection (a) shall not be construed to require any such officer or employee
to report his bona fide investments in securities traded on a securities exchange registered as a national securities exchange under the Securities
Exchange Act of 1934, in shares in an investment company registered under the Investment Company Act of 1940, or in securities of a public
utility holding company registered under the Public Utility Holding Company Act of 1935, or to report any income derived therefrom.

(c) Nothing contained in this section shall be construed to require any
officer or employee of a labor organization to file a report under subsection
(a) unless he or his spouse or minor child holds or has held an interest,
has received income or any other benefit with monetary value or a loan,
or has engaged in a transaction described therein.

REPORT OF EMPLOYERS

Sec. 203. (a) Every employer who in any fiscal year made—

(1) any payment or loan, direct or indirect, of money or other thing
of value (including reimbursed expenses), or any promise or agreement
therefor, to any labor organization or officer, agent, shop steward, or other

representative of a labor organization, or employee of any labor organization, except (A) payments or loans made by any national or State bank, credit union, insurance company, savings and loan association or other credit institution and (B) payments of the kind referred to in section 302(c) of the Labor Management Relations Act, 1947, as amended;

(2) any payment (including reimbursed expenses) to any of his employees, or any group or committee of such employees, for the purpose of causing such employee or group or committee of employees to persuade other employees to exercise or not to exercise, or as the manner of exercising, the right to organize and bargain collectively through representatives of their own choosing unless such payments were contemporaneously or previously disclosed to such other employees;

(3) any expenditure, during the fiscal year, where an object thereof, directly or indirectly, is to interfere with, restrain, or coerce employees in the exercise of the right to organize and bargain collectively through representatives of their own choosing, or is to obtain information concerning the activities of employees or a labor organization in connection with a labor dispute involving such employer, except for use solely in conjunction with an administrative or arbitral proceeding or a criminal or civil judicial proceeding;

(4) any agreement or arrangement with a labor relations consultant or other independent contractor or organization pursuant to which such person undertakes activities where an object thereof, directly or indirectly, is to persuade employees to exercise or not to exercise, or persuade employees as to the manner of exercising, the right to organize and bargain collectively through representatives of their own choosing, or undertakes to supply such employer with information concerning the activities of employees or a labor organization in connection with a labor dispute involving such employer, except information for use solely in conjunction with an administrative or arbitral proceeding or a criminal or civil judicial proceeding; or

(5) any payment (including reimbursed expenses) pursuant to an agreement or arrangement described in subdivision (4);
shall file with the Secretary a report, in a form prescribed by him, signed by its president and treasurer or corresponding principal officers showing in detail the date and amount of each such payment, loan, promise, agreement, or arrangement and the name, address, and position, if any, in any firm or labor organization of the person to whom it was made and a full explanation of the circumstances of all such payments, including the terms of any agreement or understanding pursuant to which they were made.

(b) Every person who pursuant to any agreement or arrangement with an employer undertakes activities where an object thereof is, directly or indirectly—

(1) to persuade employees to exercise or not to exercise, or persuade

employees as to the manner of exercising, the right to organize and bargain collectively through representatives of their own choosing; or

(2) to supply an employer with information concerning the activities
of employees or a labor organization in connection with a labor dispute
involving such employer, except information for use solely in conjunction
with an administrative or arbitral proceeding or a criminal or civil judicial
proceeding;

shall file within thirty days after entering into such agreement or arrangement a report with the Secretary, signed by its president and treasurer or
corresponding principal officers, containing the name under which such
person is engaged in doing business and the address of its principal office,
and a detailed statement of the terms and conditions of such agreement
or arrangement. Every such person shall file annually, with respect to
each fiscal year during which payments were made as a result of such an
agreement or arrangement, a report with the Secretary, signed by its president and treasurer or corresponding principal officers, containing a statement (A) of its receipts of any kind from employers on account of labor
relations advice or services, designating the sources thereof, and (B) of
its disbursements of any kind, in connection with such services and the
purposes thereof. In each such case such information shall be set forth
in such categories as the Secretary may prescribe.

(c) Nothing in this section shall be construed to require any employer
or other person to file a report covering the services of such person by
reason of his giving or agreeing to give advice to such employer or representing or agreeing to represent such employer before any court, administrative agency, or tribunal of arbitration or engaging or agreeing to engage in collective bargaining on behalf of such employer with respect to
wages, hours, or other terms or conditions of employment or the negotiation of an agreement or any question arising thereunder.

(d) Nothing contained in this section shall be construed to require an
employer to file a report under subsection (a) unless he has made an
expenditure, payment, loan, agreement, or arrangement of the kind described therein. Nothing contained in this section shall be construed to
require any other person to file a report under subsection (b) unless he
was a party to an agreement or arrangement of the kind described therein.

(e) Nothing contained in this section shall be construed to require any
regular officer, supervisor, or employee of an employer to file a report in
connection with services rendered to such employer nor shall any employer be required to file a report covering expenditures made to any regular officer, supervisor, or employee of an employer as compensation for
service as a regular officer, supervisor, or employee of such employer.

(f) Nothing contained in this section shall be construed as an amendment to, or modification of the rights protected by, section 8(c) of the
National Labor Relations Act, as amended.

(g) The term "interfere with, restrain, or coerce" as used in this section means interference, restraint, and coercion which, if done with respect to the exercise of rights guaranteed in section 7 of the National Labor Relations Act, as amended, would, under section 8(a) of such Act, constitute an unfair labor practice.

ATTORNEY-CLIENT COMMUNICATIONS EXEMPTED

Sec. 204. Nothing contained in this Act shall be construed to require an attorney who is a member in good standing of the bar of any State, to include in any report required to be filed pursuant to the provisions of this Act any information which was lawfully communicated to such attorney by any of his clients in the course of a legitimate attorney-client relationship.

REPORTS MADE PUBLIC INFORMATION

Sec. 205. (a) The contents of the reports and documents filed with the Secretary pursuant to sections 201, 202, and 203 shall be public information, and the Secretary may publish any information and data which he obtains pursuant to the provisions of this title. The Secretary may use the information and data for statistical and research purposes, and compile and publish such studies, analyses, reports, and surveys based thereon as he may deem appropriate.

(b) The Secretary shall by regulation make reasonable provision for the inspection and examination, on the request of any person, of the information and data contained in any report or other document filed with him pursuant to section 201, 202, or 203.

(c) The Secretary shall by regulation provide for the furnishing by the Department of Labor of copies of reports or other documents filed with the Secretary pursuant to this title, upon payment of a charge based upon the cost of the service. The Secretary shall make available without payment of a charge, or require any person to furnish, to such State agency as is designated by law or by the Governor of the State in which such person has his principal place of business or headquarters, upon request of the Governor of such State, copies of any reports and documents filed by such person with the Secretary pursuant to section 201, 202, or 203, or of information and data contained therein. No person shall be required by reason of any law of any State to furnish to any officer or agency of such State any information included in a report filed by such person with the Secretary pursuant to the provisions of this title, if a copy of such report, or of the portion thereof containing such information, is furnished to such officer or agency. All moneys received in payment of such charges fixed by the Secretary pursuant to this subsection shall be deposited in the general fund of the Treasury.

RETENTION OF RECORDS

SEC. 206. Every person required to file any report under this title shall maintain records on the matters required to be reported which will provide in sufficient detail the necessary basic information and data from which the documents filed with the Secretary may be verified, explained or clarified, and checked for accuracy and completeness, and shall include vouchers, worksheets, receipts, and applicable resolutions, and shall keep such records available for examination for a period of not less than five years after the filing of the documents based on the information which they contain.

EFFECTIVE DATE

SEC. 207. (a) Each labor organization shall file the initial report required under section 201(a) within ninety days after the date on which it first becomes subject to this Act.

(b) Each person required to file a report under section 201(b), 202, 203(a), or the second sentence of 203(b) shall file such report within ninety days after the end of each of its fiscal years; except that where such person is subject to section 201(b), 202, 203(a), or the second sentence of 203(b), as the case may be, for only a portion of such a fiscal year (because the date of enactment of this Act occurs during such person's fiscal year or such person becomes subject to this Act during its fiscal year) such person may consider that portion as the entire fiscal year in making such report.

RULES AND REGULATIONS

SEC. 208. The Secretary shall have authority to issue, amend, and rescind rules and regulations prescribing the form and publication of reports required to be filed under this title and such other reasonable rules and regulations (including rules prescribing reports concerning trusts in which a labor organization is interested) as he may find necessary to prevent the circumvention or evasion of such reporting requirements. In exercising his power under this section the Secretary shall prescribe by general rule simplified reports for labor organizations or employers for whom he finds that by virtue of their size a detailed report would be unduly burdensome, but the Secretary may revoke such provision for simplified forms of any labor organization or employer if he determines, after such investigation as he deems proper and due notice and opportunity for a hearing, that the purposes of this section would be served thereby.

CRIMINAL PROVISIONS

SEC. 209. (a) Any person who willfully violates this title shall be fined not more than $10,000 or imprisoned for not more than one year, or both.

(b) Any person who makes a false statement or representation of a material fact, knowing it to be false, or who knowingly fails to disclose a material fact, in any document, report, or other information required under the provisions of this title shall be fined not more than $10,000 or imprisoned for not more than one year, or both.

(c) Any person who willfully makes a false entry in or willfully conceals, withholds, or destroys any books, records, reports, or statements required to be kept by any provision of this title shall be fined not more than $10,000 or imprisoned for not more than one year, or both.

(d) Each individual required to sign reports under sections 201 and 203 shall be personally responsible for the filing of such reports and for any statement contained therein which he knows to be false.

CIVIL ENFORCEMENT

SEC. 210. Whenever it shall appear that any person has violated or is about to violate any of the provisions of this title, the Secretary may bring a civil action for such relief (including injunctions) as may be appropriate. Any such action may be brought in the district court of the United States where the violation occurred or, at the option of the parties, in the United States District Court for the District of Columbia.

Title III—Trusteeships

REPORTS

SEC. 301. (a) Every labor organization which has or assumes trusteeship over any subordinate labor organization shall file with the Secretary within thirty days after the date of the enactment of this Act or the imposition of any such trusteeship, and semiannually thereafter a report, signed by its president and treasurer or corresponding principal officers, as well as by the trustees of such subordinate labor organization, containing the following information: (1) the name and address of the subordinate organization; (2) the date of establishing the trusteeship; (3) a detailed statement of the reason or reasons for establishing or continuing the trusteeship; and (4) the nature and extent of participation by the membership of the subordinate organization in the selection of delegates to represent such organization in regular or special conventions or other policy-determining bodies and in the election of officers of the labor organization which has assumed trusteeship over such subordinate organization. The initial report shall also include a full and complete account of the financial condition of such subordinate organization as of the time trusteeship was assumed over it. During the continuance of a trusteeship the labor organization which has assumed trusteeship over a subordinate labor organization shall file on behalf of the subordinate labor organization the annual financial report required by section 201(b) signed by the president and treasurer or corresponding principal officers of the labor organization which has assumed such trusteeship and the trustees of the subordinate labor organization.

(b) The provisions of section 201(c), 205, 206, 208, and 210 shall be applicable to reports filed under this title.

(c) Any person who willfully violates this section shall be fined not more than $10,000 or imprisoned for not more than one year, or both.

(d) Any person who makes a false statement or representation of a material fact, knowing it to be false, or who knowingly fails to disclose a material fact, in any report required under the provisions of this section or willfully makes any false entry in or willfully withholds, conceals, or destroys any documents, books, records, reports, or statements upon which such report is based, shall be fined not more than $10,000 or imprisoned for not more than one year, or both.

(e) Each individual required to sign a report under this section shall be personally responsible for the filing of such report and for any statement contained therein which he knows to be false.

PURPOSES FOR WHICH A TRUSTEESHIP MAY BE ESTABLISHED

SEC. 302. Trusteeships shall be established and administered by a labor organization over a subordinate body only in accordance with the constitution and bylaws of the organization which has assumed trusteeship over the subordinate body and for the purpose of correcting corruption or financial malpractice, assuring the performance of collective bargaining agreements or other duties of a bargaining representative, restoring democratic procedures, or otherwise carrying out the legitimate objects of such labor organization.

UNLAWFUL ACTS RELATING TO LABOR ORGANIZATION UNDER TRUSTEESHIP

SEC. 303. (a) During any period when a subordinate body of a labor organization is in trusteeship, it shall be unlawful (1) to count the vote of delegates from such body in any convention or election of officers of the labor organization unless the delegates have been chosen by secret ballot in an election in which all the members in good standing of such subordinate body were eligible to participate, or (2) to transfer to such organization any current receipts or other funds of the subordinate body except the normal per capita tax and assessments payable by subordinate bodies not in trusteeship: *Provided,* That nothing herein contained shall prevent the distribution of the assets of a labor organization in accordance with its constitution and bylaws upon the bona fide dissolution thereof.

(b) Any person who willfully violates this section shall be fined not more than $10,000 or imprisoned for not more than one year, or both.

ENFORCEMENT

Sec. 304. (a) Upon the written complaint of any member or subordinate body of a labor organization alleging that such organization has violated the provisions of this title (except section 301) the Secretary shall investigate the complaint and if the Secretary finds probable cause to believe that such violation has occurred and has not been remedied he shall, without disclosing the identity of the complainant, bring a civil action in any district court of the United States having jurisdiction of the labor organization for such relief (including injunctions) as may be appropriate. Any member or subordinate body of a labor organization affected by any violation of this title (except section 301) may bring a civil action in any district court of the United States having jurisdiction of the labor organization for such relief (including injunctions) as may be appropriate.

(b) For the purpose of actions under this section, district courts of the United States shall be deemed to have jurisdiction of a labor organization (1) in the district in which the principal office of such labor organization is located, or (2) in any district in which its duly authorized officers or agents are engaged in conducting the affairs of the trusteeship.

(c) In any proceeding pursuant to this section a trusteeship established by a labor organization in conformity with the procedural requirements of its constitution and bylaws and authorized or ratified after a fair hearing either before the executive board or before such other body as may be provided in accordance with its constitution or bylaws shall be presumed valid for a period of eighteen months from the date of its establishment and shall not be subject to attack during such period except upon clear and convincing proof that the trusteeship was not established or maintained in good faith for a purpose allowable under section 302. After the expiration of eighteen months the trusteeship shall be presumed invalid in any such proceeding and its discontinuance shall be decreed unless the labor organization shall show by clear and convincing proof that the continuation of the trusteeship is necessary for a purpose allowable under section 302. In the latter event the court may dismiss the complaint or retain jurisdiction of the cause on such conditions and for such period as it deems appropriate.

REPORT TO CONGRESS

Sec. 305. The Secretary shall submit to the Congress at the expiration of three years from the date of enactment of this Act a report upon the operation of this title.

COMPLAINT BY SECRETARY

Sec. 306. The rights and remedies provided by this title shall be in addition to any and all other rights and remedies at law or in equity:

Provided, That upon the filing of a complaint by the Secretary the jurisdiction of the district court over such trusteeship shall be exclusive and the final judgment shall be res judicata.

Title IV—Elections

TERMS OF OFFICE; ELECTION PROCEDURES

SEC. 401. (a) Every national or international labor organization, except a federation of national or international labor organizations, shall elect its officers not less often than once every five years either by secret ballot among the members in good standing or at a convention of delegates chosen by secret ballot.

(b) Every local labor organization shall elect its officers not less often than once every three years by secret ballot among the members in good standing.

(c) Every national or international labor organization, except a federation of national or international labor organizations, and every local labor organization, and its officers, shall be under a duty, enforceable at the suit of any bona fide candidate for office in such labor organization in the district court of the United States in which such labor organization maintains its principal office, to comply with all reasonable requests of any candidate to distribute by mail or otherwise at the candidate's expense campaign literature in aid of such person's candidacy to all members in good standing of such labor organization and to refrain from discrimination in favor of or against any candidate with respect to the use of lists of members, and whenever such labor organizations or its officers authorize the distribution by mail or otherwise to members of campaign literature on behalf of any candidate or of the labor organization itself with reference to such election, similar distribution at the request of any other bona fide candidate shall be made by such labor organization and its officers, with equal treatment as to the expense of such distribution. Every bona fide candidate shall have the right, once within 30 days prior to an election of a labor organization in which he is a candidate, to inspect a list containing the names and last known addresses of all members of the labor organization who are subject to a collective bargaining agreement requiring membership therein as a condition of employment, which list shall be maintained and kept at the principal office of such labor organization by a designated official thereof. Adequate safeguards to insure a fair election shall be provided, including the right of any candidate to have an observer at the polls and at the counting of the ballots.

(d) Officers of intermediate bodies, such as general committees, system boards, joint boards, or joint councils, shall be elected not less often than once every four years by secret ballot among the members in good standing or by labor organization officers representative of such members who have been elected by secret ballot.

(e) In any election required by this section which is to be held by secret ballot a reasonable opportunity shall be given for the nomination of candidates and every member in good standing shall be eligible to be a candidate and to hold office (subject to section 504 and to reasonable qualifications uniformly imposed) and shall have the right to vote for or otherwise support the candidate or candidates of his choice, without being subject to penalty, discipline, or improper interference or reprisal of any kind by such organization or any member thereof. Not less than fifteen days prior to the election notice thereof shall be mailed to each member at his last known home address. Each member in good standing shall be entitled to one vote. No member whose dues have been withheld by his employer for payment to such organization pursuant to his voluntary authorization provided for in a collective bargaining agreement shall be declared ineligible to vote or be a candidate for office in such organization by reason of alleged delay or default in the payment of dues. The votes cast by members of each local labor organization shall be counted, and the results published, separately. The election officials designated in the constitution and bylaws or the secretary, if no other official is designated, shall preserve for one year the ballots and all other records pertaining to the election. The election shall be conducted in accordance with the constitution and bylaws of such organization insofar as they are not inconsistent with the provisions of this title.

(f) When officers are chosen by a convention of delegates elected by secret ballot, the convention shall be conducted in accordance with the constitution and bylaws of the labor organization insofar as they are not inconsistent with the provisions of this title. The officials designated in the constitution and bylaws or the secretary, if no other is designated, shall preserve for one year the credentials of the delegates and all minutes and other records of the convention pertaining to the election of officers.

(g) No moneys received by any labor organization by way of dues, assessment, or similar levy, and no moneys of an employer shall be contributed or applied to promote the candidacy of any person in an election subject to the provisions of this title. Such moneys of a labor organization may be utilized for notices, factual statements of issues not involving candidates, and other expenses necessary for the holding of an election.

(h) If the Secretary, upon application of any member of a local labor organization, finds after hearing in accordance with the Administrative Procedure Act that the constitution and bylaws of such labor organization do not provide an adequate procedure for the removal of an elected officer guilty of serious misconduct, such officer may be removed, for cause shown and after notice and hearing, by the members in good standing voting in a secret ballot conducted by the officers of such labor organization in accordance with its constitution and bylaws insofar as they are not inconsistent with the provisions of this title.

(i) The Secretary shall promulgate rules and regulations prescribing minimum standards and procedures for determining the adequacy of the removal procedures to which reference is made in subsection (h).

SEC. 402. (a) A member of a labor organization—

(1) who has exhausted the remedies available under the constitution and bylaws of such organization and of any parent body, or

(2) who has invoked such available remedies without obtaining a final decision within three calendar months after their invocation,

may file a complaint with the Secretary within one calendar month thereafter alleging the violation of any provision of section 401 (including violation of the constitution and bylaws of the labor organization pertaining to the election and removal of officers). The challenged election shall be presumed valid pending a final decision thereon (as hereinafter provided) and in the interim the affairs of the organization shall be conducted by the officers elected or in such other manner as its constitution and bylaws may provide.

(b) The Secretary shall investigate such complaint and, if he finds probable cause to believe that a violation of this title has occurred and has not been remedied, he shall, within sixty days after the filing of such complaint, bring a civil action against the labor organization as an entity in the district court of the United States in which such labor organization maintains its principal office to set aside the invalid election, if any, and to direct the conduct of an election or hearing and vote upon the removal of officers under the supervision of the Secretary and in accordance with the provisions of this title and such rules and regulations as the Secretary may prescribe. The court shall have power to take such action as it deems proper to preserve the assets of the labor organization.

(c) If, upon a preponderance of the evidence after a trial upon the merits, the court finds—

(1) that an election has not been held within the time prescribed by section 401, or

(2) that the violation of section 401 may have affected the outcome of an election,

the court shall declare the election, if any, to be void and direct the conduct of a new election under supervision of the Secretary and, so far as lawful and practicable, in conformity with the constitution and bylaws of the labor organization. The Secretary shall promptly certify to the court the names of the persons elected, and the court shall thereupon enter a decree declaring such persons to be the officers of the labor organization. If the proceeding is for the removal of officers pursuant to subsection (h) of section 401, the Secretary shall certify the results of the vote and the court shall enter a decree declaring whether such persons have been removed as officers of the labor organization.

(d) An order directing an election, dismissing a complaint, or designating elected officers of a labor organization shall be appealable in the same manner as the final judgment in a civil action, but an order directing an election shall not be stayed pending appeal.

APPLICATION OF OTHER LAWS

SEC. 403. No labor organization shall be required by law to conduct elections of officers with greater frequency or in a different form or manner than is required by its own constitution or bylaws, except as otherwise provided by this title. Existing rights and remedies to enforce the constitution and bylaws of a labor organization with respect to elections prior to the conduct thereof shall not be affected by the provisions of this title. The remedy provided by this title for challenging an election already conducted shall be exclusive.

EFFECTIVE DATE

SEC. 404. The provisions of this title shall become applicable—

(1) ninety days after the date of enactment of this Act in the case of a labor organization whose constitutions and bylaws can lawfully be modified or amended by action of its constitutional officers or governing body, or

(2) where such modification can only be made by a constitutional convention of the labor organization, not later than the next constitutional convention of such labor organization after the date of enactment of this Act, or one year after such date, whichever is sooner. If no such convention is held within such one-year period, the executive board or similar governing body empowered to act for such labor organization between conventions is empowered to make such interim constitutional changes as are necessary to carry out the provisions of this title.

Title V—Safeguards for Labor Organizations

FIDUCIARY RESPONSIBILITY OF OFFICERS OF LABOR ORGANIZATIONS

SEC. 501. (a) The officers, agents, shop stewards, and other representatives of a labor organization occupy positions of trust in relation to such organization and its members as a group. It is, therefore, the duty of each such person, taking into account the special problems and functions of a labor organization, to hold its money and property solely for the benefit of the organization and its members and to manage, invest, and expend the same in accordance with its constitution and bylaws and any resolutions of the governing bodies adopted thereunder, to refrain from dealing with such organization as an adverse party or in behalf of an adverse party in any matter connected with his duties and from holding or acquiring any pecuniary or personal interest which conflicts with the interests of such organization, and to account to the organization for any profit received by him in whatever capacity in connection with transactions conducted by him or under his direction on behalf of the organization. A general exculpatory provision in the constitution and bylaws of such a labor organization or a general exculpatory resolution of a governing body purporting to relieve any such person of liability for breach of the duties declared by this section shall be void as against public policy.

(b) When any officer, agent, shop steward, or representative of any labor organization is alleged to have violated the duties declared in subsection (a) and the labor organization or its governing board or officers refuse or fail to sue or recover damages or secure an accounting or other appropriate relief within a reasonable time after being requested to do so by any member of the labor organization, such member may sue such officer, agent, shop steward, or representative in any district court of the United States or in any State court of competent jurisdiction to recover damages or secure an accounting or other appropriate relief for the benefit of the labor organization. No such proceeding shall be brought except upon leave of the court obtained upon verified application and for good cause shown, which application may be made ex parte. The trial judge may allot a reasonable part of the recovery in any action under this subsection to pay the fees of counsel prosecuting the suit at the instance of the member of the labor organization and to compensate such member for any expenses necessarily paid or incurred by him in connection with the litigation.

(c) Any person who embezzles, steals, or unlawfully and willfully abstracts or converts to his own use, or the use of another, any of the moneys, funds, securities, property, or other assets of a labor organization of which he is an officer, or by which he is employed, directly or indirectly, shall be fined not more than $10,000 or imprisoned for not more than five years, or both.

BONDING

SEC. 502. (a) Every officer, agent, shop steward, or other representative or employee of any labor organization (other than a labor organization whose property and annual financial receipts do not exceed $5,000 in value), or of a trust in which a labor organization is interested, who handles funds or other property thereof shall be bonded for the faithful discharge of his duties. The bond of each such person shall be fixed at the beginning of the organization's fiscal year and shall be in an amount not less than 10 per centum of the funds handled by him and his predecessor or predecessors, if any, during the preceding fiscal year, but in no case more than $500,000. If the labor organization or the trust in which a labor organization is interested does not have a preceding fiscal year, the amount of the bond shall be, in the case of a local labor organization, not less than $1,000, and in the case of any other labor organization or of a trust in which a labor organization is interested, not less than $10,000. Such bonds shall be individual or schedule in form, and shall have a corporate surety company as surety thereon. Any person who is not covered by such bonds shall not be permitted to receive, handle, disburse, or otherwise exercise custody or control of the funds or other property of a labor organization or of a trust in which a labor organization is interested. No such bond shall be placed through an agent or broker or with a surety company in which any labor organization or any officer, agent, shop steward, or other representative of a labor organization has any direct or indirect interest. Such surety company shall be a corporate surety which holds a grant of authority from the Secretary of the Treasury under the Act of July 30, 1947 (6 U.S.C. 6–13), as an acceptable surety on Federal bonds.

(b) Any person who willfully violates this section shall be fined not more than $10,000 or imprisoned for not more than one year, or both.

MAKING OF LOANS; PAYMENT OF FINES

SEC. 503. (a) No labor organization shall make directly or indirectly any loan or loans to any officer or employee of such organization which results in a total indebtedness on the part of such officer or employee to the labor organization in excess of $2,000.

(b) No labor organization or employer shall directly or indirectly pay the fine of any officer or employee convicted of any willful violation of this Act.

(c) Any person who willfully violates this section shall be fined not more than $5,000 or imprisoned for not more than one year, or both.

PROHIBITION AGAINST CERTAIN PERSONS HOLDING OFFICE

SEC. 504. (a) No person who is or has been a member of the Communist Party or who has been convicted of, or served any part of a prison term resulting from his conviction of, robbery, bribery, extortion, embezzlement, grand larceny, burglary, arson, violation of narcotics laws, murder, rape, assault with intent to kill, assault which inflicts grievous bodily injury, or a violation of title II or III of this Act, or conspiracy to commit any such crimes, shall serve—

(1) as an officer, director, trustee, member of any executive board or similar governing body, business agent, manager, organizer, or other employee (other than as an employee performing exclusively clerical or custodial duties) of any labor organization, or

(2) as a labor relations consultant to a person engaged in an industry or activity affecting commerce, or as an officer, director, agent, or employee (other than as an employee performing exclusively clerical or custodial

duties) of any group or association of employers dealing with any labor organization,

during or for five years after the termination of his membership in the Communist Party, or for five years after such conviction or after the end of such imprisonment, unless prior to the end of such five-year period, in the case of a person so convicted or imprisoned, (A) his citizenship rights, having been revoked as a result of such conviction, have been fully restored, or (B) the Board of Parole of the United States Department of Justice determines that such person's service in any capacity referred to in clause (1) or (2) would not be contrary to the purposes of this Act. Prior to making any such determination the Board shall hold an administrative hearing and shall give notice of such proceeding by certified mail to the State, county, and Federal prosecuting officials in the jurisdiction or jurisdictions in which such person was convicted. The Board's determination in any such proceeding shall be final. No labor organization or officer thereof shall knowingly permit any person to assume or hold any office or paid position in violation of this subsection.

(b) Any person who willfully violates this section shall be fined not more than $10,000 or imprisoned for not more than one year, or both

(c) For the purposes of this section, any person shall be deemed to have been "convicted" and under the disability of "conviction" from the date of the judgment of the trial court or the date of the final sustaining of such judgment on appeal, whichever is the later event, regardless of whether such conviction occurred before or after the date of enactment of this Act.

AMENDMENT TO SECTION 302, LABOR MANAGEMENT RELATIONS ACT, 1947

SEC. 505. Subsections (a), (b), and (c) of section 302 of the Labor Management Relations Act, 1947, as amended, are amended to read as follows:

"SEC. 302. (a) It shall be unlawful for any employer or association of employers or any person who acts as a labor relations expert, adviser, or consultant to an employer or who acts in the interest of an employer to pay, lend, or deliver, or agree to pay, lend, or deliver, any money or other thing of value—

"(1) to any representative of any of his employees who are employed in an industry affecting commerce; or

"(2) to any labor organization, or any officer or employee thereof, which represents, seeks to represent, or would admit to membership, any of the employees of such employer who are employed in an industry affecting commerce; or

"(3) to any employee or group or committee of employees of such employer employed in an industry affecting commerce in excess of their normal compensation for the purpose of causing such employee or group or committee directly or indirectly to influence any other employees in the exercise of the right to organize and bargain collectively through representatives of their own choosing; or

"(4) to any officer or employee of a labor organization engaged in an industry affecting commerce with intent to influence him in respect to any of his actions, decisions, or duties as a representative of employees or as such officer or employee of such labor organization.

"(b) (1) It shall be unlawful for any person to request, demand, receive, or accept, or agree to receive or accept, any payment, loan, or delivery of any money or other thing of value prohibited by subsection (a).

"(2) It shall be unlawful for any labor organization, or for any person acting as an officer, agent, representative, or employee of such labor organization, to demand or accept from the operator of any motor vehicle (as defined in part II of the Interstate Commerce Act) employed in the transportation of property in commerce, or the employer of any such operator, any money or other thing of value payable to such organization or to an officer, agent, representative or employee thereof as a fee or charge for the unloading, or in connection with the unloading, of the cargo of such vehicle: *Provided,* That nothing in this paragraph shall be construed to make unlawful any payment by an employer to any of his employees as compensation for their services as employees.

"(c) The provisions of this section shall not be applicable (1) in respect to any money or other thing of value payable by an employer to any of his employees whose established duties include acting openly for such employer in matters of labor relations or personnel administration or to any representative of his employees, or to any officer or employee of a labor organization, who is also an employee or former employee of such employer, as compensation for, or by reason of, his service as an employee of such employer; (2) with respect to the payment or delivery of any money or other thing of value in satisfaction of a judgment of any court or a decision or award of an arbitrator or impartial chairman or in compromise, adjustment, settlement, or release of any claim, complaint, grievance, or dispute in the absence of fraud or duress; (3) with respect to the sale or purchase of an article or commodity at the prevailing market price in the regular course of business; (4) with respect to money deducted from the wages of employees in payment of membership dues in a labor organization: *Provided,* That the employer has received from each employee, on whose account such deductions are made, a written assignment which shall not be irrevocable for a period of more than one year, or beyond the termination date of the applicable collective agreement, whichever occurs sooner; (5) with respect to money or other thing of value paid to a trust fund established by such representative, for the sole and exclusive benefit of the employees of such employer, and their families and dependents (or of such employees, families, and dependents jointly with the employees of other employers making similar payments, and their families and dependents): *Provided,* That (A) such payments are held in trust for the purpose of paying, either from principal or income or both, for the benefit of employees, their families and dependents, for medical or hospital care, pensions on retirement or death of employees, compensation for injuries or illness resulting from occupational activity or insurance to provide any of the foregoing, or unemployment benefits or life insurance, disability and sickness insurance, or accident insurance; (B) the detailed basis on which such payments are to be made is specified in a written agreement with the employer, and employees and employers are equally represented in the administration of such fund, together with such neutral persons as the representatives of the employers and the representatives of employees may agree upon and in the event the employer and employee groups deadlock on the administration of such fund and there are no neutral persons empowered to break such deadlocks, such agreement provides that the two groups shall agree on an impartial umpire to decide such dispute, or in event of their failure to agree within a reasonable length of time, an impartial umpire to decide such dispute shall, on petition of either group, be appointed by the district court of the United States for the district where the trust fund has its principal office, and shall also contain provisions for an annual audit of the trust fund, a statement of the results of which shall be available for inspection by interested persons at the principal office of the trust fund and at such other places as may be designated in such written agreement; and (C) such payments as are intended to be used for the purpose of providing pensions or annuities for employees are made to a separate trust which provides that the funds held therein cannot be used for any purpose other than paying such pensions or annuities; or (6) with respect to money or other thing of value paid by any employer to a trust fund established by such representative for the purpose of pooled vacation, holiday, severance or/similar benefits, or defraying costs of apprenticeship or other training programs: *Provided,* That the requirements of clause (B) of the proviso to clause (5) of this subsection shall apply to such trust funds."

Title VI—Miscellaneous Provisions

INVESTIGATIONS

SEC. 601. (a) The Secretary shall have power when he believes it necessary in order to determine whether any person has violated or is about to violate any provision of this Act (except title I or amendments made by this Act to other statutes) to make an investigation and in connection therewith he may enter such places and inspect such records and accounts and question such persons as he may deem necessary to enable him to determine the facts relative thereto. The Secretary may report to interested persons or officials concerning the facts required to be shown in any report required by this Act and concerning the reasons for failure or refusal to file such a report or any other matter which he deems to be appropriate as a result of such an investigation.

(b) For the purpose of any investigation provided for in this Act, the provisions of sections 9 and 10 (relating to the attendance of witnesses and the production of books, papers, and documents) of the Federal Trade Commission Act of September 16, 1914, as amended (15 U.S.C. 49, 50), are hereby made applicable to the jurisdiction, powers, and duties of the Secretary or any officers designated by him.

EXTORTIONATE PICKETING

SEC. 602. (a) It shall be unlawful to carry on picketing on or about the premises of any employer for the purpose of, or as part of any conspiracy or in furtherance of any plan or purpose for, the personal profit or enrichment of any individual (except a bona fide increase in wages or other employee benefits) by taking or obtaining any money or other thing of value from such employer against his will or with his consent.

(b) Any person who willfully violates this section shall be fined not more than $10,000 or imprisoned not more than twenty years, or both.

RETENTION OF RIGHTS UNDER OTHER FEDERAL AND STATE LAWS

SEC. 603. (a) Except as explicitly provided to the contrary, nothing in this Act shall reduce or limit the responsibilities of any labor organization or any officer, agent, shop steward, or other representative of a labor organization, or of any trust in which a labor organization is interested, under any other Federal law or under the laws of any State, and, except as explicitly provided to the contrary, nothing in this Act shall take away any right or bar any remedy to which members of a labor organization are entitled under such other Federal law or law of any State.

(b) Nothing contained in titles I, II, III, IV, V, or VI of this Act shall be construed to supersede or impair or otherwise affect the provisions of the Railway Labor Act, as amended, or any of the obligations, rights, benefits, privileges, or immunities of any carrier, employee, organization, representative, or person subject thereto; nor shall anything contained in said titles (except section 505) of this Act be construed to confer any rights, privileges, immunities, or defenses upon employers, or to impair or otherwise affect the rights of any person under the National Labor Relations Act, as amended.

EFFECT ON STATE LAWS

SEC. 604. Nothing in this Act shall be construed to impair or diminish the authority of any State to enact and enforce general criminal laws with respect to robbery, bribery, extortion, embezzlement, grand larceny, burglary, arson, violation of narcotics laws, murder, rape, assault with intent to kill, or assault which inflicts grievous bodily injury, or conspiracy to commit any of such crimes.

SERVICE OF PROCESS

SEC. 605. For the purposes of this Act, service of summons, subpena, or other legal process of a court of the United States upon an officer or agent of a labor organization in his capacity as such shall constitute service upon the labor organization.

ADMINISTRATIVE PROCEDURE ACT

SEC. 606. The provisions of the Administrative Procedure Act shall be applicable to the issuance, amendment, or rescission of any rules or regulations, or any adjudication, authorized or required pursuant to the provisions of this Act.

OTHER AGENCIES AND DEPARTMENTS

SEC. 607. In order to avoid unnecessary expense and duplication of functions among Government agencies, the Secretary may make such arrangements or agreements for cooperation or mutual assistance in the performance of his functions under this Act and the functions of any such agency as he may find to be practicable and consistent with law. The Secretary may utilize the facilities or services of any department, agency, or establishment of the United States or of any State or political subdivision of a State, including the services of any of its employees, with the lawful consent of such department, agency, or establishment; and each department, agency, or establishment of the United States is authorized and directed to cooperate with the Secretary and, to the extent permitted by law, to provide such information and facilities as he may request for his assistance in the performance of his functions under this Act. The Attorney General or his representative shall receive from the Secretary for appropriate action such evidence developed in the performance of his functions under this Act as may be found to warrant consideration for criminal prosecution under the provisions of this Act or other Federal law.

CRIMINAL CONTEMPT

SEC. 608. No person shall be punished for any criminal contempt allegedly committed outside the immediate presence of the court in connection with any civil action prosecuted by the Secretary or any other person in any court of the United States under the provisions of this Act unless the facts constituting such criminal contempt are established by the verdict of the jury in a proceeding in the district court of the United States, which jury shall be chosen and empaneled in the manner prescribed by the law governing trial juries in criminal prosecutions in the district courts of the United States.

PROHIBITION ON CERTAIN DISCIPLINE BY LABOR ORGANIZATION

SEC. 609. It shall be unlawful for any labor organization, or any officer, agent, shop steward, or other representative of a labor organization, or any employee thereof to fine, suspend, expel, or otherwise discipline any of its members for exercising any right to which he is entitled under the provisions of this Act. The provisions of section 102 shall be applicable in the enforcement of this section.

DEPRIVATION OF RIGHTS UNDER ACT BY VIOLENCE

SEC. 610. It shall be unlawful for any person through the use of force or violence, or threat of the use of force or violence, to restrain, coerce, or intimidate, or attempt to restrain, coerce, or intimidate any member of a labor organization for the purpose of interfering with or preventing the exercise of any right to which he is entitled under the provisions of this Act. Any person who willfully violates this section shall be fined not more than $1,000 or imprisoned for not more than one year, or both.

SEPARABILITY PROVISIONS

SEC. 611. If any provision of this Act, or the application of such provision to any person or circumstances, shall be held invalid, the remainder of this Act or the application of such provision to persons or circumstances other than those as to which it is held invalid, shall not be affected thereby.

Title VII—Amendments to the Labor Management Relations Act, 1947, as Amended

FEDERAL-STATE JURISDICTION

SEC. 701. (a) Section 14 of the National Labor Relations Act, as amended, is amended by adding at the end thereof the following new subsection:

"(c) (1) The Board, in its discretion, may, by rule of decision or by published rules adopted pursuant to the Administrative Procedure Act, decline to assert jurisdiction over any labor dispute involving any class or category of employers, where, in the opinion of the Board, the effect of such labor dispute on commerce is not sufficiently substantial to warrant the exercise of its jurisdiction: *Provided,* That the Board shall not decline to assert jurisdiction over any labor dispute over which it would assert jurisdiction under the standards prevailing upon August 1, 1959.

"(2) Nothing in this Act shall be deemed to prevent or bar any agency or the courts of any State or Territory (including the Commonwealth of Puerto Rico, Guam, and the Virgin Islands), from assuming and asserting jurisdiction over labor disputes over which the Board declines, pursuant to paragraph (1) of this subsection, to assert jurisdiction."

(b) Section 3(b) of such Act is amended to read as follows:

"(b) The Board is authorized to delegate to any group of three or more members any or all of the powers which it may itself exercise. The Board is also authorized to delegate to its regional directors its powers under section 9 to determine the unit appropriate for the purpose of collective bargaining, to investigate and provide for hearings, and determine whether a question of representation exists, and to direct an election or take a secret ballot under subsection (c) or (e) of section 9 and certify the results thereof, except that upon the filing of a request therefor with the Board by any interested person, the Board may review any action of a regional director delegated to him under this paragraph, but such a review shall not, unless specifically ordered by the Board, operate as a stay of any action taken by the regional director. A vacancy in the Board shall not impair the right of the remaining members to exercise all of the powers of the Board, and three members of the Board shall, at all times, constitute a quorum of the Board, except that two members shall constitute a quorum of any group designated pursuant to the first sentence hereof. The Board shall have an official seal which shall be judicially noticed."

ECONOMIC STRIKERS

SEC. 702. Section 9 (c)(3) of the National Labor Relations Act, as amended, is amended by amending the second sentence thereof to read as follows: "Employees engaged in an economic strike who are not entitled to reinstatement shall be eligible to vote under such regulations as the Board shall find are consistent with the purposes and provisions of this Act in any election conducted within twelve months after the commencement of the strike."

VACANCY IN OFFICE OF GENERAL COUNSEL

SEC. 703. Section 3(d) of the National Labor Relations Act, as amended, is amended by adding after the period at the end thereof the following: "In case of a vacancy in the office of the General Counsel the President is authorized to designate the officer or employee who shall act as General Counsel during such vacancy, but no person or persons so designated shall so act (1) for more than forty days when the Congress is in session unless a nomination to fill such vacancy shall have been submitted to the Senate, or (2) after the adjournment sine die of the session of the Senate in which such nomination was submitted."

BOYCOTTS AND RECOGNITION PICKETING

SEC. 704. (a) Section 8(b)(4) of the National Labor Relations Act, as amended, is amended to read as follows:

"(4) (i) to engage in, or to induce or encourage any individual employed by any person engaged in commerce or in an industry affecting commerce to engage in, a strike or a refusal in the course of his employment to use, manufacture, process, transport, or otherwise handle or work on any goods, articles, materials, or commodities or to perform any services; or (ii) to threaten, coerce, or restrain any person engaged in commerce or in an industry affecting commerce, where in either case an object thereof is—

"(A) forcing or requiring any employer or self-employed person to join any labor or employer organization or to enter into any agreement which is prohibited by section 8(e);

"(B) forcing or requiring any person to cease using, selling, handling, transporting, or otherwise dealing in the products of any other producer, processor, or manufacturer, or to cease doing business with any other person, or forcing or requiring any other employer to recognize or bargain with a labor organization as the representative of his employees unless such labor organization has been certified as the representative of such employees under the provisions of section 9: *Provided,* That nothing contained in this clause (B) shall be construed to make unlawful, where not otherwise unlawful, any primary strike or primary picketing;

"(C) forcing or requiring any employer to recognize or bargain with a particular labor organization as the representative of his employees if another labor organization has been certified as the representative of such employees under the provisions of section 9;

"(D) forcing or requiring any employer to assign particular work to employees in a particular labor organization or in a particular trade, craft, or class rather than to employees in another labor organization or in another trade, craft, or class, unless such employer is failing to conform to an order or certification of the Board determining the bargaining representative for employees performing such work:

Provided, That nothing contained in this subsection (b) shall be construed to make unlawful a refusal by any person to enter upon the premises of any employer (other than his own employer), if the employees of such employer are engaged in a strike ratified or approved by a representative of such employees whom such employer is required to recognize under this Act: *Provided further,* That for the purposes of this paragraph (4) only, nothing contained in such paragraph shall be construed to prohibit publicity, other than picketing, for the purpose of truthfully advising the public, including consumers and members of a labor organization, that a product or products are produced by an employer with whom the labor organization has a primary dispute and are distributed by another employer, as long as such publicity does not have an effect of inducing any individual employed by any person other than the primary employer in the course of his employment to refuse to pick up, deliver, or transport any goods, or not to perform any services, at the establishment of the employer engaged in such distribution;".

(b) Section 8 of the National Labor Relations Act, as amended, is amended by adding at the end thereof the following new subsection:

"(e) It shall be an unfair labor practice for any labor organization and any employer to enter into any contract or agreement, express or implied, whereby such employer ceases or refrains or agrees to cease or refrain from handling, using, selling, transporting or otherwise dealing in any of the products of any other employer, or to cease doing business with any other person, and any contract or agreement entered into heretofore or hereafter containing such an agreement shall be to such extent unenforcible and void: *Provided,* That nothing in this subsection (e) shall apply to an agreement between a labor organization and an employer in the construction industry relating to the contracting or subcontracting of work to be done at the site of the construction, alteration, painting, or repair of a building, sructure, or other work: *Provided further,* That for the purposes of this subsection (e) and section 8(b)(4)(B) the trems 'any employer,' 'any person engaged in commerce or an industry affecting commerce,' and 'any person' when used in relation to the terms 'any other producer, processor, or manufacturer,' 'any other employer,' or 'any other person' shall not include persons in the relation of a jobber, manufacturer, contractor, or subcontractor working on the goods or premises of the jobber or manufacturer or performing parts of an integrated process of production in the apparel and clothing industry: *Provided further,* That nothing in this Act shall prohibit the enforcement of any agreement which is within the foregoing exception."

(c) Section 8(b) of the National Labor Relations Act, as amended, is amended by striking out the word "and" at the end of paragraph (5), striking out the period at the end of paragraph (6), and inserting in lieu thereof a semicolon and the word "and," and adding a new paragraph as follows:

"(7) to picket or cause to be picketed, or threaten to picket or cause to be picketed, any employer where an object thereof is forcing or requiring an employer to recognize or bargain with a labor organization as the representative of his employees, or forcing or requiring the employees of an employer to accept or select such labor organization as their collective bargaining representative, unless such labor organization is currently certified as the representative of such employees:

"(A) where the employer has lawfully recognized in accordance with this Act any other labor organization and a question concerning representation may not appropriately be raised under section 9(c) of this Act,

"(B) where within the preceding twelve months a valid election under section 9(c) of this Act has been conducted, or

"(C) where such picketing has been conducted without a petition under section 9(c) being filed within a reasonable period of time not to exceed thirty days from the commencement of such picketing: *Provided,* That when such a petition has been filed the Board shall forthwith, without regard to the provisions of section 9(c)(1) or the absence of a showing of a substantial interest on the part of the labor organization, direct an election in such unit as the Board finds to be appropriate and shall certify the results thereof: *Provided further,* That nothing in this subparagraph (C) shall be construed to prohibit any picketing or other publicity for the purpose of truthfully advising the public (including consumers) that an employer does not employ members of, or have a contract with, a labor organization, unless an effect of such picketing is to induce any individual employed by any other person in the course of his employment, not to pick up, deliver or transport any goods or not to perform any services.

"Nothing in this paragraph (7) shall be construed to permit any act which would otherwise be an unfair labor practice under this section 8(b)."

(d) Section 10(l) of the National Labor Relations Act, as amended, is amended by adding after the words "section 8(b)," the words "or section 8(e) or section 8(b)(7)," and by striking out the period at the end of the third sentence and inserting in lieu thereof a colon and the following: "*Provided further,* That such officer or regional attorney shall not apply for any restraining order under section 8(b)(7) if a charge against the employer under section 8(a)(2) has been filed and after the preliminary investigation, he has reasonable cause to believe that such charge is true and that a complaint should issue."

(e) Section 303(a) of the Labor Management Relations Act, 1947, is amended to read as follows:

"(a) It shall be unlawful, for the purpose of this section only, in an industry or activity affecting commerce, for any labor organization to engage in any activity or conduct defined as an unfair labor practice in section 8(b)(4) of the National Labor Relations Act, as amended."

BUILDING AND CONSTRUCTION INDUSTRY

SEC. 705. (a) Section 8 of the National Labor Relations Act, as amended by section 704(b) of this Act, is amended by adding at the end thereof the following new subsection:

"(f) It shall not be an unfair labor practice under subsections (a) and (b) of this section for an employer engaged primarily in the building and construction industry to make an agreement covering employees engaged (or who, upon their employment, will be engaged) in the building and construction industry with a labor organization of which building and construction employees are members (not established, maintained, or assisted by any action defined in section 8(a) of this Act as an unfair labor practice) because (1) the majority status of such labor organization has not been established under the provisions of section 9 of this Act prior to the making of such agreement, or (2) such agreement requires as a condition of employment, membership in such labor organization after the seventh day following the beginning of such employment or the effective date of the agreement, whichever is later, or (3) such agreement requires the employer to notify such labor organization of opportunities for employment with such employer, or gives such labor organization an opportunity to refer qualified applicants for such employment, or (4) such agreement specifies minimum training or experience qualifications for employment or provides for priority in opportunities for employment based upon length of service with such employer, in the industry or in the particular geographical area: *Provided,* That nothing in this subsection shall set aside the final proviso to section 8(a)(3) of this Act: *Provided further,* That any agreement which would be invalid, but for clause (1) of this subsection, shall not be a bar to a petition filed pursuant to section 9(c) or 9(e)."

(b) Nothing contained in the amendment made by subsection (a) shall be construed as authorizing the execution or application of agreements requiring membership in a labor organization as a condition of employment in any State or Territory in which such execution or application is prohibited by State or Territorial law.

PRIORITY IN CASE HANDLING

SEC. 706. Section 10 of the National Labor Relations Act, as amended, is amended by adding at the end thereof a new subsection as follows:

"(m) Whenever it is charged that any person has engaged in an unfair labor practice within the meaning of subsection (a)(3) or (b)(2) of section 8, such charge shall be given priority over all other cases except cases of like character in the office where it is filed or to which it is referred and cases given priority under subsection (1)."

EFFECTIVE DATE OF AMENDMENTS

SEC. 707. The amendments made by this title shall take effect sixty days after the date of the enactment of this Act and no provision of this title shall be deemed to make an unfair labor practice, any act which is performed prior to such effective date which did not constitute an unfair labor practice prior thereto.

Approved September 14, 1959.

INDEX

Aaron, Benjamin, 30, 31, 33

Adams, Sherman, 71

Administration bills: in Senate (S.748), 57, 60; in House of Representatives (H.R.3540), 133, 151

Advisory Panel on Labor-Management Law Revision, membership, 285-86

AFL, see American Federation of Labor

AFL-CIO, see American Federation of Labor–Congress of Industrial Organization

AFL-CIO Committee on Political Education (COPE), 57-58; voting records evaluation by, 143

Agricultural labor, 24, 52

Aiken, George, 108

Alford, Dale, 226

Alger, Bruce, 219

Amalgamated Clothing Workers Union, 255, 257, 260

American Farm Bureau Federation, 212

American Federation of Labor (AFL), 21, 22, 24, 25, 26; merger with CIO, 33-36

American Federation of Labor–Congress of Industrial Organization (AFL-CIO): need for labor reform legislation and, 9, 17; merger, 34-36, 273-74; attempts at purification, 40; backing of Kennedy-Ives bill, 46; acceptance of "two package" approach, 54; internal disputes and loyalties, 65-68, 116-17, 270; McClellan and, 84-85; objections to McClellan bill of rights, 101, 106-7; backing of Kuchel compromise, 111; legislative tactics of, 113-17;

denunciation of Senate version of Kennedy bill, 114-19, 123-24, 125-26; Teamsters Union and, 117-18, 127, 276-77; errors in evaluation of situation and tactics, 124, 239, 267-69, 276-77; strategy meetings with House Democratic leadership, 148-49, 163-64, 189, 192; lobbying tactics in Committee on Education and Labor, 152-58, 166; legislators versus, 156; phantom bill proposed by, 168-69; opposition to Education and Labor Committee bill, 170, 171; Shelley bill, 183-85; lobbying strategy in House, 198-200, 210-11; opposition to Landrum-Griffin and Elliott bills, 200; question of amendments to Elliott bill and, 204, 224; House debate on labor bills and, 223-24; position of, after passage of Landrum-Griffin bill, 242-44; resistance to changes, and labor image, 270-72; corruption issue and, 273-74

Anderson, Cy, 97, 116, 165-66, 246

Arends, Les, 214, 224

Assembly, freedom of, in text of Labor-Management Act of 1959, 305

Attorney General, proposals for use of injunctions by, 26

Ayres, William H., 172, 238

Bailey, Cleveland, 220

Bakery and Confectionery Workers' Union, 40

Barden, Graham Arthur, 128-30, 131, 289; chairman of House Committee on Education and Labor, 5, 42;